THE BROTHERS

THE BROTHERS

THE RISE & RISE OF SAATCHI & SAATCHI

Ivan Fallon

HUTCHINSON
London Melbourne Auckland Johannesburg

© Ivan Fallon 1988

This edition first published in Great Britain
by Hutchinson in 1988, an imprint of Century
Hutchinson Ltd, Brookmount House, 62–5 Chandos
Place, London WC2N 4NW

Century Hutchinson Australia Pty Ltd
89–91 Albion Street,
Surry Hills, NSW 2010

Century Hutchinson New Zealand Ltd
PO Box 40–086, Glenfield, Auckland 10,
New Zealand

Century Hutchinson South Africa (Pty) Ltd
PO Box 337, Berglvei, 2102 South Africa

Reprinted 1988 (twice)

British Library Cataloguing in Publication Data

Fallon, Ivan
    The brothers : the rise and rise of Saatchi
    and Saatchi
    1. Great Britain. Advertising industries.
    Saatchi Charles. Saatchi, Maurice.
    Saatchi Charles & Saatchi, Maurice
    I. Title
    338.7'616591'0922

    ISBN 0–09–170890–7

Typeset by Input Typesetting Ltd,
London SW19 8DR
Printed in Great Britain by
Mackays of Chatham PLC, Chatham, Kent

CONTENTS

For Sue, Tania, Lara and Padraic Robert

ACKNOWLEDGEMENTS

The original idea of this book came from Richard Cohen, who also talked me into doing it, while Frank Delaney first proposed me as the author. The Saatchi brothers themselves were far from enthusiastic when first I broached it; they had received many approaches from other would-be biographers and had refused to co-operate in the slightest. In the end I told Maurice that, despite his reluctance, I would go ahead anyway – unless he and Charles were so opposed that they would cut off all contact with their family, employees and friends. I was keenly aware that had they wanted to they could have closed off so many avenues that it would not have been possible to write this book; and in any case, I needed access to *them*. Eventually they agreed that they would not obstruct me and, having made that promise, Maurice in particular was generous with his own time. I had access to anyone inside Saatchi & Saatchi anywhere in the world when I wanted it, with no conditions imposed upon my interviews other than the standard one which the Saatchis insist on for all journalists before they allow any employee to be interviewed: they must not be quoted directly, although the information given can be used and attributed indirectly. I found this a small price to pay, particularly as in those circumstances Saatchi staff were much more prepared to speak their minds and add to the flow of anecdotes which every Saatchi man has collected about the brothers.

As my research progressed, I found there was a well-worn path to the doors of most of those I approached for interviews. In the past the majority of these people had respected the brothers' keen desire to stay out of the public spotlight and those doors had remained firmly closed. Often even those who had quarrelled with the brothers still checked with either Maurice or Charles before they would agree to see me; but nobody I approached refused to talk to me, and invariably they were frank, open – and often critical. The brothers must have wondered from a distance what I was discovering, but they never tried to control where I went, whom I saw or what I learnt. Nor did they make any attempt to gain or exercise any influence over what I wrote about them. I showed them the first draft of the manuscript, as indeed I showed it to several others who were centrally involved, including Tim Bell. As a result I made a number of changes, but more by way of elaboration than anything else. I was told by others that the brothers were distressed by some of the material in this book, but they never asked for anything to be removed and their courtesy to me never wavered. I am very grateful to them for that, and for all the direct help they gave me.

This book is based on more than a hundred interviews in London and New York with most of the people the brothers have ever had any close contact with in business, the arts, politics or other areas of their lives. I have been very fortunate in that, for many of these people, contact with the Saatchis was a memorable event, often the high point of their lives, and their recollection of it has usually been keen. The time-scale is also short enough for memories still to be reasonably fresh; most of the central characters are around the same age as the brothers – early to mid-forties – and because Saatchi & Saatchi only came into existence in 1970, the main events are fairly recent. A number of people I interviewed more than once, some up to half a dozen times. Where possible I have quoted them on the record, but often people talked more freely off the record and I have respected that. Where I quote a conversation, I have always tried to check it with both sides.

I am especially grateful to Naim Dangoor for his invaluable help and guidance on the history of Iraqi Jews, to Barry Day for his advice both on political advertising and on the American advertising industry, and to all those who gave me their time, particularly Tim Bell who could not have enjoyed reliving some of the events described, and to Jeremy Sinclair, Michael Dobbs, Martin Sorrell, Brian Basham, Frank Lowe, Milt Gossett, Carl Spielvogel and many others; and to Lindsay Masters and Christine Barker who besides submitting to interviews also allowed me access to the *Campaign* library. Thanks also to Gordon Phillips of The History of Advertising Trust, and to Edward Booth-Clibborn for access to the Designers & Art Directors (DAD) library.

Among those I interviewed were:

Terry Bannister	Frank Lowe

Christine Barker
Brian Basham
Tim Bell
Professor Percy Cohen
Edward Booth-Clibborn
Frankie Cadwell
John Chiene
Sir Robert Clark
Ron Collins
Ross Cramer
Charles Crane
Nick Crean
Geoff Culmer
Naim Dangoor
David Davis
Herman Davies
Barry Day
Michael Dobbs
Rodney Fitch
Milt Gossett
Kenneth Gill
Michael Green
James Gulliver
Hans Haacke
Josephine Hart
John Hegarty
Robert Heller
Michael Heseltine
Keith Hopkins
Lord King
Fred Krantz
Jennifer Laing

Sir Kit MacMahon
Chris Martin
Lindsay Masters
Marisa Masters
Simon Mellor
Victor Millar
Bill Muirhead
Sean O'Connor
Greg Ostroff
Cecil Parkinson
Sir Gordon Reece
Norman Rosenthal
David Saatchi
Alan Siegel
Nick Serota
Robert Shulman
Anthony Simonds-Gooding
Jeremy Sinclair
Violette Shamash
Stella Shamoon
Martin Sorrell
Carl Spielvogel
David Sylvester
Alan Tilby
Norman Tebbit
Vanni Treves
Michael Wahl
Ed Wax
Brian Wolfson
Marina Vaizey
Roy Warman
Lord Young

In addition there were a number of people who talked to me on the basis that their names would not be mentioned but to whom I am also grateful. I have also quoted from some of the many articles and other material that has been written on the Saatchis, and on the events related here, notably in the trade press.

A special note of thanks must go to Richard Cohen, the best editor an author can have, to Lynden Stafford who meticulously copyedited the manuscript, and to Vivienne Schuster, my agent. Special thanks are also due to Laurence Good for his research and hard work, to his father John, Francis Anderson and my daughter Tania. But above all I have to thank my wife Sue who put even more hours into this book than I did, not only on research and interviews, but in every other aspect of the book as well.

I.F.

Illustration/Credits
The Publishers gratefully acknowledge the following sources for illustrations:
1 – Popperfoto; 2, 3 and 6 – Mrs Daisy Saatchi; 4 – N. E. Dangoor; 5 – A & M Records; 7 – Camera Press; 8 – Duncan G. Audemard; 28 and 35 – *Daily Telegraph*; 10, 12, 14, 15, 16, 18, 20, 27, 29, 30, 32, 37, 38 and 45 – Saatchi and Saatchi; 11 – Bartle Bogle Hegarty Ltd; 13 – Hulton Picture Library; 17 – Mark Ellidge, *Sunday Times*; 19 – Keith McMillan; 21 – Eric Thorburn; 22 – *Financial Times*; 23 and 34 – Noorie Parvez; 24 – Tim Bell; 25, 26, 36, 39 and 40 – Sally Soames, *Sunday Times*; 31 – Camera 1; 33 – Thiel Photography; 41 – Syndication International; 42 and 44 – *The Times*; 43 – David Banks. Cartoon on p 146 – Michael Davidson, *Observer*.

PREFACE

Jeremy Sinclair's first idea that morning in the spring of 1970 was also his best. Instead of a young pregnant woman appealing for help, why not use a pregnant man? A twenty-three-year-old copywriter, Sinclair was working on an unpromising and difficult advertising brief: to promote contraception among the young, basically by producing the kind of posters that line the walls of dentists' and doctors' waiting rooms. It was the tail-end of the permissive age which had swept through Britain in the 1960s; but it was also well before AIDS made contraceptives an openly discussed subject. He had to make an impact without being too explicit.

The idea of a pregnant young man inspired the line that would go with it. Hesitantly Sinclair wrote it out:

'Would you be more careful if it was you that got pregnant?'

He was pleased with that. It fitted the brief given to the little consultancy Cramer Saatchi by the Health Education Council, the government body which was the client, and on which the whole office had been slaving for days. Sinclair imagined the rough shape of a young man with a bulging, pregnant stomach – and then decided that was going too far. He kept the copyline, but rejected the image because it was 'just a bit sick'. For the rest of the day he and Bill Atherton, the art director working with him on the account, thought about other visuals to fit the same copyline. Soon they knew they would have to show their work to the agency boss, and Sinclair, a diffident, slight young man only two years out of Watford College of Art, feared – as did the others who worked in their tiny office off the Tottenham Court Road – the wrath and scorn of Charles Saatchi. Saatchi, although not much older than Sinclair, had already made a name for himself in the advertising industry. It was Sinclair who coined the phrase 'two ads a day keep the sack away' to describe the frenetic, driving atmosphere that Saatchi had created around him. Some of Saatchi's ads were among the best of their day; but Charles continually demanded more and better work from his little team.

Finally Sinclair and Atherton climbed the few steps that led from the office they shared with four others into the spacious, bright room occupied by Charles and his partner Ross Cramer. The roughs they were about to show did not include the pregnant man – Sinclair had held that out, although he was only too aware that Charles wanted something very different for this ad. His anti-smoking campaign, with its blunt warnings about bronchitis, heart ailments and emphysema, had caused hundreds to write in protest to the Health Education Council. The *Sun* newspaper wrote a profile of Charles Saatchi under the headline: 'The man who's put the breeze up half the nation', and said that his ads 'made previous campaigns look like Mary Poppins', going for 'the punch in the guts – the body blow that stops you in your tracks'. This time, Sinclair knew, he wanted to go even further.

Charles in 1970 looked even younger than his twenty-seven years; a dark, slim man just over 6 feet tall, he had a mop of black curly hair above a lean saturnine face. His mood could swing in seconds, from fury when he didn't like something to a great and infectious joy when he did. The tinge of fear with which Sinclair now approached him was leavened with a compensating affection which Saatchi also inspired.

This was to be one of Charles's more enthusiastic days. He liked the thought that Sinclair was pursuing. 'That's a good line,' he said. 'I like that line.' He went through the visuals they had prepared, rejecting them one by one. 'Keep the line, that's good,' he concluded. 'But let's get another visual.'

Sinclair was actually turning to leave when he proffered his one remaining concept. 'I had this idea for a pregnant man.'

Sinclair had not even prepared a rough sketch, but it didn't need much description. Charles picked it up instantly. 'That's great,' he said. 'Let's see a visual.'

An hour later Sinclair and Atherton were back with a rough of a man with a bulging stomach.

'That's it,' said Charles. Then more loudly, 'That's it!!'

He burst out of the inner office to show it to John Hegarty, the young art director who had been working on the same brief. Hegarty had only got as far as lines such as 'Who taught your daughter the facts of life?' and a picture of a gymslipped schoolgirl. He needed just one look at Sinclair's sketch.

'I almost died,' he recalls. 'It was the best thing I had ever seen. Its simplicity and audacity were electrifying.' Quietly he tore up his own efforts and went home that evening 'depressed and in awe'.

Within weeks the pregnant man was the most talked-about advertisement in Britain. Its wit and directness attracted notice everywhere, and the unexpected reversal of the sexes magnified its impact. The Health Minister, Richard Crossman, raised an eyebrow when he first saw the advertisement but allowed it to pass. Others thought that even in permissive Britain no government agency should go this far. The national press took up the argument, and soon the 'pregnant man' had become a nationwide debate. The Health Education Council, a mundane government agency which had already been pushed into the headlines because of Charles Saatchi's anti-smoking campaign, found itself either lauded for its adventurousness or reviled for its lack of discretion. Then *Time* magazine discovered it and the pregnant man went international, presented to the world as one of the best examples of the daringly creative things that were happening in the British advertising world. It would go on to win a series of awards and enter all the textbooks of creative advertisements since the war as a classic of its kind.

The furore came at just the right time for Charles Saatchi. That spring, as the consultancy was working on the ad, he had reached a major decision. His partnership with Cramer had done well, putting them both among the highest paid young men in Britain; but Charles wanted something more – his own agency. The publicity that raged all summer was just what he needed.

When Ross Cramer decided he wanted to make films rather than join his partner in the new business Charles quickly picked a replacement: his twenty-four-year-old brother Maurice, then working as a young executive on Michael Heseltine's magazine group, Haymarket. Maurice, an academic high-flyer and winner of a gold medal at the London School of Economics, had rejected his professor's suggestion of a university career in favour of life in the world of commerce, then highly unfashionable among the British intelligentsia. This, however, was to be his first direct experience of an industry in which he was destined to become one of the biggest players in the world.

For days the brothers discussed what to call their new agency. The name 'Saatchi' was unusual by itself. Two Saatchis made it even more memorable. Why not make a virtue of it? That autumn Charles and Maurice Saatchi were ready to launch a business which within seventeen years would become not only the biggest but the best known advertising agency in the world. Saatchi & Saatchi was born.

1

ERE BABLYON WAS DUST

In the summer of 1985 Michael Wahl, founder and proprietor of one of America's largest sales promotion companies, was approached by a New York investment banker. Would he be interested in selling his business to Saatchi & Saatchi? 'No,' said Wahl. 'I don't want to sell out to the Japanese.' Many similar stories abound. Sometimes the Saatchi brothers are reckoned to be Italian, sometimes American; on occasion people who work for them wonder if they exist at all. In 1987 when a new office of a subsidiary of Saatchi & Saatchi opened in the Mid-West the executives posed for pictures beside full-size cardboard cutouts of the brothers. It was probably the closest anyone in that office felt they would ever get to their bosses.

Considering they are household names in business circles around the world, Charles and Maurice Saatchi are probably surrounded by more myths and misconceptions than any other businessmen. In Britain for years it was fashionable to talk about their being 'Italian ice-cream salesmen', oiling the wheels for the smooth running of the Conservative Party machine. They were the two boys who had changed Margaret Thatcher's voice and hairstyle, who by advertising and promotion had put her in Downing Street – and continued to guide her every move. They were upstarts with over-grand ambitions who would soon meet their nemesis. They were destroying the values and craft of Madison Avenue, or what was left of it, with their limitless hunger for size, power and money. Yet who really were they? Where did they come from? In a world of ambitious businessmen and corporate predators, what singled them out from the pack?

By the time they had become the biggest advertising agents in the world's history, most newspaper and magazine profiles correctly ident-ified their background as Iraqi Jewish, but invariably talked about their father emigrating to Britain from Iraq 'before the war' or even 'during

the war', implying that the boys were born in Britain after he arrived.
The only book written about them (*The Saatchi & Saatchi Story* by
Philip Kleinman) describes their family background in a single sentence:
they are 'the middle two of four sons of an Iraqi Jewish businessman
settled in North London'. Articles repeat the same anecdotes,
attempting to stereotype two men not easily stereotyped. They have
accomplished an extraordinary public sleight of hand by getting their
names known around the globe yet keeping their personal lives private.
They have not encouraged the myths that have sprung up, but neither
have they sought to correct them, being happy to let the mystery grow
and deepen. Even those who have worked with or for them for years
know little about their private lives. Everyone with a television set in
the free world has seen their advertisements; everyone in the advertising
world knows the legend. Few know the real story.

Charles Nathan Saatchi, second son of Nathan and Daisy Saatchi, was
born in Baghdad on 9 June 1943 into a large family household,
containing literally dozens of aunts, grandparents, cousins and servants.
Nathan was a prosperous textile merchant, importing cotton and
woollen goods from Europe, and shared a huge house, which had
several wings, with his brother, who was also his business partner. It
was not untypical of other Iraqi Jewish families at the time, an extended
and close family living in some prosperity and even luxury.

Charles was the second son; his elder brother David had been born
in 1937, and with the arrival of a second child Nathan decided it was
time to move house. Perhaps he had fallen out with his brother, perhaps
Nathan had become more Westernised because of his frequent travels,
but around 1943 he moved out of the old family home and bought a
house for himself in the suburbs. There too there were servants and
helpers, and by Western standards it remained a large household. It
was there in 1946 that Maurice Nathan Saatchi was born.

Between the births of Nathan's second and third sons the political
climate in Iraq changed dramatically. In mid-war when Charles was
born it was relatively peaceful, although only two years before, on 18
April 1941, Rashid Ali al-Gaylani, a man known for his Arab nationalist
sympathies and pro-German sentiments, had formed a new government, which included elements notorious for their Nazi connections
and their anti-Jewish inclinations. A month later, with Rommel's troops
advancing towards Egypt, Rashid Ali declared war on Britain: so began
the harassment of a community which had prospered and multiplied

around Baghdad from Baylonian times. In the 1920s and 1930s over 50 per cent of the trade and finance of Iraq had been in Jewish hands. Now events were in train which were to cause the second exile of the oldest community in the Jewish diaspora and end twenty-five centuries of continuous sojourn in a land fundamentally important for the culture and teachings of the Jewish religion. Rashid Ali's government did not last long – it fled at the end of May, when British troops approached the outskirts of Baghdad. But in the aftermath, and with British troops still waiting to enter, demobilised Iraqi soldiers turned on the Jewish community, killing between 170 and 180 and wounding many others.

When Tobruk fell to the Germans the news was greeted with open jubilation in nationalist circles in Baghdad. The overthrow of Rashid Ali and the battle of Alamein at the end of 1942 caused the nationalist feeling to abate again, and by 1943 there was little overt sign of the trauma that lay only a few years away. The latter years of the Second World War were actually a time of considerable growth in the Iraqi economy. 'Trade flourished, prices increased by the day, with profit margins increasing accordingly, and there was much activity in the financial sphere,' wrote Nissim Rejwan, a former Iraqi journalist, in his book *The Jews of Iraq*. The Jews, of course, were predominant in all these areas of business, and few sensed the disaster that lay ahead. 'The Jews, at least those of the older generation, virtually forgot the trauma of 1941 and became fully occupied with their daily pursuits,' says Rejwan.

The Saatchi family was not one of the very wealthy who built their castles and fine houses along the banks of the Tigris river which flows through the heart of the city, but well-to-do none the less. Literally translated, 'Sa'atchi' means 'watchmaker' or 'clockmaker', although there has never been a watchmaking industry in Iraq. The family has long forgotten the origin of the name, if it ever knew, but Nathan believes it goes back to his forebears in Vienna; others suggest it may be Venetian. Nathan himself was born in Baghdad, as was his father, so for generations the family had lived in that city. In Nathan's day there were few records of marriages and births, and what there were were either destroyed during the time of the Ottoman empire or later with the exit of the Jewish population after the Second World War.

Other Baghdad emigrants associate the Saatchis with a watch and jewellery business, but there is no evidence of this. By the time the boys were born, Nathan's operations were essentially buying his goods in Europe and exporting them to Iraq, the Lebanon, Syria and other parts of the Middle East. Contemporary pictures of Baghdad at the time show a uniform mass of unpainted two-storey houses nestling on both banks of the river, often flooded when the river burst its banks. The centre, from where Nathan (pronounced Nat-than) Saatchi and his brother ran their business was full of busy, palm-lined thorough-fares, already jammed with cars, trucks and buses: Baghdad for centuries was at the meeting point of the routes of south-west Asia, the nodal point of the caravan trails between East and West. It commanded the two waterways of the Tigris and Euphrates, close to the upward limit of navigation on the Tigris which in Baghdad was crossed by a single bridge of boats. An airport was finished before the war, but a railway linking Baghdad to the Bosporus was only completed in 1940. Even before that, however, it had become noticeably Westernised during the twentieth century. In 1947, the year the Saatchis left, one observer who knew it well mourned: 'The traveller who wishes to see a purely Eastern city will not find it in Baghdad except in the byways and in a few of the old mosques which remain.'

Some older quarters still preserved their purely oriental character, but during the twentieth century changes had taken place in the city itself which had altered it out of recognition. Some of the main roads had been straightened and a macadam surface laid down, so that most of the city had been opened up to motor traffic. There was a telephone and taxi-cab service, and a modern water system had at last replaced the old canals and insanitary methods of drawing water from the Tigris. One of David's lasting memories is of the icemen delivering ice to the Saatchi refrigerators, and the habit of sleeping for a couple of hours in the afternoons, traditional in many hot climates. The population in 1938 was 400,000, according to most estimates, having doubled in twenty years. Inside the town some of the old covered bazaars still survived, but by the time Charles Saatchi was born Western-style stores were common.

Nathan Saatchi is a short, slight man who, like most middle-class Jews of Iraq, is well educated. The predominant foreign culture was French, but the British had been in and out of the area since 1917 and had left their mark too. Many educated Baghdad Jews speak up to five languages, including English and French, but the main spoken one is Iraqi Arabic, with English taught as the second language. Nathan, like all his contemporaries, went through the age-old ritual of using a matchmaker when it came to finding a wife: the story is related of how he was told to walk past the window of a certain house at a certain time and there would be a pretty girl standing there. Daisy (many Baghdad Jews were given foreign, usually French or English, names at this time)

Ezer had been to the Alliance School for Girls, an institution sponsored by the French government, and came from a similar middle-class background. She was seventeen when they married in 1936, Nathan being twelve years older.

Nathan and Daisy had grown up in a Jewish community which witnessed few of the pogroms or anti-Semitism which their Ashkenazi brethren lived through in eastern Europe at the time. When in 1917 the British entered Baghdad, the Jews constituted the largest single group in the population – 80,000 out of 202,000. The rest were Sunnis, Shi'ites, Turks, Christians and Kurds, and for the most part they lived in reasonable harmony. The Jews were by far the wealthiest and best educated, and had a worldwide network of business contacts, much of it with fellow Baghdadi Jews who had moved on over the years to India, England (the Sassoons had come out of Baghdad) and the Far East (the Kadooris of Hong Kong also originated in Baghdad). Under centuries of Ottoman rule the Jews were given 'protected minority' status, and more recently they became full citizens, enjoying equal rights with their Muslim neighbours. To the horror of the Jewish population, the British, after the First World War, proposed setting up indigenous governments in Syria and Mesopotamia, as Iraq was then called. In 1921 the Jews asked for British citizenship but were refused, and they watched uneasily as Amir Faisal, the son of Sharaf Hussein ibn 'Ali who had led the Arab revolt against the Ottoman sultan, at the insistence of Colonel T. E. Lawrence (of Arabia), was brought from Mecca to take over the Kingdom of Iraq, the first Arab country to attain independence from the British.

For a time, however, they continued to thrive. One Baghdad Jew, Sassoon Heskel, even became Finance Minister while another was a justice of the supreme court; in the new parliament of 1925 five of the thirty-two deputies were Jews. From the mid-1930s, coinciding with the rise of Nazism in Europe, the position began to change, but there was still little sign that 2500 years of history were drawing to a close.

Few Jews of the generation of Charles and Maurice Saatchi have anything more than a superficial knowledge of the culture they left behind, yet the generation of Nathan and Daisy was steeped in it. Hebrew associations with Iraq go back to the time when Abraham, the very first Hebrew (the term meant 'from the other side', meaning he had come from the other side of the Euphrates river), set out from southern Iraq to Canaan to form a new nation which he was convinced was destined to bring the knowledge of God to the world. Twelve centuries later, in 597 BC, King Yehoyachin and many of the leading

citizens of Judah were brought as slaves to Babylon (Baghdad). Then
eleven years later, in 586 BC, came one of the major events of Jewish
history. The Babylonian king, King Nebuchadnezzar, razed Jerusalem
to the ground, but contrary to the legends neither killed nor enslaved
all its inhabitants. What he did do was take the entire aristocracy of the
Jews into exile in Babylon. They were the craftsmen, physicians and
priests – practically all the skilled and educated people in the population.
Only poor peasants remained in the war-ravaged valleys of the Judaean
hills. From this deportation most historians date the fashioning of the
real Jewish religion. 'Out of the crucible of exile and affliction, Judah
emerged, purged and purified, into a new people – the Jews,' wrote
Rabbi Isidore Epstein. 'Spreading quickly throughout the earth, the
Jews carried wherever they settled a new message – Judaism. Shaped
and nurtured by a faith which was impervious to change of circumstance
and environment, Judaism in captivity not only survived but also
developed a dynamic which in turn was destined to captivate the world.'

The Jews had always regarded Babylonia as the cradle of their civilis-
ation, the place of the Tower of Babel, Noah, the Garden of Eden and
the origin of many of their beliefs. The Babylonians spoke a language
very similar to the Hebrew of the Jews, and in some cities of Babylon
it was identical. Far from being treated harshly, the Jews in Babylon
were given fruit trees and vineyards, land and houses, and even allowed
to keep what gold and jewels they brought from Jerusalem. According
to the Jewish historian Naim Dangoor, they 'gradually took the position
of colonists rather than of captives'. When the Persian king Cyrus the
Great defeated Babylon and tried to repatriate the Jews, only 40,000
returned. Another 80,000, encouraged by the Persians, stayed and
prospered in the rich land by the waters of Babylon, though still,
according to the psalm, weeping when they remembered Zion.

Dangoor, whose grandfather was the chief rabbi of Baghdad, points
out that the Jews of Baghdad number among their ancestry such figures
as Joshua the High Priest, Ezra the Scribe, Nehemia the Prophet and
the great Rabbi Hillel, a gentle philosopher and teacher whose most
famous and lasting saying was: 'If I am not for myself, who will be for
me? And if I am only for myself, what am I? And if not now, when?'
It is a line curiously evocative of the Saatchi philosophy.

At one time Babylonian Jewry totalled a million, and may have constituted the largest part of the Jewish population. It produced one of the
great jewels of Jewish history: the Babylonian Talmud, written between
the second and fifth centuries BC. Babylonia also gave the Jews something else – their love of commerce. In Israel the Jews had been

an essentially agricultural race: peasants, settlers, cattle-breeders and tradesmen. To survive and retain their culture they had to change. Nissim Rejwan observed: 'It was in Babylonia that the occupations of merchant, trader, financier and banker were introduced to Jewry – professions which continue to be favourites with Jews up to our own day.'

Despite this background, when Charles Saatchi was four and his brother Maurice only a baby, Nathan and Daisy decided to abandon their life in Iraq and leave with whatever they could. They were the forerunners of what, proportionately, was a huge exodus. Within a few years they were followed by some 120,000 Jews, leaving only 15,000 behind. After mass executions of Jews in 1969 the others followed, leaving just a few hundred elderly Jews in Baghdad today. As the *Jerusalem Post* declared in 1986: 'No other exodus in Jewish history, except the exodus from Egypt, was comparable in terms of its drama and spontaneity to the story of the Iraqi Jews.'

Trouble for the Jews of Iraq started a few months after the end of the Second World War. Major events were happening in the Arab world which would sweep them up with them. The League of Arab Nations had been created with the principal target of preventing the creation of a Jewish state in Palestine, and in Iraq the official attitude to the Jews underwent a change. Measures were taken to reduce the number of Jews in the civil service, there were restrictions imposed on the teaching of Hebrew, all contacts with Palestine were prohibited and Jews were forced to take on Muslim partners in their businesses. Jews found it increasingly difficult to gain admittance to state schools and universities. Government ministers talked darkly about political Zionism 'poisoning the atmosphere'. Jews were forbidden to buy land. At the beginning of 1947 a new regulation insisted that any Jew leaving the country had to deposit a guarantee of £1500 regardless of the purpose of their travel. Now no Jews at all were accepted into government schools.

In 1946 Nathan Saatchi went to Britain again, bought a couple of cotton and wool mills and began looking for a house. He toyed with the idea of living in Canada or the United States, but he liked London. An uncle had gone to Britain in the 1930s, but they were not close, and essentially Nathan was proposing to put down roots in a strange land which he hardly knew. Both he and Daisy spoke English, but with a distinctive Middle East accent. He was away for the best part of a year, and missed the birth of Maurice on 21 June, 1946.

The Iraq economy was in one of its worst ever recessions, partly the result of the huge inflation of the war years, and the Saatchi family business suffered badly. Nathan was no longer leaving very much behind. In 1947 he and his brothers sold the business, and he, Daisy and their three children set off for England. Jews who left after 1949 had their assets confiscated, but Nathan was probably able to take a certain amount with him. Among the emigrants from Iraq at the time stories abound of gold coins smuggled out inside tubes of toothpaste and diamond earrings stuffed down socks. 'My father, who came out about the same time as the Saatchis, brought what he could easily carry in his pockets, which was nothing really,' says one Sephardic Jew. ' He had a big business in Baghdad, but he arrived in England with the equivalent of just a decent year's salary. My mother still moans about the jewellery she left behind. They all do.'

Nathan anticipated disaster by a couple of years. With Maurice in Daisy's arms, the family caught a train to Lebanon, then a boat to Marseille, and another boat to England. The trip took three months. Daisy had been far more reluctant than Nathan to leave, but for a wife of her generation there was no question of not going with her husband.

After their arrival they first lived in a house in Ossulton Way, on the edge of Hampstead Golf Club, one of the more select parts of North London. For a few years it was a lonely existence. They had exchanged a warm, friendly large house for a home which by British standards was big but which was no longer peopled by an extended family and servants. The climate was cold, and the boys soon discovered that they couldn't even buy chocolate: London was still in the grip of post-war rationing. Many of the Saatchi friends and callers were fellow exiles from Baghdad who began pouring into London in the late-1940s, but at home now, on Nathan's orders, only English was spoken. Even a request for food had to be made in English or it was not answered. David, aged ten, spoke only Arabic, so was sent to boarding school in Brighton to learn English ways as fast as he could. Within a few years he was wearing cavalry twill trousers and sports jacket and playing English sports; and his English, if not grammatically perfect, was at least spoken with a good English accent.

The richer Iraqi Jews of the day mostly went either to the United States or to Britain. The poorer ones on the whole went to Israel, to become the butt of another kind of prejudice: the Ashkenazi Jews, mostly refugees from Germany and Eastern Europe, looked down on

these more traditional, less Westernised people. It was a strange prejudice. As Stephen Birmingham comments in his book *Our Crowd*, which
describes the Jewish banking families of New York: 'In the unwritten
hierarchy of world Jewry, the Sephardim are considered, and consider
themselves, the most noble of all Jews because as a culture, they claim
the longest unbroken history of unity and suffering.' However, the
Sephardic Jews who set up the great banking houses in New York –
the Nathans, Hendrickes, Cardozos, Baruchs, Lazaruses and the rest
– mostly arrived after a journey which had begun several centuries
before in Spain, where they had been expelled, by coincidence, in the
same year in which Columbus discovered America. The Sephardim
who now arrived in the new state of Israel or journeyed further to the
USA and Britain were not, on the whole, Westernised, although there
had been a tradition in the 1920s and 1930s for the richer families to
send their children to English schools to be educated.

The Saatchi boys were soon to pick up English ways, but for their
parents it was much more difficult to adjust. However, it did not take
Nathan long to build up his business again, and by the time a fourth
son, Philip, was born in 1954, they were in a position to move house
again, this time to a large home in Hampstead Lane, Highgate, today
one of the most expensive and sought-after areas of London. One old
family friend from their Baghdad days recalls visiting them in 1961,
when the Saatchis already had what she described as a 'lovely home
with seven bedrooms'. In fact it had even more than that.

Like most Jewish families, the Saatchis observed their religion, and
for years afterwards colleagues of Charles and Maurice can remember
them leaving business meetings to be at their parents' home on a Friday
night. Although the Sephardic Jews in Britain have their own separate
places of worship – such as the Spanish and Portuguese synagogue in
Lauderdale Road, London, where Nathan is an elder – in London they
found none of the tension with the Ashkenazim that those who went
to Israel experienced. Britain's Jewish population, swollen in the 1930s
and 1940s, still numbered only 350,000, and any addition to it was
welcomed.

The Saatchis also found that in post-war Britain Jews were thriving
in all areas of life, from business to politics to the arts. Some Iraqi Jews
were already well established in public life, others were soon to become
so. The Sassoons had produced Siegfried, the unlikely war hero and
poet, as well as bankers and stockbrokers. Robert Sheldon became a
minister in the Wilson Labour government and is now a leading Labour
backbench MP. Derek Ezra, now Lord Ezra, became chairman of the

National Coal Board and later a leading member of the Social Democratic Party in 1984. Selim Zilkha founded Mothercare. Others like
Alan Yentob, one of the senior executives at the BBC, or the financial
writer Stella Shamoon, achieved success in the media.

As they prospered, both Nathan and Daisy moved through London
with growing confidence. Friends describe Daisy as a large, vital and
energetic woman with a huge sense of humour, involved in everything.
'She's an absolute driving force,' says one family friend. 'She'd influence anybody – she's certainly influenced me. She's got so much get-
up-and-go. For a woman with her background, born in that environment, to be so open, that bright, that intelligent, so much on the ball,
is outstanding.' Another friend from her Baghdad schooldays, Violette
Shamash, tells of Daisy shopping at Harrods. Her sons by that stage
had made the family name famous, and as she filled in her name the
assistant asked: 'Oh, are you related to the Saatchi and Saatchi
brothers?' 'No,' she said firmly. 'They are related to me.' All four boys
grew up tall and strong – each is 6 feet or more, towering over their
slight father. Nathan is described by family friends as 'a lovely man,
very cultured and dignified, proficient in languages, still going into his
office daily' (he is eighty).

In the early days of their sons' education the Saatchis found the
children of other Iraqi emigrants at the same private nursery school,
but the atmosphere was very English. There is a picture of the three
elder Saatchi brothers at a birthday party in 1951, the year of the mass
emigration from Iraq, among other children who had left: Jonathan
Bekhor, now a leading stockbroker in the City, the Shamoons and
others. Interestingly, of the fourteen children in the picture all are Iraqi
Jewish, an indication of how close a community they were at this time.
'None of us was really subjected to Baghdadian influences,' says one
Iraqi Jew of roughly the same age as the Saatchi brothers. 'We all
arrived at around the same time, but like Charles and Maurice my
earliest recollections are of England. We assimilated very rapidly.'

In the mid-1950s, however, financial crisis overtook the Saatchi
family. Pakistan and India were producing cheaper textiles than any
mill in Britain, and Nathan, for all his shrewdness and hard work, faced
ruin. David remembers sitting on the stairs when one day his father
came home and emptied out his pockets. A few coins fell out. 'This is
all the money I have in the world,' he said. Yet the financial crisis was
short-lived. Within months, Nathan was back on his feet with a new
business, using his old contacts in the Middle East to open up new
trades and new lines of exports.

Soon the Saatchis had moved on into the North London state school system. David was not an academic success. His father desperately wanted his eldest son to go to university, but he had no interest in doing so. He went through the stage of having ferocious fights with his father, then joined the air force for his national service, compulsory at that time. Like many similar young men, David loved it for the first year or so, and from that moment on became progressively more independent of his father. Over the next three years he studied accountancy, which he hated, but it provided him with the opportunity he needed. One of his clients owned a small pharmacy, which he wanted to sell – and David reckoned he was valuing it too cheaply. He suggested to his father that they bought it, and Nathan, impressed with his son's enterprise, lent him the money. He duly purchased the business, selling it two years later for a considerable profit and repaying his father. He was left with a small fortune by the standards of the day. Nathan was upset when, freed from accountancy, David then chose to go to Israel to live on a kibbutz instead of joining the family business. In fact David did not settle in Israel, and spent the next four or five years travelling about the world, living in Paris for six months, going to Egypt and elsewhere. In between, he bought himself an apartment in London and began writing 'this bad play'. At last, at the age of twenty-seven, he went to work for his father, but he didn't like the world of business. In 1968 there was a family drama when David set off to join the Israeli army in the Six-Day War. By the time he got there it was over. It was, however, the excuse he needed to get out of his father's business without another row. He drifted on from Israel to America, went back to Britain for a while, and finally emigrated to the USA where he still lives in New York, a prosperous commodity broker, who plans eventually to become a sculptor.

Charles, although clearly bright, was equally not an academic success. Half a century earlier the Sassoons had sent Siegfried to Eton and Cambridge; Charles went to the more modest Christ's College, Finchley, an all-boys, nineteenth-century state school of no great distinction. Nor did he leave much of a mark, although he is remembered with a certain affection. His French teacher, Ron Oliver, recalled him thus: 'I taught him all I knew about French, and he still seemed to learn absolutely nothing. He just couldn't grasp languages. But if Charlie wasn't outstanding, he was the sort of boy every mother wanted to cuddle because he was angelic looking. He was certainly not academic but, like a lot of other Jewish boys, he was a real go-getter.'

Charles was no more distinguished in maths. His teacher remembers him as 'the boy who was always struggling, always getting detention for bad conduct. He took no interest in school activities, clubs or sport. He was the sort of boy who made you wonder what would ever become of him.' A school photograph taken in 1956 shows Charles as a well-built thirteen-year-old, his face round and serious beneath a mass of black curly hair, already one of the tallest boys in the school.

Both teachers and fellow pupils remember his driving energy and impatience, a kind of pent-up force which set him aside from the others and which was clearly going to be channelled into something – but what?

2

THE JOURNEY UPWARDS

From numerous quarters one gathers the impression of Charles as one of those people who seem to be born already set on their own track. When he was growing up, nothing seemed to deflect him from what he wanted. David recalls that in the middle of their bad financial patch Charles wanted two comfortable chairs and Nathan refused to buy them. So Charles designed and made one; it was rough, clearly amateur, but David was astonished when he saw it. It had been put together with much thought and an extraordinary eye for balance. 'There was really a lot of activity within that chair design.' Charles was a continual worry to Nathan, who had major rows with him over his clothes – very early on he wore jeans – his hair, which he wore long before it was widely fashionable, his rock'n'roll music and his indomitable will. Nathan was no weak character himself, so confrontations with his wilful teenage son were inevitable.

For all that, it was a loving and happy household. Nathan and Daisy allowed the boys considerable areas of freedom; they could invite girls home, just so long as they were out by breakfast time; and they could have parties downstairs, just so long as it didn't affect the whole household.

Charles left school at seventeen, having done little or no work in his last months there, and after that friends recall a period of wild party-going when Charles would lead a group of them around London, leather-jacketed and often on motor bikes, crashing parties to which they were not invited, staying out late and generally leading the life of the wilder teenagers of what was then the early days of the so-called 'swinging London' era. Charles, one friend recalls, would always make a beeline for the prettiest girl in the room, even if she was the host's girlfriend: evenings often ended up in a fight. Soon he was in the USA, and he seems to have spent about a year there working his way around the country. All the while he was an avid TV watcher, absorbing both the modern TV culture and the advertisements. Quite what Nathan and Daisy, brought up without television in a strict, work-oriented religious community, thought is not recorded, but Charles remained attached both to them and to his home. He would continue to live with them long after he was a millionaire, leaving only when he got married, at the age of twenty-nine.

Charles developed another enthusiasm, which he passed on to Maurice. 'They were real car freaks,' says a friend. 'They used to go motor racing all over England every week; Silverstone, Aintree, Brand's Hatch, anywhere there was motor racing.' Charles did more than watch: he raced. When he was twenty and Maurice seventeen they persuaded their mother to swap her ordinary Mini for a Mini Cooper S, a souped-up version of the transverse-engined Mini which was very much in fashion for rallying and saloon-car racing in the 1960s. It was not the most useful of cars for shopping and became even less so after Charles and Maurice had transformed it into a racing Mini, stripping out the seats and the padding and fitting it with a straight open exhaust. Their mother seems not to have minded. Charles raced it, but Maurice went along as his faithful supporter and mechanic. Several times Charles crashed, but never seriously.

Maurice, by contrast with his elder brother, was quieter, shyer, academically far brighter. He went to a different school – Tollington Grammar, which has now disappeared into one of the modern comprehensives put together by successive governments after 1974 – where he was continually in the A-stream. In 1964, to Nathan's and Daisy's great joy, he won a place at the London School of Economics, which was the academic institution probably more in tune with the times than any other. In common with other universities, it was rapidly expanding. That autumn, as Maurice began his academic life, the institution was bursting at the seams with a huge intake of new undergraduates, and a growing population of postgraduates from all over the world, particularly the USA.

In the autumn of 1964 an election was looming and the *Beaver*, the LSE's weekly magazine, like many student publications, welcomed the Labour Party's promise of a 'scientific revolution and new technological frontiers' led by the man it hoped would be the next prime minister, Harold Wilson. The Parliamentary Labour Party, which duly ended thirteen years of Tory rule on 10 October, included sixteen LSE graduates, and among the articulate students of the day there was a distinct bias to the left. This was analysed by one of its own academics,

Thomas Bottomore, who said that there was a strong association between sociology and socialism and that the LSE had the biggest and best sociology department in Britain (in which Maurice was majoring). Bottomore proclaimed himself a radical socialist, well to the left of the Labour Party and claimed that the LSE, as a university in which Laski and Tawney had taught, was a left-wing institution.

During Maurice's three years there, enthusiasm for the Labour government, the Beatles, Mary Quant (who first made the mini-skirt fashionable) and 'swinging London' were all at their height. The college was to become, in the words of the LSE professor, Kenneth Minogue, 'the eye of the storm which was about to burst over universities'. In harmony with the growing volume of student dissent there was an LSE student demonstration against UDI in Rhodesia; twelve students were arrested outside Rhodesia House and LSE students marched on Downing Street. In the course of the winter of 1965–66, Maurice's second year, there were student union rows between left-wing and right-wing factions over a resolution to send delegates to a 'council for peace' in Vietnam. Professor Minogue would later dismiss the LSE political debate of the 1960s as 'all Marxist stodge – there was no Plato, no Hobbes, no Mills . . . anaemic, under-intellectualised, drawing on only a single tradition of political input.' But for those there at the time, caught up in the regular demonstrations against apartheid in South Africa, or the war in Vietnam, or in favour of the Campaign for Nuclear Disarmament, it was strong stuff.

Maurice recalls being remarkably untouched by it. He was not disinterested in politics, but it was far from a passion with him. He watched, says one of his professors, 'with a sceptical eye the political turmoil at the LSE and the student demonstrations'. Professor Percy Cohen, who has remained Maurice's main link with the LSE, was his sociology lecturer at the time and says that the young Saatchi was 'no gullible consumer of political ideologies'. He remembers him as an outstanding student, but a person who did not draw attention to himself. Cohen got the impression that Maurice did not want to be noticed. In tutorials he spoke rarely, but when he did he was always worth hearing. His professors noticed many of the same characteristics that his colleagues would later remark on. Cohen remembers Maurice's habit of listening and observing and not committing himself too quickly. 'You could never imagine him panicking.' Yet Cohen would miss something else: Maurice was absorbing his tutor's style and methods, as he would absorb the best of other people's teachings through his life. Cohen was very skilful at developing an argument, carefully pulling in the detailed analyses and facts he needed to support each point. He never made a statement or generalisation without instantly giving apposite, particular examples. Maurice found his style of exposition extraordinarily effective, and would later use it time and time again in presentations and arguments.

Curiously, it was sociology rather than economics or politics which Maurice seemed to enjoy most, and in his final year he won the sociology prize. Cohen ascribes Maurice's interest in the subject to his Iraqi origins: sociology, with its study of class structures, hierarchies, institutions and the whole complex structure of society, is an ideal way of understanding and coming to terms with a host society.

Cohen was sufficiently impressed with Maurice's academic abilities and his capacity for self-discipline to attempt to persuade him to become a full-time academic – even twenty years later he gives the impression he would have counted it a personal triumph had Maurice become a professor of sociology rather than an advertising magnate. Maurice, however, insisted he wanted to go into business, and was impervious to the prevailing distrust, even contempt, in academic circles (particularly the LSE) for business and capitalism in general. When he finished his final exams, Saatchi gave his tutor his telephone number and asked Cohen to let him know his results. When Cohen rang the Saatchi home with the news that he had got a first, it was another member of the family who answered, and the response, Cohen recalls, was of great pleasure; he had the impression of great family solidarity.

Meanwhile Charles was establishing himself. He had joined his first agency in 1960, and hated it. 'It was a very bad agency and he thought what they were doing was garbage,' said a colleague from his early days. Possibly an impatient young Charles just couldn't get along with smallness and inefficiency, but more likely he hated his lowly status. *Fortune* magazine, in a profile on the Saatchis in 1986, said that 'Charles got an old-fashioned start in advertising by going to work at eighteen as an agency office boy and rising quickly to star copywriter', but that is a considerable over-simplification. The same magazine two years before had reported that the Saatchis were 'sons of a modestly prosperous North London textile manufacturer whose Sephardic Jewish forebears arrived in England generations ago.' Charles had left that agency and, for a time, the whole advertising industry; he was unemployed for a while, and there was also a period at a college in Charing Cross Road where Charles had briefly studied design, probably at his father's insistence. Even when he had no job, friends always remember his interest in clothes – which Maurice shared – and Charles always seemed to have a tailor in a back-street who would make him West End standard suits at a fraction of the cost, and in a design which usually only became popular several years later. Charles got his first proper break in the advertising world when he was twenty-two, two years before Maurice's graduation. In 1965 Jack Stanley, the creative director of Benton & Bowles, a large American-owned agency based in Knightsbridge, took him on as a junior copywriter. John Hegarty, then a twenty-one-year-old art director, was working at his desk one morning when Stanley poked his head into Hegarty's tiny office. He had hired a new man, he said, as a copywriter. 'I'd like him to work with you, so see what you can do with him.'

At Benton & Bowles Charles found something he could do well. Hegarty, young as he was, was already being singled out as a talented art director. Stanley must have been impressed with Charles to have put them together as a team. 'In those days good art directors were hard to find,' says Hegarty. 'But good copywriters were even harder. This was Charlie's first job in copywriting, but he was obviously very good.' Jack Stanley knew he was taking a risk. He says, 'He had never done any work as a copywriter. He didn't talk a lot but what he did say made sense. What most impressed me about him was his sense of purpose.' Stanley soon felt vindicated. It is often difficult, twenty years later, to evaluate the assessments of early contemporaries of Charles Saatchi, since people tend to exaggerate their own role in his career, or to suggest that his reputation was overblown. Others still like to be over-flattering. Stanley, however, was interviewed for *Campaign* in 1968, long before Saatchi's reputation had moved outside the advertising world, and gave this view: 'Charles is a really good copywriter. He has a lot of heart about people, which is important if you are not going to treat consumers as a lot of faceless buyers. He has great colour and a sense of salesmanship.'

It was not long before Charles was the senior figure on the two-man team, but Hegarty greatly enjoyed working with him, remembering the flow of ideas and energy that came from him. 'He was terrific, and we had a great time.' But they were both inexperienced youngsters in an agency not renowned for its interest in imaginative ideas. 'While he was working with me he was considered a junior and we would only get half-baked briefs,' says Hegarty. 'We'd just be tossed things to see what madness we'd come up with.' Not many of the Saatchi–Hegarty ideas even got to the client, let alone into finished ads. Hegarty remembers the atmosphere as stultifying and claustrophobic for the new gener-

ation joining the business in the mid-1960s. 'Agencies were dominated
by a management who were basically account handlers of some kind,
and were not sympathetic to our outrageous creative ideas, and thought
they would rock the business, upset the clients.' He and others like him
were among the first generation in Britain who had chosen advertising as
a career while still at art school or college, and found their elders and
superiors were often former journalists, army officers, marketing men
or others who had drifted into the industry as a second choice. 'Only
we weren't just passing through. We weren't on our way to the first
novel, or working on some canvasses in a garret in Chelsea. We actually
wanted to be in advertising.'

After just two and a half months at Benton & Bowles Charles met
Ross Cramer. Cramer was five years older and a senior art director.
The two met almost by accident one day when Cramer was at his
drawing board working on a large poster which featured Biggles and
Dan Dare. He barely noticed the tall young man looking over his
shoulder until he spoke.

'That's terrific,' said Charles Saatchi. 'I really like that.'

The two began discussing their ideas about advertising, and Cramer
responded to Charles's interest and his analysis of the material that was
being produced by London agencies at the time. He divided most of it
into two categories – it was either 'terrific' or 'shit' – but beneath
that simple assessment was a keen analytical mind. Charles frequently
stopped by Cramer's desk, and soon joined him as the other half of his
team. They did so with Jack Stanley's active support. Stanley recalled
it was his initiative to team them up, 'and my hunch paid off. They
made a very good team.' John Hegarty, abandoned by Charles, did not
resent it. 'It was good for him,' he said, and the two remained friends
for years afterwards.

It was the beginning of the most important business partnership
Charles Saatchi ever had other than that with his brother Maurice.
Cramer was a witty, attractive man, always the centre of whatever group
he was in. He was a perfect foil for Charles. 'We just got on terribly
well,' says Cramer. 'He was so enthusiastic about everything.' Cramer
was the diplomat of the two, and for the next five years they would
work together to produce some of the best ads of the time. That would
not happen at Benton & Bowles, however, which even Cramer had
come to hate. 'It was one of the worst agencies to work for,' he says
now. The B & B management was taking on bright young men, but
with no idea what to do with them. In common with many of the other
big agencies, they had little interest in creative work, yet perceived

dimly that their clients required it. Of the many awards the two men were later to accumulate, none was won at B & B.

There was another person at the agency to whom Charles would become even closer. Doris Dibley, described by colleagues as 'a cool Hitchcock blonde', was an American who had read French and art history at Smith, the fashionable East Coast college, married a racing driver called Hugh Dibley and moved to London. She was three years older than Charles and, like him, was employed as a copywriter. If there was a relationship between them at Benton, no one seems to have noticed, but in April 1973, when Charles was twenty-nine and Doris was thirty-two, they would marry.

Cramer and Saatchi did not stay at Benton and Bowles for long. Cramer recalls the two of them sitting in their 'awful office' one day trying to get on with some work. Very little was getting past the executives and they were both increasingly frustrated. 'Benton & Bowles treated the creative department as if we were rubbish,' says Cramer, 'while spending huge amounts on the executive floor.' In an attempt to placate the two men, a firm of interior decorators had been hired to brighten up their work area. It proved the last straw. 'Paint was dropping all over our work,' recalls Cramer, who was at boiling point when an old friend, a photographer called Bob Brooks, walked in. Brooks had been an award-winning creative advertising man in his day, and had always taken a keen interest in Cramer's career. As Cramer and Saatchi moaned, he said, 'Go to Colletts,' meaning Collett Dickenson Pearce, then a new and creative agency. He would set up an interview with Colin Millward, the creative director. Cramer knew all about Millward – 'he was the best creative director in London.' Within half an hour Brooks rang back to say he had arranged a meeting. Cramer did all the talking, showing some of the work the two men had done together, with Charles nodding respectfully in the background. Millward wanted Cramer all right, but he had no interest in Charles. However, Cramer insisted they came as a package, and finally Millward commented: 'Well, hell, if you want the organ grinder you've got to take the monkey!' They got the job, and Millward soon came to appreciate the monkey. Benton & Bowles made a token effort to hold them. 'I knew we couldn't keep them,' said Jack Stanley in a 1968 interview. 'We kept upping their money but with talent like that some other agency is bound to come along with more.' He wished them well, remarking that they were 'one of the few teams working together who will stay together for a long time. They are both highly critical of each other, and aren't easily satisfied. This is a great virtue in the advertising business.'

When they joined Collett Dickenson Pearce in 1966 the agency was breaking new ground as probably the most creative agency of its kind. Founded by John Pearce (ex-Colman Prentis & Varley), it was British-owned, small enough to be hungry, and big enough to have some good accounts. It also attracted some of the brightest talents in the business. A young David Puttnam was there, and so was Alan Parker, later, like Puttnam, to make his mark on the world film industry. So too was Ron Collins, an art director who would form his own agency, Wight Collins Rutherford Scott, and who already had a considerable reputation when the Cramer–Saatchi partnership arrived. Even among this creative group, however, Charles stood out, not only for the originality of his copywriting and his often outrageous ideas but also for his impatience with both his clients and his bosses. One copywriter remembers a side of Saatchi's character which soon began to emerge: 'Charlie was the brooding kind of manic copywriter who would literally tell the clients to go screw themselves and would storm out of meetings if they didn't buy his work. He had mad long hair, and really eccentric suits – and crazy cars.'

In fact the long hair and suits only emerged after Saatchi had been at Colletts for some months. Before that, he had dressed remarkably soberly. Cramer remembers him being 'vaguely Ivy League' with conservative suits and ties. Cramer introduced Charles to the man who made his suits, a celebrity tailor called Major, who also made suits for the photographer Terence Donovan, one of the most successful photographers of the day. Charles was so impressed that he had Major run off half a dozen three-piece suits, with wide lapels and padded shoulders, the trend at the time. He and Cramer even sported watch-chains. But in contrast to the suits Charles let his wiry black hair grow out uncut and untamed. 'He looked like a gollywog,' says Cramer. 'Just like the one on the label of Robertson's jams.'

No one seemed to mind, least of all Colin Millward, an art man whom Charles later untypically recalled as an 'advertising genius'. That did not stop them having their differences. Ron Collins, five years older than Charles, remembers walking into Millward's office as Charles was steaming out, still shouting obscenities at the startled Millward. The creative director, says Collins, had not liked one of Charles's ads. 'If he didn't like what I did,' said Collins, 'I would go away and redo it, as would anyone else. But if he criticised Charles's work, Charles told him to stuff it and walked out.'

None the less Charles's reputation as one of the best copywriters in the British advertising industry in the past twenty-five years dates from his time at CDP. 'He erupted there,' says Cramer. 'Really took off.' In that first year, 1966, the two won an industry award for their work for the London store Selfridges, with ads such as 'A warning to the under-12s. Be on your guard when your parents volunteer a trip to Selfridge's toy department. It could be a bribe to get you inside our barber shop.' Or: 'The most valuable things shoplifters get off with in Selfridges are the girls on the cosmetic counter.' Trite stuff now, perhaps, but effective in its day. Certainly it caught the eye of the industry.

The next year they made their mark more forcibly, working on the Ford account. Ford was no ordinary account; it was not only large and prestigious but much sought after, and it had been won by the small creative agency CDP against the big Mather agency (later Ogilvy & Mather), its first multinational account. The fact that Charles and Cramer were put on to it says a great deal for their reputation at the time.

Rick Martindale, then the head of marketing at Ford, remembers the CDP pitch well. Mather's produced a straightforward, low-key, technical series of ads. Then came John Pearce, the head of CDP, and another senior executive, Geoffrey Pattie, later a minister in the Thatcher government, with a much more imaginative approach. Even the highly conservative chairman of Ford, William Batty, and his managing director, Terence Beckett, were impressed.

Batty was a martinet, legendary for his dislike of suede shoes, long hair, or any hint of incorrect attire or address. Martindale describes how he would stand at the top of the escalator as the Ford executives appeared for work at 8.15 in the morning, and send people home if they were wearing the wrong shoes. 'Underneath he was really a very nice fellow,' says Martindale. 'But he put on this attitude and everyone was in fear and trembling of him.' At some stage he was going to have to meet the Cramer–Saatchi team, who were now turning out some first-class ads. They were mostly what were called 'long copy ads', with lengthy captions by Charles and not much illustration. For example:

Parking is a lot of fun, especially afterwards
when you want to get the car out again, and
you find you've been left four inches in front
and five inches behind to play with,
and it's hot, and the sun has turned the car
into a Turkish bath, and you're working the
wheel one way, and then the other,
and you're perspiring and turning the wheel,
and cursing and turning the wheel,

and crunch there goes a tail-light, then finally
you're out, and feeling just marvellous,
when a little old lady in a big Zodiac
tries getting into your space, and she's
spinning the steering wheel with one finger,
and for Pete's sake, she glides in in one go
and you wish you were dead.

There were others in the same genre; and there were others which won awards, such as the ad showing a new Cortina overtaking an older, slower model: 'They appear the same – but disappear differently.' The Ford people were greatly impressed with them, as was the industry. Charles Saatchi was being noted as a rising star.

Martindale finally organised an evening where Charles Saatchi and Ross Cramer could go down to Essex and meet the senior Ford team, including Batty. The head of CDP, John Pearce, with his respectable air and his little pince-nez glasses, and Geoffrey Pattie, arrived first at the Ford country club chosen for the occasion. 'Everything was going smoothly, and they were all talking about the cars and things, when I saw Charles arrive,' says Martindale. 'And he had this Afro hairstyle, really freaky way-out hair, it stood about six inches off his skull all the way around.' Martindale did the introductions, and Batty controlled himself long enough to greet him courteously. 'But I could see Bill's face freeze,' says Martindale. 'And I could see he was really wondering what to do. He was going through this schizophrenic thing in his own mind, because *Time* had written this thing about the swinging sixties and we were all supposed to be on a great modern up-beat, and here it was in front of him, and maybe he should be joining it rather than fighting it.'

Batty took his head of marketing aside. 'How did *he* get here?' he asked, nodding in Charles's direction.

Martindale was ready for that one. 'In his Ferrari, I believe, Bill,' he replied.

'And that absolutely broke him up,' says Martindale. 'He thought, Oh well, that does it, I know it's me that's wrong. I'm the one that looks strange.' And he almost took his REME tie off and threw it away. And the evening was a great success.'

It was while working on the Ford account that, for the first time in his career, Charles Saatchi found himself in the centre of a controversy. The rules of the Institute of Practitioners in Advertising (IPA) forbade 'knocking copy', ads which attacked competing products (the rules have since been changed). For Ford the Cramer–Saatchi team produced an ad which displayed the merits of its top model, the Ford Executive, against the much dearer Jaguar, Rover or Mercedes, with the copyline: 'The Ford Executive compares quite favourably with these grand cars.' It created a considerable fuss, which only added to the effectiveness of the ad, and persuaded Cramer and Saatchi of the merits of knocking copy, which they would use often over the next few years. 'What is a knocking ad?' asked Cramer in an interview at the time. 'How can you push one product without saying something bad about its competitors? If knocking ads work, then we use them.' Less controversial were other Ford ads such as 'With some 2 litre cars you pay for the name. Ford only charge you for the car.' Even twenty years later, those Ford ads look and read well, and compare favourably with many of today's. Alan Parker had a hand in a number of them, as did Robin Wight, later of Wight Collins Rutherford Scott.

By now Cramer and Saatchi were acquiring significant reputations. Charles was also one of the most highly paid men in the agency. Ron Collins, although older and more senior, recalls how Saatchi would go in to see Pearce or Millward, insist that he was worth more money, and 'usually get it, basically just by asking. And he was always asking.' He and Cramer had gone to Colletts for £3500 a year each, a reasonable although not spectacular salary for the day. Charles got this up to £9000 a year when Cramer went to the USA to look at some of the ads being done there, particularly by Doyle Dane Bernbach. Charles let it be known – wrongly – that Cramer was doing the rounds of the big agencies with a selection of their work and that the two would probably soon be going to Doyle Dane. Cramer returned to find he had been given a big rise in salary.

About that time Charles drove an open-top Lincoln Continental, an ostentatious car in any part of the world, but particularly in London, where there were few imported American cars. He was living at home in his parents' house, so had few expenses, and seemed to lavish most of his money on his cars. A Jaguar 3.8S cost £1741, a Mercedes 200 cost £1895, and the Ford Executive, which Charles was promoting so heavily, was £1567, so on his salary he could afford what he wanted. Friends also remember a Ferrari at this time, but there were so many cars that no one, not even Maurice, was able to keep track.

Interviews around this time describe Charles as 'dark and broody' and are sprinkled with comments such as 'Cramer does most of the talking, while Saatchi merely interjects with affable indifference.' Close as Charles was to Cramer, it was an essentially work-orientated relationship. The two seldom saw each other in the evenings or at weekends.

Cramer was married with young children, while Charles was a bachelor with many casual girlfriends, but no one steady, at least that Cramer ever remembered. He had the impression that Charles had a close group of friends whom he saw in the evenings, usually to play cards, or with whom he would go to the cinema. Charles visited Cramer's house a number of times and became fond of his children and Cramer recalls an incident when his wife rang him to say one of the children had been hurt in an accident at home and was being taken to hospital. Charles, he recalled, was 'as worried as I was' and insisted on driving him in his Ferrari, burning up through the London traffic, to the hospital. All was well, but Charles worried for days about the child.

Charles hugely enjoyed the atmosphere at Colletts. In contrast to his teenage years, he became – and remains – extraordinarily shy with people he did not know but he made some life-long friends at CDP. He and David Puttnam became particular friends, going to Majorca on holiday together. Charles even overcame his natural shyness enough to have a party at his parents' house. Cramer, Puttnam, Alan Parker and others from the office went up to Hampstead to the large house almost opposite the gates of the Kenwood stately home. An enormous table was set out with a variety of food. 'The table was so large that Puttnam and I and a few others pushed all the food down one end.' Charles himself was ill at ease, and Cramer had the impression he had never poured a drink before. 'Someone asked for a gin and tonic and Charles just filled up the glass with gin.' No one can recall Charles drinking anything at the time, and even later he would at most sip a glass of wine. The room was peopled with family photographs, some showing the Saatchi grandparents in their traditional Iraqi clothes, and the food had a definite Middle Eastern taste.

And yet Charles didn't stay at Colletts. The man responsible for his next move was John Hegarty, his old friend from Benton & Bowles. Hegarty had been fired from Benton for being, he says now, 'a pain in the arse', and had ended up in a small agency called John Collings & Partners. It was not a particularly impressive agency, although it had one or two talented people, notably Richard Cope, who at that stage was trying to set up a division with good creative people. Cope asked Hegarty who were the best. 'The two that I know best, and that I've got the highest regard for, are Ross Cramer and Charles Saatchi,' said Hegarty. 'Why don't we talk to them?'

They did, and in 1967 Cramer and Saatchi decided to make the move. It was a disaster for all concerned. Some said that the pair could never get on with the boss of Collings, Andrew Blair, but Hegarty gives another reason. 'It all went foul because nobody there could understand how it operated. . .understand what Ross and Charlie wanted to do, and what I wanted to do, with it.' Charles himself later referred to it in an interview with *Campaign* in 1968. 'It was a badly aborted attempt. Basically I think we had no real desire to fight for minute clients. There's too much talk and intellectual chat in agencies.'

The alliance lasted six months before Cramer and Saatchi decided they had had enough. They had also had enough of working for other people. Neither of them liked the agency scene, although for different reasons: Charles because he hated taking orders from anyone else, Cramer because he didn't much like the system under which agencies worked.

They had a new idea: they would form a consultancy which would offer to do creative work on a freelance basis to anyone who wanted to hire it. Both Cramer and Saatchi had considerable confidence in their own ability to produce creative advertising, of which there was a considerable shortage in the industry at the time. They would put together a small team, find an office, and set up on their own.

3

SWINGING GOODGE STREET

When Charles Saatchi and Ross Cramer set off on their own, they could not have known that they were launching themselves at what was one of the most interesting and stimulating times of British post-war history, particularly in the advertising industry. The satirical revue *Beyond the Fringe*, starring the talented quartet Dudley Moore, Peter Cook, Jonathan Miller and Alan Bennett, was transported via Oxford and the Edinburgh Festival to London, where its form of humour became a cult among the young. It was soon joined by an even more powerful voice: television satire, which lampooned the old order and had a powerful impact on the youth. *That Was The Week That Was*, a weekly snook cocked at the establishment which brought David Frost to fame, and later *Monty Python's Flying Circus* epitomised a new style of irreverent humour which would influence the ads made in Britain over the next decade and later their style of wit and humour made an impact on the straighter ads of the New York agencies.

Much of it would not last, but for a decade at least it was exhilarating. The age of television exposed for the first time the weaknesses of the old order, in the shape of Alec Douglas-Home in the 1964 election campaign, and the skills of the new, in the shape of Harold Wilson. Another grammar school product, Margaret Hilda Thatcher, was making her way up through the political ranks to rule over a government cabinet which for a few months, until the old order fought back, would contain no Old Etonians for the first time in living memory.

Britain seemed in these years to be the most 'swinging' of all countries. In the music world, the Beatles, the Who and the Rolling Stones led the way, and even the fashion scene, for so long dominated by the chic and expensive Parisian designers, switched to London. Mary Quant and Ossie Clark became international names, and Carnaby Street, just off Oxford Circus, became one of the best-known fashion spots in

Europe. The King's Road and Portobello Road were also international
meccas. It was an extraordinary time for fashion photographers born in
London's East End: Brian Duffy, Terence Donovan and David Bailey.
There was a new sense of liberation, a break with formal styles which
Charles Saatchi and his contemporaries could relish.

The late 1960s saw the first man on the moon, the first heart
transplants by Dr Christiaan Barnard, the legalisation of homosexual
acts between consenting adults, Concorde, Mao's cultural revolution.
They also witnessed the student explosions of 1968, the year of battles
on the streets of Paris that almost brought down de Gaulle, bloody
confrontations at the Chicago Democratic Convention, the Soviet
invasion of Czechoslovakia, a massive anti-Vietnam War rally outside
the American embassy in Grosvenor Square that destroyed the myth
that such political demonstrations could not happen in London, and
university occupations everywhere. At the LSE, the *Beaver* exorted the
class of '68 to tear down the walls, and expressed its disappointment
when the students did not want revolution as much as it did.

It was a culture change that Charles Saatchi could swim in with great
enjoyment. His father, like many fathers then, found it hard to cope
with the changes, and the attacks on so many of the old shibboleths:
patriotism, religion, monarchy. But Charles, with his love of new
fashions and ideas, his instinctive desire to see change and his dislike
for the status quo, was in the forefront of it, not in the actual physical
revolution that was taking place but in the cultural and emotional one.
So were his friends and partners. Maurice watched it with a more
detached and academic eye, responding cerebrally rather than emotionally; but in his own different way he was no less a part of it than
Charles. And the lessons he took from it would prove deeper and longer
lasting than for most of his generation.

From the outside, the building on the corner of Goodge Street, just
north of Oxford Street, was unprepossessing. On the ground floor was
a restaurant called the Golden Egg, one of those American-style chains
of eating houses which appeared around Britain in the 1960s, offering
a menu that was halfway between fast food and proper restaurant fare.
Around the corner, Tottenham Court Road was fast developing into
London's centre for cut-price electrical goods, sold in 'pile 'em high
and sell 'em cheap' fashion. To the west were expensive restaurants
such as L'Etoile and the White Tower, haunts for some of the advertising executives from the big agencies which had settled in the area.

To the east was the City, Britain's financial district, which would later prove crucial for the Saatchis.

The time was January 1968 and, wholly by coincidence, some of the most talented men in the media world gravitated to the offices in Goodge Street that were entered by a door to the side of the Golden Egg. David Puttnam, intent on getting into the film world, left advertising to set up a photographic agency. At the age of twenty-six he was already the leading photographers' rep in Britain, taking twenty-five per cent of the earnings of some of the leading photographers in the country, including David Bailey, David Montgomery, Sid Roberson and Mel Sokolsky, none of them grossing less than £35,000 a year – which meant that Puttnam was already earning well into six figures. Alan Parker, who had originally taken over at Collett Dickenson Pearce as the golden boy after Charles Saatchi departed, would soon join Puttnam to try his luck in the film industry.

On the top floor was a design agency called Klein Peters, which was composed of Lou Klein, a highly talented American, and Michael Peters, who was to become one of the leading designers, particularly of shops, in the 1970s and 1980s. Then there was a young advertising man called Martin Boase, who through the 1970s and 1980s was to become one of the leading rivals to Saatchi & Saatchi with the agency he founded, Boase Massimi Pollitt.

In early 1968 Ross Cramer, now aged twenty-nine, and Charles Saatchi, aged twenty-four, moved into their first ever offices in that Goodge Street building.

Puttnam, Parker, Cramer and Saatchi were all young, energetic and creative, with bags of self-confidence and plans for changing a world which they felt, despite the image of swinging London, was still decades behind what was happening in New York and elsewhere.

That year the leading British creative figures in the film, television, design and advertising worlds were taken to New York for a major exhibition called 'It's Great! Britain'. Another bright young designer of the 1960s, Rodney Fitch, was asked to design the presentation. 'I met all the top advertising, design and commercial film people. And that's where I made my first contact with Puttnam and Cramer and Saatchi.' Puttnam was sufficiently impressed by Fitch's work to hire him to do his office. Puttnam wanted something special. 'I did him a really nice office,' Fitch recalls. 'All done in green baize, like a billiard table.' As Cramer and Saatchi were just moving in, Fitch designed both offices at the same time, organising a joint reception area for the two operations. For Cramer and Saatchi he used white Formica, a material which

Charles would use in all his offices thereafter, but new to the advertising world at the time.

The space Fitch had to work in was not large: basically two rooms, the larger and brighter one approached by a small stairway where the two principals would have their office, the smaller space occupied by the four or five people they would collect around them. Yet, despite the size, those who worked there remember it as the ideal spot for what they wanted to do. Charles would later say that it was only when Saatchi & Saatchi had become the biggest agency in the world and he moved to Lower Regent Street that he had an office as good as he had at Goodge Street. 'Until then copywriters and art directors had worked on different floors,' says Fitch. 'They were brought together by account directors and for conferences and things like that. But the Saatchi people were introducing new work, and they were concerned with the words as much as the visuals. So I created these large white desks where the art directors and copywriters worked together.'

Charles was by now a prosperous young man about town. He had graduated to a dark blue Rolls-Royce Corniche and he also had an Aston Martin around this time; he wore the latest suits, and had his hair groomed in the best salons. The gollywog style was gone, and his hair was fashionably long, a mass of curls sitting tightly on his head, his sideburns level with his ears. He was still living at his parents' house in Hampstead, but would spend most of his evenings with friends, playing cards or chess, or simply going out on the town.

In the advertising industry he was already renowned not just for his ads but for something else: his ability to generate personal publicity. Charles had learned from his earliest contact with the industry that publicity could provide him with a short-cut to success. No one either before or since in the advertising business – and not in many others either – has worked on his publicity as assiduously as Charles Saatchi. Most of it appeared in the advertising press, particularly the weekly magazine *World Press News*, forerunner of *Campaign*, but occasionally it would spill over into other media: for instance, Charles appeared in the London *Evening Standard* as the young man earning the most money in the late 1960s. Colleagues early on noticed that somehow it always seemed to be *his* ads about which the trade press wrote, *his* controversies which caught the headlines. Curiously shy of direct contact, Charles conducted his one-man press campaign by telephone, establishing a discipline and routine whereby he got to know the times when the trade magazines *Campaign* and *Ad Weekly* were going to press and he rang through with his stories. They were not always about himself or even his friends – far from it. He picked up all the ad industry gossip he could, stories about accounts changing hands or executives moving or being fired, processed it and rang it through to the magazines. In return he expected some favourable interest in his own activities – and got it.

He cultivated fame in another way too: through recognition for the quality of his creative advertisements. Edward Booth-Clibborn, chairman of the Designers & Art Directors Association (D & AD), set up in 1962 to encourage high standards in visual communication, remembers Charles as one of the most active of the young advertising men in trying to get his work accepted by the jury which each year selected the best advertising work, and which published it as an annual, awarding prizes for the best. In 1967 the Selfridges ad, written at CDP, was included; the following year the Ford ad. Appearing in the annual got Charles more attention than anything else in the quarters that mattered to him: the industry, marketing men and clients. Anyone looking for a new advertising agency – and in those days there were rules against poaching clients – would look at the annual and see the name Charles Saatchi.

There was more to it than that, however. Charles has always been fascinated by the creative process, even while being equally interested by its commercial application. He had discovered in himself a talent for copywriting that he was not even aware he had before he started – although he always had the view that he would be good at *something*. It could just as easily have been channelled into, say, screen writing if circumstances had taken him in that direction – as they nearly did. Writing advertisements does not rate highly as a creative activity even today, and in the 1960s Charles would have been treated contemptuously for suggesting it was an art form. Yet he regarded it as such, approaching it with the same passion he would later apply to his art collection. Booth-Clibborn has no doubt about Saatchi's talent. 'He was very exceptional,' he says. 'This was very much the period of what I call "the breakthrough" of creative work in this country. Up to that time we were copying American slang, and now for the first time we started to use our own language in advertising. And these people, particularly Alan Parker and Charles Saatchi, started using colloquial English that gave a special identity to their work. Charles Saatchi was very conscious of doing work that got visibility, particularly through the D & AD awards, but he and some of the others at the time really believed in D & AD and what we stood for. They were still an isolated group in the industry, but they believed in improving creative standards; that was the important thing.' Booth-Clibborn used to make regular trips to the USA, study the latest advertisements and come back to give lectures about them. Charles would be there in the audience.

The consultancy, which they agreed to call Cramer Saatchi, was an idea more common in countries such as Japan, where the habit is for the large firms to contract out to consultancies. Cramer and Saatchi dealt direct with agencies, who sub-contracted their creative work to them, then passed it off as their own. In theory there was to be no contact with clients – but it did not turn out that way. Those who know Charles believe that he was at this stage – it would not necessarily be true later – more interested in enjoying a creative free rein than in making money. 'He must have known that people really don't pay you for having ideas,' says John Hegarty. 'You make money *making* ideas, not having them.' Cramer was the business end of the partnership, Charles for a while at least being content to get on with the creative side.

Hegarty soon joined them at the consultancy. So did an even younger man, straight from Watford Art College. A diffident Jeremy Sinclair turned up for an interview, showed Cramer and Saatchi some of his work, and was told: 'Come back – but don't stop taking the dole yet.' When he did return he was offered a job and started work at £10 a week as a junior copywriter.

The idea was that they would work in pairs, each pair consisting of a copywriter and an art director: Cramer and Saatchi would continue the partnership they had already carried across three agencies in less than three years; Hegarty, an art director, initially hired Mike Coughlan as his copywriter, but when he left after a year he teamed up with another young copywriter who also came from Colletts, Chris Martin; and Sinclair, who could never have dreamed he would one day become the head of the biggest agency in the world, worked with Bill Atherton, another youngster straight out of the London College of Printing – which had also produced Hegarty and Martin. There was a secretary called Gail – and that was the full team.

The consultancy allowed Charles to try his hand at something he had always wanted to do, something which fascinates him to this day: to get into the film business. Working in the same building as David Puttnam and Alan Parker, both clearly talented, was the ideal opportunity, and within months of the consultancy starting Charles was embroiled in his first venture. Creative consultants could do more than write creative ads – they could write film scripts as well. Ross Cramer joined in with equal enthusiasm.

'You know, deep down Charlie always felt he got David Puttnam into films,' says one of the team at the time. Charles himself would not agree – it was Puttnam who nearly sucked *him* into films. He and Cramer had a go at it, developing three story-lines that Puttnam then proposed to sell to the movie world. 'One of the stories was an idea that Puttnam had, a story about a little girl who'd run off at the age of eleven with her boyfriend to get married. It was originally called *Melody*, but it was changed to *SWALK* – "sealed with a loving kiss". Ross and Charlie developed the script, wrote the scenario, and then Alan Parker wrote it as a film script,' says Hegarty. The film was made, but sank without trace. 'Terrible film – but rumoured to have done well in Japan!' says one of the team. However, Puttnam, in trying to launch it, went to New York, made connections, and used them to get his own career started.

Charles would later look back on his own efforts and cringe. There was, for example, a satire on *The Carpetbaggers*, for which Charles and Cramer roughed out the story, which neither is proud of. Hegarty is kinder about the scripts than Charles or Cramer. 'They were good. Charlie is a very good writer, not just of ads.' For a time some of the others thought the consultancy would veer away from advertising as Charles became more and more interested in the film business. Possibly if some of the scripts he worked on had become successful he might have done, and Saatchi & Saatchi would never have existed. Charles himself would not contradict that view. The problem was that the three scripts he worked on were, by his own admission, poor efforts. If one of them had been even half good, he would say, then he might well have taken the road to Hollywood with Puttnam. It is a thought that still intrigues him, and years later he would closely follow Puttnam's career, discussing the films he was working on, listening to the gossip and problems of Hollywood, half wishing he were there. Ross Cramer too was hooked, already looking to film-making as his career.

But the work poured in for the consultancy, and Puttnam and Parker later went their own way to make films such as *Midnight Express, Buggsy Malone, Birdy* and many others. Charles, whether he seriously considered a change of direction or not – he was still only in his mid-twenties – was driven by events and his own success into an even bigger step into the advertising world. Some fifteen of the top twenty agencies in London had hired the services of the consultancy. The money was rolling in, and their reputation growing. Then, slowly but significantly,

Cramer Saatchi broke its own rule about not taking on clients directly. The account it broke it for was the Health Education Council, which like the Conservative Party account a decade later was not worth a great deal of money but was to do more for the Saatchi reputation than any other.

The HEC, working on a small government budget, was responsible for putting out brochures and posters, warning people of the dangers of not cleaning their teeth or not washing their hands. The account came in through Ross Cramer, whose child went to the same school as the child of a woman who worked for the council. As they waited for their respective children they talked about advertising, and the woman said that her boss, Hilda Robins, might be interested in more professional ads. She would mention it.

Charles Saatchi could have had no idea how important this little account would be for him. This was still several years before the Royal College of Surgeons produced the most comprehensive report yet showing the clear links between cigarette smoking and cancer. But even so there was already pressure on the Labour government in Britain to curb tobacco sales, even though duties on cigarette sales constituted a key element of the Treasury's revenues. The task of persuading the public to cut back fell to the Health Education Council – and passed on to Cramer Saatchi. Charles took to it with enthusiasm.

It was one of his most productive periods. The most memorable ad was one of a hand holding a glass saucer into which a liquid stream of tar was being poured. The caption read: 'No wonder smokers cough.' Below that was the line: 'The tar and discharge that collects in the lungs of the average smoker.' There was another which featured a stained hand being scrubbed by a nailbrush under the heading: 'You can't scrub your lungs clean.'

Many of the anti-smoking ads were good enough for the D & AD jury to select them for its annual. They ran through most of the life of the consultancy, creating a media stir and attracting even more publicity for Charles. Again he was adept at cultivating it. The whole consultancy worked on the ads at various times, but Charles was centrally involved, writing many of them himself and overseeing the others. 'There were spreads in the *Evening Standard*, full pages in all the nationals – they were everywhere,' says Chris Martin. 'It was at a time when a full page in the *Daily Express* was probably the pinnacle of advertising media, rather than sixty seconds on *News at Ten*, which is the top now. And we won all sorts of awards.'

The anti-smoking ads got him into the national papers as well. The

Sun, then just a few years into its relaunch by Rupert Murdoch, in April 1970, devoted a whole page to him and Cramer, with a five-column picture of the two working on new ads in front of a huge 'You can't scrub your lungs clean' poster. 'Once a week Charles Saatchi plays poker with a few friends,' it began. 'But in the last month or so he's been less interested in the game than in the fact that it's getting easier to see the cards. The cigarette haze that used to hang over the table is thinning noticeably.' Everyone, said the *Sun*, seemed to be giving up smoking because of the 'remarkably successful' Saatchi campaign. Charles, in what is about the only direct quote he ever gave to a national paper, is quoted as saying of his ads: 'Of course they're shocking. But the truth is shocking. What we did was dig out as many facts as possible about what smoking can do to you, and present them baldly, ruthlessly, clinically.'

The *Sun* writer was taken with Charles's assertion that these same facts had so impressed him that he had cut down from thirty a day to only two, and that several of his team had given up completely. (Charles, alas, has slipped back since – he probably smokes thirty a day again.)

The fuss over the anti-smoking advertisements, however, was only a foretaste of the publicity which Charles created for another HEC ad: Jeremy Sinclair's pregnant man ad, written in 1970, just in time for the biggest event yet in Charles's life. He was planning to go into business with his brother.

As Charles was building his business and his reputation, Maurice was making his way in life too. He had his first class honours degree in sociology, and a gold medal for academic achievement, and now went looking for a job. With his personality and his ability to marshal complex thoughts and present them coherently, Maurice could probably have been taken on more or less anywhere he wanted. The mid-1960s was a time in Britain when the big companies toured the universities in search of bright young managers, and there were far more jobs on offer than there were suitable graduates to go round. Even an average graduate could end up with half a dozen job offers – and Maurice was well above average.

Perhaps influenced by his brother's affinity with the trade press, he chose Haymarket Publishing, a small but rapidly growing group which owned several publications of great interest to Charles. Haymarket at the time was controlled by Michael Heseltine, one of the brightest of the younger generation of Conservative MPs and one of the best orators on the Tory benches, and his partner Lindsay Masters. They had bought most of their publications out of the near-bankrupt British Printing Corporation. One of these was *World Press News* which Maurice remembers as exceptionally dull – it had been around for years, writing about happenings on Fleet Street and the world of advertising. It contained no scoops or interesting gossip, and was going nowhere.

Maurice arrived for an interview as a graduate trainee just as Heseltine and Lindsay Masters were deciding to revamp and relaunch it. It was Masters who interviewed him, and he still remembers the occasion well. After the usual questions, he was impressed enough with the young Saatchi to offer him a job.

'Right, when can you start?' They discussed that for a few minutes before Maurice blinked and said:

'We haven't talked about salary yet.'

It was Masters' turn to blink. There was a standard starting salary for graduates through most of British industry at that stage of around £1000 a year. That was what he was offering, he explained.

'Ah,' said Maurice. 'I couldn't possibly afford to come for that.'

Why not, asked Masters.

'You see, I've got this frightfully expensive car and I couldn't run it on that.'

Masters blinked again. Then he asked him how much he *would* come for.

'It would have to be at least two thousand a year,' said Maurice firmly. Meekly, Masters agreed. It is a story that he tells, years later, to emphasise the impact that the young Maurice had on him from the very first day.

Maurice worked as a junior assistant to both Masters and Heseltine, but mostly to Masters, assisting in the planning for the magazine they decided to call *Campaign*. Later many would give the credit for the success of the product that emerged to the new editor, Michael Jackson, but Maurice always attributed it to Heseltine and Masters, who developed a format which would work successfully on a series of other magazines, transforming the financial fortunes of Haymarket, where Heseltine ended up with a shareholding worth over £25 million, making him one of the richest Members of Parliament in the country. *Campaign* was an editorial success from the start, featuring news of the advertising industry on the front page, with well-written features and columns inside. It was also classic territory for Charles Saatchi to place his stories in, and for the next seventeen years it was his main outlet for the items of news and gossip he tirelessly gathered, in turn receiving a steady supply of favourable stories about his own business.

Dozens of young graduates have been through the hands of Masters and Heseltine before and since Maurice Saatchi. He was with them for only three years and was effectively gone from their lives by the time he was twenty-four. But both recall him clearly.

'I remember this bright as a button guy, really contributing,' says Heseltine. 'He wasn't just taking orders, or carrying out instructions; he was in the dialogue. His ideas you listened to, and his perception and analysis were valuable. I can certainly remember feeling we had an ace here.'

It was with Masters that Maurice worked most closely, and both Masters and his Italian wife, Marisa, became genuinely fond of him. With Masters he was involved in the launch of other magazines, particularly *Accountancy Age*, which Masters says he more or less launched by himself. Maurice was in charge of the co-ordination and, according to Masters, he did it brilliantly:

'Maurice learned a lot about how to sell here,' says Masters. 'He was one of those people who instinctively seemed to know the whole business of publishing. Some people learn by staggering around and falling over all the time, and then pick themselves up. Maurice doesn't fall over very much. He seemed to be born with it.' He was given the title of "business development manager" but in reality he had to do just about everything, from planning to selling ads. 'He was our one-man R & D department,' says Masters.

Haymarket, unlike most other publishers, had a system of client cards in tin boxes, and Maurice, along with others, had to use them to make a certain number of calls every day to potential advertisers. Today it would all be computerised, but by the standards of the day this was an advanced and streamlined method. It was hard and sometimes humiliating work, but invaluable experience which Maurice would later use when he joined his brother. Haymarket in those years had a considerable impetus and indeed eventually became a company making many millions of pounds a year. But Maurice later felt that, if Heseltine had not, in 1970, become a senior minister in the new Conservative government of Ted Heath, Masters and Heseltine could together have turned it into a Murdoch-sized company. He watched Heseltine at work looking for new magazines to take over, and helped identify potential targets. 'What we did', explains Heseltine, 'was we wrote a standard letter to the chairman of every publishing house offering to buy them. We sent out hundreds of letters, and if we bought two magazine groups in a year that was fine. In fact you only need one a year to make it worthwhile.' Heseltine cites the example of a phone call which came in from a man in Canada as a result of one of his letters. 'We're just about to sell to Thomson and I've got your letter. He's a bit big and I don't want to sell to him. Are you really interested?' Heseltine leaped into action, worked through the night and ended up buying a medical publishing company which has made considerable profits for Haymarket since. For Maurice it was an eye-opener, and he absorbed the systems and style like a sponge. Just as he had learned presentation and how to marshal arguments from Professor Cohen at LSE, now he learned from Heseltine and Masters.

Like his brother, Maurice was still living at home. He was far less well paid – he was on £3000 a year when he left – but he had enough to indulge his passion for cars. Much to the astonishment of everyone at Haymarket, the tall, owlish Maurice travelled to work in his 1966 Corvette, an American sports car almost unavailable in Britain. He also sported smart suits, although they were rather more conservative than Charles's.

Maurice was no ordinary twenty-four-year-old. It was clear to Masters in particular – and he knew him best – that he was heading straight for the top of whatever he wanted to do. Already his consider-able charm, cloaked underneath his slightly diffident and shy manner, was at work in the organisation. He worked hard and thoughtfully, concentrating his energies and intelligence, and he had that flash of original thought which already set him aside from others of his age, and which would prove so crucial for the future of himself and his brother.

In early 1970 Charles began to itch for his own agency. He found it irritating that his creative work should appear as the work of the agencies who hired his consultancy services. He now had the kernel of a team and something of a track record, and the success of the anti-smoking ads made him confident he could attract new clients. He had seen enough of the agency world to despise most of it. Other than the work produced by his old house Collett Dickenson Pearce and one or two others, he felt nothing creative was happening in the British ad world.

At home at the weekends Maurice, observing the ad scene from the outside as a customer and through his connection with *Campaign*, encouraged his brother. And in turn Charles was impressed by Maurice's ability to analyse the business, to pick out the weaknesses and the strengths, and by his disciplined hard work.

Quite when Charles decided to make Maurice part of his new venture neither of them now remembers precisely, but by early 1970 Maurice was preparing to join him. Ross Cramer to Charles's surprise proved less enthusiastic. 'Look, I'm growing away from all this,' he told Charles. 'I think I want to go off and direct. I'm getting more involved with films, and with this scriptwriting we've been doing. I've decided that's where my love is.' He would, he said, direct commercials for a living, and maybe move into feature films if it went well. (He never did – but has made a successful career in the commercial ad world.)

'Charlie pleaded with him not to,' says Hegarty, 'because they were a great team, they were great buddies and everything. Ross was a terrific guy, a smashing bloke. But Ross said, "No, I won't like what's going to happen, it'll be boring", and he decided to leave. And Charlie got his brother in to start the agency.'

The idea, says Hegarty, had been to call the agency Saatchi, Cramer & Saatchi. Now Cramer would not be there, it would have to be called something else.

4

'A BLOODY GOOD NAME'

In the middle of May 1970 Charles Saatchi emerged from the office he shared with Ross Cramer. He paused on the top step, looking down at the room below, and called for attention. He had some news to announce which affected them all. The days of the consultancy were coming to an end, he said. They were no longer going to work for other agencies who passed off the best creative work coming out of Cramer Saatchi as their own. They were now going to work for themselves in their own new agency, with a new type of thinking and approach to the business. The two years of running the consultancy, which had been a novel idea when it was started, had proved not only that they could do it but that there was a need for a hard-selling creative agency. They would need some more people, and he had some ideas on that. And they would have to move – he was already looking for new offices, he added.

It was a short speech, one of the few that Charles Saatchi has ever given. He had some bad news as well as good. Cramer wanted to leave. He had been in the agency world before and didn't want to enter it again. Working in the same building as David Puttnam and Alan Parker, with their burning enthusiasm, had given him a taste for the film world. He was going to join the photographer Terence Donovan, to make commercials, and maybe other kinds of films.

That caused some dismay. Cramer, although only in his early thirties, was a veteran compared with the others. He was also a calming, stable influence on a young group of copywriters and art directors, none of them aged above twenty-six. All of them liked as well as respected him; he was the only one of them capable of standing up to Charles, the only one who could talk him out of some of his wilder and more extravagant ideas. He would be a loss.

Charles Saatchi, however, already had ideas on who would step into his shoes, he said. Cramer would be replaced – and here there was a moment of held breath on the part of the audience – 'by my brother Maurice'. The others looked at each other blankly. They knew the younger Saatchi worked for Haymarket, and had never worked in an agency. How could he replace Cramer? Charles none the less seemed to have little doubt. Maurice had other virtues. However, with Cramer going the name would have to be changed. Cramer Saatchi, he said, would become Saatchi & Saatchi. 'It's a bloody good name for a new advertising agency,' he went on. 'Saatchi & Saatchi – it's so bizarre no one will forget it in a hurry.'

'I remember him making a joke of the name,' says Chris Martin, then a junior copywriter at the consultancy. 'He said they had to have a name that people would remember, so he had got his brother in to make sure they had the right name, almost as if that was the only reason he was joining.'

Martin had never even met Maurice at the time, but raised no objection; he was twenty-three, doing well, and was attached to a man he regarded as one of the most creative in the British advertising industry. If Charles Saatchi wanted to start his own agency, Martin was happy to follow. John Hegarty, who although only in his mid-twenties at the time had known Charles Saatchi longer than any of the others, did voice a protest. Unlike Martin, he had met Maurice, but only a couple of times. 'I thought he was a terrific chap, a really nice guy. But I didn't see what he could contribute to us.'

Hegarty took Saatchi aside. 'Charlie, are you serious?' he began. 'He's only twenty-four. Are you sure you're right? It's bad enough that we're just creative people and there's no senior management, but you know . . . what's your brother going to add to that? Are you sure this is correct?'

Charles Saatchi liked and respected Hegarty and was anxious that he joined him in the new venture. With Cramer going, Hegarty could reasonably expect to be made a partner. Charles realised that not everyone was going to welcome his brother immediately. 'Well, it might not be correct,' he said finally, 'but I tell you something, John. Whatever happens I know I can trust Maurice. And he won't put a knife in anybody's back. That's worth a dozen of another type of business person that might screw it up for us.'

Hegarty did not press the point, nor did he take it as a reflection on his own loyalty. He too was enthusiastic for the new venture, and if Charlie reckoned his brother would add to its chances of success he would accept that. A third member of the team, Jeremy Sinclair, raised no objections. As he would do for the next seventeen years – and is still doing – Sinclair remained loyal and supportive of Charles Saatchi.

'The Saatchis timed their arrival perfectly – or rather their parents did,' wrote Jeremy Bullmore, chairman of J. Walter Thompson in London, in the *Guardian*, in October 1987. 'Before the Saatchi phenomenon, those of us in the surprisingly small industry (only 15,000 people in the whole of this country) were accustomed to obscurity. No agency was a household name, very few people knew what agencies did, the City of London had never met us and didn't want to and the feeling was mutual. More importantly, we'd all been brought up to believe that the function of agencies was to make brands and clients famous and profitable while remaining decently anonymous ourselves.' This last, slightly carping note would be echoed for many years by the older generation of advertising men. It would be a long time before agencies realised, as Charles Saatchi did from the beginning, the value of publicity for the agency itself.

Bullmore, however, make another point which also only slowly became apparent. In the early 1970s, he said, the conventional wisdom in the thinking classes, in both Britain and the USA, was 'still mostly conditioned by the title of *The Hidden Persuaders* (few had actually read it), Priestley's 'Admass' and Galbraith's *The Affluent Society*. Few observed at the time that this sector of British business was faster, more responsive, more competitive and more efficient than any other.'

The Saatchis believed this was true only for a small sector of the industry. Charles was unimpressed with the organisational or creative capacity of most of the big agencies, and Maurice had seen enough to know that the advertising industry could learn a lot from the methods practised by Michael Heseltine and Lindsay Masters at Haymarket. The structure of the business was disorganised and ripe for the type of semi-financial acquisitive operation the Saatchis would run. Even with the multinational agencies so dominant, concentration in the industry was remarkably low: there were over 600 agencies, none with more than 5 per cent of billings. The stock market despised the industry, dismissing it as one largely run for the benefit of the partners in the agencies, with low-quality earnings likely to disappear as clients changed agencies or creative talent left for fresher pastures (wrongly, as we shall see later). It was an industry remarkably vulnerable to a person as determined as Charles Saatchi, but even more so to someone as bright and organised as his younger brother.

*

The name 'Saatchi & Saatchi' had not come about as readily as Charles made it sound that day in Goodge Street. Originally the plan was simply to change the Cramer Saatchi consultancy into an agency with the same name. Then Charles, impressed by the obvious business acumen of his younger brother Maurice and aware that creative advertising people were not necessarily good at the commercial end of the operation, decided to bring him in, and to call the business something like Saatchi, Cramer & Saatchi. When Ross Cramer refused to join him he had to think again. At the home of their parents the two Saatchis had long discussions, often involving their parents and brothers. Saatchi was such a strange name for the ordinary client. What would it mean to them? On the other hand the agency had acquired such a reputation among those who knew about advertising that clients were approaching them direct. They should not lightly abandon the name.

They discussed all sorts of other possibilities. In the end they agreed that Saatchi & Saatchi was a 'bizarre' name, and since they couldn't change it they would have to capitalise on it. 'The name Saatchi is something we can't bury,' insisted Charles. 'We're stuck with it, so let's make it an asset.'

Those discussions took place well before Charles made his speech to the staff. Now that it was out in the open, preparations for the agency began in earnest. Hegarty, Martin and Sinclair all willingly agreed to become part of the new venture, which meant that from the beginning it would have a nucleus of talented, creative men with their own reputations. Although he was still a half-owner of the consultancy, Cramer quietly disappeared from their professional lives, and the tall boyish-looking bespectacled figure of Maurice began to be seen bustling in and out, carrying bulging briefcases and files. The offices in Goodge Street, still used in this transitional period, were comfortable, airy and had suited them all well, but were clearly unsuitable for the new venture. The new office would have to contain more people, be easily accessible to clients who could not be expected to climb the four floors up to the old offices, and it would have to have a boardroom and projection room for making pitches to clients. Most important of all, Charles was looking for premises which could be cleverly disguised to make it seem as if his little firm owned the whole building rather than the single floor which he knew was all he could afford. Within these constraints, the Saatchis did well, and by midsummer a suitable office had been found.

Golden Square is an oasis in the throbbing, multicultural world of London's Soho district, surrounded by a mixture of seedy streets full of striptease clubs, cinemas showing pornographic films and shops selling sex videos and hard-porn magazines. Nearby is London's China-town, offering an array of restaurants which serve up some of the best Chinese food in the world. To the south, just a couple of blocks away, is Piccadilly Circus. The square itself is leafy and surprisingly secluded, the headquarters of some of Britain's largest textile companies and television groups, its respectable Victorian frontages concealing the offices of firms of lawyers, consultants, the better class of wine and spirit merchants, a tailor's shop making tweed suits and dresses for the gentry and the odd textile gallery. Hundreds of studios and film processors used by the film and television industries are only minutes away. There were better addresses in Adland, but this was fine.

Charles liked the look of Number 6 Golden Square the first time Maurice and the agent showed it to him. It was one of the most elegant buildings in the square, with carved stone pillars and a high fanlight over the doorway conveying a feeling that the residents of this office were respectable, solid and had been around for a long time. The Saatchis took the ground floor and a basement below it, the whole area not much bigger than the Goodge Street premises, but with the poten-tial, with a little creative design, of appearing much larger. The design was again entrusted to Rodney Fitch, by now making a reputation for his work with Terence Conran; Conran in turn was making a major impact among the younger and trendier middle class with his Habitat shops specialising in stripped-pine furniture and stainless-steel and glass-topped kitchen furniture. Fitch soon started on Golden Square, working to Charles's and Maurice's detailed instructions. The main area on the bright ground floor would basically be open plan, with everything designed to give the impression there was more of it hidden away somewhere that the client couldn't see. 'It was very clever,' says John Hegarty. 'It looked really smart, sort of elegant. You went in, and as always with agencies you want the feeling of energy, of people doing things, and it was designed to give you that.' Some of the best ads were blown up, and hung on the walls, an unusual feature then in agencies, but now an essential feature in Adland reception areas. Fitch installed partitions about 5 feet high so that it was possible when sitting down to have some privacy, but anyone standing could still see what was going on across the room. The reception area had a higher partition, so that it was difficult to see over, but the waiting client could hear sounds of activity inside. The room had a high ceiling and windows fitted with modern blinds. The basic working area was divided by four large white-topped tables to serve as desks, the passageways running between them. At the back were three partitioned-off offices, still part of the main room, where clients could be interviewed or phone calls made. In the furthest corner was a spiral staircase leading down to the basement which had a projection room and a long table for conferences and meetings.

The final touch was typical of Charles. He had a brass plate made similar to others around the square which announced firms of solicitors or accountants. Picked out in subdued black lettering were the words 'Saatchi & Saatchi'. It was all that would signal to the outside world what went on within.

The office, however, was a minor matter compared with the need to get some clients aboard. At that point the Cramer Saatchi consultancy had only one prestige client which Charles could safely rely on carrying with him: the Health Education Council. In those final months before the launch, Charles Saatchi exploited the reputation he had built on the health ads for all he was worth.

In fairness, he had something to boast about. The Health Education Council had initially involved designing brochures and posters, work which Charles left mostly to the young Jeremy Sinclair, to Hegarty, and Mike Coughlan who could produce adventurous ads from the most unpromising of material. But the others acknowledged that it was often his input which turned their ideas into startlingly good ads. This was true of the pregnant man ad, and was equally true of the 'fly in your food' poster which in its day created considerable notice. It was one of the first ads Cramer Saatchi produced for the HEC and Charles wanted something bold. The brief was to show in the most graphic way the dangers of allowing flies anywhere near food. Charles found some text in an old medical book, describing how flies vomit on food to soften it up, then 'stamp the vomit in until it's liquid, usually stamping in a few germs for good measure. Then when it's good and runny they suck it all back again, probably dropping some excrement at the same time.'

Coughlan added the finishing touch. He wrote at the bottom: 'And then, when they've finished eating, it's your turn.'

More celebrated of course was the 'pregnant man' ad, with which Charles Saatchi to this day is often credited and which was one of the key factors behind his reputation when the Saatchi & Saatchi agency opened. 'Years later, when we were first buying an agency in New York, the only thing they knew about us was the pregnant man ad,' says a Saatchi man. The ad was just coming off the drawing-board as Charles Saatchi was finalising his plans for the agency, and he seized upon it as a heaven-sent opportunity for publicity for the new business. For what was to be the best-known ad they would ever produce, there is more myth about it than any other. In 1987 the Harvard Business School did a case study on Saatchi & Saatchi and noted that 'The agency's first breakthrough came in 1975 when it produced the famous "pregnant man" advertisement. This established Saatchi & Saatchi's reputation as the UK's "creative" agency.'

In fact, as we have seen, the pregnant man ad had been written five years earlier at a time when the consultancy was evolving into the agency. And Charles's own involvement in it, although important, was by no means as central as legend later had it. The ad was the work of Jeremy Sinclair, with the artwork done by Bill Atherton. What was all due to Charles, however, was the clever exploitation of the publicity. There was considerable criticism from the quarters that Sinclair originally feared; but there was much favourable comment too. No one mentioned Cramer Saatchi – in those days the client got the credit or brickbats for its advertising and the agencies stayed in the background. But the industry knew – or thought it knew – who had written it, and Charles made sure prospective clients knew too. He never attempted to deny Sinclair credit for it, or to claim it as his own. But he did make sure it was associated with the name Saatchi. The story ran in the press for months, right through the last days at Goodge Street and the first months in the new office at Golden Square. It continued to crop up afterwards in the most unexpected ways: a year later the model was involved in a bicycle accident and taken to hospital with broken bones. The *Sun* newspaper caught up with him there, photographed him and ran a story with the headline: 'MAN WITH A HUMP GOES DOWN WITH A BUMP'.

The Health Education Council was only one client; the brothers desperately needed more. Charles had a friend at his old agency, Collett Dickenson Pearce, called Danny Levine, a junior copywriter who admired the work coming out of the Cramer Saatchi consultancy. Levine's father was the marketing director of the Citrus Marketing Board of Israel, which sold its oranges and lemons around the world under the Jaffa name, and had decided on a big push in Britain designed to take advantage of the growing boycott of South African oranges. Levine suggested to his father that he try this bright new agency; they were creative and hungry; with everything at risk they would put their best work into the account, which none of the big agencies would. The Saatchis were asked to pitch, and spent days preparing. They won the account, but never got to run what they reckoned was their best advertising: Jeremy Sinclair and Bill Atherton produced a campaign with a biblical feel, along the lines of 'And the Lord said: let there be oranges . . .'. This ended with the line 'Jaffa: the Chosen Fruit', but this was turned away by the ITCA, which controls all advertising on British television, because it was 'anti-Jewish'. The authority was unmoved by the pleas that 'we're Jews and we like it – and the Israelis like it too.'

Now they had two clients, but the brothers wanted at least three significant accounts before they opened: otherwise the financial gamble they were taking was going to be even more of a wild one. Another prospect soon appeared. Granada TV was not one of the big accounts by the standards of the multinational agencies, but that summer it was looking for a new agency and a new campaign for its television rental side. The man running it was Brian Wolfson, now chairman of the company that owns Wembley Stadium, then a young executive carving a reputation for himself in the tough world of television rental. Maurice heard about him from his contacts at *Campaign* and rang him. Could Saatchi make a pitch? Wolfson, surprised by the approach, agreed. Again the team worked hard on the presentation material, but as the day approached Charles began to worry about another problem: they had no suitable premises in which to make their presentation to the client. At Goodge Street where they were still running the consultancy they had no projection facilities, because they had always been able to use those of the client agencies. Golden Square was not finished yet. What to do?

By a coincidence one of the last jobs done at the Cramer Saatchi consultancy was some creative work for a tiny agency called Bowman Harris. It was intended for an Australian client, and as soon as it was finished the whole of the Bowman Harris team, only three or four strong, were to fly off to Australia with it. As it happened Bowman Harris had smart offices just off Berkeley Square which included projection facilities. 'Suddenly Charlie thought, this is it,' says Chris Martin.

Knowing they were all in Australia, he rang up the receptionist and said, 'I'm just phoning to make certain that everything's all right for the presentation to Granada TV next week.' 'I don't know anything about that," said the girl. 'Oh, didn't Arnold Bowman tell you? I'd agreed with him that we could borrow your conference room to make the presentation to a client, because of course everyone's away.' Naturally she said 'Fine' and Charlie went on: 'Will there be a slide projector? And could someone bring in tea and biscuits?' So this wonderful bit of opportunism takes place where the client is directed to these very smart offices, and they actually put a Saatchi & Saatchi sign over the door, and Charlie meets them outside, and then John

Hegarty and Maurice make the presentation. And they came back having got the client! It was wonderful.'

As important as the clients were, getting the right people to work in the new agency was even more important. Charles decided to do away with account executives, the salesmen most agencies place between the creative team and the client. They were, he insisted, an unnecessary and damaging layer which got in the way of direct discourse between client and creative team. Everyone would have to join in to do that work (much of it would fall to Maurice). However, he needed other specialist skills, and his intention was to fill the team with the same type of person he had working at Goodge Street: young, creative and aggressive. The secret of much that was to follow was Charles's skill at getting such people to work for him. Later most of the seven whom he hired as the initial team at the agency went on to found their own agencies or reach the top in another profession. They are now almost invariably wealthy men, established proprietors themselves, although still only in their early forties.

Not everyone he wanted joined, however, and the the list of those who didn't is almost as interesting as the list of those who did. For instance, Maurice had the idea of hiring a food retailer in order, he suggested, to give them an edge in getting some of the big food and consumer accounts. (The idea was not entirely new – a number of other agencies already employed ex-supermarket men, with mixed results.) He spent weeks trying to woo a young supermarket manager called Ian McLaurin. Still only in his twenties, McLaurin was already head of the northern division of Tesco, then the most aggressive food retailer in the country. McLaurin was tempted, but in the end was persuaded by the Tesco management that he had a good career there. He did – today he is chairman.

Maurice had other imaginative ideas. Even before the agency began, he proposed offering clients another service, management consultancy, arguing that it went together with advertising.

With his analytical mind, he could see trends perhaps more clearly than his brother, and to him it was obvious that one of the faults of the advertising industry was that it had an image of being 'very polite and superficial, even a bit silly. People in it think about it as a hobby.' Management consultancy, on the other hand, had a different type of person working in it, a more professional and intellectual type whom he felt could make a contribution at a business level. It says something for the relationship between Charles and his twenty-four-year-old brother at this stage that Charles not only listened to him but told him to go ahead.

In between pitching for clients, Maurice approached a young consultant at McKinsey's, then probably the leading consultants in the world, called Peter Foy. Maurice deployed all his persuasive charm, but Foy in the end decided to stay with McKinsey's – and is now senior partner.

There was another failure which would later have considerable – and beneficial – significance for the agency. A key role in the new firm would be what is called the 'media man', the executive who buys space and time from the newspapers and television stations. Charles that summer was propounding to anyone who would listen his theories about how much better a service advertising companies could give their clients by buying media time cheaply, and charging their clients a proper fee, instead of the system then (and still) in existence.

Recognised agencies were allowed a 15 per cent discount on the price of advertising space; they in turn charged the client the full price, in effect making their profit from the discount. It was an anomaly that dated back to the time when advertising agencies worked for the newspapers and magazines actually selling space rather than buying it. Although their role had reversed from seller to buyer well before the Second World War, the system had carried on, basically because the advertising industry, which ran itself almost as a cartel, found it comfortable and clients didn't object.

To make his plan work – and there were many who told him it was unworkable no matter what happened – he needed a good media buyer. Paul Green, then regarded as the best media buyer in the business, was tempted by the thought of the new agency, and by Charles's idea of what could be achieved in the media-buying field by some really aggressive and imaginative bargaining, in particular with the television companies. However, he was even more taken by the idea of working for himself. Several media men had left to start their own media-broking businesses, and that route appealed to Green. Just weeks before the agency was to launch he backed out. Today the operation he set up, Media Buying Services, is highly successful.

Green's withdrawal came as a bombshell to the Saatchis. 'Paul Green came to a meeting, he met the people from Jaffa who we were pitching for at the time, and then at the eleventh hour, really almost the twelfth hour, he pulled out,' says John Hegarty. Charles Saatchi that very day had dictated a letter to be sent to the media authorities with whom every new agency has to be registered, listing Green as a director of the new agency. Chris Martin recalls:

> Charlie suddenly said to Gail [his secretary], 'Don't send that letter.' 'Gail said, 'I've posted it.' Charlie said, 'Where?' 'Well,' she said, 'it was either in the box in Goodge Street or the one in Tottenham Court Road, or did I post it on my way?' She couldn't remember. It was about six letter boxes she came up with in the end. So Charlie went berserk, and he handed three or four people fivers, and he said, 'Go and stand by the box until the chap comes and bribe the postman to get the letter back.' And Maurice, Charlie, Gail and Hegarty all went off. And they got the letter back. And Paul Green was heard of no more. And enter Tim Bell.

When the Saatchis asked who was the best media man after Green, Bell was mentioned. A phone call from Maurice brought him round within hours; Bell needed little persuading to join – he was already a fan. 'Charlie Saatchi was my god,' he says today. 'I thought he was a genius – I still do. As far as I was concerned, he was the man who had written the pregnant man ad, the best ad I had ever seen. Only later did I discover that was untrue. At the time I saw him as the new Bill Bernbach. The advertising world in those days was terribly boring and stultifying. Charles to me represented excitement and creativity.'

'Lady Luck really smiled on Charlie and Maurice when Paul pulled out and they got Tim in,' says Hegarty. 'Like a lot of things in life, you're dealt what you think is a blow but what in fact is a great piece of luck. Paul Green was an outstanding media man, but in personality terms he didn't balance Maurice and Charlie. The great thing that Tim had was that balance, and without him they never would have built the agency to the size they did.'

Bell at the time was twenty-eight, nearly two years older than Charles. Six foot tall, slim and good-looking, Bell was already heading rapidly up the ladder at Geers Gross, one of the newer and brighter agencies in the industry – and one of the few that Charles Saatchi respected. He also possessed a charm that over the years would become legendary well beyond the bounds of the advertising industry – years later a profile of him would talk about his being the sort of person 'even the dogs cross the street to be kicked by'. To the others he was as near a replacement they could get for the popular Ross Cramer. 'Physically they were very alike; they had that kind of fairish hair,' says Hegarty. 'And Tim, personality-wise, was very similar to Ross. They were both amiable, and neither ever showed if they were down. They were always in the centre of what was happening, very good at remembering the little things that kept people happy, and great at rallying the troops.'

5

'TIME FOR A NEW KIND OF ADVERTISING'

By the end of the summer of 1970, the Saatchi brothers had persuaded most of the talent they wanted to join them. Ron Collins, twenty-nine, was regarded by the others as one of the leading art directors of the day – as he later proved when he went on to found the agency Wight Collins Rutherford Scott. Alan Tilby came from Colletts, where he too had a considerable reputation. With Hegarty, Sinclair, Atherton and Martin, it was a young team, entirely creative except for Maurice and Bell. But how exceptional was it? Each individual member would almost certainly have risen high in whatever agency he chose to join – as indeed most of them did when later they left Saatchi. But there were dozens of other equally talented men and women in the London advertising world at the time; the industry was offering high salaries, it was recruiting young people direct from art schools and universities, there were many like Hegarty and Sinclair who had chosen advertising as their career. As manufacturing industry continued its decline and the City of London financial service sector was in the doldrums, advertising offered an attractive and glamorous career.

So what singled out the nine-man team that Saatchi & Saatchi put together that summer? Several factors emerge. A major part of the answer, certainly in these initial stages, has to lie in the character, energy and drive of Charles Saatchi himself, and in the way he could motivate and bring the best out in others. Hegarty still talks about the special atmosphere Charles could create, a climate touching on fear, but fear in a positive sense. 'Creativity is, I believe, an expression of insecurity,' says Hegarty, 'a desire to win approval. It is in a climate of self-doubt that the creative spark is forced and cajoled into fire.' Charles had a way, he says, of 'daring your ability to create a piece of work of even greater artistry'.

But the role of Maurice should not be underestimated. Over the years the relationship between the brothers would change. In my research for this book I initially formed the view, based on interviews with the early Saatchi team, that Charles had most of the ideas, that the broad strategy and concepts were his, and that Maurice for the first four or five years at least was essentially a bright and obviously able assistant, who carried them out. Only when one analyses the key decisions taken at this early stage, and even more important ones taken later, does one realise it was never quite like that. The huge ambition, the overpowering desire to be bigger, richer, more famous – just to be *more* than anyone else – mostly came from Charles. But Maurice was equally ambitious in his own different way. The business plans and systems that took Saatchi & Saatchi out of the ordinary run-of-the-mill agency within months of its starting were all Maurice's – Charles did not even try to understand them. The takeover plans already being hatched were his too. So were many of the wider concepts, such as the management consultancy service. It is probably true that in these early days Charles was the 'X' factor, but without Maurice he would never even have thought about public companies, altering the City attitude to the advertising industry, spreading the network worldwide, or so much else that made Saatchi & Saatchi what it is today. Without Charles, Maurice would still probably have built a big business, whatever he had gone into. Lindsay Masters says he would still have raised money for him, whatever he wanted to do – and at one stage he even believed Maurice had plans to create his own publishing business. Over the years people would come to find it impossible to imagine one without the other, so well did they work together. But it was never, even in these very early days, the dominant-Charles/little-brother-Maurice relationship that even those who worked closely with them believed it to be.

At this early point, this was not yet apparent, even to Hegarty or Sinclair. None of them had any real idea what they were venturing into, just that they were bright young people starting their own new business with some good ideas, something of a bumpy but creative reputation, a trio of clients and not much else. Sinclair was undoubtedly a highly talented copywriter, probably one of the most talented of his age; Tim Bell would soon emerge as an exceptional advertising executive whom any agency boss would have loved to have had work for him. But advertising history is full of examples of bright young men setting off on their own to form what in a single generation became successful agencies. Without Maurice, there was nothing especially new or dramatically different about their beginnings. They may have *said* that they were different, that they were going to break the mould, build an entirely new form of advertising agency; but then they would, wouldn't they? What new company does not? But it would have been terribly difficult at this point to spot the chemistry that would make this small agency, above all the other little businesses beginning around that time, grow to such monumental proportions, and become so embedded in the corporate folklore of the 1980s. Eighteen years later, Charles could now put his finger on what that catalyst was: his younger brother. But he had no way of knowing it then.

Both Charles and Maurice have also displayed a remarkable ability to choose good people, each time suitable to the particular stage of the organisation. They would be right for one stage of the company's development, do their job and leave – or lag behind the advance of the brothers. Of the team now assembled only Jeremy Sinclair would live with the brothers' pace for the next seventeen years. All the others, including Bell, would drop away or assert their independence. For each new stage of the company, different specialities and areas of expertise would be required, and the Saatchis did not hesitate to go out and hire it.

Charles was always contemptuous of his own industry, voicing again and again that summer his view that most advertising was just a waste of money; the clients might as well dig a hole and bury it for all the good it did them. He would point to full-page ads in the papers that he reckoned no one, 'literally no one', would read. His team was going to be genuinely creative, he kept insisting, and would produce the best ads ever seen in Britain. The very fact that his consultancy had done so well showed how big were the problems inside the big agencies. They had no creative ideas of their own, and had to turn to him to help them. Look what he had done for the Health Education Council. Look at his anti-smoking campaign which had been so effective it had made even *him* cut down.

There were many who found Charles arrogant and overbearing, full of hubris and not very likeable. The realities of running his own agency and dealing with clients would soon bring him down a peg, they prophesied. Anyway his ideas were unworkable, they warned. He was planning to break with a whole series of industry traditions, but others had tried that too and retreated again. No account executives? Well, Geers Gross managed to get away with it, but it posed an intolerable burden on the creative staff having to deal with clients as well as produce imaginative advertising. Bigger discounts from the media, and pass the rebate back to the client? That was just a gimmick, fiddling with figures. The clients wouldn't understand anyway, and couldn't be bothered to try (the team would soon discover that with Granada Television Rentals). Cold-calling clients? That would just annoy them and wouldn't produce a single extra one, or at least a good one. The big accounts were not going to move because some twenty-four-year-old rang up and said, 'Hey, we're a new agency with some creative ideas and we'd like to have your account please.'

Charles either didn't mind the criticisms or ignored them. What he did care about was being noticed, and he was achieving that. No new agency had received such publicity in the trade press before a launch. That summer he made sure that *Campaign* in particular received a steady supply of stories, whipping his staff to greater efforts. 'He used to go around every Monday before press day on *Campaign*', says Chris Martin, 'and he'd say "Give me a story for *Campaign*. Get out there and get in the pubs, any titbit you heard this week, give it to me and it will be passed on. If you don't know one, make it up!" And every single week he'd ring *Campaign* with a story. Not necessarily about Saatchis. They made the front page week after week. It was incredibly time-consuming to do it, but that's what Charlie used to do.'

That summer was a busy one for both brothers, as they prepared pitches at the Goodge Street office, hounded Rodney Fitch about the new premises in Golden Square, and worked out their business plan. Hegarty, Sinclair and Martin were used to Charles's pressure, and didn't worry too much as long as his irritation wasn't directed at them. During the years they had known him they had seen him work himself up into a fury, the invective and obscenities pouring forth in a great stream on top of the unfortunate recipient. They already talked ruefully about being 'beaten up' by Charles, not physically but verbally. They had seen him rip up bits of artwork that had taken days to prepare when he didn't like them, hurling the pieces around the office, shouting that it was 'fucking crap'. He was uncompromising about the product that came out of his agency. Several times someone had shown art-work to the clients who liked it, only to have Charles throw it out because *he* didn't. "Fuck the client, what does *he* know about it?' But he would take infinite pains to get it right if he was unhappy with an ad. 'He could argue all night about a point,' says one of the team. 'He would continually say: "I don't understand what you're trying to do. Tell me what it is you're trying to say." He has an incredibly clear mind that gets right to the heart of it.' Sinclair, like the others, soon learned to keep the conversation with Charles to a basic level. He had no interest in philosophising or intellectualising about advertisements, replying impatiently to any such attempt: 'Yeah, yeah, you keep your philosophy, just tell me what you're trying to say.'

Getting the money together was Maurice's job, and he took to it with flair. The brothers had to find most or all of the £25,000 capital themselves; they would take a few of the others in as partners, but their intention from the beginning was to keep control. Charles had for several years been a big earner, able to command a high salary even before he moved into his own consultancy. He lived at home, but even so had saved little. His earnings in 1970 were £25,000, a huge salary for a twenty-six-year-old in Britain at the time; but he ran a Rolls-Royce Corniche, dressed well and generally lived the good life. Maurice's £3000 a year at Haymarket, good for a twenty-three-year-old, did not allow him to save any capital, particularly with his Corvette Stingray. They would not ask their father for capital, but would raise it outside.

It is an indication of Maurice's relationship with his then boss Lindsay Masters that he chose him as the person to ask for capital – and a manifestation of Masters's affection for him that he should respond. When he told Masters he was leaving to join his brother, the Haymarket boss first tried to dissuade him, then, seeing that was hopeless, decided to help him with advice, contacts and office space until such time as he was ready to go. 'I liked him very much,' he recalls. 'He had done a wonderful job for us and one felt very warmly disposed towards him.' For some months after he had offered his resignation in the transitional months between the consultancy and the agency, Maurice remained at Haymarket, and Masters would occasionally discover him working on budgets and plans for the Saatchi & Saatchi agency. 'I didn't mind – it was fine.'

When Maurice came to see Masters asking him for £25,000, Masters told him he had a problem. Because Haymarket owned *Campaign* he was concerned about the propriety of investing in a company about which the magazine would be writing. He would, he decided, bring in others. Masters of course was a wealthy man, and had some even wealthier friends.

It is perhaps typical of the Saatchi & Saatchi story that these investors were not faceless people. Mary Quant in 1970 was at the height of her fame -or notoriety – having just come up with a new idea she called 'Make-up to Make Love In', a range of cosmetics which a girl 'could kiss and cuddle in all night without looking smudged'. She had married one of her original partners, Alexander Plunket-Greene, and it was to them, and another partner Archie McNair, that Masters went that summer. Maurice Saatchi, he explained, was a very bright young man who worked for him, and he needed £25,000 to start a new business with his brother. Would they help him? 'Would *you* invest?' he was asked. Masters explained that he would indeed, but he had a problem with his conflict of interest, and preferred not to. Mary Quant and her husband agreed – but only if Masters invested too. Reluctantly he accepted, and took a share of the investment (and conscientiously never spoke to any of his *Campaign* editors about the company). 'The thing was done by all of us as a sort of well-inclined and friendly gesture, and not really as an attempt to get massively rich,' says Masters. His partner Michael Heseltine was much keener to invest, but it was just too late for him – the Heath government was now in power, and Heseltine was one of the bright young ministers in it. There are strict rules governing the investments of government ministers, and Heseltine ruled himself out.

There is a revealing little tale that attaches to Masters's particular investment. Much of the talk between him and Maurice took place at Masters's home, and his wife Marisa admits she developed other designs on the younger Saatchi. Her eldest daughter was about Maurice's age, and she thought he might be an ideal match. On several evenings she brought the girl into the room where the discussions were being held; but as the evening wore on, and Maurice developed his plans and arguments for the agency, she fell asleep. Romance never blossomed.

Mrs Masters herself listened to Maurice's plans with considerable interest. She had worked in London as a translator, and kept her savings in a beautiful Victorian box she had found in an auction room. It was, she explains, 'my little nest-egg', which all good Italian women put by without telling their husbands. In this instance, the Victorian box had been safely deposited in Coutts Bank, in the Strand, and in it she had £6000. She would invest it, she decided, in Maurice's new business.

Her husband wouldn't hear of it. He had gone to the Quants because of his worry over his conflict of interest, and she could not invest for the same reason. Recalling the events, Marisa becomes quite emotional. 'I wanted to give my money to Maurice because I loved him as a human being, and I trusted him so much. I really loved him. I begged Lindsay. I said I would invest in my Italian name, Lassandro. It is the first time in my life I want to use my money, the first time in my life I know that I can trust someone completely. But he wouldn't let me. I said, I will give my money to Mary, and she can invest in her name, and I won't even have any documents. I begged, I cried. But no, he wouldn't.'

Just in case he weakened, she took Lindsay's driver to Coutts Bank and got her Victorian box out. She hid it in a cavity under her bath, and waited. The discussion between Masters, Maurice and Mary Quant went on for weeks. Lindsay still refused her the chance to invest, partly for ethical reasons, but also because he didn't believe that a new company was the right place for her 'nest-egg'. Some months later she and her husband went to a reception. When they got home, they found that a back window had been forced. The burglar had found her box, smashed it open with her own tools, and taken her nest-egg. 'I cried for three months with anger and shame.' She never knew until years later that Lindsay had, after all, invested.

The brothers now had the capital they needed, found entirely by Maurice, another example of how crucial he was at this point. Maurice had also completed a detailed five-year plan, which he hoped would take them up to a stock market quotation. With that in mind, he drew up a projection of what profits would need to be to hit that target. The company would have to make £25,000 in the second year, then £50,000, then £125,000 and £250,000 in the fifth year. It was the plan he showed to Masters and to Mary Quant. Now he showed it to the manager at Coutts Bank, who was even more impressed. 'He said it's the best new company plan he's ever seen,' Maurice later told Charles.

Everything was going to plan. By another stroke of luck the economy was picking up under the new Heath government. Neither brother had much interest in politics at the time, Charles in particular dismissing all politicians as useless. The economy was still in poor underlying shape, but the advertising industry could cope with foreign or British companies alike; it didn't matter who made the goods, just so long as someone had the money to buy them.

Many years later there would be a great deal of speculation about what was in the Saatchis' minds at this point. Were they setting out to become the biggest ad agency in Britain, the biggest in the world? Were they set on revolutionising advertising, taking not just London but Madison Avenue by storm, making themselves into household names, while building a 'business services' conglomerate that would be the biggest of its kind in the world? Years later, the 1987 study by the Harvard Business School of Saatchi & Saatchi stated that 'their initial strategy was to shake up the staid British advertising world and to produce the most creative advertising in the country'. In 1970 when they started that would have seemed a considerable ambition, but by the standards of what they have achieved it now looks modest.

'They always seemed to believe the total market was theirs,' says Chris Martin, 'and not just advertising.' That is supported by the attempts to bring in a supermarket executive and a management consultant from the first day. Jeremy Sinclair recalls the ambitions for the new agency as being threefold: 'We were going to be big, we were going to be good and we were going to be profitable. Everyone was keenly aware of those three things.' Mary Quant and Lindsay Masters thought they were backing a couple of bright young men who with a bit of luck might do a little more than survive in the advertising world. There was nothing in the business plan, presented to them by Maurice with all the carefully rehearsed skills of pitching to a client, which indicated that theirs was going to be anything more than a medium-sized agency. Even those involved did not seriously believe that what they were doing was fundamentally different from what other agencies did.

What they did grasp was that Charles and Maurice were extraordinarily ambitious, imaginative and energetic. Yet even this is exaggerated with hindsight. 'With gargantuan ambition burning behind his owlish spectacles, [Maurice] went into the advertising business with his brother in 1970,' wrote *Fortune* magazine in a profile of the Saatchis in 1984. No one who knew them then would recognise that picture; but it was not hard to see they were going places. Working around them were a group of bright young men who had picked up the fever, and it was infectious. All the newcomers knew from their own experience how vulnerable the rest of the advertising world was. Given a fair wind, it should not be impossible, they reasoned, to carve out a niche and make a decent living – and enjoy it at the same time.

Robert Heller, then the editor of *Management Today* and someone who knew them better than most, attributed to them rather grander ambitions. Writing in 1987 he said: 'They arrived at a time when rising American domination had been accompanied by a pervasive blandness and repetition in the actual creative work of advertising. It gave British agencies, mostly new, the chance to become the Greeks to the Romans of Madison Avenue. A rolling tide of brilliant British advertising reset the standard and the style. The Saatchis shared in the flood. The difference was that their ambitions were Roman in scope. They wanted an empire.'

There is no evidence that this is so. Years later, the brothers themselves have difficulty recalling what their motives were. They had no thoughts about 'globalisation' and only dimly perceived moves beyond the advertising industry, and even then only as an extra service to get more advertising business. An international agency seemed a long way away, and their ambitions on that score, says Maurice, only began to develop a couple of years into the agency. 'We were just hoping that it wouldn't fail,' says Maurice. That is almost certainly a rationalisation at the opposite pole to Heller's, or *Fortune*'s. The Saatchis had greater ambitions than Maurice cares to remember.

'I never recall thinking, Wow, this is going to be enormously successful,' says Martin. Yet he was aware of an extra dimension even before the agency started.

> Charlie loved playing poker with his mates – that was his great thing in those days. And his mates were all the guys from North London that he'd gone to school with, grown up with. I know that he was very strongly influenced by the fact that most of these guys had gone off into the City or property or whatever and they were making big, big money. I can remember him saying one day that the motivation for Saatchi & Saatchi was the fact that he'd gone to school with a lot of Jewish boys who were now all millionaires, all really going for it. Although he had a fast car and a big salary, he wasn't accumulating the sort of wealth that they were putting together. So I think Charlie said: 'Okay, I've come into this business, I think my pride tells me that I can't admit that was a mistake and then go off to the City and do anything else. I'm going to bloody make some money.'

Maybe that was a factor too. But if it was, it was not an important one, because this was not Charles's preserve at all, but Maurice's. He instinctively understood the financial side of it in a way that Charles never would; he could learn to pull the right levers that made the City of London react; he would in time become skilled in handling bankers, brokers and City editors; people would like him in a way they would never like Charles, and Maurice in turn would move through the financial and advertising communities in London and New York making many more friends than enemies. The brothers are both, when they want to be, attractive, clever and witty men; the essential difference is that Charles never had the patience or the desire to cultivate new friends, or even to keep up old ones. Maurice still let very few people get close to him, but assiduously courted a wide circle of acquaintances and contacts; born with a natural charm, he polished and perfected it, using it on colleagues and potential clients alike. As the agency grew into a company, and then into a multinational, these are the qualities that were crucial; Maurice was born to cope comfortably with a big organisation, big business and big money. Charles too would grow with the business, and his imagination, energy and ambition looked over horizons; but his best day was now, when the agency was young and the product was essentially his – with some input from the clever creative people, such as Sinclair, Hegarty and Collins, that he had gathered around him.

A number of the Saatchi friends and distant relatives were emerging around this time as leading City figures, and all the talk was of share prices and takeovers. This was the era of City figures like Jim Slater, when young men were making fortunes taking over staid old companies with nothing more than high-priced paper and stripping out the assets. Charles Saatchi lived in that world as much as he did in the advertising one, but it was Maurice who saw that the route to really large money lay in the City, and the best way to get there quickly was by takeover. In the USA advertising agencies were going public at a rate of almost one a month, and although almost all of them were now hitting trouble the principle was appealing. In London a stock market quotation was still relatively novel for an advertising agency, and the two that had followed that route were held in low esteem by the investment community, with consequent low ratings. One of them was Dorland Advertising which was taken over by John Bentley, a young whizz-kid, who bought it in 1971 for the property assets it contained. Bentley sold it three months later, minus its properties. (Dorland eventually became part of the Saatchi empire, and today, under their banner, is the second largest advertising agency in London – after Saatchi & Saatchi.) The Bentley move frightened the only other quoted company, S. H. Benson, which immediately sought shelter under the corporate umbrella of Ogilvy & Mather, an American agency founded by a Scot, David Ogilvy.

In 1970, however, both were still quoted, and despite their modest rating Maurice had fixed his eyes along that route. Even from the earliest days he talked to the others about takeover plans. At the time it all seemed absurdly ambitious.

That summer Maurice came to know Vanni Treves, a solicitor who represented the Quant consortium, very well. Treves is now senior partner of McFarlane's and in 1987 joined the Saatchi & Saatchi board. The solicitor carefully worked out a share structure and articles of association designed for a public flotation. Maurice incorporated it all carefully into his five-year plan. That summer he made frequent visits to the City to show it about. At home the brothers also showed it to family and friends, seeking their reaction. They were never too concerned about raising the money – that was the easy part. On the other hand they were very concerned about keeping the equity tight, ensuring that backers such as Quant and Masters received only a nominal amount of shares while still getting a good return on their money.

They divided the shares out on the basis that each of them had 40 per cent; another 15 per cent was owned by the Mary Quant consortium; and they spread 5 per cent of the shares between Ron Collins, Tim Bell and John Hegarty, with Collins and Bell getting the biggest slice. The details were gone over again and again by Maurice and Treves, with Charles continually asking for progress reports, for changes, for the inclusion of often unworkable clauses which would ensure the brothers always kept control.

Most new businesses would feel that they had now done enough to ensure they had a reasonable chance of success. The publicity in *Campaign* almost every week that summer made sure there was an air of expectation in the industry. Three good clients were aboard, guaranteeing that most of the bills could be paid even if there was no new business. The team was in place. The offices were developing nicely, with Fitch now laying the floor covering: diagonal linoleum in two shades of beige in great wide strips. The £25,000 had been raised, and bank facilities arranged. The 'pregnant man' story was still doing the rounds, adding to the reputation of Charles Saatchi as the creative genius of the advertising world.

Charles still wanted more. There had to be yet another gesture, something which would make an impact beyond Adland, something which would establish the agency from the beginning as something genuinely different, set it well aside from the run of advertising companies, and catch the imagination of the world beyond. Early in September 1970 he hit on it.

The result appeared on the morning of Sunday 13 September, the day before the agency was to open. It was a full-page advertisement on page 7 of the *Sunday Times* with the headline 'Why I think it's time for a new kind of advertising'. It cost the Saatchis £6000, nearly a quarter of their capital. Later Maurice Saatchi would say, 'That ad put us on the map,' but that is a high claim for it. The general readership of the *Sunday Times*, which then (as now) had a circulation of about 1.4 million, almost certainly ignored the ad. It was of no interest to them, nor was it aimed at them. What it was designed to do – and what it achieved – was to surprise the industry, get itself talked about, and gain for the new agency a reputation for boldness and imagination. In all of that it succeeded. 'I can remember reading that ad,' says Bill Muirhead, who joined Saatchi early in 1972, 'and how it sent a cold shiver down my spine. I was an ambitious young account man, and here was this ad telling me I was about to become a waste of space. The account man was redundant.'

No one had ever done anything quite like it before. 'That caught people's breath. It was the forerunner of their becoming a household name, a prelude to their leading advertising out of a closed shop industry,' says Chris Martin. He remembered the lesson well. Years later, when he set up his own agency, Martin did almost exactly the same thing with a full-page advertisement announcing 'Now the famous brothers represent the "mega" agency. They are no longer the little wooden balls, but are themselves the coconut shy.'

The *Sunday Times* ad, although costly, thus proved another clever bit of self-promotion. For it to work effectively the brothers decided that the piece had to be attributed to a named writer. The person chosen was Robert Heller, whose *Management Today* was another Haymarket publication. Heller wrote a management column in the *Observer* every week and had also written a series of management books. The brothers gave him a rough draft of what they wanted to say and Heller pulled it into shape. 'It was about the easiest assignment I ever had,' he says.

For those who knew Charles and had listened to him and his brother that summer, it was familiar stuff. Its starting point was that most advertising is a waste of money. The central philosophy of Charles's simple approach to advertising was set out in the third paragraph: 'Expenditure of shareholders' money is only justified if it ultimately produces a quantifiable and adequate return in the same terms – money. In advertising language, this means that a campaign only succeeds if it ultimately helps to create new sales for a client, and does so effectively and economically.'

Heller quoted a recent survey in *Management Today* which showed that most advertising did not even set out with this objective but was aimed at improving a company's image or improving brand awareness. 'Images and brand awareness are meaningless if they fail to achieve greater turnover: the test is the cash in the till.' Heller then went on to set out some of the points which Charles insisted on stressing as singling the new agency out from the rest. There was an attack on the role of the account executive, 'the middle-man between the advertiser and the people who are paid to create the ads'. Others in the industry were trying to come to terms with this: KMP had a new open-plan office where creative people and account executives all worked together; Lonsdale Crowther had split itself into self-contained units, each one with its own creative and account-service staff. Saatchi & Saatchi would go further: it would totally abolish the account executive and replace him with a 'co-ordinator who is not briefed by the client, does not brief the creative people, does not pass judgement on ads and does not present ads to the clients, but works with the creators as a day-to-day administrator.'

This was an exaggeration. There weren't any 'co-ordinators' among the staff – unless one counted Maurice. The copywriters and art directors were in effect being asked to take on the role of servicing the client, something people such as Jeremy Sinclair felt singularly unfitted for – and rightly so. Within weeks of the new agency opening on 11 September 1970, Charles Saatchi was already busily hiring account executives, and a year or so later he had six, doing almost exactly the job his ad condemned so roundly.

The ad went on to quote the 'hard-selling creative' record of the Cramer Saatchi consultancy, making the point that it had thrived because it could take a fresh approach to tired old advertising problems – just as Bill Bernbach 'came back to Avis with the unwelcome news that the only thing which he could find to say about Avis was that it was Number Two: the rest is advertising (and selling) history.' Saatchi & Saatchi intended to extend that 'freshness' from consultancy into agency.

Then came the bit that made the advertising industry sit up and take note. Saatchi & Saatchi would not take the traditional 15 per cent commission on billings. Its charges, it said, would average 22 per cent which would be paid by the client. What traditionally happened was that if an agency placed an ad costing, say, £10,000, it demanded and got a 15 per cent discount. So it paid £8500 for it. But it charged the client £10,000, taking its profits on the difference. The agency therefore had a vested interest in the newspaper or television company making the highest possible charge for its space or time. (The actual costs of making the ad were already charged direct to the client.) The quid pro quo that Saatchi was now offering for its 22 per cent fee was 'a promise of the cheapest possible buying of space and time'. This would have been the role of Paul Green, but would now be for Tim Bell to achieve. 'Our ploy was that we were going to buy media cheaper than anyone else,' says John Hegarty. 'We were saying we'll make your media money go further. Charlie was going to baulk the 15 per cent commission fee and charge 22 per cent, but guaranteed he would save you money on your media – which meant that you were in fact paying less than 15 per cent. In practice that's not how it worked out. It was really a brilliant

Why I think it's time for a new kind of advertising.

By Jeremy Sinclair

The first Lord Leverhulme, Britain's original margarine and soap king, won undying literary fame by observing that half of the money which he spent on advertising was wasted, but that he didn't know which half. For all he knew, Lord Leverhulme may have wasted still more of his advertising money, and many of today's advertisers doubtless waste more than Lord Leverhulme.

Wasted ads are the ones which nobody sees, reads or notes. Ads are unseen unless the agencies which create and place them, and the clients who approve and pay for them, remember the prime purpose of advertising. Lord Leverhulme never forgot that prime objective. In his day, the age of the entrepreneur, the great ads and the great advertisers were the great sellers. They still are.

Expenditure of shareholders' money is only justified if it ultimately produces a quantifiable and adequate return in the same terms – money. In advertising language, this means that a campaign only succeeds if it ultimately helps to create new sales for the client, and does so effectively and economically. This self-evident truth rests on another: advertising cannot create sales unless (first and above all) it catches the consumer's attention; then, interests the consumer; then, changes the consumer's attitudes; and finally, sells to the consumer. These are the four Stages of Man in advertising; Attention, Interest, Desire and Action.

The sheer power of advertising is so great, anyway, that it can triumph over a lack of penetration which would kill off many other industries. Research by Gallup shows that only 26 per cent of readers of a national newspaper read the average *full page* ad: in other words, if the ad pulls, it does so despite the 74 per cent of the readership which completely ignores the advertiser's expensive message, and which never passes advertising's Stage One. Gallup's files also contain examples of full-page colour ads in a national daily which were noted by only 5 per cent of the readers, and actually read by none of them. Plainly, an ad which everybody reads is far superior to one which somebody reads: but an ad which nobody reads does nothing except cost money. Oddly enough, some companies expect little else from their advertising.

A familiar management failing...

This emerged in a recent survey in *Management Today* by Simon Majaro, director of Strategic Management Learning, and a partner with management consultants, Urwick Orr. He found that many manufacturing firms glibly claimed advertising objectives (making no attempt to measure their achievement) like "improving image of company's products", "improving company's image" and "creating brand awareness" – these objectives were put above "increasing sales", which was regarded as somehow inferior. This is an example of a familiar management failing – putting the means before the end.

Images and brand awareness are meaningless if they fail to achieve greater turnover: the test is the cash in the till, and passing that test is far harder than image-building or winning awards. The great split between so-called creative hot shops and the big marketing agencies is wholly fictitious. A creative ad is only an exercise in self indulgence unless it achieves the client's marketing purposes, expressed in concrete terms of sales penetration; and a marketing agency cannot achieve any result, except the expensive duplication of its clients' own marketing and merchandising skills, unless it creates ads that seize the public mind.

The proper role of the middle-man

The self-induced schizophrenia in the advertising world can create confusion in the agency itself. For example, what is the proper role of the account executive, the middle-man between the advertiser and the people who are paid to create the ads? It must not be to block the creators from direct access to the client: for the risk then is that ads will get created, not to sell more *for* the client, but to give the middle-man something which he can sell *to* the client.

The current experiments with internal agency organisation point to this anxiety: the famous open plan offices at KMP, with creative people hopefully jostling against account executives to some better effect than bruised shoulders; or the division of Lonsdale Crowther into self-contained groups of creative and account-servicing staff; or the total abolition of the account executive by the new Saatchi and Saatchi agency, which adds to its gratifying start of almost £1 million of initial billings, a self-declared role as "just salesmen". The account executive's replacement is a coordinator who is not briefed by the client, does not brief the creative people, does not pass judgement on ads and does not present ads to the client, but works with the creators as a day-to-day administrator.

Obviously, the mode of organisation counts for nothing compared to the results and, in the agency world, there is always a fashion of not being in fashion. No new agency, bursting with all the usual bravado would dream of appearing without new organisational clothes. The Saatchi and Saatchi salesmanship dress gets its individual cut (what you might call a Unique Selling Proposition) from the peculiar nature of its birthplace – a hard-selling creative consultancy called Cramer Saatchi.

Two years ago, creative consultancy itself was a virgin idea. Its subsequent flowering also points to problems inside the big agency. An agency presumably calls in consultants because of doubts whether its own creative staff can produce effective advertising unaided. Several causes arise naturally from time to time even in the best-regulated shops like simple shortage of able bodies; or else thinking on an account gets too inbred, until the agency realises it cannot judge campaigns objectively – it is trapped by its total immersion in the client's own business philosophy and prejudices.

Great advertising nearly always involves looking at a marketing problem in a totally new light – often from a viewpoint which is distasteful to the conventional client. Thus Bill Bernbach of Doyle Dane Bernbach came back to Avis with the unwholesome news that the only thing which the agency could find to say about Avis was that it was Number Two: the rest is advertising (and selling) history. The consultant trades on his blissful ignorance – on coming in fresh to every account, unexposed to the client's sales objectives, marketing problems, management preoccupations and fixed ideas.

Diminishing the power of the retail chains

The major snag when consultants, like Saatchi and Saatchi, proliferate into agency form, is how to preserve this freshness. Their device is to split the agency into two groups on every campaign. The so-called working group, advised by an ex-supermarketeer whose role is to tilt at the growing power of the big retail chains, gets fully involved with the client; its Siamese twin, the control group, knows nothing about the marketing ideas behind the campaign, and asks only one awkward question. Will these ads sell to a consumer who knows equally little about the marketing logic behind them and cares even less?

The potential for what is euphemistically known as "creative tension" between the groups is enormous, but again the results are the only criterion. For this particular agency, that criterion looms especially large, since it is not cheap – charges will average about 22 per cent of total billings – far above the norm: it results from dropping that dear, dying, illogical commission system in favour of cost-plus fees. Its clients pay the agency's costs, amortised over the period of expenditure and net of commission; the quid pro quo for the 22 per cent touch is a promise of the cheapest possible buying of space and time. The growth of the new media brokers has shown how far shrewd and determined media buying can stretch a budget (and stretch a middle-man's profit).

The mechanical task of placing ads most effectively, in terms of price and impact, has been most curiously neglected. For instance, back covers of magazines are seen by far more people than inside pages: yet all media owners know that most back covers are hard to sell. Advertising is beset by other hoary prejudices – for instance, that there's no point in advertising in August and January. Prevalence of myths, which could be smartly destroyed by investigation (or even by common sense), means a disregard for fact – and fact is the foundation of all successful advertising.

A salesman's job

You cannot, except for the briefest span of time, persuade consumers to buy a bad product. If the product is genuinely good, the most effective method of selling and advertising that product is invariably to present the facts about its advantages. Advertising which does its salesman's job presents accurate, meaningful facts about the goods or services of the client: and these few factual ads must be bold or original enough to persuade readers or viewers to pay attention to the facts.

Similarly, effective advertisers must judge agencies by the facts of their own sales performance – and many don't: Saatchi and Saatchi make the unlikely boast that their salesmanship line will cut them off from half their potential clients. Certainly, it is folly to hide behind the smoke-screen of Lord Leverhulme's celebrated dictum (another non-factual myth) and the intangibles of the image. What should concern all advertisers are the tangibles of their advertising expenditure and of the revenue which that spending generates or (as in the Case of the Wasted Ads) fails to generate.

Saatchi & Saatchi and Company

6, Golden Square, London, W1R 3AE.

01-734 9111

kind of juggling with figures.' Like so many other ideas offered in the ad, it was soon abandoned. Saatchi & Saatchi from the beginning was certainly aggressive at media buying, and that has remained one of its hallmarks, but its methods of charging never caught on, and the system it said was 'dying' has remained remarkably intact.

The ad finished by making 'the unlikely boast' that the salesmanship line would cut Saatchi & Saatchi off from half their potential clients. As others remarked, that still left a few to go for.

Heller delivered his copy, but as it got towards publishing time he suddenly had second thoughts. He consulted Lindsay Masters and others at Haymarket and decided that by putting his name on the ad he was endorsing the new agency, something that an independent editor probably should not do. That left the brothers with a problem: whose name would go on it? They chose Jeremy Sinclair.

The brothers later claimed the intention had always been to put Sinclair's name on it, but that is an example – there will be many others cited – of what their critics call their 'ability to rewrite history'. Sinclair was bemused when he was told the ad was to be signed by him. He had very little to do with the advertisement which was now to be seen by nearly four million *Sunday Times* readers. It is symptomatic of so much to come that neither of the Saatchis would put his own name to the ad, although theirs was the name on the agency and they were largely the authors. As far as the outside world was concerned, the author of the ad was an unknown copywriter (at least outside the industry) called Jeremy Sinclair. The advertising industry, on the other hand, knew full well who was really behind it.

The brothers were too excited to wait for the *Sunday Times* to be delivered. On Saturday evening, as the presses of the paper began to roll on what was – and is – the biggest print run in the Western world, Charles, Maurice and John Hegarty went to the Gray's Inn Road print-works to watch. 'We went right down into the press-room,' says John Hegarty. 'And I can remember thinking: Bloody hell, that's us. When we launched we really did launch!'

6

GOLDEN DAYS IN SOHO

The Saatchi brothers started their little agency only dimly aware of the seminal changes going on around them. Even historians seldom recognise change until long after it has occurred, and there was little of the historian in either Saatchi. What they could see was an industry growing fast – total expenditure on advertising in Britain had trebled in the 1950s and doubled again in the 1960s. That growth was visible even from the worm's eye view, and Charles and Maurice both had a natural instinct for taking a higher perspective.

'The joke at the time in the advertising industry was: what do you want to do, fall off a log or make money? Answer: make money – it's easier,' says a senior Saatchi executive. Charles was keenly aware that the industry was only on the threshold of still bigger change and, even more importantly, greater opportunity. For Britain was taking to colour TV in a big way, and the agencies which exploited the new medium best were going to dominate. In retrospect that seems an obvious view, but even by the late 1960s there were agencies in London which were having trouble adapting to commercial television, let alone to colour TV. The men running the agencies had grown up in an age of print, and, although they had seen the importance of commercial TV for their industry (as J. K. Galbraith put it, television 'allows of persuasion with no minimum standard of literacy or intelligence'), they would never be comfortable with it. It was the generation which had been brought up on television, which had learned as children to love the advertisements and sing along with the jingles, which was now impatiently coming up through the business. Charles has always been a compulsive TV watcher, a devotee of the soaps and the serials, and from his earliest memories a fan of catchier commercials. Those who worked with him remember him combing through the TV listings in the daily papers, muttering: 'What's on the box tonight?' Although he had until this point done most of his work in print, his day had arrived.

The 1970s promised to be a boom time for consumerism, which would be spearheaded by advertising on television; and while colour TV was still in its infancy in Britain, a decade after it was widespread in the USA, and only 10 per cent of British homes had colour sets, they were the fastest-selling items in electrical stores. In June 1970 the Conservatives had come back to power with renewed promises of returning the country to economic health and expanding consumer spending. In this new era, and with a new medium, the old-fashioned agencies would be at a disadvantage compared with the younger, who were offering the type of creative work which touched a chord even in the most traditional of clients. At least, that is how the newer agencies perceived it, and up to a point they were to be proved right.

Charles Saatchi and his friends had already detected a movement away from what they saw as the staid multinational houses towards a new kind of advertising. A hunger among clients for more creative thinking had become apparent in the three years of the Cramer Saatchi consultancy. Britain in the 1960s had changed and the Saatchis told each other it was high time for advertising to reflect it. What they failed to perceive was that the larger agencies were changing too, and that no business, however it might appear to the outsider – and Charles Saatchi was never an 'insider' in the sense of being privy to the strategic thinking going on in the bigger agencies – is static. Their picture of the industry, which was never wholly true, was of a business that was 'soft', in the sense of being poorly managed, poorly capitalised and vulnerable, both creatively and financially, to newcomers willing to work hard and who were unencumbered by the baggage of traditional advertising values. They would never have agreed with the view of Jeremy Bullmore of JWT that in 1970 the industry was more responsive, competitive and efficient than any other.

If Bullmore is correct, then the Saatchi achievement has been all the greater, for over the next decade they were to slice through their industry, not only challenging the might of JWT which then stood atop the advertising world but actually toppling it. Bullmore's view, however, is not supported by others of the Saatchi generation who even in the better-run agencies felt stifled. John Hegarty might have been joking when he said that at Benton & Bowles, where he and Charles first worked, 'a full point at the end of a headline was considered a creative breakthrough', but there was an element of truth in that too. There was a joke in the early 1960s that all JWT's press advertisements had a headline, a squared half-tone illustration, a few lines of copy and a pack shot in the bottom right-hand corner. But if that is an unfair jibe, and if in fact JWT in London was competitive and efficient – it was no accident that it was number one – not every agency was. At any rate, it proved remarkably easy for Charles Saatchi to establish his new agency with a reputation as 'creative'. It should not be forgotten that Charles had already been at least partly influenced by his experience at CDP and by working with Cramer. Nor should the input of some of the older hands he came across, such as John Salmon and Colin Millward at CDP, be underestimated, although Charles himself was never free with his gratitude. There was a number of bright young men, of similar creative experience and ambition to Charles, working in the same direction at the same time. Unlike the older generation, they were unapologetic about their profession, rising for the first time above the social stigma that had attached itself to advertising.

Kenneth Galbraith's *The Affluent Society*, on the bestseller list in 1958, was followed by two further parts of his trilogy, reinforcing the point that advertising was the method used by large companies to 'manipulate' the consumer into desiring goods and services primarily because it suited the objectives of the large organisations. In the late 1960s Galbraith was still a powerful liberal voice. The new generation, however, was more influenced by Bill Bernbach and David Ogilvy than by Vance Packard or Galbraith, and Charles Saatchi, who seldom read books, was also blessed with a total lack of introspection.

The point is that 1970 was a new era in other areas besides advertising. It was at the end of a long chain of other changes which came together. Powerful consumer, social and economic trends were moving into new phases too. In the early days, the sheer novelty of TV ads meant that they had a major impact on viewers and produced some dramatic effects on sales. By 1970 the novelty had worn off, and clients and public alike were looking for a new kind of advertising. It had already happened in the USA where the 1960s had seen a much more imaginative approach to advertising than earlier decades, but had largely missed Britain, where many companies were still debating, not which advertising house to go to, but whether they should advertise at all. The 1950s and 1960s had been decades of bumpy but considerable growth in consumer spending in Britain, which would slow in the 1970s. The nature and habits of Britain's workforce had changed sharply in the post-war years, with many more women going out to work, resulting in a demand for convenience foods and one-stop shopping. Britain during the 1960s had replaced the corner shop with the supermarket, which was much more responsive to brand success, and showed a marked preference for products which were promoted on television. The significance of that was not lost on the Saatchis, which is why they had tried to persuade Ian MacLaurin to leave Tesco and join them.

It was still a time of reasonably full employment (at least by today's standards), but despite the promises of Heath and his new chancellor, Tony Barber, the country was about to move into a long period of inflation and an even patchier economic record than the previous decade had seen. The late 1960s saw a huge merger boom in corporate Britain, encouraged by the Labour government which had set up a special agency, the Industrial Reorganisation Corporation, to create larger units to take on continental and American competition. Under Heath, Britain would join the Common Market, and for a few years at least the 'bigness is best' doctrine ruled. British products were seen to be suffering at the hands of competitors who had the advantage of much larger home markets, and only mergers, preferably on an international cross-border basis, could change that. The idea was right but the execution of it all wrong, and within a few years many of the big mergers had fallen into disrepute, notably that between the two leading automobile makers, Leyland and the British Motor Corporation in 1968, and the many more controversial takeovers sponsored by Jim Slater and the financial whizz-kids in the City. Although few knew it at the time, by 1970 this trend was already passing and within a few years would give way to the idea of 'small is beautiful', equally short-lived.

In 1970 another trend had also reached its zenith, again without anyone noticing or recording it. The age of the great multinationals was changing, to be replaced by what the Saatchis would later adopt as their own doctrine: globalisation, a word then seldom heard outside the study halls of the Harvard professor Theodore Levitt, who would later become very important to the brothers. In 1970 the multinational corporations such as IBM, Ford, Shell, Bayer and the Swedish group SKF were generally regarded in Europe as sinister organisations to be feared and loathed. Their annual sales, it was pointed out, were as large as the gross national products of many countries, their growth rate much faster. They could – and did – transfer vast quantities of money between currencies, precipitating financial crises. They could, in theory at least, transfer production from a factory in one country to an identical one in another in the event of either a strike or a better deal being offered – a power which made them greatly hated by the unions.

Most of the multinationals were American, and dislike of them became inextricably mixed with anti-Americanism, less prevalent in Britain than in other European countries but none the less a growing factor. In 1967 Jean-Jacques Servan-Schreiber had published his classic attack on American business, *Le Défi Americain*, and it had aroused as much interest in Britain as everywhere else. The following year there was an attempt at a British equivalent, *The American Takeover of Britain*, written by two *Daily Express* journalists, James McMillan and Bernard Harris, which listed all the American brand names marketed in Britain, and raised the question: 'How far does Britain's economic dependence on the United States compromise her ability to remain politically independent?' In retrospect many of the fears and forecasts raised in *Le Défi Americain* by McMillan and Harris and by subsequent books and articles were absurd, but then critics of Galbraith, particularly when market and supply economics came to dominate the politics of both Britain and the USA in the 1980s, would say the same about him.

It is worth pausing for a moment to reflect on some of the fears that McMillan and Harris set down, not to ridicule them but to record the generally accepted view at the time. It was not, they said, the fact that eight out of the fourteen largest agencies in the UK were US-owned that concerned them, nor even that many of the remainder had associate links with US companies, 'but rather that the development of twentieth-century advertising has coloured British lives and twentieth-century advertising is overwhelmingly American in its origin'.

They gave examples: packaged meat had originally appeared in supermarkets because American researchers in American advertising agencies had discovered that women 'were secretly scared of entering discussions about cuts of meat in the butcher's shop'. Cake mixes had also been introduced into Britain from the USA after research 'based on a psychiatric study of women's menstrual cycle and emotional state'. Even 'swinging London' had been made more swinging by the American introduction of ads for underwear: 'I dreamed I stopped the traffic in my Maidenform bra.' In the late 1960s Britain was going through much the same phobia about new research and marketing methods that the USA did after Packard's *The Image Makers* and *The Hidden Persuaders* were published. 'Advertising in the US has long had practitioners in the esoteric realms of motivational research and deep analysis,' wrote McMillan and Harris. 'They are now at work in the UK. In advertising, more than any other business, it is true to say "What America does today, England will do tomorrow".'

In 1970 this was a familiar argument, one which may in the event have made progress easier for the Saatchis, in the sense that more

British companies may have felt, if they had to advertise at all, they might as well choose a British agency.

The rise of the big American agencies had gone side by side with the rise of the multinationals – as well as American banks, accountancy firms and various other services which went international behind the big manufacturing companies. In his book *The Multinationals*, written in 1971, Christopher Tugendhat writes: 'The advance of the multinationals can be likened to that of an army with a large band of camp followers. When the company settles in a new market, it likes to have familiar faces around it, and to seek advice from the local subsidiaries of the same firms who provide it at home.' Thus, he pointed out, the Chrysler and Gulf Oil subsidiaries in Britain employed the US-owned Young & Rubicam for much of their public relations, while Young & Rubicam in turn had an account with the London branch of the First National City Bank of New York (as it was then called). In 1937 only four US agencies had branches outside the USA. By 1960 the number had grown to thirty-six with a total of 281 offices. Before the rise of the Saatchis, only four of the top twenty agencies were still British-owned. J. Walter Thompson had started in Britain in 1899 and by 1960 was twice the size of its nearest rival with £14.7 million of billings, compared with the £6.9 million of the next in line, S. H. Benson. JWT's dominance of the big American accounts came under threat only when the other established US agencies arrived in the 1950s: Young & Rubicam, Foote Cone & Belding and Ted Bates all set up shop in London, offering their services to their own clients back home.

Tugendhat reflected the widespread fear among the commentators and politicians of the day that the multinationals, particularly the American ones, would grow to the point where they were a serious challenge to national governments. Professor Howard Perlmutter forecast in 1968 that by 1985 world industry would be dominated by 200–300 large international companies responsible for the greater part of industrial output. Giovanni Agnelli, Fiat's chairman, warned that the concentration in the world auto industry would be greater. 'Eventually there will be the three American companies, and one British. The rest will wind up together – as one or two companies.' No one had told Agnelli about the Japanese; or about the state of the British car industry which would never again seriously feature on the world scene, except as 'niche' players. Nor did many foresee that by the mid-1970s the great American multinationals would begin to retreat and the threat to governments, always more imagined than real, would subside.

The multinationals functioned by having largely autonomous

companies operating in different countries of the world, their relationship with the parent back home being essentially a financial one. Ford in Britain made a different range of cars from that of Ford of Germany, and both ranges bore little relationship to the cars made by the parent company in Dearborn. From the late 1960s on, however, everybody in the world wanted common products. The result, wrote Professor Theodore Levitt, was 'a new commercial reality – the explosive emergence of global markets for globally standardised products, gigantic world-scale markets of previously unimagined magnitudes'. The world's aspirations would level both outward and upward through the 1970s and 1980s, he forecast. The companies that recognised that would 'devastate competitors that still live functionally in the disabling grip of old assumptions about how the world now works'. Levitt was preaching this message long before the Saatchis ever heard him, and it is only with hindsight that it is possible to recognise the change from multinational to global.

The Saatchi projections in 1970 stopped some way short of the 'global', however. In preparing his five-year plan, Maurice had studied the growth of advertising revenue and broken it down into its various sources, more to add support for his money-raising exercise than for anything else. Everyone could see how commercial TV was benefiting the business. For the agencies it was a wonderful medium: they could, for the first time, use both sound and movement to state their proposition, could reach audiences in their own homes and could repeat a message several times in the same evening. With a press ad, readers could choose whether they wanted to read it, or decide what parts of it interested them. With the television set, particularly before the days of remote control, the only choices to be made were whether to turn the set on and which of the two channels, BBC or ITV, to watch. Sophisticated new research methods had already made it possible to estimate the size and composition of a TV audience at any given time. Moreover, television considerably boosted the profits of agencies who received 15 per cent commission every time an ad was screened.

Yet the advent of commercial TV found the British agencies woefully unprepared. Although it should have been clear that the trends which had already emerged in the USA in the 1940s and 1950s would eventually come to Britain, even the new generation, including Charles Saatchi, had achieved most of its more creative work in print. The early TV commercials made in Britain reflect their creators' uncertain approach to the new medium: they were longer, used middle-class actors, values and accents, had a painfully slow delivery and spelt out the message several times. They were also black and white, and invariably used poor lighting. They were, in short, adaptations of press advertisements, and not very good ones at that.

Seeking to improve them, the agencies turned to the one influence that meant anything to them: the USA. 'Broadcast advertising was an American invention,' wrote David Bernstein in an essay on the television commercial. 'UK agencies studied US reels. If the agency was US-owned, producers and writers taught their British associates.' Agencies imported British producers, and this was not always helpful: their experience was often in sponsored programmes, and there was no sponsorship in Britain. Alternatively, says Terry Nevett, a marketing academic, in his book *Advertising in Britain*, the British-based agencies 'engaged ageing British thespians whose contribution was even more doubtful'.

Much of that changed in the 1960s as the agencies learned the lessons through trial and experience. In 1963, for instance, Jim Garrett set up his own production company to make ads for the agencies and soon he and others were producing high quality work for the first time. By the time the Saatchis were ready to launch their agency the TV commercial had come of age. 'We were all awaiting the 1970s, when the creative revolution would be unleashed ten years after the one in the USA and yet become much more significant in its long-lasting effect,' said Tim Bell later. 'It has always fascinated me that the US agencies which dominated British advertising in the 1960s never imported the good work being done in their home country to the colonial outpost of the UK.'

Again the Saatchis only dimly glimpsed another trend which was to prove central for them: the move towards greater financial sophistication. The late 1950s and most of the 1960s may have been expansionary times, but not many advertising people had much interest in running agencies as if they were businesses. That was soon to change. The smaller agencies were sometimes partnerships, and under the British tax laws a partnership cannot accumulate capital. Even where they were incorporated they had usually been founded at a time when a large working capital was not needed; but, with expansion, capital was essential, and many of the agencies had to borrow heavily to finance their clients' growing media expenditure. In their attempts to compete with the Americans the British agencies offered an increasingly wide range of non-advertising services free: marketing, public relations and other services, often provided by people imported from America, where most of the experience in these new areas existed. As McMillan and

Harris remarked in their book, the British industry was fighting back vigorously, 'but it is, perforce, fighting with weapons chosen and perfected in America.'

A downturn in economic fortunes in the second half of the 1960s, together with the new and hated Selective Employment Tax, caused unemployment and mergers among the agencies. By 1970 most of the agencies not American owned, even those with big names and reputations, were financially so weak that they were easy prey to an aggressive takeover-bidder. Charles and Maurice Saatchi were fully aware of that from the moment they launched their agency, and always intended to take full advantage of it.

One or two agencies had tried to go public, but that was an even more dangerous game. The City had a low opinion of advertising agencies, with their high costs, small assets and a business which could disappear at the whim of the client. David Ogilvy had taken Ogilvy & Mather public simultaneously both on Wall Street and in London in 1966, the first agency to be quoted in both markets until Saatchi & Saatchi some fifteen years later; but even his shares never acquired glamour stock status, and Ogilvy, despite doing much to build the image of the advertising industry worldwide, never understood the importance of a high financial rating. The predatory instincts of John Bentley, already described in the last chapter, lay ahead but were always a danger at the back of any agency's mind. It was inevitable, for instance, that at some point someone – and it didn't have to be Bentley – would recognise that the property value of S. H. Benson, founded in 1893 and one of the most firmly established in the business, was greater than its own stock-market value. In that instance, it was Jacob Rothschild who stepped in, buying Benson's for £4.9 million and then selling, by prearrangement, the advertising agencies to Ogilvy & Mather, run by that same David Ogilvy who would later be so critical of the big mergers in the industry in the 1980s. Rothschild, like Bentley, kept the property, and his deal with Ogilvy allowed him to carry out a highly effective job of asset-stripping. When Bentley had done the same thing there had been an outcry; Rothschild was greeted as a saviour.

That was several years away, but may have been another factor in the development of Saatchi & Saatchi: they would never, if they could avoid it, invest in buildings or purely material assets. They were determined not to become vulnerable to takeover.

For the moment, however, the Saatchis could concentrate their attack on the obvious weak points of the advertising business. They could – and did in the *Sunday Times* ad – cite research showing how ineffective was most of the current advertising. Maurice turned up figures produced by Gallup which showed that some four-colour ads in a daily newspaper had been noted by as little as 5 per cent of their readers. 'The sheer power of advertising is so great, anyway, that it can triumph over a lack of penetration which would kill off many other industries,' he noted. Further research confirmed another view: many manufacturing firms talked about objectives such as 'improving image of company's product', or 'improving company's image' or 'creative brand awareness', putting them ahead of 'increasing sales'. It was, the Saatchis said in their ad, 'an example of a familiar management failing – putting the means before the end'.

In later years Saatchi & Saatchi would not refrain from doing similar advertising itself, but in September 1970 it was set only on attacking much of the accepted wisdom and myths of the business.

Probably what was changing more than anything else in London Adland was the people. By 1970 the generation that had joined the ad industry before the Second World War was almost gone. The inrush immediately post-1945 often consisted of men already in their thirties, who had often drifted into advertising because they could think of nothing else. With commercial television, the advertising industry for the first time became an exciting place to be in. 'It was the generation who entered advertising in the late 1950s and early 1960s who transformed not only television advertising but, in doing so, the agencies themselves,' says Bell. The emergence of Collett Dickenson Pearce as the pre-eminent creative agency, then Saatchi & Saatchi and Boase Massimi Pollitt, was to have a permanent impact on the business. By 1970, print media had been relegated to a supporting role, used only when the details of the product or an offer were so complicated that they needed explanation at length. In an average agency handling many new consumer products, television was given 85-90 per cent of the budget. There was a small amount of cinema and radio advertising, but television was predominant.

It is interesting to contrast the relative positions of the agencies as the Saatchis set off. Between the wars J. Walter Thompson stood head and shoulders above the competition. By 1970 it was still number one, with a turnover of £24 million-plus and profits of over £300,000 (although others were now closing on it). Charles Saatchi was proposing to open an agency employing just nine people; JWT in London alone employed nearly 1000. Saatchi had five accounts (and that was stretching it); JWT had 100. JWT had offices around the world, with thousands more employees. Saatchi had that one office, with its ground-floor room and basement. It was inconceivable that Saatchi could ever challenge JWT – or was it? Douglas C. West, writing a history of JWT from 1919 to 1970, maintains that in 1970 'rivalry with the then fledgling Saatchi & Saatchi was to commence and continue to the present day'; so he at least took it seriously, albeit retrospectively. In 1970 JWT did not see it that way, and nor did its clients.

The news broke where Charles Saatchi wanted it to – and exactly according to plan. The new agency, Saatchi & Saatchi, would open for business on the morning of Monday, 14 September 1970. The *Sunday Times* ad was set for Sunday, 13 September, so the previous Friday *Campaign* carried a front-page lead story under the headline 'Saatchi starts agency with £1m'. It dominated that week's issue, with pictures of the brothers – Charles, his hair now a respectable length, wearing a light-coloured suit and striped tie, and Maurice, his hair longer, more soberly attired in a dark suit. The story announced that Charles, 'the copywriting partner of the highly reputed Cramer Saatchi creative consultancy', was setting up on his own. He would have five accounts, with billings worth £1 million, it said. Maurice was not mentioned until the fourth paragraph, where he was said to be responsible for new business and 'marketing the agency'.

The story contained a number of fallacies which would become parts of the myth. For instance, even the most generous of accounting could not add up the billings to anything approaching £1 million; those who worked for the Saatchis suggest that they were worth no more than £250,000 and that 'Charlie was anticipating events – as he always did.' It was a trait that has characterised him ever since: announce that you have made such-and-such a figure, then go out and make it right. Then there was the financial backing: no mention of the Quants, or Lindsay Masters. 'The agency is being backed by a City financial group plus a considerable investment from the elder brother.' It would have been slightly embarrassing for *Campaign*, even if it had been aware of it, to reveal that its own proprietor, Lindsay Masters, was a shareholder, although Masters had invested only reluctantly and with the best of motives; his involvement, brief as it was to be, remained secret for years.

There was, of course, no City group, unless one counted the Plunket-Greenes as 'City' – they did meet in Vanni Treves's office in the City for regular reviews of their investment. Nor had the 'elder brother' put his hand in his pocket – Charles had not put up any of the capital.

Inside, *Campaign* carried a full-page feature on the agency; the two

campaign

The newspaper of the communications business — September 11 1970 — 3s

Why Campaign is first

Campaign celebrates its second birthday this week with the inside story of the setting up of an important new agency. Over the last 12 months, in fact, all the major events of the industry have been recorded first and frequently only in *Campaign*.

At the same time *Campaign*'s appointments pages, now designed in six columns, are carrying more job ads than any similar paper. The story is the same with display advertising.

More and more companies are realising that the best medium in which to advertise is *Campaign*. Because *Campaign* is the only publication to give a full, in-depth coverage of advertising and marketing

Home news 2-7, International news 8, Leader 11, Letters 11, Criticism/Press 13-15, Criticism/TV 16, TV Ratings 19, The Saatchi and Saatchi agency 21, Charles Marowitz on advertising 23, Campaign Interview—George Cannon of Alliance Cash and Carry 25-29, Advances 32-34, Appointments 35-43, Diary 44, Philip Kleinman 44

Ex-Pritchard Wood director goes to Eden Vale

BASIL HOOPER, a former director of Pritchard Wood, has been appointed marketing director of Eden Vale, the dairy foods subsidiary of Express Dairies. He replaces Fred Barker who retired in July.

Hooper, who joined Pritchard Wood after the Boase Massimi Pollitt breakaway in 1968, was in charge of account services and was thought at one time to be successor to Austen Barnes, then managing director of the agency.

But he left the agency in April last year following a top management reshuffle, when Barnes became chairman and was succeeded by account director Ian Pavitt and creative director Bill Jenkins. Since then he has been doing consultancy work.

Saatchi starts agency with £1m

CHARLES SAATCHI, the copywriting partner of the highly reputed Cramer Saatchi creative consultancy, is setting up his own agency.

It will start with five accounts and a billing approaching £1 million.

The accounts are Jaffa oranges, Granada TV rentals, the Health Education Council, a division of the Amoco oil company and a cosmetic and fashion company for which it will launch a new range of products.

Saatchi, 27, is starting the agency, Saatchi and Saatchi and Company, with his brother Maurice, 24, business development manager at Haymarket Press and a former promotions manager of *Campaign*. Maurice will be responsible for new business and "marketing the agency". The agency is being backed by a City financial group plus a considerable investment from the elder brother.

The agency is strongly orientated towards the creative side and much interest will centre on whether it can be as successful as the Cramer Saatchi consultancy which is now folding.

For while admiring the work of Saatchi and art director Ross Cramer, critics have claimed that it is one thing to run a consultancy doing new presentations in a marketing vacuum and another to run advertising that must appear in the open market. Charles Saatchi points out, however, that he has produced campaigns, which have run, for a number of packaged-goods clients.

The Cramer Saatchi consultancy was formed over two years ago when Saatchi and Cramer left Collett Dickenson Pearce. Cramer will now direct commercials through the Terence Donovan production company (Hotline, June 26).

The split appears to be an amicable one. Cramer, who will make most of the commercials for the new agency, says: "When it came to the point of forming an agency I realised I didn't want to go on working in an office for years. And I had become far more interested in the television side of advertising."

The consultancy specialised in presentation work for agencies and, according to Saatchi, worked for 15 of the top 20 agencies in London and helped move more than £6 million of billing. It became best known for its creative work for the Health

Charles Saatchi (left) and his brother Maurice . . . on their own

Charles Saatchi : We'll cut ourselves off Page 21

Education Council, creating the anti-smoking campaign, the Pregnant Man ad for contraception, the award-winning Fly poster for food hygiene and the controversial venereal disease posters.

The consultancy also worked direct for a number of clients and, though the agency has not pitched for the business, it hopes that these clients will use it.

The agency will have three directors in addition to the Saatchi brothers: Tim Bell, 30, media manager at Geers Gross, a supermarket executive whom the agency will not yet name and a financial adviser still to be appointed.

Two new creative people are joining those already at the consultancy. They are Ron Collins,

31, senior art director at Doyle Dane Bernbach, and Alan Tilby, 25, a copywriter at Colletts. Collins will be an associate director with John Hegarty, an art director at the consultancy.

Collins was responsible for the famous Martell brandy campaign with French scenes such as an outdoor wedding reception, Dunn's suits which won the DADA ad of the year award in 1969, and Acrilan.

Tilby has worked on Hamlet cigars, the launch of Mellow Virginia Flake, Pretty Polly stockings and Ford.

The agency will have an unusual structure with working and control groups for each account. When a new account is taken on there will be a general discussion with all the staff after which a working group of six or seven will be appointed. The group would consist of four creative

TURN TO PAGE 5

Let the radio sponsors in, says Bow Group report

THE ban that prevents advertisers from sponsoring TV programmes should not be applied to commercial radio, says a report published today by the Bow Group, the independent group of left-wing Tories.

The report, prepared by eight Bow members including advertising and Press people, says: "If BP wanted to finance an opera performance in London and sponsor it on radio, as Texaco does with the New York Metropolitan, why forbid this?"

Stations should carry a maximum of six minutes of advertising an hour, plus a specialised ration of time for advertising magazines of the shopping guide variety, says the report.

Commercial radio should be supervised by a Central Radio Authority operating through a Local Radio Authority in each station's area. Content should lie between "the pap and paternalistic extremes."

To help the bigger advertiser the central authority would have under it a central time-selling agency offering deals for national or regional coverage, says the report.

Authors of the report are David Weeks, a Bensons account director; Donald Etheridge, marketing director of the Davidson Macaulay agency; Max Hann, an IPC marketing research executive; Pamela Dyas, an IPC research and development administration officer; Eric Reynolds, marketing executive at Sadler Wells; Terence Kelly, journalist and broadcaster; John Costello, a TV producer; and Patrick Hodgson, formerly of the Conservative research department.

Commercials firm to close down

THE Runnymede production company is to fold at the end of the month. Gordon Murray, the commercials director and founder of the firm, says: "We have not gone broke and all commitments will be met when we stop trading."

Murray started Runnymede with lighting cameraman Sam Martin in 1959. In production company terms this makes it one of the old established commercials shops. It has made films for Coca Cola, Dunlop, Philips, Ambrosia sago and the Dutch Dairy Bureau.

It was regarded as an efficient and low cost company but suffered from a lack of fashionable image and a general slowing of commercials production in recent months.

brothers were interviewed and in contrast with their later legendary reticence were positively loquacious. 'Both are excitable, sound very much alike, use the same expressions (most advertising is either "terrific" or "shit"). If one stops talking the other instantly takes up the script. Each is caught up in the infectious enthusiasm of the other.'

Charles made much of the concentration on creativity, stressing the importance of two newcomers to the agency: Ron Collins from Doyle Dane Bernbach and Alan Tilby from Collett Dickenson Pearce (where Collins had also worked, at the time Charles was there). 'The creative function is the main one, and one of only two services an agency should provide: the other is media buying,' said Charles. 'They are the two services necessary to fulfil the agency's one function – to sell the clients' goods. We don't understand any other service.' Charles also made the point, which he had been expounding all summer, that there would be no account executives, insisting that the creative advertising people would work directly with the client. 'All our creative people have to act as if they were salesmen,' said Charles. 'They have to imagine themselves in the client's position all the time. They have to see themselves with a warehouse full of the product which has to be sold. Most agencies have replaced the basic function of selling with myths and mystiques about marketing and research. But agencies and clients have become too sophisticated, whereas advertising is not a sophisticated business at all. It is a simple business.'

It is worth examining this comment, not least because it is one of the longest on record from Charles. There is a certain amount of hypocrisy in it, since Charles always hated having any contact with a client, and would become progressively more distant from such contact as time went on. Charles might have intended that his creative staff should talk to the client rather than going through the traditional account executive; but he had no intention of doing it himself. *Campaign* allowed itself a sceptical note here: 'It will be interesting to see whether this is as meaningful in practice as the Saatchi brothers fervently believe.' As events would prove, it wasn't.

There is another point of interest about the interview. By 1970 most London agencies were, as Charles said, offering detailed research and measurements of results. In 1964 JWT had set up 'creative workshops' to try to substantiate how advertising worked, and from this had evolved a complicated system, which it called its 'T-plan', which talked about advertising being a 'stimulus' which produced a 'response'. Other agencies had their own variations, their attempts to provide a technical discipline to what had been until then a far from scientific industry.

Charles wanted none of that. Research? If he needed it he would buy it. Advertising was about selling more of the clients' products or services. Good creative work and good buying of media space – that was what it was all about. 'They will say we don't offer the services. We will say "We don't understand what other services there are." But whatever we say they will never understand.'

It is easy enough to spot the holes in Charles's quotations to *Campaign* that day. He had never run an agency, and was about to learn some important lessons. Today, Saatchi & Saatchi offers its clients every service it can think of, from advertising to management consultancy, legal research, packaging, direct selling and public relations. Yet there is a fair amount of consistency here too. To Charles, advertising was, and remains, essentially a simple business. His own special genius was his ability to distil a complex argument into a single-minded message. It was what he trained himself to do in his best creative moments, and what he dinned into his executives. His extraordinary ability to see through the jargon and the complexity that inevitably creeps into any industry has been one of the strengths behind Saatchi, not just as an advertising agency but as a fully-fledged public limited company. Charles felt then, and still to some extent feels, that research and other modern methods can get in the way of the purpose of advertising, which is, after all, to sell.

Saatchi & Saatchi had been going a week when John Hegarty met Doris Dibley at a business reception. Hegarty was somewhat in awe of her. The tall, long-legged American copywriter was increasingly being seen in Charles's company, and Hegarty was aware they were more than friends.

'How is it, John?' asked Doris.

'Doris, it smells great,' said Hegarty. 'You just feel it's going to do something. It just isn't like anything else. The way the office is laid out, the way the whole thing looks, the way it feels like a new idea in advertising – I just have a feeling something great is going to happen.'

That did not mean it was comfortable at Golden Square. From the beginning there was an air of tension which was not always positive, but which most of the Saatchi team would later recall as the 'golden era' of Saatchi & Saatchi, named after both the period and the Soho address. Ron Collins, several years older than anyone else, found it hard to adjust and never settled to the pace demanded by Charles. Others, however, thrived on it. Tim Bell, although brought in as the media space buyer, soon moved to centre stage, more because of his personality than anything else. Within a matter of months he had assumed as of right the position of number two to Charles and Maurice – not that it meant much. There was no question who was running the place.

From early morning to late evening, Charles strode the floor of his little empire. Although he had assigned himself and Maurice two of the little offices at the back of the big open plan floor where all the others sat, he was seldom in it. 'Charles's office was where he happened to be – which was sometimes in the middle of my desk, sitting up there cross-legged, with everybody sitting around, shouting suggestions at him,' says Hegarty.

Although Charles was as volatile as ever, there was a new aspect to him which Hegarty, who had known him longer than anyone except his brother, now noticed. 'From the day Charlie decided he was going to start the agency, he changed totally,' he says. 'From being this lunatic creative guy who screamed and shouted and stormed out of meetings, he became a businessman. He cut his hair short, he wore sober suits, he bought club ties that he had no right to wear, went to Turnbull & Asser and got shirts made. It was incredible.'

Charles emphasised again and again to the others the importance of giving the impression the agency was bigger, busier and more established than it was. The offices were designed around that principle. Maurice added a little touch too. He had Bill Atherton design their 'Saatchi & Saatchi' letterheading in very sober type. 'Make us look like a bank,' he told him.

In these early days, Charles handled clients himself – and did so with skill and courtesy. No one in the agency had any doubt how charming and convivial he could be when he chose; but all had seen him change abruptly into a raging, contemptuous figure, as liable to wheel on a client, however large, as he was on one of his own staff. For several months, however, even while he stormed around the office shouting for more effort, more business and better ideas, with clients he was remarkably restrained. 'It was like somebody threw a switch,' says Hegarty. 'He was terribly concerned to get the right image and the right publicity. When a client walked in, they thought, "Gosh, I've got to see these mad creative people and they'll probably be wearing pyschedelic shirts", and instead they met Charlie, and he looked like a NatWest bank manager – but a very elegant one.'

While Charles was dominating the creative output, preparing pitches and even presenting to clients, Maurice was drumming up new business. He had learned a great deal at Haymarket and had soaked up the cheeky but effective methods he had observed work so well for Michael Heseltine. The principal one was that the more phone calls you made the more business you got in – something unheard of in the advertising industry, where agencies traditionally relied on contacts, word of mouth and reputation. Maurice enthused about this method to Charles, who saw the possibilities for the new agency. Haymarket, under Heseltine and Masters, was probably the most advanced publishing house of its day in terms of organised selling of advertising space. The Saatchis would employ exactly the same technique, even using the same files of names and telephone numbers, to solicit for new accounts. Haymarket required its advertising salesmen to make twenty-five calls a day, the optimum number they reckoned anyone could reasonably handle. From the first day of Saatchi's Maurice was in one of the small offices at the back working through a Rolladex file of company names – making twenty-five calls a day.

Years afterwards, Maurice still has his little introduction off by heart: 'Hello, my name is Maurice Saatchi, and we're a new advertising agency. Although you're probably very happy with your present advertising agency, I think it would be worthwhile your coming to talk to us, and seeing a presentation we have prepared for you.'

Even to the younger members of the team, this method of getting business came as a shock. None had ever seen it before – or even heard of it being done. It broke all the rules of the industry, which expressly forbade poaching clients. The Saatchis, however, never much cared for the conventions, and soon Tim Bell was joining in the phone calls. Charles himself, in a quiet moment, would also grab a Rolladex and begin calling, invariably giving someone else's name – Bell's or Ron Collins's or Jeremy Sinclair's, or a wholly imaginary one. No one ever remembers him making a call under his own name.

And it worked. 'They got streams of people in,' says Hegarty. 'It was phenomenal.' Translating that into actual billings was another matter, and the brothers knew it would take time. They were laying the groundwork, sowing the seeds. 'You get someone in, and three months later they remember you and they come back. Six months later they're reviewing their account, and maybe they come and see you again,' Maurice explained to the others, just as Michael Heseltine had expounded it to him.

Many marketing directors were affronted to get a 'my name is Maurice Saatchi' phone call, but no one in Golden Square minded. Bell and Maurice made it into a game to relate the best reason yet for being turned down, and the others would roar with laughter when they staggered out of the back office to relate the latest refusal. In those early weeks the others quickly learned to appreciate and respect the younger Saatchi for his discipline, his devotion – and also his humour.

'Maurice was great,' says Hegarty. 'He'd come out saying, "Another one just slammed the phone down", and he'd be dying of laughter. And Charles would join in and then say: "Back in, Maurice – another twenty-four calls today." And he'd go back and get the old digit going.'

If the marketing manager at the other end of the phone responded, Maurice would invite him to Golden Square for what the Saatchis called a 'house presentation'. Marketing directors were used to this, and there was enough talk around about this new agency for them to be sufficiently curious to go. There they got a surprise. The normal system was that an agency in a house presentation would tell the client all about the agency – and nothing about its views on the client. Maurice, however, did his homework assiduously, and when the client appeared would give him an analysis of the position as he saw it. 'It became something of a joke in the agency, because people would say: "Good God, you must have seen our latest research," ' says a Saatchi man. It was a simple yet effective bit of marketing; Maurice knew his way around the company card index and press cuttings files, and an hour's research was often enough for him to identify a company's basic problems or opportunities.

Maurice himself recalls this particular period with mixed feelings. It was tough, but also exciting. He and his brother were building their own business, and their own fortune. They brought in David Perring to look after the financial detail (he is still there), but Maurice, in between chasing new business, preparing presentations and filling in wherever there was a gap, was also the man who had to report to the shareholders' group, represented by Lindsay Masters and the Plunket-Greenes. It meant that every few months he made the journey to the office of Vanni Treves to explain how the company was doing. Treves remembers the youthful Maurice, tall and gangling, with a curious mixture of diffidence and confidence, presenting the latest set of accounts at these meetings. Years later the minutes make interesting reading: 'Maurice Saatchi reported that he was concerned about the rent bill of £1100 a month . . . .' But if Maurice was concerned Treves reckons he was the only one who was. The shareholders were more than happy with their investment, and with the quality of the reporting. From these meetings Treves developed a lifelong relationship with the Saatchis, and a considerable respect for Maurice in particular.

From the first day, everyone was busy. The main account was still the Health Education Council, now in full flight with a new anti-smoking campaign. The 'pregnant man' ad had raised expectations high, and Charles was conscious of how much depended on getting the new campaign right. It was not a simple campaign: it was what is known in the jargon as 'attitude-change' advertising, one of the first times it had been done in Britain in this way. The first commercial from the new agency – for television – showed lemmings leaping off a cliff, intercut with London commuters walking across Waterloo Bridge, smoking cigarettes. The voice-over said: 'There's a strange Arctic rodent called the lemming which every year throws itself off a cliff. It's as though it wanted to die. Every year in Britain thousands of men and women smoke cigarettes. It's as though they want to die . . .'

The campaign, the work of Jeremy Sinclair, proved as controversial as some of Charles's earlier efforts – which is what he wanted. 'It was the making of Saatchi's,' says Tim Bell, 'because the controversy got them talked about in the national press – something which happened more and more as the years went on until the agency itself became a household word.' There was another series of ads featuring a quiz-master saying that if you smoked forty cigarettes a day you could win a case of chronic bronchitis, and an ad written by Jeremy Sinclair with the line 'I gave up smoking by eating prunes', followed by three columns of text with helpful suggestions on how to give up, including eating prunes, chewing gum and even hypnosis. 'Every ad got talked about,' says Bell.

There was an element of hypocrisy to all this. Several of the Saatchi team, including Bell, were chain-smokers, and Charles, although he had announced he was giving up, was still an occasional smoker. Ron Collins recalls a TV crew coming round to film Charles about the anti-smoking campaign. He was hesitant and nervous, and it took him several takes to make his righteous condemnation of smoking. Exhausted by the experience, he waited for the camera crews to pack up, then said, 'Shit, someone give me a fag. I'm dying for a smoke.' In those early days, Charles could – and did – make a virtue of being anti-smoking, even while the room he worked in was heavy with cigarette smoke.

It was fashionable for some agencies to boast they had no cigarette accounts. In New York Bill Bernbach maintained that boast for thirty-three years, but his agency, Doyle Dane Bernbach, took on Philip Morris eleven weeks after his death, in 1982. Similarly Ogilvy & Mather had a policy of no cigarette accounts for many years. It would be 1983 before Saatchi & Saatchi, after parting company with the Health Education Council, took on its first cigarette client, Silk Cut, for which it then produced some award-winning ads, featuring a pair of scissors slicing across a bed of silk. And right to this day, the conflict between running anti-smoking campaigns and at the same time acting for cigarette companies remains. In April 1988, Saatchi hit the headlines again when RJR Nabisco, the American food and tobacco company, removed $84 million of its advertising because a Saatchi agency produced a commercial for Northwest Airlines showing passengers applauding a ban on smoking. The fact that Saatchi did not handle any of Nabisco's tobacco products made no difference.

Ron Collins and Alan Tilby were regarded as the 'heavyweights' on the creative side: they had been hired to add depth and strength to the reputation of the team which otherwise consisted of mostly unknown youngsters. Collins and Tilby were assigned the Jaffa account. They soon discovered they did not get on, although they shared one of the four large square white-topped tables in the room. Collins had won a number of awards at Colletts and at Doyle Dane Bernbach. His work on a Martell brandy campaign with French scenes including an outdoor wedding reception had gained him a considerable reputation. Painstaking and thorough, he liked to research and think about a campaign for some weeks. He resented the fact that in most agencies the art director was regarded as junior to the copywriter, and wanted to change that at Saatchi's. Tilby, a short, square man, considerably less polished than the style-conscious Collins, irritated him by sitting with his feet on the desk, endlessly snipping bits out of newspapers and magazines. Like Collins, Tilby liked to work meticulously, and he too found it difficult to respond to the speed and urgency that Charles demanded from him.

The other two teams, Jeremy Sinclair and Bill Atherton working at one table and John Hegarty and Chris Martin at a third, were familiar with the Charles Saatchi work pattern, the pressure to produce rapidly and well – the 'two ads a day keep the sack away' syndrome – the continual drive and impatience, the sometimes savage dismissal of material which had taken weeks to produce and Charles's uncanny way of seeing through to the heart of a campaign. Collins and Tilby, the only two newcomers to the creative team, were not sympathetic to the Saatchi style. The others regarded them as 'prima donna-ish'. Chris Martin says neither of them was 'very impressed by the Saatchi thing', a statement borne out by interviews with both men. The concept of the Jaffa ads was to persuade the British public to eat more Israeli-produced citrus, particularly the humble grapefruit. They produced the line 'And all you ever did was sprinkle sugar on it', with the suggestion that the grapefruit could be used in a variety of ways. It was dull stuff for a person with Collins's gifts, but he tried hard; and when Charles contemptuously dismissed his work he stalked out of the office for a couple of days. When he came back he discovered that Charles had given the go-ahead to his campaign, which later won an award.

This was nothing in comparison with a row which blew up when Tim Bell, by now working as an account man, altered one of Collins's lay-outs. In one of those incidents which has passed into trade mythology, Collins stormed into Charles Saatchi's office and threatened to resign. In the outer office there was a hush, as the voices inside grew more heated. Three people, including Collins himself, relate the climax, Charles suddenly shouted: 'Who the hell do you think you are, Ron – Michael-fucking-Angelo?'

Collins, however, often glimpsed another side to Charles. One of the new clients was a London store called Escalade, which was a small account. Collins remembers going to see the client to work on the latest press ad, which would feature some new French-made jeans which they would sell at £5.25 – expensive for jeans in those days. He came back complaining that he didn't see how he could get much out of that. Charles immediately grabbed his pad and pencil and said:

'Well, let's see. French jeans, are they? What's "French jeans" in French?'

Collins's schoolboy French was good enough for the Franglais, and he produced 'Les Jeans Français'.

Charles wrote it down. 'Now, what else can we say about them?'

Tentatively, Collins proffered the information that they were for both men and women.

'Right,' said Charles. 'What's that in French?' At Collins's dictation he wrote down 'pour un homme et une femme', then added 'Escalade'. Then between them they added the final line: 'Un belle bargain à £5.25.'

It had taken about ten minutes. Charles threw the pencil down and said, 'Right, get a nice picture of a couple wearing the jeans and get it off.'

Like many things that Charles did, it attracted notice – and won an award. 'People came up to me and said "That was a sweet ad" ', says Collins.

Despite such moments, Collins did not have the temperament to enjoy the frenetic existence of the early days of Saatchi & Saatchi. Hegarty, although exhausted by it, remembers events differently. 'Charlie stimulated great tension to create better work. It was always constructive tension, if that makes sense. In the creative process, if you had a violent disagreement, it wouldn't be because he thought the work was too daring. He would say "I don't think it's creative enough. I don't think you're going far enough on it." You might feel creatively exhausted, because you've put everything into it, and he's just saying to you: "I think you can go further." '

This is a familiar message about Charles, and central to answering the question: 'What is special about him?' There is no doubt he had – and has – exceptional creative talent, but there were others who were talented too who have not achieved anything like his success. What was evident from these early days is the extra dimension to Charles, what one person calls 'the spark', which displayed itself as a ferocious drive to go one step further than anyone else. One of his lifelong friends, a man as successful in his own business as Charles is in his, says: 'Charles is a visionary. He's got tremendous balls, more courage than anyone I've ever met. He tells you about an idea, and you think he's just joking because it's so unbelievable. And then he has the guts to go ahead and do it.' What of the other side? 'Everybody fights with Charles,' says the friend. 'There are times when he can be unbearable and do the most terrible things, but you always forgive him, because he's Charles. At the end of the day you just have to say, this guy is different, the normal rules don't apply.' These characteristics would become more apparent in the corporate leaps Charles would take once he got into the takeover game.

The person driven the hardest was Maurice, regarded by Charles in these early days almost as an extension of himself. The others soon realised that it was no accident that the name on the door was that of the two brothers; they had a relationship which only brothers can have, particularly brothers brought up in a tight family environment. Their fights would become legendary, and every Saatchi man has a 'Charles beats up Maurice' story. Most articles on the Saatchis recount incidents of Charles hitting Maurice with a chair, and all those who were there describe such occasions, with variations. Several remember hearing Charles shouting at Maurice, 'We never came out of the same womb' (another incident deep in the Saatchi mythology), and Tim Bell was once just in time to see a chair hurtling across the office with Maurice ducking – too late. As one Saatchi director relates:

> The level of violence between them was sometimes awful. They were two Jewish brothers and no one else was allowed to interfere. They had forgotten all about it minutes later – or at least Charles had. Tim always thought of

himself as the third brother and could never understand why they would not accept him. He was the only one who tried to get between the two brothers when they were fighting, but all that would happen is that they would wheel on him. Tim once got hit with a chair when he got in the way. The brothers would always round on the interloper. So few people were trying to do so much, and there was great tension, but people understood it, and we could all live with it.

Others recall having to explain to visitors what the row was. 'Don't worry, it's only the proprietors having a fight.'

'The clients loved it,' says one director. 'It was the type of creative tension they couldn't get in their own lives. They would come down from the Midlands or wherever and they would walk into the type of madness that wouldn't be tolerated in their own world, and they thought it was great.'

Charles was no means the only one who shouted; the others picked up their tone from him, and sometimes there would be major slanging matches going on around the office. Maurice, unable to bear the tension any more, would go for a walk. So would Bell. This gave rise to a new competition: the 'how far did you get?' battle. Maurice got halfway down Piccadilly one day, possibly half a mile from the office; Bell got further. Charles would be waiting for them when they got back, probably having forgotten the row.

All of them soon learned that Charles's bouts of anger could give way within minutes to a mood of great friendliness and charm. Ron Collins says there really were three brothers in the firm: Charles, Maurice and Charles. 'Charles was two people: one, the nicest, most charming and wittiest man you could meet; the other a terror.'

Maurice never took mortal offence. Bell suffered far more, as much at the rejection of him as 'the third brother' as at the insults thrown. 'But everyone always came back,' says Bell. 'You can't win an argument with Charles. He shouts at you, his invective is often amazing, and he never admits he's wrong.'

Even those who didn't much care for Charles Saatchi still found the atmosphere in that little office in Golden Square exhilarating. 'You had to learn to take criticism,' says Alan Tilby, now the creative director at Boase Massimi Pollitt. 'You held things up and people would say "shit!" It was a great way of working really because it knocked all the rubbish out of you. You had to accept the fact that you were in a highly competitive environment.' Tilby found it very different from Colletts, where most of them had come from, either directly or indirectly. 'In Colletts we'd learned to live in a kind of spoilt environment, where you could go away and reshoot things. Or send the account man back down if he failed to sell the work. It was an elitist organisation, and Ron Collins was used to that mode of existence, and I got quite used to it. Saatchis was different – it was cheapskate, it made you work hard.'

Cheapskate or not, Tilby was impressed by Charles Saatchi's refusal to compromise, at least at the beginning. On one occasion Escalade refused to sign off one of the ads Saatchi's had prepared, and he and Collins came back to the agency to explain.

'Look, we've been down to see them, and they won't accept it,' Tilby told Charles.

Saatchi exploded. 'Tell him if he doesn't sign it off he can roll it up and stick it up his arse!'

Tilby and Collins trooped back to Escalade to tell this to the client, albeit in a slightly censored version. 'That's strong talk,' said the Escalade executive; but he signed it off.

Hegarty, on the other hand, who was a Charles Saatchi admirer, felt that compromise had begun to creep in within that first year. Only a matter of weeks after getting the account, everyone realised that Saatchi should not be working for Granada TV Rentals. The TV rental business, which was for many years an industry unique to Britain, was booming with the growth of colour television, and Granada, immediately after it had given its account to Saatchi, had taken over the much bigger Robinson Rentals. It could rent out every set it could lay its hands on. Robinson was a much more conservative company, and had only ever done local advertising before – not unnaturally, since it wanted each local population to go to its nearest shop. The Robinson team didn't see much point in a national campaign, and had no interest in the creative ideas coming out of Saatchi. On the other hand Charles was loath to abandon any account, however unpromising. Relations became strained as the Granada marketing men turned down anything other than the staidest of ads, but Charles managed to remain civil to the client. Back in the office, John Hegarty remembers him saying angrily: 'Right, if they want shit, I'll give them shit. I'll give them the best shit they've ever had. If that's what they want, that's what they'll get.'

By now the agency was getting bigger, and more staff were being taken on. Bell was doing some of the presentations, and as he and Maurice proved far better at them than anyone could have hoped Charles began to do fewer and fewer. He would still undertake them if forced, however, and the others recall the occasion when the marketing director of the German car maker Audi insisted on Charles himself making the presentation before he would consider the agency. Charles was furious but went along, dropping little anti-German jokes into his presentation and generally making himself as offensive as he could. It was a major client, and a prestigious one, but Charles seemed not to care. They were offered the account, but in the event didn't accept it – on the same day it came through, they were also offered the British Leyland corporate account. They took BL.

Another Saatchi man remembers a pitch to Hygena, one of the leading kitchen manufacturers. Considerable preparation had been done, and Charles joined the others to make the presentation. One of the team described the event:

> He could feel that it wasn't going down particularly well, so he stopped. It was just a wonderful piece of theatre, because he had a huge pile of ads to show, and he put the ads down and walked around the table. And I thought: "He's going to do something barmy here, something's going to happen." Everybody just stopped, and watched him. He picked up a pack of cigarettes – he never smoked enough to have his own – took one out and lit it. This seemed like hours, the tension was terrible, and he walked back. Then he began again and I could see the client immediately begin to pay attention. Charles finished, then walked out of the room, ignoring the client, and he hid until the rest of us came out to see if we had got the account.

This time they hadn't.

Soon Bell was being used everywhere in the agency, and could no longer cope with the media side on his own. It was he who hired his own number two, Roy Warman, a tall, thin media specialist, from Geers Gross. Warman took to the Saatchi atmosphere from the first day (he is now joint head of the agency). The others could hear him on the phone in his odd slack moments: 'My name is Roy Warman, that's W-A-R-M-A-N, from Saatchi & Saatchi, that's S-A-A-T-C-H-I, and again. And we are a new advertising agency with ideas we think can help you and I wonder . . .' In 99 cases out of 100 the reply was 'No', sometimes vehemently, but Warman joined in the Bell/Maurice game of topping the others with the latest reason for rejection, laughing along with the rest.

When Warman joined in January 1971 the agency was four months old. Another man who was to go high up the Saatchi ladder was Bill Muirhead, a tall, blond twenty-four-year-old Australian. He was interviewed early in 1971 as the first full-time account man, helping out Maurice and Bell, whose work had spilled over into that area. On the appointed day Muirhead turned up at Golden Square and was immediately taken with the atmosphere. It was in Soho, which is

Bohemian, but this was respectable Bohemian. The brass sign on the door was worthy of a dentist or solicitor; he knew little of the company's history and it struck him as an establishment which had been there for some time. Inside, there were large ads which had been blown up – common enough in agencies today, but then unusual in London. There were two attractive girls in mini-skirts at the reception desk. The reception area was screened off from the main room, but a tall person could see across the whole room, although he could not see the other people inside if they were sitting behind other screens. It was impossible to know that there were just four large tables, three small cubicles at the back and a conference room in the basement. To Muirhead it looked solid and large, and he was under the impression that Saatchi & Saatchi occupied the whole building.

The effect of the office on Muirhead, mirrored by others, is worth noting. Charles and Maurice had spent some time with Rodney Fitch, and all who worked in Golden Square remember the offices and the atmosphere as perfect for the image they wanted to create: young, creative, dynamic, thoughtful. David Ogilvy had long preached that the physical appearance of an advertising company's offices was important: 'If they are decorated in bad taste, we are yahoos. If they look old-fashioned, we are fuddy-duddies. If they are too prestigious, we are stuffed shirts. If they are untidy, we look inefficient.' Ogilvy's text was almost a bible to aspiring advertising men; but Charles Saatchi arrived at what he wanted much more intuitively than through any conscious learning process. At Golden Square he set a tone for the agency which it has never quite lost, even in much more institutionalised circumstances.

While Muirhead was sitting in the reception area a head peered over the partition and examined him intently. Before he had a chance to speak it was withdrawn, and a few minutes later Muirhead was ushered down a spiral staircase and into an oval room with no windows; it had aluminium chairs and rushmat carpeting, and a long, black table – very modern and clean. There he was interviewed by Maurice Saatchi, whom he remembers as 'charming and intelligent'. Tim Bell 'hovered', passing occasional notes to Maurice. Everyone seemed young and energetic, and there was a discernible buzz. On the way out he passed the same head that had watched him over the partition, now complete with body and sitting at one of the desks. Charles Saatchi did not spare him another glance; he must have been satisfied with what he had seen the first time. Muirhead was soon working on his first account, the *Daily Mail*, which arrived at Saatchis more or less the same time as he did in 1971. The young recruit was made the account executive and a few weeks later went down to Fleet Street for a meeting with the client. An hour later he was back in the office again, searching frantically for the *Daily Mail* ad: the man who had taken the clients' brief, Mike Johnson, had forgotten to pass it on. John Hegarty, the art director involved, eventually produced an ad, and Muirhead went back to the *Mail* to do his presentation with material he had never seen before. He was now very late for his meeting, so he took a cab – something unheard of for junior Saatchi men, who were required to travel by bus or underground. In the cab, he looked at the ad for the first time – and found to his horror he could not understand it. Going up in the lift he prepared his opening gambit. He would say: 'This is an extraordinarily difficult brief, and we've been struggling with it, and I don't think we've really cracked it. This is as far as we've got.'

A few minutes later he made this little speech to the marketing director of the *Daily Mail*, produced the ad and waited for the flak to hit him.

'It's brilliant,' said the marketing man. 'Marvellous! I love it.'

It was a bemused and shamefaced Muirhead who arrived back at Golden Square to relate this event. He still didn't understand the ad, but he had made a sale and he decided there was a new technique here which he could develop, if only he could work it out. At that moment Charles Saatchi appeared. He picked up the ad.

'What is this shit?' he shouted.

John Hegarty was on the next desk, watching with some trepidation. Muirhead explained it was the ad the *Daily Mail* was using the next day to promote itself.

'It's crap,' said Charles. The ad was stapled to a strong cardboard backing, but even so he ripped it apart and hurled it on to the floor.

'But the client loves it,' Muirhead managed.

'You'll just have to ring him and tell him you're going to do something better.'

Muirhead rang the *Mail*. 'You know that ad you loved? We've done something better now.'

Charles sat down opposite and calmly asked, 'What's the brief?', and worked on it. Muirhead went back with it yet again, to be received with even greater enthusiasm. 'It was the most amazing thing I'd ever experienced in my whole life,' Muirhead told a friend later. Another Saatchi man who witnessed the incident says:

Bill loved Charles for that, because the most wonderful thing about him is that he has instant judgement which confirmed Bill's initial thought. People look at a painting and they say 'great' but they don't really mean it, because they don't really understand it. Charles said, 'I don't understand this – it's crap', and was prepared to say to the client that something he liked was rubbish.

Everybody who worked in Saatchi's has heard the story of how Charles posed as an office cleaner. As with the chair-throwing story, it crops up again and again in the profiles and the feature articles on the company. As with most other anecdotes, it has at least some truth in it, although over the years has tended to become embroidered.

It happened in 1972, when the agency was bulging out of the original Golden Square building but had still not moved to larger premises. One of the big clients the agency was after was Singer, the sewing machine group which in the early 1970s was a considerable advertiser. It had taken some hard work, but eventually Singer had been persuaded to come in for a pitch. Immediately Maurice and his team went to work, doing considerable research, and Charles sat in on a full-scale rehearsal the night before. The office had to look busy and full, and he was anxious that when the Singer team arrived, just after lunch, there should be plenty of people around. Everyone, he instructed, must ring their friends and contacts and get them to come in around that time. They must all be on the phone, or pretending to talk to clients. The story is told that when he was still not happy with the general air of busy-ness the next day he sent people out into the street, offering passers-by £5 a time to come in and look busy. 'We got cleaners, lorry drivers and shop-assistants in, and said, "Pretend you're talking on the phone",' says one Saatchi executive. Tim Bell also confirms the incident, and the brothers themselves chuckle when they are reminded of it.

At any rate, the Singer team arrived at three in the afternoon to find an office buzzing with activity. They were taken down to the conference room in the basement, and Bell and Maurice began their pitch. It was to be a marathon eight-and-a-half-hour effort, going on until 11.30 that evening, the longest pitch anyone could remember. Charles had been very much caught up in the preparation for it, but by now he seldom saw clients (and soon would not see them at all, no matter how important). Every so often he would enter the little projection room behind the main conference room and peer in through the thick glass. He could not hear, but his own team inside could see his head, with its distinctive mop of black curly hair. Finally, he got bored hanging around, went home, changed into jeans and jacket and came back. He had just entered the main room when he heard the others coming up the spiral staircase. Unable to get out without being seen and heard, he had a sudden fear that one of his own team would not resist stopping beside him and introducing him, which at that moment was the last thing in the world he wanted. Quick as a flash he grabbed a cloth and began dusting down the partitions. All four of his own team, including Maurice, Bell and Roy Warman, recognised him and began to giggle, while Charles, his head bent, furiously went on polishing. It was too much for Maurice to resist. Very deliberately, while showing the clients out, he paused beside Charles. 'When you've finished that, could you make sure you clean my office,' he said. A glower promised trouble for Maurice but he ignored it, enjoying for these few minutes a fleeting ascendancy. 'God knows what hell Charles gave him later for that!' says one of the Saatchi men there that night.

Chris Martin has another anecdote – 'the Golden Square chairs'. Before moving to Soho, Charles had sent the office secretary, Gail, out to Habitat to buy cheap, light and modern chairs. 'They were fold-up chairs, with canvas backs, the sort you print "director" across the back of,' says Martin. They were not sturdy enough for the punishment they received in their new home, and one by one they broke, and were piled up at the back of the conference room basement. 'When you've got someone the size of Charlie bringing them down on his brother's head, they don't last long,' explains Martin. 'So after a few months there was this pile of matchwood and canvas which had been these chairs. And then one day Charlie saw them, and I heard him say: "Gail, take those bloody chairs back to Habitat and get our money back on them." '

All this time the agency was expanding. Maurice's relentless twenty-five calls a day, which he kept up for about a year, were bringing in clients, some better than others. They were also being tested. Great Universal Stores, one of the canniest companies in Britain, asked them to pitch for an account, with a view to giving them more if they did well with it. It was a rundown jeans manufacturer that the company had acquired as part of a larger takeover. There was a denim surplus, and the jeans factory was a loss-maker; but the Saatchis were continually asking GUS for accounts – and here was an opportunity to discover their mettle. 'There was an attitude towards us that said: "OK, you're arrogant sods who reckon you're better than anyone else. Well, see what you can do with this one," ' says a Saatchi executive.

They responded to the challenge. Designer jeans were just coming in, and the Saatchi team reckoned this was a promising area to explore.

Why not turn out more fashionable, higher-priced jeans, and market them hard? Roy Warman was given the job of making the presentation for the account, and he travelled up to Speke, near Liverpool. He had made a token protest to Charles before departing. 'I don't fancy doing this, it will be a completely hostile crowd.' Charles to his surprise was conciliatory. 'Look at it this way: if they hate it, you'll never see them again. If they love it, we'll get the account. All you can do is your best. Go for it.'

Another Saatchi man remembers similar encouragement from Charles. 'It's typical of him. It's his "Don't look down" syndrome. Let people make their mistakes. Kill them for dumbness, but not for trying.'

Warman got the account, then a few months later, just as the sales began to lift off, GUS sold the company – as it had always intended to do. 'GUS very cleverly thought that if they gave us the account, and built up the image for a very small amount of money, they could flog it for five times what they paid for it,' says Hegarty. However, GUS became – and still is – a client for some of its larger businesses.

There were other tough accounts, some of which Saatchi's could do nothing with, some of which grew into much larger ones. 'The big corporations would say, "Well, these guys might be mad, they might be bright, or they might be daft – let's give them this nitty-gritty problem we've always had and see what they can do with it," ' says Hegarty. 'That way you had to prove yourself with them.'

To help their expansion Charles worked on spreading the word through the constant drip-feed of stories to *Campaign* and the rest of the trade press. From the start they had ignored the rules of the industry that you did not poach another agency's clients (the rules were later changed because of the activities of Saatchi & Saatchi). There was another factor which increasingly was helping them win accounts: Tim Bell, now the main presenter. Even so it was still Charles who set the style for presentations, paying considerable attention to the way in which they were done. 'Charles insisted we had to counter this thing that people just thought we were a mad group of creatives,' says Hegarty. Presentations were full of charts and plans, and Charles also insisted they showed a chart of the structure of the company, and the presenter would talk about organisation. He insisted on introducing more and more titles into his small group. 'I was deputy creative director,' says Hegarty, 'and someone else was creative director, and he was account management supervisor. And right down to the guy in the studio, Melvynne Redford. Someone spelt his name M-E-L-V-I-N, and we were doing a rehearsal, and somebody said "That's not how Melvynne spells his name." And Charles said: "Don't be daft, that sounds like a lunatic, I want it spelt like this". And from then on that's how it was.

All this time Maurice was filing monthly trading statements, a profit-and-loss account and a balance sheet with Vanni Treves. Treves in turn reported back to the directors of Mary Quant Ltd. These reports contain fascinating glimpses of the state of the business in these early years. On 3 May 1972, for instance, when Saatchi & Saatchi had been going twenty months, Treves wrote to Archie McNair, Quant's partner, to say that the Saatchis were now 'working very hard to get the first really big client which they all regard as the breakthrough' (this would be Singer). Treves in this letter already conveys something of the impression that the younger Saatchi brother had made on him. 'If one believes Maurice (and there is no reason for not doing so) the company's reputation is spreading quickly and the quality of its work and ideas is thought by many people as second to none.' The Saatchis, he went on, were proposing to spend money on advertising 'to maintain this momentum of nascent goodwill'. Their only misgiving, he added, was 'the prospect of spending in one shot such a large proportion of the presently available balance on profit-and-loss account (£13,480).' Treves was convinced by now that the Saatchis were going to achieve their breakthrough and told McNair that they 'deserved it'. He also reminded Maurice around this time that the interest on the money from Mary Quant had not been received, but seemed satisfied with Maurice's response that the original invoice from Mary Quant 'was wrong and a corrected one took a long time to arrive'. Treves was not uncritical of the way in which the Saatchis carried on business. 'Saatchi & Saatchi keep all their creditors waiting for not less than one month as a matter of policy,' he noted. 'I personally do not think it is a very good one, but it is for the board to decide' – the 'board', of course, being the Plunket-Greenes and Archie McNair.

By the summer of 1972 Maurice had good news to report to the board and to Treves. The agency was on target. It had made a profit of nearly £20,000 in its first full year, and now had enough clients to make it viable. The second year was looking good. It was expanding and taking on extra premises around Golden Square. It was being talked about more and more, and its reputation for creative advertising was established. The first hurdle – survival – had been jumped. Now it was time for bigger things.

7

THE THIRD BROTHER

By 1972 Charles Saatchi had discovered he had two unsuspected assets. The first was Maurice, who had taken to the advertising industry as if he had been born to it. He was not greatly involved in the creative side, although he often shyly offered suggestions; but it was his other attributes which now came to the fore. Within weeks he had earned the respect of the others by grasping the more complex tactical and strategic points of running a business and an account. He was the only university graduate among them, although several of the others had been through art college, and they soon learned to respect his intellect even if they worried about his inexperience. He also proved to be an excellent new business-getter, and presenter; although quiet-spoken and younger-looking even than his twenty-five years, he had a curiously persuasive power which in later years he would employ to considerable effect. He was also a natural organiser, making the simple machinery of the office function in between the myriad other tasks Charles set for him.

The second asset was as much good fortune as good judgement. Tim Bell had been a late choice for the job of media director, and nobody, not even Charles, could have guessed how important he would prove. Unlike most of the others, Bell had a middle-class background, and had not set off for the world of advertising as his first choice for a career. He was born in 1941 and brought up in London. His mother was Australian; her second husband, Tim's stepfather, was an alderman, and Mayor of Marylebone. Tim went to a North London grammar school, and in his late teens set his heart on becoming a jazz musician – he played a variety of instruments, including the trumpet, piano and vibes, though none of them well enough to make a living. When he was nineteen, he says, 'my mother decided she did not want me hanging around at home', and he was sent off to the Stella Fisher Employment Agency in Fleet Street. It was a time of full employment in Britain, and for a bright, personable young man finding a suitable job was no problem. He came back with a choice of three interviews: one in publishing, one in insurance and the other with ABC Television. Bell chose the last. 'It was my generation who could, almost unconsciously, see the power of television and, by inference, the power of advertising in it.' However, when he presented himself at ABC, advertising was the last thing on his mind: 'I saw myself as a star in the making – an actor or a producer.' Instead he was put to shifting bits of cardboard about on the big board in the advertising department: his first introduction to the industry.

Two years later he moved to the agency Colman Prentis & Varley (which, among other accounts, did some work for the Conservative Party) as a junior media buyer. His next move was to Hobson Bates (taken over by the American agency Ted Bates, which would later become part of Saatchi) as media group head, then as media director of Geers Gross. It was at Geers Gross that Bell, now twenty-eight, got a call from the Saatchis. From all accounts, during this time Bell was arrogant and flashy but very popular.

At the new agency, he rapidly established himself as the person round whom most of the others gathered. John Hegarty took to him instantly, as did most of the others, except perhaps for Ron Collins who resented him.

Media buying – negotiating the best deals for TV time and newspaper space -was designed to be one of the key jobs in the new agency when it was launched, but Bell outgrew it within three months. He gloried in the pressure, happy to camp in the office overnight or sleep under a desk when they worked – as they often did – through the night on preparations for a pitch to a potential client or on a new campaign. He established a routine of being one of the first in and the last away, a routine he would maintain most of the time he was at Saatchi.

It was at presenting that Bell excelled. Charles was awkward, impatient and often rude to clients; Maurice was much better, although he had not yet the self-confidence to put himself out front. Bell, by contrast, turned on potential clients a charm that would later often be remarked on. Charles and Maurice soon put it to good use.

'Tim was the best presenter I've ever worked with,' says one of the Saatchi team. He remembers Bell presenting a pitch he had written. At the end the client turned to the younger Saatchi who had sat silently watching.

'Maurice, you have a brilliant presenter here,' he said in front of Bell.

Baghdad (*above*), where once
80,000 Jews lived and prospered.
The Saatchi family left in 1947,
to be followed by almost the
entire Jewish population of Iraq.

1951, the year of the mass
emigration of the Jews from
Iraq. The Saatchis were already
part of an Iraqi Jewish
community forming in London.
Maurice, aged five, is at the back
left, beside his eldest brother
David, aged 14. Charles, aged
eight, is on the right, at the end
of the back row.

The parents: Nathan and Daisy Saatchi (*right*), at their comfortable London home where Charles and Maurice lived until they were married.

Charles (centre back) at age 13 (*below*), at his North London school, Christ's College, Finchley, October 1956. In contrast to Maurice, he was not an academic success.

The eldest brother: David (*above left*), seven years older than Charles, lives in New York where he is a successful commodity broker, and soon to be a full-time sculptor. He arrived in London unable to speak a word of English.

The youngest brother: Phil (*above right*), the only one of the four brothers to be born in England. Seven years younger than Maurice, he worked as a journalist before going into the music world, first with his own recording studio, then as a songwriter, singer and guitarist; he supported Joan Armatrading on a tour and released his first album in April 1987.

The original backers: Mary Quant and her husband Alexander Plunket-Greene (*below*), who put up the bulk of the £25,000 to start Saatchi & Saatchi. Lindsay Masters (*below left*), who gave Maurice his first job at Haymarket Publishing, put up the rest. Michael Heseltine (*below right*), Masters' partner at Haymarket, did not invest – although he wanted to do so – because he had just become a government minister.

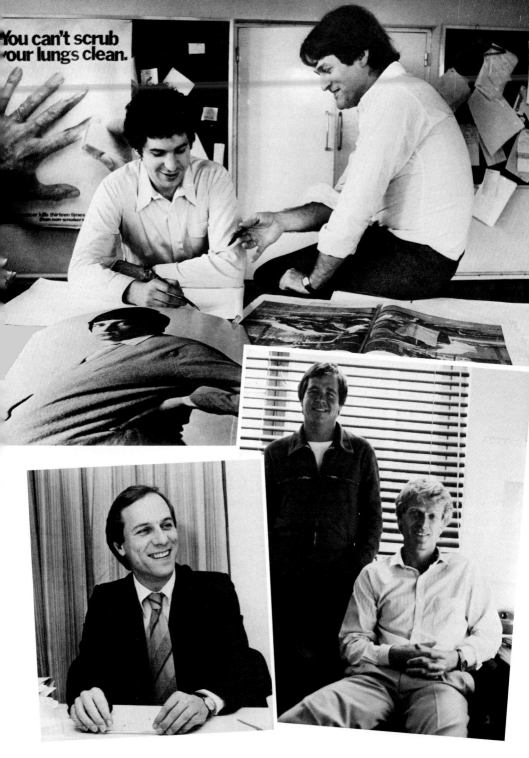

Top: Charles and his partner, Ross Cramer, in April 1970; their Cramer Saatchi consultancy business, the forerunner of the Saatchi & Saatchi agency, worked for the Health Education Council, for whom they produced a highly successful Stop Smoking campaign – and the 'pregnant man' poster.

Above left: Jeremy Sinclair, who wrote the 'pregnant man' ad in 1970 – and many others over the next twenty years. Charles Saatchi hired him as a copywriter in 1968, straight from Watford College of Art, and he is still there, now joint deputy chairman of the worldwide group, number three to the brothers.

Above right: John Hegarty (seated), an art director who was one of Charles's first recruits; Chris Martin (standing) joined soon afterwards. Both men are now directors of their own agencies.

'I know,' said Maurice simply.

'Tim, I knew, had not seen the work before, so he was looking at it new,' says the Saatchi man. 'I mean, we've got a lot of strategy, a lot of logic, objectives and preparation that go into a presentation for a major piece of business, and he hadn't seen any of it. And he's pitching it, and he's doing it for the first time, and I'm thinking to myself: How can this man do it? This is an act of sheer brilliance.'

There is an element of hyperbole here, since pitching to a client, whatever the circumstances, is not technically a difficult business. What the Saatchi men could often see was that Bell was better at it than they were, and he seemed to do it without apparent effort. He seldom needed to prepare, although he usually did. The harder the task the more he relished it; yet the others noticed that despite his considerable self-confidence he seemed to depend on the brothers. 'I sometimes used to think that his brilliant presentations were more to please Maurice than they were to please the client,' says one of the early Saatchi men.

'Tim completely revered Charles,' says another. 'In the later years Charles became very, very important to him, but in the early days of the company it was both Maurice and Charles.' Most of those who knew Bell well say there is something incomplete about him, as if he could not function without the brothers, and Charles in particular. 'The agency in those early days had something special – and I think what it had was Charles. Until 1978, he was the catalyst, the centre, all the energy,' says one senior Saatchi man. 'On the other hand, Tim likes things to be nice, and for people to get on. He hadn't the guts needed for starting a business of his own.' 'You got the impresssion that Charles didn't mind if the whole business went down the drain – he was prepared to take that sort of risk,' says another Saatchi man. 'He was a real entrepreneur. Tim never had that.'

Bell was prominent in developing one of the agency's major accounts, British Leyland. In 1970 Keith Hopkins, the head of public relations for British Leyland – which still had over 40 per cent of the British car market – first met the Saatchi brothers. Leyland's advertising manager, David Welch, had heard about them and suggested to Hopkins they were people he ought to know. Welch (who now works for Saatchi), Hopkins and the brothers met at a restaurant in Shepherd Market. There was, Hopkins believes, no question of Saatchi & Saatchi doing any advertising for him at this stage, but soon afterwards the Saatchis managed to get a foot in the BL door, with a tiny corporate advertising account, working to the office of the chairman, Lord Stokes, in Berkeley Square.

From that followed a bigger but still small account: Triumph Cars, one of the smaller selling ranges of the BL empire at the time. It was Welch who was involved in giving them that account. Martin and Hegarty prepared the creative work, and Charles himself decided to present it in the basement at Golden Square. It was another of those days when the office had to be especially filled with passers-by. 'Charlie went out and got people in off the street,' says Chris Martin. 'He just went up to them and said, "Come on, here's a quid, come and make this place look lively." '

Welch appeared with a number of senior Triumph executives, and the party was ushered down the spiral staircase, with Charles, immaculately clad in blue pinstripe, at his most engaging. When they emerged a couple of hours later he was the perfectly mannered host – but they hit an unpleasant surprise. It was now around 6.30 and the office was nearly empty, except for the man Charles probably least wanted to meet at that moment. Joe Andrews ran his own photographic studio and frequently dropped into the Saatchi office where he was one of the outside contractors. His appearance was extraordinary. Chris Martin describes him: 'He had long streaked hair down to the waist, like a gypsy, with a great bald pate in the middle, huge piratical earrings, make-up, jeans that showed more leg than was covered, leather combijacket, huge cowboy boots with jangly spurs, all topped off with a stetson hat. And he was deaf – he had a huge hearing aid.'

He was also loud, cheerful and very Cockney. He was in the reception area collecting some work when he saw Charles's head appear over the partition, and he greeted him in his usual effusive manner. 'Cor blimey, Charlie, still at it are we?' he shouted. According to Martin, he then grabbed Saatchi round the neck and gave him a huge kiss on the cheek, leaving lipstick – although the others do not remember it going that far. Says Martin: 'Charlie says under his breath, "Joe, lovely to see you, but I've got some clients here." And Joe says: "Sorry, Charlie, have I cocked it up for you?" And these Leyland people fell about. It was so funny, I'm sure that's what won the business.' Both Hegarty and Martin remember Charles carrying the whole thing off remarkably well, formally introducing the Triumph executives to Andrews and retaining his good humour and his manners. It would be one of the last presentations he would do.

It was to be another year before Keith Hopkins entered the picture again. BL's problems, severe enough at the end of the 1960s, became catastrophic in the early 1970s, when its share of the mass car market plummeted. Its hopes for recovery were pinned on a key new model: the Austin 1800-2200, later rechristened the Princess, into which it had poured its best design skills and engineers. Before its launch, Stokes reshuffled his management, putting Hopkins into the all-important role as head of the mass car division, Austin-Morris. If the Princess failed Austin-Morris would never recover, so the launch of the car was going to be a major event.

Hopkins invited the company's existing agencies to make a pitch for the launch account. Benton & Bowles, Masius Wynne-Williams, Dorlands and Murray Parry all duly travelled up to Longbridge, near Coventry, to try to get the account. At the last moment Hopkins included Saatchi & Saatchi in the 'beauty contest' on the grounds that they were creating a stir in the advertising world, seemed to be doing a good job for Triumph, and he thought it might be worth seeing what they could do for him. 'People said they're having a go, they're good – watch these people.'

The pitch took place in a conference room in the huge Longbridge complex, then one of the biggest factories in Britain. When Hopkins entered he was taken aback by the size of the Saatchi contingent: 'There seemed to be the world and his wife there, whereas my team was three or four.' Hopkins noticed one vaguely familiar face in the Saatchi crowd, 'a rather pubescent young man with large glasses who hardly said anything' – Maurice. Otherwise he knew nobody, and wasn't sure what to expect.

At that point Hopkins had never heard of Tim Bell, who rose and began the introductions. Then he launched into his presentation on how to sell the new car to a reluctant public. 'He was absolutely spellbinding,' says Hopkins. 'By the end of it I knew I wanted this guy on my side. None of the others featured, except to pass him a couple of bits of copy or a drawing. It was the best presentation I've seen, either before or since. And of course I decided to award them the account, and subsequently gave them a lot more business. It was Tim that did that, Tim and Tim only.'

In the event the Princess was never a great success, but that was the fault of early design and production faults rather than the advertising. Saatchi produced not just advertising but a marketing strategy as well, which Leyland adopted for its whole range of cars. 'We had a thing called Superdeal, which was the most successful extended campaign of all time,' says Hopkins. 'We had an awful lot of cars to sell, and we did in fact accomplish some phenomenal sales results. Superdeal was fundamentally dreamed up, at least the sharp end of it, between Tim and myself. We worked very closely indeed. Then we had a very big television campaign, which was drafting the Leyland Cars identity on to all our diverse brand names.'

The decision to turn down Audi had been justified. But unfortunately for Hopkins, and the British car industry, almost every car of his Superdeal was sold at a loss, and through the 1970s and 1980s what remained of the company was kept going only by large injections of state cash. As an important and prestige account, it dribbled away. No amount of advertising could sell models that were seen as out of date, unreliable and technically inferior to the flood of Japanese and European cars which soon came to dominate the British market. Today different Saatchi agencies handle Renault, Nissan, Saab, American Motors, Mercedes, Toyota and Chevrolet around the world.

Behind all the shouting, no one ever doubted that Charles Saatchi had an inner coolness, a clear-thinking business brain. He would take risks, but they would be calculated ones. The scale of his ambition at this early stage was steadily rising, and was being matched by that of Maurice. Perhaps their ambition is always destined to stay several stages ahead of what is achievable. Charles's impatience to get up there among the big players was even greater after that first year than it had been before they started. He said again and again that Saatchi & Saatchi would be the biggest agency, first in Britain, then in the world, at a time when it seemed absurd, and his listeners turned away in confusion and embarrassment. But he was always a shrewd, hard businessman, unwilling to surrender an inch if he didn't want to. There are many examples of his tough business stance in these early days, either in holding expenses down or in bargaining with contractors. Hegarty cites an episode when some artwork for Jaffa didn't turn up on time and Charles refused to pay for it. 'They brought their lawyers in to discuss it, and they just didn't realise who they were dealing with – they thought they could sit down and have a reasonable argument. Basically he told them to fuck off. He wasn't going to pay their bill, and if they wanted to sue him, go ahead. "You didn't deliver and I'm not paying. You should have told us you couldn't deliver." And there might have been a grey area where somebody said, "Look, it's going to be tight, but we'll do our best for you." But not with Charlie.'

Bell could observe with a certain degree of humour Charles suffer the odd humiliation. There was, for instance, the incident of Rodney Fitch's bill. Fitch reckoned he was still owed money for his work on Golden Square, and Charles either wouldn't or couldn't pay. The sum involved was small – about £1800. 'It was my first introduction to the world of finance. Until then I was just – perhaps I still am – a designer.' Charles refused to talk to him, and Tim Bell kept putting him off. 'Eventually my lawyer suggested that we put something called a garnishee order on them, which duly was served. And the solids hit the fan!'

Bell remembers it very well. 'Charles didn't know what a garnishee order was, and threw it in the wastepaper basket. He didn't tell anyone about it – until the men from the Sheriff of London's office arrived.'

A garnishee order is not something to ignore. It froze the Saatchi bank accounts, and meant they could not pay either staff or suppliers until they had paid Fitch. Bell learned this when he rang his father, a lawyer, who explained how serious it was. 'Charles was furious and went around shouting about it for days,' he says. Fitch, on the other hand, learned a valuable lesson. 'It's the most marvellous scheme, and I've used it several times since. We got paid very promptly. There was a great deal of bitterness from Charles about that, yet what I found amusing was that when they moved to Lower Regent Street they asked me to help out.'

Bell relates this story (he actually told it in an after-dinner speech at the London Hilton with Fitch on the top table beside him) to emphasise how naïve they all were in business matters in those early days. They were learning fast, but Charles and Maurice had a natural instinct for it, and Bell didn't. He watched with a hint of awe the hard-headed way in which they tackled suppliers and creditors, and with genuine respect their approach to new accounts and to expansion through acquisitions.

By nature Bell is gentler and softer than the brothers, and was willing to trade a great deal for a happy atmosphere and a pleasant working life. He hated their fights, and always felt obliged to intervene when the brothers shouted at each other, unable to understood that it was second nature to them and meant as little to them as a husband and wife having a shouting match. 'Tim used to say, "They only hired me as the referee", as he went in to try to part the brothers and stop them tearing each other apart,' says Chris Martin. 'And he'd come out with the broken chairs. But Tim was very important to the whole agency; he was a complete ad man. As it grew, he was the catalyst.' Others don't agree with the 'complete ad man' bit. One senior Saatchi man (not one of the brothers) notes one major gap in his armoury. 'Tim couldn't judge an ad to save himself,' he says. 'He could neither judge them nor write them. His clients would get the impression that he wrote them, art-directed them, and did all the work. Not that he would have said that, but he would give that impression. His judgement was sometimes dangerously out, and if you did the opposite to what he said you'd probably be right. But once you told him the work was great, then he'd go out and sell it superbly.'

What Bell wanted more than anything else was to turn the duopoly of Charles and Maurice into a triarchy, not just in working terms but in personal terms too. Given his contribution and the tiny size of the agency, it did not seem an impossible request; but the brothers would not even consider it. The more he tried the more hurt he became; as the years rolled by, that sense of humiliation and hurt would grow. To this day, Bell has never understood why he was shut out. The reasons are probably complex, but possibly go back to the brothers' early background – they were very conscious of their Iraqi-Jewish background, and Charles in particular always found it hard to share his private interests and passions with anyone who was not family. Bell, try as he might, would never be family. Martin noticed something which others have remarked on: the more junior you were, the less you got shouted at by Charles; the higher up you went, the more you were subject to his wrath. Maurice got the brunt of it, but Bell increasingly moved into that area too. 'He used to beat you up in the morning, not speak to you in the afternoon, then ring at ten in the evening to make peace – but not to apologise. He never, ever, did that.' For Bell, the 'beating up' was purely verbal, except when he got between the brothers; but he found it exhausting just keeping up with Charles. 'He plays mind games with people, all the time. It's innate in his character. He's always totally in control of things, and he thinks with the speed of light, seeing your sentences finish before you do, often just playing with you for the intellectual hell of it.' However well he did, Charles always wanted more from him.

At the end of the second year he and Maurice decided the company was doing well enough to buy Charles a car. He had owned most models, and it had to be something special – a Rolls-Royce to replace the model Charles had sold when they started the agency. 'He had been so bloody-minded, and we thought it might make him behave better towards us,' says Bell. 'But it never made any difference.'

As it happened, the thought of a Rolls-Royce had already occurred to Charles. The others can remember him frequently throwing the rhetorical question at David Perring, the company secretary, every time the question of money came up. 'Can I buy a Rolls-Royce yet, David?' And Perring always said no – until one day he said, 'Yes – a second-hand one.'

Chris Martin recalls Charles bursting in the door saying, 'Let's all go for a drive.' Outside on the pavement was a second-hand Rolls-Royce, on test from Jack Barclay's of Berkeley Square, the main Rolls-Royce dealer for the West End. It was not a successful trip. According to Martin, they stopped at a set of traffic lights in Shaftesbury Avenue, and another Rolls pulled up beside them, driven by the photographer Terence Donovan, an East-Ender who had already established himself as one of the leading – and highest-paid – photographers of the 1960s. Charles recognised him, and began winding down the window to greet him. According to Martin, he never got the window all the way down. 'Terry's got one of the new ones, with electric windows, and he just goes BZZZZZ, and leans over and says: "What's up, Charlie, can't you afford one of the newer ones?" Then he went BZZZZ again, put the window up – and drove off. Charlie drove straight back to Berkeley Square, parked outside Jack Barclay's, and told them he didn't want it.'

Finally Maurice and Tim Bell ordered him a Rolls-Royce Corniche – and Bell got a Porsche. He wrecked it within two days, impatiently reversing into a ramp in an underground car park. But the company was doing increasingly well, able now to pay larger salaries, and reward those whom the Saatchis thought were doing good work. Bill Muirhead came in one morning to find an envelope on his corner of the desk. Inside was a cheque for double his monthly salary – a present from the brothers. On another occasion his wife told him that a swimming-pool firm had been in to measure the garden: Charles had asked what Muirhead might like, and someone said he was an Australian and all Australians swim. Muirhead was hugely embarrassed – they couldn't fit a swimming-pool into his little semi-detached house in Bromley.

Bell by now was the most favoured employee, but he was still an employee – he had a small stake in the agency, but it was still the brothers' agency, with their name on the door. Yet it never seriously occurred to him, as it was now occurring to Ron Collins, Alan Tilby and even John Hegarty and Chris Martin to look elsewhere, start their own agencies, seek their own fortunes. The Saatchi & Saatchi agency was clearly going places, and Bell was going with it.

Towards the end of their second year the Saatchis decided to buy out the original investors, Lindsay Masters, Mary Quant and her husband Alexander Plunket-Greene. The brothers had been clever enough to structure the company in such a way that most of the outside money

was in the form of a debenture, with no rights to shares. The Masters/
Plunket-Greene holding, held through Cannon Holdings, was 15 per
cent, and the Saatchis wanted it back before the agency became too
valuable. They were heading for a market quotation at some point, and
15 per cent might be worth a great deal of money then. It had been
nice to have the backing of Quant and her husband, but they had never
been asked to do anything other than invest; now perhaps they could
be persuaded to sell – if there was enough incentive.

Maurice began a careful but firm negotiation through Vanni Treves.
The Quants were in no hurry to sell, Lindsay Masters even less so.
'Look, you're showing a good profit on your investment, and we'd like
to buy back the shares,' said Maurice. Quant and her husband
succumbed, but Masters hung on a bit longer – 'he had to persuade
me a bit harder' – but eventually he agreed to sell too (his wife, Marisa,
later told Maurice that her faith in him was such that she would *never*
have sold, which would have cost him a great deal of money in the long
run). None of the parties involved can recall exactly how much was
involved, but most agree on a figure in the region of £100,000. The
investors had quadrupled their money, and went away reasonably satisfied, while the Saatchis had consolidated their position.

Later of course they would all look back and try to calculate, as did
Masters's wife Marisa, how much they would have made had they
kept their holding. It would have been well into the millions. Michael
Heseltine too muses on this. Masters had offered to take him in as a
partner when he first invested – as they were partners in most things.
He had refused then because he had just become a minister in the new
Heath government; later he decided he had been far too scrupulous:

> Having read the rules of ministerial behaviour perhaps more cautiously than
> I should, and wishing to remain 100 per cent within the spirit of them, I
> thought it would not be right to have been involved. That was rubbish.
> Having read them again now, when I have had time years later, in a detached
> way, it would have been absolutely right and proper for me to have been
> involved in such an investment. Nobody could have said that I was influ-
> encing it, or that it was a high proportion of the shares, or anything of that
> sort. I wasn't going to play a managerial role. It was the sort of investment
> ministers are fully entitled to make.

He had, he believes, 'misunderstood in the anxiety of a new ministerial
life the restraints that are imposed on ministers'. He said no to Masters,
and took no shares in the Saatchi business – a misunderstanding very
beneficial to the Saatchis. Heseltine observes:

What is of real interest is that Maurice very rapidly wanted to buy out this significant shareholding; and although I was never involved in the negotiations – as I had no money in it – I heard about them, the offers and the counter-offers, the blandishments and the persuasion used by the Saatchis to buy out the original investors. The interesting question which historians can pose – and no one can answer – is: if I'd had shares in it, would they have actually succeeded in buying us out? If I'd been with Lindsay and there had been two of us, instead of Lindsay on his own, we might have reinforced each other. Whether Maurice would have got away with it – I've often laughed about that.

The question of others' shareholdings turned out to be less tricky. Ron Collins tells the story of being summoned to Charles's office, where he was abruptly told that he 'had a problem'.

'You've got more shares than Tim Bell.'

'Yes, Charles, but that was the agreement on which you hired me.'

'You're not understanding me. You have a problem. Now I want to know what you're going to do about it.'

Only gradually did it dawn on Collins that he was being asked to transfer some of his shares to Bell. Shaken by it, he refused. Charles, says Collins, presented it as *his* problem, although as far as he was concerned it had nothing to do with him. Bell was clearly the senior in the hierarchy, although Collins was older and more experienced, and when he had been hired he had been the senior.

He decided to go. When he told Charles this, he brought up the question of the shares. Collins – and the others – had even less idea about financial matters than Charles, and he had never seen these legendary shares which Maurice seemed to keep locked away somewhere. When he was hired he had been given a lengthy contract which looked impressive. 'He was always arguing about points in his contract,' says Hegarty. 'He consequently never signed it.'

The legend among old Saatchi hands is that when Collins asked about his shares Charles told him they were still only 'share options'.

'Well, how about my options?'

'Oh – we've decided not to take them up,' Charles is reported to have said casually.

Collins himself does not deny this outrageous version, although reckons, 'financially naïve as I was', he was never quite that silly; but he still left Saatchi & Saatchi without his shares and without any compensation. Bell later received over £3 million for his smaller holding. Collins did see a lawyer, who told him the contract, signed or unsigned, was barely worth the paper it was written on. He could still have sued Saatchi, but decided it was not worth the hassle. Collins has since made his fortune through his partnership in Wight Collins Rutherford Scott, and lives in a comfortable house in Essex, from where he acts as a consultant.

Collins was not alone in drifting away. Alan Tilby lasted just over a year; he had been brought in to do TV ads, and Saatchi in those early days did not have much TV work. He had fallen out with Charles when Alan Parker's first feature film was screened, and Parker, a close friend, invited him to the preview in the middle of the afternoon. Charles was less than enthusiastic. 'Right, you can go. But you're going to have to make up the time after work.' A furious Tilby stomped out. He, like Collins, could never tune into the atmosphere at Saatchi & Saatchi, and was discouraged both by his own prospects and by the agency's. 'To be honest, I couldn't see it going anywhere.' Tilby, from behind his huge desk in Boase Massimi Pollitt (from where he again moved on in the summer of 1988), laughs uproariously at his own short-sightedness.

The Saatchis didn't mourn long for either Collins or Tilby, but when John Hegarty and Chris Martin decided they were going that was a different matter. Hegarty had worked for Charles for more than five years when in 1973 he decided to move on, and the brothers were genuinely fond of him. 'I suppose I left because I thought, quite rightly, that it was called Saatchi & Saatchi. Charlie was going to run it, it was his agency, and he'd run it his way and there wouldn't be the opportunity for me to do the things I wanted,' says Hegarty. 'I resigned, and Charlie didn't speak to me for two years. It was about family, and I was leaving the family.' Hegarty was called an 'associate director', but he was wise enough to know he would never be considered a partner. Like Collins, he went off to found his own agency, Bartle Bogle Hegarty, where he too has grown wealthy.

'Charlie was terribly upset when we left,' Chris Martin recalls. 'He was actually shaking – the most upset I've ever seen him. Not for me, but for Hegarty, who had played a big part in his career. He saw that John was also very talented, which he has gone on to prove, but it was more than that; I think Charlie had this Jewish family feeling that you kept everyone together, and you were loyal to them and they were loyal to you, and now we were going.'

There was a time when Jeremy Sinclair, the longest-serving and (today) the closest person in the organisation to Charles other than his brother, decided he was leaving too. Unlike Hegarty, Bell and Collins, he had received no shares (or even 'options') when the agency started.

By now it was well known that he was the creator of the pregnant man ad, and he got an approach before most of the others. Ron Collins recalls Charles taking Sinclair out into the little park in the centre of Golden Square and talking to him for hours. They were still there when dark descended. When they came back Sinclair was aglow. He wasn't going after all. 'This agency is going to be the biggest and the best in the world,' Collins remembers him saying.

New staff were being taken on all the time: Terry Bannister, later to become joint managing director of the agency, came from a client, Fisons; Ron Leagas, who would later also rise to become managing director of the agency, joined. There were now just a few of the original nine left, with Roy Warman and Bill Muirhead coming through as men with considerable potential.

The departures left Tim Bell even more firmly installed as the number two to the brothers than ever. He was taking his role more and more seriously, trying hard to apply to Saatchi some of the disciplines he had learned at other agencies, behaving as he believed a good executive should, although he had limited experience of management. Hegarty, before he left, recalls Bell badgering the Saatchis to hold proper board meetings.

> Charlie would never have them. He'd say, 'What for?' And Tim would say, 'Charlie, you've got to do this, we're building a big company.' And Charlie would just refuse, insisting, 'What do I need to go to a board meeting for? We've made all the decisions, haven't we? Just go around and tell them.' You had to kind of respect him, because he just wouldn't have bullshit. And he thought boards were bullshit. As he said, 'Power is doing a great ad. That's power in this business. If you want power, do a great ad.'

It was around this time that the trade press began to refer to Bell as 'the third brother'. Bell loved it – in fact he may even have initiated it, although he now denies it. 'It was the trade press that started it,' he says. 'I thought it was a great compliment. But they hated it, to think that this middle-class guy should be attributed to them.' The Saatchis probably never spared a thought for Bell's class; like him, they have classless accents, particularly Maurice (the brothers have uncannily similar voices, and on the phone, or if one closed one's eyes, it is almost impossible to tell them apart). But it would be another ten years before Bell discovered he never could be the third brother, not even an adopted one. He began to mock himself by describing himself as the ampersand in 'Saatchi & Saatchi' rather than the third brother.

Others would have their views on Bell's contribution at a later stage.

Would Charles and Maurice have built such a big agency without him? Hegarty, who had no contact with Bell after he left in 1973, that year gave his own view:

> I do genuinely believe that Tim was the third Saatchi. Much as Charlie may disagree, I think he'd agree on his contribution. Charlie was terrific at bringing out the best in whoever he worked with, and he used Tim's abilities to the full, and Tim's abilities in turn helped him build an even better agency. Just as Maurice was a marvellous counterbalance to Charles, so Tim was a marvellous counterbalance to the two of them. And they all worked as a marvellous trio.

By the end of 1973 the shape and structure of the agency was altering rapidly. Saatchi & Saatchi now had space in offices all over Golden Square to house the overflow. Maurice and Bell were making it run more and more as a business, and Charles was already pulling back, seeing much less of the new staff who came in than he had of the old. He no longer saw clients, even when they insisted they would take their business elsewhere unless he did. The company was growing as much from acquisition as from new business. It was time to move to new and bigger premises. The Golden Square days were over, and with them went the 'creative hot-shop' atmosphere in which it was founded. Saatchi & Saatchi was now a business – which would bring its problems as well as its rewards.

8

REVERSE TAKEOVER

At the end of its second year of operation, Saatchi & Saatchi showed a profit of £90,000, after paying salaries, rates and expenses – not at all a bad result for a new business, and certainly enough to cover the cost of Charles's new Rolls-Royce. The third year, 1973, was also a good one, although profits only rose by £10,000 to £100,000. Then came 1974, and the advertising industry dived into its worst recession for years. It was not just advertising – the period from November 1973 through to the spring of 1975 was one of the gloomiest in post-war Britain. The Saatchis were about to hit financial troubles for the first time in their corporate lives.

The Yom Kippur war and the immediate threefold increase in oil prices caught Britain at a bad moment. Long before the first oil crisis, Britain's economy had been running into serious problems. The Conservative government of Edward Heath had overreacted to a rise in unemployment in the winter of 1971–2 by slashing taxes and freeing public expenditure from restraint; and by rescuing first Upper Clyde Shipbuilders and then Rolls-Royce the government had, in the words of the economist Sam Brittan, handed an invitation card 'to every lame duck to call on the Department of Trade and Industry'. The result was that from mid-1972 onwards the economy began to run faster and faster and by mid-1973 was growing at 6 per cent – a desperate overheating which was already causing the rate of inflation to rise. There was a huge overloading in the construction industry; Hoover rationed its washing machines to retailers; industry reported shortages of reinforced concrete, steel and timber; electrical motors were in such short supply that there was a twelve-month delay on deliveries. In the job market vacancies were at a record low, and despite a government incomes policy wages were starting to rise rapidly. Economists, including Brittan, warned of the serious consequences of letting money supply expand at 20 per cent, and in the summer of 1973 there was another sterling crisis which the government countered by pushing the Bank of England's minimum lending rate up from 7½ per cent to 11½ per cent.

It was still a boom time for advertising, and the Saatchis, as caught up in the euphoria as everyone else, spent lavishly on a move to new offices (in Lower Regent Street), on new cars and on taking on further staff. To the man in the street it was a time of plenty – there was more spending on everything, particularly by the government. House prices boomed to the point where a new phenomenon entered the scene, 'gazumping', where a buyer persuaded the seller, for an extra consideration, to sell to him, breaking a contract the seller had already made with someone else. Commercial property was enjoying its biggest-ever boom too, with prices well past the point where the rents could meet the interest payments. And a raft of new and largely unregulated hire purchase companies and fringe banks were pumping out loans to anyone who would take them, offering the extra incentives of TV sets and free holidays.

It had to end, and it did – abruptly. Panic in the Heath government set in early in November 1973 when the effects of the Middle East war became apparent. The price of oil had gone through most of the 1960s at between $2 and $3 a barrel, had risen to $3 in the middle of 1973 and now lifted straight to $12. The OPEC cartel organised itself effectively for the first time and cleverly cut its supply so as to have the maximum impact on price. Britain, still without its own North Sea oil, was hit by rationing as well as price increases. And by something worse still: the National Union of Mineworkers, which had already won a national strike two years before, in November began an overtime ban. In December Heath declared a state of national emergency, and Britain entered a three-day working week, with the lights going out even in offices in the City. Heath reluctantly called a general election at the end of February on the basis of who was running the country: the government or the unions? He narrowly lost, then lost a second time, more convincingly, in another election in October.

The new government was perhaps the most left-wing that Britain had ever seen, at least in its first eighteen months of office when, in the words of Sam Brittan again, it gave the impression that 'irrespective of wage claims or restrictive practices, union leaders would be saved by government cash if they priced their members out of jobs.' The Labour government of 1964–1970 had left behind social and libertarian reforms which were sensible and would last; and its economic aims were growth without inflation. By contrast the new Labour government's economic policies had two major aims: redistribution of wealth and the furtherance of trade union objectives. There was a sustained attack on wealth, with the introduction of a poorly prepared Capital Transfer Tax; and increasingly industry and the financial community felt the effects of the antagonism flowing from Whitehall. Much of it was more imagined than real, but the rhetoric left the clear impression that profits and wealth creation were under genuine attack. Industrialists and the City were demoralised. The new government continued the Heath policy of bailing out 'lame ducks', notably British Leyland and the British end of Chrysler; and in its attempt to expand its way out of inflationary recession borrowed hugely from overseas.

The result of all this was the biggest financial crisis and stock market crash Britain has seen this century – far worse than the 1929 crisis. The economy plunged into recession, and it would be more than a dozen years before industrial production recovered to its pre-1973 level. Share prices fell by over 70 per cent in nominal terms, nearly 90 per cent in inflation-adjusted terms – the equivalent of the Wall Street crash of 1929–1933. It was against this background that the Conservative Party, early in 1975, rejected Heath and elected its first ever woman leader, Margaret Thatcher, who gathered around her a group who were increasingly influenced by the monetarist doctrines of the Chicago school of economists, led by Professor Milton Friedman and propounded in Britain by Ralph Harris and Arthur Seldon at the Institute of Economic Affairs. This event was to have profound importance for the Saatchis in the years ahead.

At that point in their career, however, the brothers did not spare much thought for Thatcher and monetarism; they had their own problems. For Saatchi & Saatchi, like so many businesses in Britain, was in trouble.

The brothers had actually coped well with the early months of the recession, and ended 1974 with billings of £10.8 million, profits of £190,000 and a nineteenth-place ranking in the billings league table. However, the whole of Adland faced a tougher and tougher time as the year wore on. In inflation-adjusted terms total expenditure on advertising in Britain had grown from £554 million in 1970, when the brothers started their business, to £716 million in 1973 – an increase of 30 per cent. In nominal terms it had grown from £554 million to £874 million – nearly 60 per cent. No one in the industry could have known that it would be nearly ten years before advertising expenditure in real terms matched that 1973 figure again – or that, for three years in a row, it would fall steeply, reaching its low point in 1976.

If Charles and Maurice Saatchi had known it, they would certainly not have hired Rodney Fitch again to design the new office in Regent Street. The brothers had taken advantage of the property crash to purchase a lease on the building, and it was typical of Charles that he would ignore the battle of the garnishee order at Golden Square and ask Fitch to design his third office. Fitch's brief was the same as it had been when he designed the office at Golden Square: 'Make us look bigger than we are.' The offices had once been occupied by Cunard in the days when it ran the *Queen Mary* and *Queen Elizabeth* liners across the Atlantic, and the shipping company had left behind a handsome reception area, with considerable quantities of marble, while the proportions of the building were far more generous than the tiny Soho premises. For its part Saatchi & Saatchi now had a great many more people to go inside – it was becoming a respectably sized agency.

That Christmas, however, Maurice suddenly became aware of the scale of some of their mistakes. The particular cause for worry was a company called George J. Smith, which they had bought for £90,000 only to discover its liabilities were far greater than they appeared on the balance sheet. They also discovered that the money owing to the company was not as great as the figure shown. They had, in short, bought a company which was virtually insolvent.

The implications of this were just coming through when someone – the various suspects have denied it to me – decided to play a practical joke. December was normally Christmas bonus time, but in 1974, given the troubles ahead, the brothers decided to cut back. Tim Bell, now installed as managing director, sent a memo to all the staff. There would be no bonus this year, he said, but to show the company's appreciation of their efforts everyone would receive 'a small gift'. A few days later came another memo, this time under the name of the office manager, Tony Hewitson. This stated that further to Tim Bell's memo he was now writing to say that, instead of the Christmas bonus, everyone could have a choice of gifts: shares in the company, or a turkey. 'Please get your order in quick,' it went on, 'because we're running out of turkeys.'

Even some of the more senior executives believed it. Bill Muirhead put it aside, making a mental note to ask his wife if she had yet bought their Christmas dinner, while several secretaries asked Maurice where could they get hold of the turkeys. No one asked about the shares. Maurice was not at all amused. Hewitson, completely innocent, was summoned, and under Maurice's withering attack became so flustered that he admitted authorship. He was close to being dismissed – a very rare event in Saatchi & Saatchi – before the truth dawned.

It was Christmas Eve when the full impact of the business downturn finally hit the brothers. On 21 December, three days earlier, they lost their biggest account: the Singer sewing machine group, won so strenuously two years before, pulled out. It was nearly half the agency's billings, and Maurice and the accountants calculated the impact on profits for the coming year. The figures arrived on Christmas Eve: the agency was heading for a major loss in 1975.

They could see no hope of relief from the British business world that year. In the world outside, the financial crash was nearing its worst, and there was much talk that the London stock market would cease to exist altogether by the spring. Young men whom the Saatchis had grown up with and who had made fortunes in the City in the 1967-73 period were falling even more rapidly than they had risen, their paper wealth melting away to be replaced by impossible borrowings. Maurice went home that Christmas Eve feeling the world was coming to an end.

The strength of the Saatchi brothers is that they have a facility for thriving in adversity. They don't actually seek it, in the way some entrepreneurs (Tiny Rowland, for instance) do, but they are not afraid of it; and once they have a problem they have an exceptional ability to solve it. 'The brothers don't actually see obstacles,' says Anthony Simonds-Gooding, who got to know them a decade later. 'They simply go straight ahead, and then look back and say, "Oh, that was an obstacle?" ' It is entirely consistent with their later history that they should see in their current troubles lessons to be learned – and opportunities for expansion.

They tackled their problems in the best way they knew – by going even more aggressively for new clients, by getting more out of the business they had and by cutting costs. January 1975, with the bankruptcy of Burmah Oil, marked the bottom of the worst bear market on the London stock exchange in a century, and from that point on the recovery began.

By the end of September and the end of their financial year, Saatchi's were not only solvent, they could show excellent profits. During the year, far from going bust, they had raised profits from £190,000 to £400,000, a 113 per cent increase. They would weather this crisis, but it was a clear lesson that expansion could lead them astray.

The brothers had begun trying to take over other agencies in 1973, their third year of operations, applying a similar technique to their search for new business. Besides his twenty-five calls a day Maurice was also responsible for writing a series of letters to other agencies. He worked out the wording very carefully, aiming to avoid giving offence – which was difficult enough, considering the enormity of this tiny agency's expressing interest in buying some more established businesses – but at the same time indicating a genuine interest. Michael Heseltine had adopted a similar approach at Haymarket, and Maurice had seen how effective it was. The concept was to approach the maximum possible number of people, to make sure one covered the ground, and, although the failure rate would be high, one had a good chance of finding someone who just at that point was suddenly making up his mind to sell; or who would keep your letter, and come back a year later when he decided it was time to find a buyer.

Maurice's letters were polite but to the point. 'I am sure this will be the last thing on your minds, but I wondered if you felt it would make sense to dispose of your company,' he began. These letters went out in large batches and even went to the giants of the day, causing much ribald laughter in the industry. The story is told of how Jack Wynne-Williams, the august head of Masius Wynne-Williams (now, after a series of mergers, called D'Arcy Masius Benton & Bowles, and American-owned), which was JWT's only serious competitor for the top position among British advertising agencies, received just such a letter. He is said to have written back to say that he had looked in the petty cash to see if he had enough to buy Saatchi & Saatchi. Maurice does not remember this incident. There is another story, probably true, of how at an IPA meeting one agency head pulled out a letter from Maurice and boasted of the takeover approach he had received that day. Three other agency heads pulled out an identical letter.

Saatchi's held talks with a number of agencies. There was an approach to Boase Massimi Pollitt, old friends from the days with Ross Cramer at Goodge Street; and with Murray Parry. Charles also leaked a story to *Campaign* that he was about to buy an agency in the United States – big talk indeed for such a tiny business. There was another *Campaign* story about the creation of a subsidiary in Paris called Saatchi Damour, which never happened. Intentionally or not – and it probably was – the advertising world got the message that Saatchi & Saatchi was developing into a bustling international agency.

There was another set of talks which also came to nothing at the time but would later lead to perhaps the most important deal the brothers would ever do. S. T. Garland Advertising Service was started in 1928 by a former *Daily Mail* ad salesman, Sidney Garland, and in

1960 was one of those old British agencies which the big American multinationals looked for to give them a place in London. In this case, it was Compton Advertising of New York, which bought 49 per cent with an option on another 2 per cent, thus giving it effective control of a new company which was called Compton UK Partners, and which owned 100 per cent of the agency Garland-Compton. But by the early 1970s a group of its managers began to chafe at the American control, and they worked out a plan for taking the company to the stock market, diluting the Americans' holding but giving them a substantial profit. Ken Gill was the Garland man behind this, and it was he who talked the Americans into accepting it. The method of going public, however, was not his, but that of one of the sharpest City entrepreneurs of the day: Pat Matthews ran the First National Finance Corporation, one of the new-type fringe banks and finance companies which was to run into spectacular financial troubles a few years later, to be bailed out by the Bank of England.

Matthews employed a roomful of young men who eagerly examined every public company, looking for hidden value, or a way of making a quick profit. One of the companies they had come across was the Birmingham Crematorium company, which was exactly what its name suggested: a burial company based in Birmingham, except that most of its assets, with the grisly exception of a bone-crushing machine, had now gone. It was what is called a 'shell' company, one without assets or earnings which for historical reasons retains its stock market quotation. Before the rules changed, 'shells' provided a convenient short-cut for a company to avoid the lengthy process of getting a stock market quotation in its own right, with all the requirements and regulations it had to meet.

The popular game among entrepreneurs such as Matthews was to buy a company, strip out the assets, then inject another company into the 'shell' that was left. In this instance, Compton UK Partners was reversed into Birmingham Crematorium which issued new shares for it, and which then changed its name back to Compton. By this little device it had transformed itself from a private company into a public one with its shares quoted on the stock market. Gill, who now became chairman, found himself for the space of a day owning the bone-crushing machine. He hastily sold it without ever seeing it.

Matthews emerged as a shareholder, appointed one of his men to the board and began looking for other acquisitions for Gill to make. Gill was happy to let him do so: he had seen, at an early stage, the advantage of size to an advertising agency, and also realised that many agencies had no idea of their worth. He himself was on the takeover trail, and put out feelers to a variety of smaller agencies, several of which were absorbed into Compton. It was during this period that the Matthews men invited him into the City to meet two young men also keen on mergers who might be of interest to him.

It was in a banking parlour in Fenchurch Street in the City that Ken Gill first met the Saatchi brothers in 1973. They questioned him closely: how had he gone public, what differences had it made to the agency, what accounts did he have, how did he find working for Procter & Gamble? Compton had a number of clients the Saatchis would have given a great deal for: Procter & Gamble, the biggest advertiser in the world, with its exceptionally well-organised marketing set-up and its huge list of brands, was their dream. Compton also worked for Rowntree, United Biscuits and a variety of other Blue Chip clients. He in turn was interested in them, but not as a potential acquisition – not then. The brothers talked brightly about how they saw the industry developing and about international networks – the word 'global' had still not crossed their lips. They parted, and didn't see each other for another three years.

The Saatchis did make a couple of acquisitions in 1973. There was a small company called Brogan Developers, which was used to house Charles's growing art collection, and they paid £130,000 for a Manchester agency, E. G. Dawes, which allowed the brothers to expand their Manchester office, which they had started in 1973 to service Great Clowes Warehouse, owned by GUS.

The bad times of 1974 offered them more opportunity. The acquisition of Notley Advertising, now an almost forgotten incident, was actually both highly successful and significant. It almost doubled Saatchi's size, cost almost nothing, and the Notley people were absorbed into the Saatchi agency (some of them are still there), boosting both business and staff numbers substantially. The appearance of so many new faces at once was a culture shock to the old hands like Jeremy Sinclair, and also meant that even with the additional premises around Golden Square they had to move. It was that acquisition which finally pushed them to Lower Regent Street.

Then came George J. Smith, which was based in Manchester, with a division in London. Charles is said to have blamed the disaster on Maurice, and more than one Saatchi man dates the chair-throwing incident to this event.

None the less they had learned enough to know what to do – and what not to do – in future takeovers. By the autumn of 1975 they were contemplating one which, with a single bound, would make them a major agency. No other future takeover would ever have the same thrill, or the same impact.

The Saatchi & Saatchi takeover of Compton, the eleventh biggest agency in Britain at the time, with some strong clients and billings of £17.44 million, started in a bizarre way. The brothers were not even thinking about a takeover when Maurice rang Ron Rimmer, managing director of Garland-Compton, which was the operating subsidiary. He was looking for a business manager, and wondered if Rimmer would be interested. Intrigued, Rimmer told Ken Gill about it, who in turn recounted his own meeting with the brothers.

'Go there, and see what they say,' he advised Rimmer. 'Let's find out what we can.'

Unknown to Maurice, Gill was looking hard for a way of expanding his agency. He felt it had got into a rut and lacked 'bite', and to reinvigorate it he wanted to inject some of the bright young advertising talent emerging on the London scene in the 1970s. He had held lengthy talks with Ronnie Kirkwood, who had started his own agency, Kirkwood Company, in 1970, at the same time as the Saatchis. He had talked to John Pearce at Collett Dickenson Pearce; to Martin Boase at Boase Massimi Pollitt, and to others, often coming across the footsteps of the Saatchis who were following the same route. Were they now after him? For some reason he had not received one of the letters that Maurice had sent out to the other agencies, and had felt offended. But the position had now changed.

Rimmer reported back that what the Saatchis wanted was to hire him – as an administrator. It was puzzling: surely Tim Bell was the managing director? Why did they want an administrator? Even more intrigued, Gill decided to follow that up. His operation was full of good administrators. What he did not have were bright young creative people to inject a spark into his somewhat staid and respectable agency. From what he remembered of them, the Saatchis seemed ideal for the purpose.

It was now Gill who approached the Saatchis, and within days they were in serious negotiations. These lasted for months, with both sides carefully thinking through the implications of the move, and arguing intensely over the structure of a new group, should they be able to agree terms.

It was to be a complex deal, particularly for Gill, who had to persuade his major clients, his staff and his shareholders to accept the merger. Of these groups the most difficult would be the shareholders (although the staff were not easy either). Compton of New York still owned 49 per cent, and the deal needed approval from the biggest shareholder. Gill placed a call to the New York office of Milton Gossett, the fifty-year-old president of Compton, and an old friend.

Gill outlined the problem that faced him. The London end was a good, solid, day-to-day agency, he explained, but he could not see anyone among the younger people who could provide the new burst of energy needed; he had no obvious successor, and that worried him. Profits that year had fallen, and the agency was only eleventh in the 1974 billings table. But he had met these two young men producing some of the best advertising he had ever seen; they were financially bright as well as creative. He was thinking of taking over their business, and getting them to set the direction of the agency. He would like Gossett to meet them.

Gossett, like Gill, was also to play a major role in the business lives of the brothers. Compton in New York, the agency where later that year he would be promoted to chief executive officer, was a reflection of its client list: Ivy League, conventional, conservative. Gossett himself, though, was not Ivy league at all, and unlike most people in the agency not a university graduate. What college education he did have was in engineering, which was of little practical use in his career as a copywriter or as president. He had joined Compton in 1949, originally 'pushing a cart around the halls delivering mail and learning that media was not a Greek goddess'. He is still there today.

At Gill's invitation, Gossett went to London to meet the Saatchis. Before meeting the brothers, he was introduced to Tim Bell and was immediately impressed. Bell, although not on the main Saatchi & Saatchi board, was managing director, and if the deal with Compton went through was to be in charge of the joint agency. Bell, according to the brothers' version, was initially against the merger, but Gossett never got that impression. Bell showed him some of the best Saatchi advertisements, and Gossett recalls being bowled over. 'I fell in love when I saw the advertising the Saatchis were doing,' he told a friend later. And so Gill arranged for him and for Compton's chairman, Stu Mitchell, to meet the brothers.

It did not go off well. The meeting took place in Gill's flat in Down Street, just off Piccadilly. Mitchell was far more conventional than Gossett, and he needed some convincing. He was not about to get it. The first impression made by the Saatchis was not what Gill had planned. 'These two young dark-haired and very emotional young men walked in like wild creatures,' says one of the Compton party, 'and we were the enemy. We represented convention. Stu Mitchell said about three words, and they stalked out of the room.' No one remembers what the three words were: ' "rule of order" or something like that,' quips a Compton man.

It was a major setback for Gill, who had set his heart on the deal. Mitchell went back to New York and announced he was against any such thing. But Gossett, under Gill's persuasion, didn't agree. 'All I see is superb creative work, a couple of guys who are very volatile, and a fellow, Tim Bell, who is marvellous. As far as I'm concerned they're great – why shouldn't we do it?' Gill brought the brothers back to his flat for more meetings, and the talks got back on the rails.

The more the Saatchis considered Garland-Compton the more they liked the idea of getting hold of it, merging their own agency into it and running the whole show. It made sense to them for reasons other than size. A number of lessons were coming home to them. The shock of losing Singer still haunted them, but there was a longer-term consideration too. They had, they felt, established their reputation as the creative hot-shop of the industry; but they had always known that wouldn't be enough. They had hardly any clients in the fast-moving packaged-goods area: no soapflakes, packaged foods or supermarket goods, which belonged to the big accounts. They had no reputation for marketing skills, although when they started in 1970 they had identified the fact that this was essential. And they were just beginning to realise that it was very hard to get a reputation both for creativity and for marketing. The two are in many ways opposed to each other. The perception among clients was that the world divided into bright creative people, of which Saatchi & Saatchi was a good example; or bigger, more conservative operations which were strong on marketing. Garland-Compton was very much in the latter camp, while Saatchi & Saatchi on its own, no matter how fast it grew, could never get there. The thought of putting together its own creative skills and Compton's marketing reputation under the same roof became irresistible. Later the brothers would be stung by criticisms that the conflict between the creative and the marketing skills meant that the merger was a 'marriage made in hell', and forecasts that it would disintegrate annoyed them. 'It's a marriage made in heaven,' Maurice, who could see the possibilities even more clearly than Charles, told his brother that summer. Reluctant at the beginning, they began to push the negotiations on faster.

Compton was not the only shareholder whose view Gill sought. In 1975 James Gulliver was generally seen as one of the brightest and most able managers in Britain. The son of a grocer, he came from the small distillery town of Campbeltown, in Argyllshire, had studied engineering at Glasgow University, then won a Fulbright scholarship to the Georgia Institute of Technology. In his twenties, he became the protégé of the Canadian food retailer Garfield Weston, owner of the Fine Fare supermarket chain in Britain, as well as Fortnum & Mason. By the age of thirty-three Gulliver was managing director of Fine Fare, and shortly afterwards Ken Gill came along to make a pitch to him for his advertising account. After a bumpy first few years the two men became friends, and the relationship survived Gulliver's eventual break with Weston. In 1975 Gulliver had set up his own company, called James Gulliver Associates, which among other services offered management and investment advice. He had bought into Compton when it went public, and now owned just under 10 per cent of Compton's shares. He too would play an important part in the merger.

Gill enlisted Gulliver's help, asking him to advise on the Saatchi business and to suggest how the deal might be structured. Should it be done at all? Gulliver, who had a small office on the third floor of the Compton building in Charlotte Street, was initially far from keen. He was busy at the time with a series of investments he was making; but he assigned one of the bright young men he had gathered around him to the project. That young man was Martin Sorrell.

Sorrell is a short, black-haired, heavily spectacled man, born into the North London Jewish community thirty-one years earlier. His father ran a profitable electrical retail business, and Sorrell, an only son, grew up in a comfortable middle-class home, not greatly different from that of the Saatchis. As a teenager, he travelled to the USA to see the Kennedy clan campaigning and developed a lifelong interest in marketing and advertising. He took an economics degree at Cambridge, then went to Harvard Business School. Back in London he worked for Mark McCormack's sports and personality management firm. Then in 1975, just as the Compton/Saatchi saga was developing, he joined Gulliver.

Within days Gulliver told him: 'Look, I have this personal interest in Compton, and Kenneth Gill has asked me to give him advice on whether they should take over this company called Saatchi & Saatchi.'

Sorrell did a double-take. Saatchi & Saatchi? He knew the name, because he had seen it on the office in Lower Regent Street, but he didn't know it was a London advertising agency. 'I thought it was a new Japanese hi-fi firm,' he said.

Impatiently Gulliver explained who the Saatchis were, and what he wanted done. Gulliver went on to say that he was opposed to the deal, although he hadn't told Gill that, but that Sorrell should take a hard, clinical look at the whole thing.

Meanwhile the negotiations with the brothers continued. By the end of the summer of 1975 they were close to a deal, under which the Saatchis would sell their business to Compton for shares. They would own 36 per cent of the combined equity of the enlarged group, and Compton of New York would be diluted down from 49 per cent to 26 per cent. Gulliver still didn't think much of it, but Sorrell was becoming increasingly interested in the Saatchis, and their quick minds and different way of doing things. Gill's commitment never wavered, and Gossett, who had succeeded Mitchell, was prepared to go along with it.

As the deal progressed, Gill decided it was time to check with the major clients. They, like the big shareholders or the staff, were also in a position to veto it. If, for instance, Procter & Gamble told him it would take its business away, there would be no merger. P & G is in fact very punctilious about not interfering in the corporate affairs of its advertising agencies – unless it feels its brands will suffer. But it had to be convinced. The P & G people knew and liked Gill, and listened politely as he explained the proposed deal.

'Well, Kenneth, if that's what you want, we won't try to stop you,' said a senior P & G executive at last. 'But I hope you're right.'

'I'm sure I am,' said Gill. 'You'll get a tremendous service out of this, a real shot in the arm. Good creative stuff – you'll enjoy it.'

The P & G man knew enough about Saatchi's reputation to have his doubts. 'Well, we'll see.'

'You *will* see,' said Gill. 'You're really going to like it, I give you my word. And if you don't you'll fire me anyway, so it's in our interests to see that you do.'

P & G demanded a larger team to work on its account, and Gill was happy to oblige.

Rowntree Mackintosh and other big accounts took the same line. 'If that's what you want to do, we'll back you.' Only one client, Ideal Toys, didn't like it, and withdrew its account.

The brothers insisted on one condition, and refused to move on it: the name Saatchi & Saatchi had to be retained. It was a difficult point, because technically Compton was taking over Saatchi, although everyone had long accepted it was a 'reverse' takeover, in the sense that the Saatchis were going to emerge on top. Gill fought against that, and Gossett didn't like it either. Gill, however, could see the value of the name and the cleverness of Charles in making a virtue of its strangeness in the first place. So the operating subsidiary company, the merged agency, it was agreed, would be called Saatchi & Saatchi Garland-Compton. For a decade there would actually be no advertising agency called Saatchi & Saatchi, yet so powerful was the image and reputation of the two brothers that even those who worked for it called it 'Saatchi & Saatchi'.

For his part, Gill would not give way on one point: the brothers were going to have to move lock, stock and barrel into *his* offices in Charlotte Street. They had been purpose-built for Hobson Bates as the premises for an advertising company, and he did not think much of the Saatchi office in Regent Street (which, ironically, is where he has his office today). Charles did not want to go, but reluctantly gave in. Only later, after he had moved in, did he become enthusiastic.

By September 1975 the deal was ready for signing. So far there had been no rumours, and by keeping the meetings to Gill's flat they had managed to retain security. Then, with only a week to go before the announcement, Gill, opening his copy of *Ad Weekly*, suffered one of the worst shocks of his career. Charles Saatchi was quoted as saying how much he admired Garland-Compton's work – not a remark he would normally make. Angrily, he rang Charles.

'Christ, you've blown it,' he said. 'This is far too specific – everyone will know what you're up to.'

A few minutes later he had a call from Bob Gross, chairman of Geers Gross. 'Congratulations,' said Gross.

'For what?' Gill tried to sound innocent.

Gross laughed, and rang off.

But he was the only one to see through it – and the only one of Gill's peers in other agencies to support what he was doing. Within hours of the news being announced, Gill was besieged by calls from almost every agency head in London, telling him how much he was going to regret it. The Saatchis were not popular, and the thought of one of the oldest and most conservative agencies falling into their hands sent a large ripple of unease (and also of envy) through the industry. In a single step, the Saatchis had moved from London's thirteenth biggest agency to fifth biggest. They were getting into the big time.

The shocks for Gill, and for Milt Gossett in New York, were not over yet. They had insisted that the deal should be presented to the outside world as a merger, giving Garland-Compton its dignity and pride of place as the senior of the two partners, but also bringing out the importance of the Saatchi presence. 'An agency with a much higher profile than ours had come in and it was to be billed as a wonderful marriage,' says one of the old Compton people. 'Good creativity on their part, and sound marketing on the part of Garland-Compton.' It was to be done delicately, so as not to upset the Garland-Compton staff, and also to give Compton of New York some face.

That Friday's *Campaign* therefore came as a bombshell. Across the front page was the headline 'Saatchi swallows up the Compton Group'. The actual story was factually correct, but the headline did the damage. The shock wave spread to New York, where Gossett was angrier than anyone had ever seen him. In London, Kenneth Gill was devastated: friends reported he had tears in his eyes as he tried to explain the deal. It was a sour beginning to what was to prove a successful and harmonious deal.

9

NUMERO UNO

In Maurice Saatchi's office on the sixth floor of that same Regent Street building from which they had moved a decade before – and to which they moved back again in 1985 – Maurice and Jeremy Sinclair look back on the Compton merger. To them it is perhaps the most successful deal they ever did, a move that worked better than they could have dared hope, although in 1975, as they moved to Charlotte Street, just around the corner from that first Cramer Saatchi office in Goodge Street, they had travelled very hopefully indeed. On the other hand there was a certain nervousness. When they had moved out of Golden Square to Regent Street they knew they were leaving behind for ever the days when they all sat in the same room and shouted insults and ribald comments at each other, gave each other absurd nicknames and joined in the success and failure of every individual ad. In the Compton building the atmosphere would be even more different.

In Charlotte Street, Garland-Compton employed 180 people. Following its own growth and the Notley takeover, Saatchi & Saatchi employed about 100. Between them they would still be less than a third the size of JWT and several of the other big agencies in London – a minnow in world terms. Compared with a total staff of nine just over five years ago, it was a lot.

Maurice and Sinclair say that one of the main reasons they were able to cope was because they had already had a practice run – with Notley's. The takeover of this agency is seldom mentioned in the company profiles, nor is it seen by outsiders as an event of any importance. The brothers and their close colleagues, particularly Sinclair, see it as crucial, the prototype of a long production line. Maurice had used it to pioneer his own form of takeover – the 'earn-out', whereby a down payment was made and the rest, dependent on performance, was paid over five or ten years. That would be vitally important for the future. He also discovered, only after he had bought it, that Notley's at one stage had been the biggest agency in Britain, but had declined slowly over the years. Before they took control the brothers thought of it as one of the deadest agencies in the business, but to their surprise they found a number of able and talented people, some interesting ideas which they adopted quickly into their own system, and disciplines and procedures which were sometimes better than their own seat-of-the-pants methods. If Garland-Compton had been the first takeover, says Sinclair, it would have been much harder to adapt. Because of Notley's, the Saatchis and their team had adjusted to the notion that it was easier to embrace other backgrounds than to attempt to impose their own – yet another important lesson.

There is another reason for looking back on the acquisition of Compton with some satisfaction. In 1975 the Saatchis ignored the accepted wisdom that creative shops and business disciplines did not belong in the same camp. They put the the two businesses together, not just as subsidiaries owned by the same group, which is how they would later control many of their acquisitions, but as a physical merger of the agencies, making a single larger one. Until that time, as mentioned earlier, the Saatchis had never been able to offer a skilled marketing service. They had set off in 1970 with the intention of growing their own, but at that point could not attract the right person. If Ian MacLaurin had joined perhaps it would have been different, though probably marketing skills did not belong in that frenetic atmosphere. The big packaged-goods clients, such as Procter & Gamble and Rowntree, would not necessarily have appreciated Golden Square.

By accident or not, with Garland-Compton the brothers completed a merger which made good strategic sense – and then they made it work. The combined entity could now be positioned in a way that would give it a major competitive advantage over the opposition. Perhaps it was the fear of this which caused the other big agency heads to attempt to dissuade their old friend Ken Gill from having anything to do with the Saatchis; but it is doubtful if many of the others, steeped as they were in the traditions of their industry, could see the sense in it. They could see the difficulties certainly – they told Gill about them; but in the event those difficulties melted away before the Saatchi frontal assault. Once again the Saatchis were either unable to see obstacles or else chose to ignore them. In this case they saw an opportunity for doing what they had always wanted, and went straight for it. It was to be the most successful corporate move they would ever make.

*

Shortly after the announcement of the merger, Milt Gossett held a meeting in the Compton boardroom. He and the other Compton directors were still shocked by that *Campaign* headline. The complaints from the Garland-Compton staff, passed on to their friends in what they regarded as their New York parent, were plaintive and heartfelt. They had gone along with the Saatchi deal on the assumption that they were taking over Saatchi & Saatchi, that Gill was buying an injection of new talent and new energy, but that Garland-Compton, as the biggest agency, would still be in the ascendant. Saatchi, after all, were moving into their building, Gill was still going to be chairman, and they were the longest established, with a stock market quotation and all the big clients. Now they read that it was *they* who were being taken over.

Gill was so shaken that he did not want to attend the board meeting, but Gossett calmed him down and insisted he come. Gossett was not a little disturbed himself, but he took a pragmatic approach. Like Gill, he had fallen under the Saatchi spell and wanted the merger to work. There was also a good fallback in these situations, which few can pass up: blame the press. He could say that *Campaign* had got the wrong end of the stick, had taken the whole thing out of context, and point to their own press release which put the whole matter in proper perspective. Pay no attention to that headline and that story, Gossett told the directors. This was going to be a great marriage and these are great guys. He persuaded the rest of the board to support the deal, but it had been uncomfortable. 'That was a tough one,' he told Gill afterwards.

Did *Campaign* get it wrong? There was no question in the minds of Charles and Maurice nor of Tim Bell about what they were doing: they were taking over Garland-Compton. The actual mechanism and details of how it was done were immaterial. The substance was crystal clear.

However, it would have taken even an experienced journalist some time to work that out. The announcement and public statements were all designed to avoid humiliating the Compton side, and to persuade them that this move was a marriage of equals. For instance, on 25 September 1975 *The Times* reported the deal with the headline 'Merger forms one of UK's largest agencies', and went on to talk about Compton Partners, 'a quoted company with more than 70 years of trading', merging with Saatchi & Saatchi, 'formed only five years ago but with a remarkable growth record'. It said that Charles Saatchi and Kenneth Gill would be joint chairmen, that it would give Saatchi's access to a New York office, 'a long-held ambition', and added that both companies welcomed the merger, Saatchi because it gave it access to the Stock Exchange as well as a 'greatly expanded scope of operation' and

Compton because it 'injects new and aggressive young management and creative expertise'. That was the line taken by most other papers who reported the merger, not because of any interest in Saatchi's, but because Compton was a quoted company and therefore merited attention.

Campaign, in contrast, cut through the public relations flim-flam, and declared that Saatchi & Saatchi had indeed taken over Garland-Compton. The assumption in Adland was that *Campaign* had been briefed by Charles – which almost certainly it had. Everyone had seen that comment from him the week before, and the whole of Adland knew – and resented – his closeness to the trade press. Inside Garland-Compton the *Campaign* piece had done damage to him. But outside it certainly hardened the view that Saatchi & Saatchi was aggressively on the march, that it was taking the initiative, rather than the other way around.

This was the first time the brothers had ever received attention from the financial press. From now on it would become a regular event, yet curiously Charles, so keen on being mentioned in the trade press, never transferred his attention to the financial pages, where he could probably have achieved a great deal more. It was a role that would bring Maurice out from under his elder brother's shadow. By the mid-1970s many company chiefs had discovered that a good press image worked wonders for their City reputation too – and therefore for their share price. A high share price meant one had to pay less for acquisitions. There were plenty of public-relations firms around to advise the Saatchis on how to set about it. James Gulliver could have done so, if he had been asked, since Gulliver, in many ways not dissimilar to Charles in his speed of thought, his huge ambition and his drive, had learned to cope well with the financial press. But to this day no more than a couple of financial journalists in London have ever met Charles Saatchi. There is none in New York. It is not that Charles, like many advertising people, is not good on figures – he can find his way round balance sheets perfectly well. It is that, while he is wholly at home discussing ads and ad campaigns, he is less eloquent in other areas, and self-conscious about it. He is also shy with people he does not know well – and as he has grown older, he has increasingly made less effort to get to know new people.

Although neither of them recognised it at the time, this was probably a turning point in the relationship between the two brothers. Until now, Charles, with his volatile and forceful personality, had dominated not just the agency but his younger brother. Maurice had more than earned his place as a partner, but he was still the junior partner, the one who ducked when the chairs were flying; he might have argued with Charles, but it was always Charles who seemed to get his own way. Charles had been totally dominant in the hothouse atmosphere of Golden Square; he had still been the major influence at Regent Street. But now Saatchi & Saatchi was a public company, with outside shareholders, a staff of nearly 300, and aggressive plans for using its share quotation to advance its position. It required new disciplines and new thinking, and Charles would never learn them. For one thing, they didn't interest him – and Charles has probably never in his life done anything that doesn't interest him. And secondly, he had his younger brother, whom he still probably viewed as an extension of himself, to do it for him.

It is worth pausing here to note the significance of this. Both brothers today firmly believe that their ability to use the stock market in the way it should be used – for providing risk capital to new and growing businesses – was the most important factor in their growth from this point on. Charles in his more reflective moments freely acknowledges his debt to Maurice in this area in particular; if he had gone into business with Ross Cramer, with Martin Boase, his friend Frank Lowe or even Tim Bell, he would have created a decent-sized business, perhaps even become the biggest in Britain (although even that would be doubtful), and lived a prosperous life. His qualities were those of leadership, creative imagination and an ability to find and motivate other talented people. But there are others in the advertising world who have similar abilities, maybe not always as pronounced, but good enough to mean that Charles was not dramatically different from his peers. What now emerged was that Saatchi & Saatchi had not only Charles's talents but the much more important corporate abilities of Maurice as well. Just as Charles would always have made a good living, so Maurice would almost certainly have created a large company, no matter what area he had gone into. Lindsay Masters and Michael Heseltine recognised that from the beginning, and even those with the exceptional financial skills of Martin Sorrell came to admire him.

Charles probably never had any real intention of becoming joint chairman: he could not bear the thought of having to stand up in front of shareholders and handle a meeting, or talk to the City, as chairmen of quoted companies are expected to do. All of that side of the business he would leave to his brother. It was not just that Maurice was good with figures; he had the interest and the ability to apply the same intellectual process that had him so fascinated when used by Professor Cohen at LSE to advertising as an industry. Thus he wondered why advertising had such a low City image and stock market rating, and whether this was justified. He did the research to find out; and when he had proved to his own satisfaction that it was not deserved he set out with his strange mixture of self-effacement and charm to convince others of his findings. It would take him several years, but it worked far better than perhaps he ever hoped. In doing so he opened the way for Saatchi & Saatchi's expansion far beyond what Charles, despite his huge ambition to be number one, could ever have achieved on his own. To change the investment image of Saatchi & Saatchi, Maurice had to change the view of the whole advertising industry. The fact that he succeeded made it possible for many other advertising agencies to follow Saatchi & Saatchi into the public arena over the next ten years. And it would be entirely through the process of using a high stock market rating to raise capital that the bastions of Madison Avenue would eventually fall to the British.

Jennifer Laing was among the staff of Garland-Compton who had gathered to hear an address from their new employers. The daughter of a plastic surgeon, Laing always called her decision to join Garland-Compton her 'first lucky break'; she had rapidly worked her way up from being a trainee on the accounts side to become account handler for Rowntree when the merger with Saatchi & Saatchi took place. She was twenty-four at the time, but was already seen as one of the brightest people on the London advertising scene. Now, along with all the others, she was anxious to find out what lay in store for her. That *Campaign* headline had given everyone the jitters.

A few minutes later she caught her first glimpse of Tim Bell. He appeared suddenly from the back of the room, and strode confidently through the waiting Compton staff to the front. He wore a light brown suit and a golden suntan, and his hair was bleached. With him was Charles Saatchi, more soberly attired in a pinstripe suit. Bell, a cigarette in one hand, told the audience that the merger was the most exciting thing that had ever happened in any of their lives; it was going to be the greatest and most famous agency in the world; the combination of the two teams would be unstoppable, and they would win major new business and huge new accounts. He was going to be in charge of putting the two businesses together, and he was looking forward to working with everyone in the room. 'He put it all across in this wonderful sexy voice,' says Laing. 'It was fascinating watching the effect on the audience.'

When Bell had finished, Charles stood up very quietly and gave the longest speech anyone can ever recall him making. He did it well, insisting that this was a merger, and said he was looking forward to working with Kenneth Gill and everyone else. By the end the damage done by the *Campaign* headline had been more than reversed. 'It was a landslide,' says Laing. 'Everyone walked out of that room feeling they really wanted to work with these guys. I remember someone turning to me and saying, "Well, Jen, you just went into the advertising industry." '

An early casualty of the merger was Ron Rimmer, the man who had inadvertently brought it about. He had readily accepted Tim Bell as his boss, and had shifted sideways to a financial role; but within months he left, and went to McCann Erickson. 'It was the methods of working that worried him,' says a former colleague. 'He didn't understand all this fiery behaviour at all.'

There was a successor to hand, however. The deal had been completed in September 1975. Four months later, in January 1976, Martin Sorrell suggested to his boss that they offer the services of the James Gulliver Associates consultancy business to the Saatchi brothers. They had seen something of them during the bid negotiations and Sorrell had got on well with them. Gulliver was agreeable. He had set up office just outside London, in Welwyn Garden City, and was starting a company which within ten years would make a £2.5 billion bid for the Scotch whisky group Distillers, only to be beaten, through unfair and probably illegal tactics, by Guinness, in what became the financial scandal of the decade. Maurice went to lunch with Gulliver, Sorrell and Alistair Grant, then Gulliver's joint number two (today the chairman of Argyll Foods, owners of Safeway supermarkets, and the third biggest food retailer in Britain). Gulliver, particularly in his own lunch-room, was always formal, and invariably served the same food: Dover sole. Sorrell watched with some amusement his expression as Maurice, who sported bow-ties in those days, took off his jacket. Gulliver simmered, but let it pass, but Maurice had not risen in his estimation.

The Gulliver approach came at the right time, because the Saatchis were indeed looking for advice. Maurice was now coming to grips with the problems of running a public company, and wanted some ideas on how to use the stock market quotation. He was already hitting the frustrating wall of the City's dislike for advertising agencies, and for 'people businesses' in general. Saatchi & Saatchi could not borrow as easily as an industrial company, which, with concrete assets and a predictable business, can always raise money from a bank. The company's shares sold at around three times its earnings, a miserable

rating by any standards, less than a third the average rating for the rest
of the stock market. It meant that raising money, or making acquisitions,
by issuing new shares was prohibitively expensive. Maurice was casting
around for a way out of this problem, and knew that Gulliver was well
qualified to help, and Gulliver in turn assigned the project to Sorrell,
who began spending a day a week in the Saatchi office; gradually it
became more.

The financial set-up at Saatchi's at this time was far from sophisticated. David Perring had joined as a company secretary when they
started at Golden Square, and he still had that role (as he has to this
day). He was competent, but was not a qualified accountant. Mike
Johnson was the nearest they had to a finance director, although with
the merger Ron Rimmer and Douglas Blaikey had expanded the team
to four. However, Rimmer was never a proper financial director, in the
sense that most companies understand that position; nor was Johnson.
They were administrative officers, the men who looked after expenses,
chased overdue accounts, paid bills and salaries and generally made the
group work. Both Rimmer and Perring were meticulous, but neither
would be much use to Maurice in talking to the City and organising
new takeover bids. Tim Bell, Jeremy Sinclair and of course the brothers
themselves were capable of developng new skills as the business
expanded; but that did not apply to all the people taken on at Golden
Square.

The first advice that Gulliver and Sorrell gave to Maurice, therefore,
was to hire a finance director. Maurice readily agreed, and a firm of
headhunters was appointed. Finance directors of advertising agencies
in those days, in London at least, were not high-powered people, and
the headhunters went to the traditional trawling grounds: other agencies
and Fleet Street papers. 'These guys came in to see Maurice mostly in
the morning, because if they had come in after lunch it would have
been embarrassing,' says one former Saatchi man. Finally, Maurice,
who had lost Rimmer at this stage, snapped at the headhunter: 'What
I want is someone like Martin Sorrell.' 'Well, have you asked him?'
said the headhunter. Maurice did – and Sorrell came aboard.

Ken Gill relished the new atmosphere in the agency. To the other
agency heads, who expressed their forebodings whenever he met them,
he was uncompromising in his praise. 'It's wonderful,' he said, and
meant it. It was a new lease of life for him, and for the agency. Tim
Bell was working from early morning to late at night, often right through
the weekend, putting the two agencies together – and doing it well.
Other than Rimmer there was a limited fallout; the Saatchi men moved

in to take most of the key positions – Bell as managing director of the agency, Jeremy Sinclair as creative director, Roy Warman as media director, with Terry Bannister and Bill Muirhead also moving into more senior roles. Above the agency was the holding company, which had Gill as chairman (Charles never did join him as joint chairman, although there was no doubt in anyone's mind who was the real boss of the business), David Perring and Mike Johnston, and of course Maurice.

The brothers found rooms for themselves on the sixth floor, and had them redecorated. They were far from grand: Charles's looked out on to the roofs and enclosed courtyard at the back of the building. Across the corridor Maurice's office was no larger, but he made it bright and pleasant with the now traditional Saatchi style: everything, including the desk, gleaming white. Bell moved into an office on the ground floor. At Regent Street his office had been only a single flight of stairs away from theirs; now there was a considerable physical separation between him and the two brothers. That, too, may have been significant. By the standards of the day the brothers were running a medium-sized public company and were increasingly thinking in strategic terms, working on more takeover bids, on expanding the network into Europe, the USA and the rest of the world. Charles still involved himself in the creative side, but his presence was more and more remote. Many of the Garland-Compton people complained they had never seen him, and some never would, except perhaps fleetingly in the lift or walking across the foyer.

For those working in the agency in these years Tim Bell was the hub – and the brothers let him get on with it. Although Bell did not realise it until it was too late, he and the brothers now began to go their separate ways, gently at first, but more rapidly as time went on. Once Saatchi & Saatchi had become a public company, the agency was a subsidiary. In these early days, it was effectively the only subsidiary, all there was to the public company, and Bell in effect was responsible for generating all the profit. If Maurice's plans came to fruition, however, there would be other subsidiaries, other businesses, which would eventually reduce the importance of the Charlotte Street agency. Bell, relishing the role of running the business, did not pause to consider the wider implications of what was happening. It was a time of extraordinary growth, when the agency seemed to be able to get almost any client it pitched for. And a new phenomenon emerged: clients would come to Saatchi's, asking them to take on their accounts without even a 'beauty contest'.

Yet it was Ken Gill rather than the Saatchi brothers or Bell who got the new business off to a flying start. For months before the merger and all the way through it he had been talking to Schweppes about moving its account to Garland-Compton. The Schweppes account was one of the biggest and most prestigious in Britain, having become something of a legend in the 1950s and 1960s with its 'Schh...You know who' campaign. The marketing director, Keith Holloway, was an old friend, and he had finally been persuaded by Gill that it was time to move his account from Ogilvy & Mather. He had also quietly let it be known that he favoured Garland-Compton, although the agency would still have to pitch. Holloway knew nothing about the Saatchi deal, but as luck had it the Garland team was preparing for the pitch when the merger took place. Jennifer Laing was one of the team involved, but she now had the added contribution from the Saatchi side. She went along with Tim Bell and two others to make their presentation – and they got the account. To the outside world, it looked as if the magic name of Saatchi had clinched it for Garland-Compton, and Gill quietly let the Saatchi team have the credit. He could see the impetus this would give to the new agency – and he was right. The Schweppes account had a galvanising effect, both internally and externally. 'That really was a turning-point for the doubters,' says Laing.

The first report and accounts of the public company Saatchi & Saatchi Compton Ltd makes interesting reading. The format was carefully thought out, and would not be altered until the most recent accounts, for the year ended September 1987, which were sent to shareholders in late February 1988. The cover was white, with an embossed rising-step formation, signifying rising profits (or at least rising something). Across the top was the name 'Saatchi & Saatchi Compton', written in that restrained and ultra-conservative script which Bill Atherton had chosen back in 1970 to make the fledgling agency look respectable and established. Subsequent accounts replaced the word 'Compton', with 'Company', but only the sharp-eyed would ever spot it. Within a year the parent company was called Saatchi & Saatchi Company Ltd. This marked a major and complex reconstruction, which had the effect of removing the Americans as shareholders in the parent company and leaving them with shares in the subsidiary, Saatchi & Saatchi Garland-Compton. The scheme was the creation of Martin Sorrell, who worked on it for six months; a new public company was formed to bid, on a one-for-one basis, for the old. Compton would agree not to accept the offer, thus forfeiting their position as shareholders in the new parent, and removing them as a threat to the control of the brothers – the whole object of the excercise. The brothers' shareholding would therefore rise proportionately. Ken Gill, Sorrell and James Gulliver, highly nervous about the reaction they would receive, went to New York to sell it to the Compton board. In the event they got their reaction much more quickly than they expected. 'We've had this proposal,' said Milt Gosset, 'and we're perfectly happy with it.' Compton was already being Saatchified.

Maurice used the early report and accounts to tell the world how much faster the agency was growing than any other. He also identified the best campaigns they had run during the year: Leyland Cars' Superdeal, Schweppes, Brutus jeans, the launch of a new soap powder, Fairy Snow, for Procter & Gamble, Kronenbourg lager and many others. He also made some wider points. The first report declared: 'The fact is that the advertising industry is a cornerstone of the survival of a free enterprise mixed-economy in Britain.' There should be more acquisitions and mergers in the industry 'to bring about the much heralded concentration that the industry needs'; advertisers should stop complaining so much about 'account clashes and conflicts that are often more apparent than real' (the Saatchis that year had been forced to resign one beer account when they took on another). The final two pages were aimed shrewdly at the City. They pointed out that the Saatchi stock market rating was a miserable one: their shares sold at 3.9 times earnings, which meant the whole company was valued at only £1.3 million (and their own stake at 36 per cent of that). Their record was far better than the average, yet 'we are still "rated" only half as well as the average listed company!'

Even half was an improvement on what it had been at the beginning. The Saatchi share price was beginning to lift off at this time (it started at the equivalent of 6p and hit a peak of 700p in 1986), but too slowly for Maurice. In the previous year, partly as a result of his continual campaigning, shares in the tiny advertising sector had risen by nearly 60 per cent, almost twice as fast as the rest of the market. Over the years, Maurice's efforts would pay off. 'There has clearly been a change in investor sentiment towards advertising agencies,' wrote the *Sunday Times* in April 1978, and picked Saatchi & Saatchi as 'standing out from the crowd' in terms of the quality of earnings, track record and prospects. But there wasn't much of a crowd. Other than Ogilvy, Brunnings and Geers Gross (Collett, after an Inland Revenue investigation, disappeared from the quoted sector), there wasn't a quoted sector – all the big agencies were American subsidiaries.

The brothers had been struck by the difficulty of persuading major clients to change their agencies, regardless of the work produced for them; for instance, Kellogg's and Lever Brothers had been JWT clients for forty-one and fifty-two years respectively in 1979. Procter & Gamble and Rowntree Mackintosh had been with Compton even longer. Maurice calculated that, on average, accounts worth only 2 per cent of total advertising moved agencies each year. It came as a revelation to him, and then to the others when he related it. Here was his key for opening up the City. Quality of earnings, he could argue, was not at all bad in advertising, and contrary to the accepted wisdom the business did not go down in the lift every evening. It was actually remarkably stable, far more stable than anyone had realised before. He began making the point that once you were up there with the big accounts you were there to stay, even if your hottest creative people and best account managers left. Size really did matter in the industry. On the other hand, that 2 per cent was worth £1 million a week – well worth chasing. Saatchi & Saatchi still had less than 5 per cent of the total British advertising market, so there was plenty to go for.

In that first year of owning Garland-Compton, Saatchi's profits were just under £1 million, which the Saatchis could record as an increase of 145 per cent, although that included Compton for the first time. The following year they made £1.2 million, then £1.9 million, and by 1979, the year they became the number one agency in Britain, profits were £2.4 million, and the stock market was really beginning to take notice in a big way. By that stage the rating had not only caught up with the stock market average but had actually passed it. In 1980 Saatchi & Saatchi would become a glamour stock, dragging with it the advertising sector, which by then was starting to become larger as other agencies sought quotations.

Already the brothers were looking for more acquisitions, and Martin Sorrell was deputed by Maurice to find them. Initially Sorrell was appalled by the Saatchi acquisition policy. He had been schooled by James Gulliver, who was, and is, probably the most thorough man in Britain when it comes to planning a bid – his detailed examination of Distillers before he made his bid in 1985 is a classic example. Gulliver was working on a number of acquisitions at the time, and his method was to send Sorrell and his own finance director, David Webster, into the City to the offices of County Bank, a subsidiary of National Westminster. There they were required to go through the Exchange Telegraph cards, a widely used company information system which lists the financial history and details of every quoted company. By applying the special criteria that Gulliver had worked out, they then built a list of fifty possible candidates, studied them in greater detail, and whittled that down again to produce a shortlist of perhaps five. That list would then be subjected to an even more detailed study before Gulliver would even begin opening up talks or buying shares. Compton had been a target in his sights at one point, which was why he bought the shares (he had sold them in the market after the bid was announced, still not convinced it was a good deal).

At Saatchi it was different. 'Maurice's approach was very much to have the whole universe,' says Sorrell. 'Then it was like Weight-Watchers: you'd have a regular weekly meeting, and people were called to account. The list was divided up, and we all had to go to talk to these companies and see whether anybody was interested in selling their business. People were chastised if they didn't contact a large number.'

To Sorrell it was the blunderbuss versus the fine-rifle-shot policy of Gulliver. But once he realised that Maurice was working to his own carefully thought-out plan he changed his mind about it. 'It's actually a very intelligent system because what it does is register your calling card. What you're saying to people is: I'm interested. Any decent business should not be for sale the day that you ring up; but one day it might be. The best deals that I've ever been involved in all took three, maybe five, years.' Charles became deeply involved – the only time anyone can even remember him doing so – in detailed bid talks for CDP. He stayed up all night with Sorrell at one session, but Warburgs, advising Frank Lowe at CDP, advised that the price was too low. 'We got very close,' says Sorrell.

Even without acquisitions, Saatchi & Saatchi was expanding rapidly. The advertising accounts continued to pour in: Allied Breweries, new accounts from British Leyland, BP, Black & Decker, Dunlop, more from Procter & Gamble. The gap with JWT at the top was narrowing. Then, in 1979, Saatchi & Saatchi declared billings (the equivalent of turnover in a conventional firm, used as the yardstick for measuring size) of £67.8 million and claimed the top position. It was the front-page story in Campaign and the rest of the trade press. Charles was uncharacteristically modest when he told Campaign: 'as the positions of the four leading agencies are so close, it is not especially meaningful which one emerges at the top for any given period.' In Charlotte Street, however, there was jubilation. For years Charles had been openly talking about being bigger than anyone else – and had been laughed at. It was therefore very 'meaningful': Saatchi & Saatchi was no longer a little hot-shop to be despised and jeered at for its precociousness by the rest of the industry. It stood at the top of the castle, and from now on would acquire a different reputation: it would be the target for everyone else to try to topple. There was a still another year or so while other agencies, notably Masius and McCann as well as JWT, disputed that top position, but finally the impetus that Saatchi still enjoyed left no doubt. JWT, after a reign of twenty years at the top, was number four in 1978-79, and since that time Saatchi's position, if one includes all its acquisitions, has looked as unassailable as JWT's once seemed.

At the end of 1979 Saatchi & Saatchi employed 744 people, earning average salaries of £6041 each. Its turnover was £71 million and its profits £2.4 million; every year from its start it had increased its profit margins, so that by 1979 they stood at 3.4 per cent, more than twice the industry average. It was by now a proper business, its stockmarket rating rising every year. The 'twenty-five calls a day' system of getting new business had long been replaced by a sophisticated and systematic one, where companies were approached on a well-organised and rotational basis which Maurice had put into place. Maurice had visited Procter & Gamble and discovered a whole new world of management and organisational techniques which he had copied and absorbed into Saatchi.

Meanwhile the advertising industry was no longer the same business the brothers had entered in 1970, but had become much more professional, bigger and better managed. The economic crisis of the mid-1970s had caused all agencies – even Saatchi – to contract or even go under. British industry was still trying to rebuild itself after the ravages of those years, and was hitting new problems in the shape of a strong pound, pushed up from $1.53 to over $2.40 by the second oil crisis of 1979 (when Britain *did* have its own oil), and by the emergence of tight monetary controls and high interest rates under the new Conservative government. Advertising expenditure in real terms had increased by 17 per cent during the 1970s, which did not make a great growth industry, but that was actually faster than most businesses grew in Britain during that decade. Within that overall figure, whole new sectors of advertising had emerged: in 1970 detergent and food manu-facturers dominated TV advertising; by the end of the decade the retail sector was the largest, and entire new categories of advertising had emerged. Record companies, films, cars, savings and finance and travel were the growth areas.

Another factor, which again Maurice's analytical mind fastened on and played some part in encouraging, was the advertisers' change of attitude to recession. Traditionally at such a time the first items of expenditure a company cut were research and development – and advertising. Maurice argued that this was the worst decision a company could make: it merely made the downturn worse, and damaged the images of the brands. Without strong brand images, consumers would simply switch to more aggressively marketed goods or take the own-brand labels from the supermarket shelves. To compete with the advertising being done by the big retailers, such as Sainsbury and Tesco, the manufacturers should not cut back. By 1979 many manufacturers had arrived at that conclusion in their own right – and the Saatchis willingly gave them a further push. 'Brand reinforcement', they forecast, was going to be the priority of the 1980s. They were right.

Every year in their annual report the Saatchis published their views on the trends in the industry; they were far from the only people doing it, of course, but no one did it so effectively. Maurice delivered the message to the City of London, explaining how and why Saatchi believed it had accomplished only a fraction of what it was capable of.

There was little retrospection in Charlotte Street. Charles had set a target, achieved it and moved on. What had happened yesterday was gone, and he didn't even want to talk about it. Maurice was now setting the pace, with Charles urging him on from behind. Tim Bell may have been running the agency but Maurice was busy too, thinking beyond the British advertising scene to advertising in the rest of the world, and laying plans for other industries to be conquered. Here again is another part of the answer to the question 'What was different about the Saatchis?' It was Maurice who pointed out that advertising at the end of the day was still a small industry, even if you became the biggest in it. Charles on his own would probably have stayed in it, and would not have dared – or been able – to make the jump beyond. But Maurice was not wedded to advertising, and already saw it as a strictly limited industry. Charles, with all that pent-up energy, still drove and Maurice responded to his impatience, and his demands for more, always more. More what? More clients, more markets, more share of the market, more profits, more quality, more people – and more acquisitions. 'Charles was the goad,' says a senior Saatchi director at the time, 'the grit in the oyster that produced the pearl.' He was distant, but he was there – and everyone knew it, even if they were not aware that a subtle but significant change had taken place, and Maurice was now the brother framing the ambitions and controlling the direction.

The acquisitions continued to flow: Hall Advertising gave the group a major presence in Edinburgh. Then there was O'Kennedy Brindley in Dublin which took them into Ireland. This latter was an interesting buy, bringing in another fifty people and some good Irish accounts, but also beginning, in a modest way, the march to an international network.

The brothers had used N. M. Rothschild, the London merchant bank, to advise on the Compton merger, and still went to them with their ideas of takeovers. Martin Sorrell soon got fed up with this. 'We used to go along to these marvellous portals in St Swithin's Lane in the City, of which our fees wouldn't cover one square foot, and see James Joll [now finance director of Pearson, the group which owns the *Financial Times*], and he used to read us the book of Jonah and the Whale. He always thought we had these insane ideas – he was probably right.' Jacob Rothschild still talks with regret of how 'we let them get away from us'; they were too small for Jacob himself to get involved, and Joll, a former financial journalist, never glimpsed their full potential.

The brothers were not in the least deterred – there were other banks willing to take a more imaginative view. So far they had not used their stock market quotation to any advantage, but they were building towards it. That year's annual report informed shareholders: 'We are currently exploring opportunities for the company in the US market – though we regard this as a long term move and our plans are still at an early stage.'

By 1979 the Saatchi brothers were beginning to become quite wealthy. In 1976 they paid themselves less than £25,000 each and their dividends came to £64,600 – the top rate of tax then was 83 per cent. In 1979 their earnings were still less than £45,000 each, and their dividends had doubled to £120,000 (shared between them). Others in the industry were paid larger sums, but the brothers were far more interested in watching their capital value climb through the increase in their share values – they had over 2 million shares between them, now worth over £1 million, and they could borrow money against that. They also had, like every other senior manager in the agency, their company cars and other perquisites.

Both men were now married. Charles in particular had had a variety of girlfriends from his teenage years, and Maurice, in his quieter way, was also attractive to women. Maurice's marriage in 1972 to Gillian Osband, daughter of Samuel Osband, a wealthy North London property man, had been a lavish occasion, attended by most of the Jewish community with whom they had grown up.. The Osbands were near neighbours of the Saatchis in Highgate, and Nathan and Daisy must have been pleased with the match. Maurice was twenty-five at the time and Gillian was twenty-four. They moved to a gracious house in North London, where Maurice kept some of his growing collection of cars, including his great pride: an AC Cobra sports car of 1950s vintage, capable of speeds of over 150 mph, which he had lovingly restored and which he drove sparingly on Sunday mornings. A friend visiting them was later surprised to discover they had no children: the house seemed to be full of toys and children's books, but that is probably explained by the fact that Gillian worked as a children's publisher. Or maybe because Maurice collected toy trains and antique toys.

Charles married a year later, in very different circumstances. Maurice's wedding had taken place at his father's synagogue, the Spanish and Portuguese, in Lauderdale Road, North London. Charles's was a much quieter affair, at the Kensington Register Office, with only a handful of guests there. His bride was Doris Dibley (née Lockhart), whom he had first met at Benton & Bowles where she was a copywriter. At the time he and Doris were living together in Bedford Gardens in Kensington; Maurice was best man. Charles was twenty-nine; Doris, whose previous marriage had been dissolved, was three years older. Charles's marriage cannot greatly have appealed to his parents. He had married outside the Jewish religion, something unthinkable in the old days in Iraq, but which was happening with growing regularity among the younger generation of Jews who were more prosperous, better educated and more assimilated than their parents.

Marriage did not greatly alter the lifestyle or habits of either brother. Charles continued to meet his male friends several evenings a week for their regular games of snooker or poker. He also discovered, late in life, the sport of tennis, playing with a level of aggression wholly unsuited to his ability; opponents tell of Charles's insistence on serving both first and second serves at the same reckless speed, often double-faulting four times in a single game. He hated to lose, and is today often accused by those he plays with (Frank Lowe for instance) of invariably choosing a semi-professional for his partner to make up for his weaknesses. For all that he could be tremendous fun on court – as he can be in the small group of friends he has gathered around him.

Maurice was more domestic, and developed an interest in interior decoration and design that would later blossom; he and Gillian were more gregarious than Charles and Doris, often seen at cocktail parties and other gatherings. They also entertained at their own home, particularly at week-ends. Neither brother had any children at this stage, a point which often distressed Daisy and Nathan (neither David nor the youngest brother Philip, then developing as a promising pop singer, had any children either), so marriage brought no great culture shock for either of them. They had always lived in a comfortable and relaxed home, and they continued to do so.

In the late 1960s Charles developed another interest which in the 1970s, fanned by Doris who initially at least was keener than he was, turned into a passion: contemporary art. It was the age of minimal art, when New York artists such as Sol LeWitt, Don Flavin, Donald Judd and Carl André with his neat rows of bricks were beginning to emerge at the centre of a major art movement. Charles began to collect it, at first desultorily and then with growing conviction and excitement, buying works for a few thousand dollars ahead of the big rush of American investors who recognised it several years later (when prices had soared). As he became more prosperous and his collection grew, he moved back to North London, to Langford Place, near Regent's Park. He bought an old chapel and then added the ground floor of the house next door which he used as a private gallery for himself and Doris. The house, far from opulent, was behind a wall, and the visitor, coming in through a gate, was greeted by a massive tubular sculpture. Inside there was a sitting-room about 25 by 30 feet, and a high ceiling, the apse of the chapel. The room had built-in sofas, a table-full of magazines – Doris was a magazine addict – and a television. The rest of the room was taken up by one of Carl André's brick arrangements (literally 120 firebricks, the colour of dirty sugar, in a two-tiered rectangle, five bricks wide by twelve bricks long) which had caused such a sensation when a similar André brick sculpture was exhibited in the Tate Gallery. There was art all over the place: a crushed car here, a Warhol there. Then there was a dining-room, decorated in ceramic tiles by the young American-born artist, Jennifer Bartlett. Most of the floors were old stone, a relic of the chapel. The modern kitchen contained transparent glass fridges, looking, says one visitor, 'like something straight out of Fortnum's'. Those fridges and the rest of the kitchen often excited as much interest among visitors as the art did.

There were another four or five rooms, all of them devoted to more paintings and sculpture. Upstairs there was just one bedroom, a bathroom and a dressing-room. One visitor remembers being struck by the bedroom in particular. 'It had this enormous double bed with a fur rug on it, which was underneath a great Anton Kiefer painting – a very dour, strong German painting, which had an almost uncanny echo of this almost-wolf rug on the bed.' There was no spare bedroom, no space for visitors to stay. On the stairs were life-sized figures; and out the back was a tiny garden, with a swimming pool. It was a house which would have been impossible to live in as a family. 'It was like a marvel-lous theatrical set,' says one frequent visitor.

Charles drove himself into the office every morning, using in those days a jeep, an E-type Jaguar or one of the other cars from his sizeable stable. Maurice too drove himself in from his Hampstead house, often using a Mini-moke, a jeep version of the British Leyland Mini. Neither of them had chauffeurs, although Tim Bell and Kenneth Gill did, and sometimes Maurice would either ride with them to meetings or use their cars if they were available. Alternatively, he would go by taxi. Neither of the brothers, according to those who worked with them, was interested in corporate status symbols of the kind which interested more ordinary executives; but then with their names above the door they didn't need any more symbols of their status.

Their lifestyles had obviously changed since the early 1970s, but not to any significant degree. Those who know the brothers well say they are much the same people today as they were eighteen years ago. Maurice in particular worked hard, unwilling even to take holidays. 'His idea of a holiday was going to Capri for a five-day break, or, if he had a meeting in America, taking a few days off and going to Long Island. But he had to be forced to take a holiday,' says a former Saatchi director.

Charles, on the other hand, was keen on his holidays. Each summer he hired a boat in the Mediterranean and went there with Doris and a close friend, the chairman of a thriving company called Carlton Communications, Michael Green and his wife Janet. Then every Christ-mas the two of them flew to the Caribbean, calling off in New York on the way to see Doris's parents and visit the art galleries. Janet Green, daughter of Lord Wolfson of Great Universal Stores, was almost as keen a collector of modern art as Charles, and today the two of them have the best collections in Britain, if not in the world (the Greens have since separated).

Nor had Charles's style of working changed much. He may have been more remote than he had been when they started, but he still had around him a group of people largely the same as he had then. His attention span had not lengthened with age, and his executives knew that they had about three minutes on average to tell him what they needed. Kenneth Gill cannot recall Charles being present at a board meeting, and remembers him at only one annual general meeting, when he was due for re-election as a director. Charles had no title, and nor had Maurice until he took over as chairman in 1986 when Ken Gill had a heart attack.

'They never worked in another large company in any senior position, so they never had a ladder to climb,' says Nicholas Crean, who was their personal assistant in the late 1970s and early 1980s. 'They made their own ladder. They weren't aspiring to be one day on the board of a company, so they didn't think in terms of hierarchy. They could never understand the fuss people used to make about wanting to be directors of Garland-Compton, the advertising agency, or associate directors. Maurice and Charles were just Maurice and Charles. And because they were not particularly aware of hierarchies or position, they didn't have the trappings of what you would call corporate status.'

Outside the business Charles maintained his lifestyle much as before: playing snooker with his friends one night a week, playing cards another, usually playing chess with Jeremy Sinclair in his office at lunchtime. His impatience and low boredom threshold spilled into his private life too. He loved going to see films, but often walked out well before the end. If he managed to see a film all the way through he would bounce into the office the next day and enthusiastically insist that everyone went. He often went to the theatre, but again seldom stayed for the whole show. He was still a TV buff, insisting that his staff video serials such as *Star Trek*, his favourite, the tapes of which he would take home to watch later. 'If we forgot to record *Star Trek* it was like turning up to a presentation with the wrong programme,' says Nick Crean.

Charles made other odd demands of his staff. One night he went to the Embassy Club in Bond Street, which was very popular in the 1970s with the younger set, of which by that stage Charles was at the upper reaches. The next day he gave Crean the task of getting all the records he had heard the previous night. Crean had to ring the club, get a list, then track the records down, even getting some flown over from New York.

Being personal assistant to the brothers was an unusual job. Maurice would send him to the City to do some detailed research on potential acquisitions, combing through the Exchange Telegraph cards in the way Martin Sorrell had done for James Gulliver. 'You'd be doing this when Charles would ring up and say: "Where are my records?"' says Crean.

The personal assistant also had to look after the Charles Saatchi dog, a schnauzer named Lulu which most days was brought into the office. The dog was Charles's rather than Doris's, and contrasted oddly with the rest of his lifestyle. Some saw it as a child substitute, but Charles, although fond of other people's children, never indicated regret he had none of his own. The switchboard operator normally had charge of

Lulu during the day, but the personal assistant might be required to take her for walks, or even mind her in the evenings.

This, then, was the brothers' lifestyle in the late 1970s; it was, at least on Charles's part, idiosyncratic perhaps, but many of the most successful people in business don't fit the conventions. Saatchi & Saatchi was clearly an unusual company by any standards, with talented young people running it in a way which had had a galvanising effect on the whole industry. The Saatchis were much talked about in Adland, and becoming better known, at least by reputation, in the City; but outside those worlds the name meant nothing. Many may have thought about them, if they thought about them at all, as Japanese or Italian.

However, in 1978 and 1979 something else was happening to the brothers and to their agency, something which would have a far greater effect on them than anything they had done so far. Among all the accounts they had taken on, one in particular was about to propel them into the public arena in a quite new way.

10

'LABOUR ISN'T WORKING'

The day in early March 1978 when Saatchi & Saatchi won the Conservative Party account neither Maurice nor Charles turned up. Nor did Tim Bell, who was to make his reputation running it. A young account executive was the only member of the Saatchi team who appeared on time at Conservative Central Office for the formal appointment to what was to be the most important account the agency would have.

Gordon Reece, just appointed by Margaret Thatcher as director of communications at Conservative Central Office, waited impatiently. Charles Saatchi, he had recently learnt, would not appear – he simply never met clients and would not make an exception even for the Conservative Party. Reece had yet to lay eyes on him. Maurice, normally punctilious and prompt, was to represent the agency, but at the appointed time of 9.30 am he was not at Smith Square.

Reece had already cleared Saatchi & Saatchi's appointment with Mrs Thatcher. The company meant nothing to her, and she had simply told Reece that if that was what he wanted it was fine with her. However, it still had to be cleared formally by the party chairman, the former Chancellor of the Exchequer, Lord Thorneycroft, who would have to pay the bills and was, strictly, the client.

Reece had promised Thorneycroft that he would bring along the team that would be working with the party for his approval that morning. Tim Bell would be running the account, but he was on holiday in the West Indies. In any case, his name meant little even to Reece, who had simply identified Saatchi & Saatchi as the brightest and most suitable agency for the job. Now he had only one junior account executive to show Thorneycroft. Reece decided he was not going 'to bugger about waiting for Maurice Saatchi'. He brought the young Saatchi man in, and introduced him to Lord Thorneycroft 'as the top man who handled all these matters at Saatchi & Saatchi'.

The meeting was something of a formality. Reece had already persuaded Thorneycroft that the party must have a proper advertising agency. Having made that decision, Thorneycroft was quite happy to leave the choice of agency to the professionals. The aristocratic Old Etonian, a minister in Harold Macmillan's government, did not concern himself with the world of advertising. He nodded distantly as Reece and the Saatchi man explained what they wanted to do, and at the appropriate moment agreed that the account should indeed go to Saatchi's.

As they emerged, a taxi drew up and out bounded a flustered Maurice Saatchi, full of apologies, all primed to make his pitch.

'Well, we're finished that now, you can go home again,' snapped Reece. 'You've got the account.'

For all this apparent casualness, the brothers were fully aware of the importance of working for the Conservatives. Vanni Treves met Ken Gill that day at the Carlton Club and Gill was ecstatic. Treves could not understand what was so important about the account, but was impressed with Gill's enthusiasm. Over lunch Gill explained that this was the first occasion that a British political party had hired an agency to run its advertising on a full-time basis, that it was going to attract an enormous amount of publicity, and that it would establish Saatchi & Saatchi at a new level.

Even then both Gill and the Saatchi brothers wholly underestimated the impact the new account would have on their lives, both private and business. Within six months the name Saatchi & Saatchi would be a household name closely identified with all that Mrs Thatcher and her new-look Conservative Party stood for, a key component in an election campaign which was almost certainly the most important in British politics since 1945.

It all began a few weeks before when, in February 1978, Thatcher summoned Gordon Reece back from California to help her prepare for an election which everyone assumed would take place later that year. Reece was forty-six, a professional TV producer who had been hired by Armand Hammer as a vice-president of Occidental Oil, based in Los Angeles, to advise him on publicity. Reece's role in the Saatchi story is a vital one, for without him the brothers would almost certainly never have gained the Tory Party account, never have become anything like so well known, and their task in New York a few years later would have been that much more daunting.

On the other hand, there are those, notably Reece, who would claim that without the Saatchis and their advertising campaign the result of the 1979 election might well have been different, and so would the course of British political history. No one at this stage anticipated that the agency itself would become one of the issues, not just of the forthcoming election, but of the two elections that followed in 1983 and 1987.

Reece's links with Thatcher go back to the 1970 election when, on a purely voluntary basis, he was the man responsible for the technical job of putting the Conservatives' party political broadcasts together. A team of professional advertising men, led by Barry Day of McCann Erickson and Jim Garrett, a close friend of Edward Heath, wrote them and produced the artwork, and they were filmed in a little studio in Soho. Reece, who had produced numerous TV programmes in the 1960s ranging from *Emergency Ward 10* to series with Eamonn Andrews, Dave Allen and Bruce Forsyth, acted as 'a sort of editor, putting the whole thing together'.

Thatcher was one of the Tory politicians filmed for the broadcasts, but the footage ended up on the cutting-room floor. By common consent, she was awful, stilted and shrill, unable to project herself. When the Tories, led by Heath, unexpectedly won the June election, she became Minister of Education. Reece, in partnership with the veteran BBC presenter Cliff Michelmore, formed a video cassette company backed – and later acquired – by EMI. In the four years of the Heath government, Reece got to know her slightly, and then in 1974 Thatcher, by now more proficient but still far from perfect in her TV performances, played a more prominent role in the two elections, both of which the Tories lost. Again Reece had the job of editing the party political broadcasts and schooled her on how to present herself to the camera.

After the second defeat in October 1974 the move to replace Heath as leader gathered steam, with Sir Keith Joseph as the ostensible challenger from the right wing of the party. Reece, however, made another suggestion: Thatcher herself, the person who had once forecast that Britain would never see a woman prime minister in her lifetime. 'I think that I was the first person to mention that she should run for the leadership of the party,' said Reece. 'She didn't want to do it, she wanted Keith Joseph. And it wasn't until Keith stepped down that she agreed to run.'

Reece was given a leave of absence from EMI to help her with her campaign. When she won, she asked him to stay on, and for the next three years he advised her on her public relations and appearance. It brought him a considerable amount of publicity; Reece was widely credited with persuading her to change her hairstyle and clothes, lower her voice and pause more for effect. 'There has been something intriguingly professional about the panache and growing confidence of Mrs Thatcher's public appearances,' observed the *Daily Telegraph* soon after Reece had begun his work. The paper went on to reveal some of Reece's secrets on how he got Mrs Thatcher to seduce the cameras: 'It is important not to wear a lot of fuss on television. Edges look good but scoop necklines are out. The ideal outfit is a tunic dress with a shirt underneath.' It is not clear where the *Daily Telegraph* got this information: Reece kept his secrets to himself, insisting when pressed that a person like Margaret Thatcher had to have someone she could confide in without feeling it was going to end up in a newspaper or a new set of memoirs. Privately, however, he was offended by the image of himself as Mrs Thatcher's private Norman Hartnell, 'mincing around with a strategic powder puff', as the *Telegraph* put it. He had not redone her hair; she had done that herself, advised by people far more expert in hairstyles than he was. Nor had he softened her voice. What he *had* done was urge her to act naturally, relax more in front of the cameras, follow her own political instincts. He had certainly schooled her in speaking to the microphone, getting her to slow down and talk more deliberately – made her 'more effective', which was the whole object. 'It was really straightforward editing stuff,' says one of the people involved. 'He corrected her as a director would correct any performer, making her redo things, showing her how to act in front of the camera.'

Later the belief that Saatchi & Saatchi had restyled and repackaged Mrs Thatcher became almost unshakeable, and the brothers, although pointing out the real story in private, did little to discourage it. It became part of the folklore, to be denied when it was damaging, but generally to be enjoyed, particularly after Mrs Thatcher began winning elections. The truth, of course, is that advising on Thatcher's appear- ance was never part of their brief, and the changes had already occurred before they appeared on the scene.

In her years as leader of the Opposition Mrs Thatcher came to rely heavily on Reece, and he in turn was said to regard her with 'near veneration'. His influence during these years in opposition was considerable. 'If there is such a thing as "Thatcherism", Reece, because of what he did in 1975-80, is at least partly responsible,' wrote the *Observer*. His work attracted a considerable amount of flak and even ridicule: Mrs Thatcher, it was said, was being moulded by the media men and was no longer entirely herself. However, that criticism did not last long once she became prime minister, when it was replaced by complaints that she was too strong a character, dominating a cabinet of yes-men.

Reece was born in Liverpool in 1930, the son of a car salesman. He went to school at a Roman Catholic establishment, Ratcliffe, where one of his seniors was Norman St John Stevas, later one of Mrs Thatcher's ministers. Stevas, then known as simply Norman Stevas, at one stage reported him to the headmaster for alleged atheism, which was an unfair charge: Reece was a devout Catholic, sometimes visiting churches up to four times on a Sunday, largely to hear the sung mass. 'Church services', he would enthuse, 'are so wonderful that they ought to charge for them.' At other times he forecast that 'religion is the coming thing. People are ready for it.'

He graduated from Cambridge with a law degree and went into newspapers, working for the Staffordshire *Evening Sentinel* in Stoke, the *Liverpool Post* and, for a brief period, the *Sunday Express*. In the early 1960s he made a critical break into television. Now in 1978 Thatcher had brought him into Central Office in a key role, and Reece immediately began making changes. One of his first moves, he decided, would be to find an advertising agency to replace the voluntary efforts which had gone before.

Reece was a man of some style. Slight and dapper, always immaculate with pocket handkerchief matching his ties, well-cut suits complete with watch-chain, and an ever-present cigar, he was referred to variously as the 'image maker' or more often, in what became a well-worn Fleet Street cliché, the 'champagne-tippling Svengali'. He certainly liked his champagne, preferably one of the better vintages. Alastair McAlpine, the Tory Party treasurer, still tells the story of how Lady (Janet) Young, then deputy chairman to Thorneycroft, complained that it was disgusting that Reece spent so much in expenses on the drink, and said it must be stopped.

'Do you have a car, Janet?' McAlpine asked.

'Yes, a small one.'

'But you have to buy petrol for it. You see, if you have a Gordon Reece, you have to run him on champagne.'

Unknown to either Maurice or Charles, Reece had come across Charles's work before. In the late 1960s he was making a TV commercial when the client, the *Daily Mail*, decided it wanted a different slant to it, some new writing. 'And they hired a strange person by the name of Saatchi who had his own creative shop. And he was jolly good.'

Reece thought no more about it until a decade later he began his search for an advertising agency to work for the Conservatives. It had never been done before by any party, but Reece had learned a great deal from his time in the USA and wanted to import some of the techniques used so successfully by Johnson and Nixon. There was – and is – one crucial difference between promoting politicians in Britain and in the US: in the latter, a party can simply buy space on television or radio (there is no limit in either country on newspaper or poster advertising), but in Britain the political parties are allotted, free, a set number of political broadcasts. Even within these constraints, however, Reece had persuaded Thatcher that a bright creative agency could make all the difference.

Until 1978 the Tories, like Labour, had relied for political broadcasts on the voluntary contributions of supporters in the advertising industry. That by no means meant they were bad. Barry Day and Jim Garrett in 1970 had studied the advertising in the Nixon-Humphrey race of 1967, and made a series of party election broadcasts for Heath in 1970, featuring the twin anchormen of Geoffrey Johnson-Smith and Chris Chataway, both Tory MPs and broadcasters, which marked a major change in TV promotion of political parties, and probably contributed to Heath's unexpected victory. As Saatchi & Saatchi would be later, Day had been particularly impressed by one ad in the Johnson campaign, made by Bill Bernbach, which showed a small girl picking the petals off a flower while the soundtrack used the countdown to a nuclear blast – a reference to Barry Goldwater's hardline policy. The techniques of commercial advertising became an accepted part of electoral communications in the USA in the 1960s, and Day in 1970 used some of them in projecting the Tories. It was, says Day, 'the first *conscious* effort to use the established techniques of commercial marketing on the British political scene'. The Tories did employ an agency, Colman Prentis & Varley, but it only produced the posters and newspaper advertising which were at that stage not much talked about, while Day and his team wrote the broadcasts which were finally edited by Reece.

The same team had been involved again in the two elections of 1974, but by then no one, including Day, was pleased with the product. Too many people had become involved in the process of making the ads, and the 1974 Tory campaigns were essentially gloomy affairs. Reece wanted a new approach.

I've always thought a committee approach to running a political campaign is a very bad idea. One of the reasons is that they're all chiefs and there isn't a single indian there. And when you end up trying to get rid of someone it's the Battle of Hastings, because he resigns in a huff and you have to explain it to the newspapers and it becomes a major *cause célèbre*. If you've got an agency, you simply tell the managing director to change a chap because you don't get on with him, and he is changed.

Saatchi & Saatchi, says Reece, virtually picked itself. He had to have an agency that was big enough to have muscle, but not so big it wasn't hungry. 'You wanted somebody who said: God, we could get really famous if we did this properly.' He also decided the agency had to be one 'whose talent was on the creative side, not the media-buying side', because, by contrast with the USA, there was no media buying involved. Finally, he thought the agency should be British – which ruled out most of the others.

Reece soon settled on Saatchi. The reputations of Tim Bell, Jeremy Sinclair and of course Charles now stood very high in the industry. A friend of Reece's, Terry Donovan, the photographer and director of commercials (and the man with the electric-windowed Rolls-Royce which Charles had envied in the Golden Square days) told Reece he must talk to Charles Saatchi, so he called the agency. 'I want to see Charles Saatchi. When will it be convenient?' The reply was instantaneous: 'This morning.'

When Reece arrived at Charlotte Street there was no sign of Charles, and it would be another six months before he met him; but he saw Maurice, who greeted him politely on the sixth floor. Reece did not know enough about the brothers to understand Charles's reticence, but he was happy enough to meet at least one of the Saatchis. He announced he was no longer willing to make do with a few volunteers to run the advertising for the Tory Party. He wanted an agency to handle the account, and he had narrowed the list down to two; he didn't name the other one.

Maurice's interest in politics at the time was 'above average' but no more, and his immediate reaction was a commercial one. Saatchi, he said, was certainly interested in the account, but would not act on a voluntary basis. It would run it in the same way as it would run any other account, although obviously it would assign its best people to it, and at election time would give it all the commitment it needed. However, Reece recalls him saying, 'We would like it very much; and we are all Conservatives.'

Reece never did have two agencies in mind. He had toyed with the idea of the Masius Wynne-Williams agency, but it was renowned more for its ability at media buying than for its creativity. 'I didn't want a beauty parade. I can't understand why any company in its right mind asks agencies to pitch. The best work goes into the pitch, and is therefore wasted. Anyway, as far as I was concerned, here was this wonderful agency and I went down into the engine room to see who was running it. I had heard about this chap Tim Bell, who was so frightfully clever, but he wasn't there.' Reece was introduced to Jeremy Sinclair, Andrew Rutherford, a copywriter, and a few others. Even without Bell and Charles, Reece was impressed. The more he saw, the more he decided here was the place to go. 'There was a dynamism about the place. It was the coiled spring, the kettle bubbling. I felt I had to get them appointed.'

Charles and Maurice easily saw through Reece's ploy about the second agency. Once they knew what he wanted they realised there was no other agency which fitted the specifications as well as they did. The account was theirs – if they wanted it.

In Barbados that same day Tim Bell had a phone call from Charles. 'What do you think?' Charles asked.

Bell didn't think much of it at all. 'It's a bad idea,' he told Charles. 'It will be completely disruptive to the whole agency. I don't think we should do it.'

Bell had been a young media buyer at Colman Prentis when they had handled just a part of the Tory Party account, and he had seen the problems it caused there at election time. 'I knew perfectly well it would fall to me to run the business, because Charles and Maurice didn't handle accounts. I reckoned it would be tremendously disruptive and I didn't think it was worth any money. I was just vaguely negative about the whole thing, but they were extremely enthusiastic, particularly because Gordon Reece was asking us to take on the account without our even having to make a pitch.'

Bell was by far the most politically involved of the team. His step-father had been an alderman in the City of London, and Mayor of Marylebone when Lord Hailsham, then Quintin Hogg, was Maryle-bone's Member of Parliament. He had canvassed for Iain Macleod, who died just weeks after he became Chancellor of the Exchequer in 1970, for Reginald Maudling, a previous Chancellor, and even for Mrs Thatcher, although at that stage he had not met her. 'I was a very committed Conservative, but it's not something I ever discussed with the brothers. We never talked politics at all. We were businessmen influenced by the political environment, and it never occurred to us to think about how we could influence the politicians.' Now he was being given that opportunity and was less than enthusiastic.

By the time Bell arrived back in London, Thorneycroft had confirmed Saatchi's appointment. Sure enough, Charles and Maurice asked Bell to handle it. Bell had had time to think about it, and had changed his mind. He could see that handled properly, in the way Reece proposed, it could be a very interesting account indeed. 'I'd be delighted,' he said. Reece was anxious to recover from the first meeting at Central Office and was insistent that the whole team, particularly Bell, parade before the party chairman as soon as possible. They all went down to Central Office, where Reece introduced them to Thorneycroft. It was there he met Tim Bell for the first time. 'And of course he was brilliant, absolutely brilliant,' Reece comments.

That day there was nothing for Bell to present, but he never needed much time to work up ideas. Reece wanted a party political broadcast to go out on television in April, only a month away, so time was pressing. He also had other ideas which he bounced off Bell.

We had a major political problem. The Labour government had been unpopular for some time, but we all believed an election would come that autumn. I was sure of it. And my experience of politics was that during the summertime governments do extraordinarily well, particularly if it's warm. People say: 'Things aren't so bad, perhaps we shouldn't have a change, perhaps we should leave things as they are.' Therefore I wanted to have a campaign right in the middle of summer, hit them with everything we'd got in August. But it was now March, and it takes three months at least for an agency to pick up. I wanted to get things moving quickly.

Back in Charlotte Street, Bell and the team set to work. Even as they started, the polls suddenly showed a fall in support for the Conservatives, putting the Callaghan government ahead for the first time in two years. Labour, which had appeared dead only months before, was recovering. After the economic crisis of 1976, when Britain had been forced to call in the IMF, living standards were again improving. The government had made cuts in public expenditure, been defeated on key parliamentary votes and no longer had an assured majority in Parliament as its pact with the Liberal Party was coming to an end. It had presided over a period of record inflation and soaring unemployment. Yet, with an election nearing, its political position was improving. Conservative morale was sagging.

It was against this background that Saatchi's first-ever party political broadcast (PPB) for the Tory Party appeared in the spring of 1978.

Saatchi's had come up with a novel idea for attracting extra interest: they ran a 'teaser' in the tabloid press with the message that if one missed television at 9 o'clock that night one could regret it for the rest of one's life. The 'teaser' would have been far more effective if the name of the advertiser could have been left off, but the law in Britain requires the name to appear; none the less it attracted the interest the Saatchi team was looking for.

The ad itself was Saatchi at its most creative. Scripted largely by Jeremy Sinclair, it depicted everything in Britain going backwards. There were shots of people walking backwards over Waterloo Bridge, of Stephenson's Rocket steaming backwards, of the Comet, the world's first jetliner, landing in reverse, climbers inching their way *down* Mount Everest, and so on.

'This country was once the finest nation on earth,' intoned the voice-over. 'We were famous for our freedom, justice and fair play. Our inventions brought the world out of the Middle Ages to industrial prosperity. Today we are famous for discouraging people from getting to the top. Famous for not rewarding skill, talent and effort. In a word, Britain is going backward.'

The final sequence showed Michael Heseltine delivering the line: 'Backwards or forwards, because we can't go on as we are. Don't just hope for a better life – vote for one.'

It was slick, fast-moving and attention-catching. The short takes of different politicians, often just delivering one line, had never been used before: the public had been accustomed to seeing 'talking heads' on its party political broadcasts. This they found to be more fun.

Although there is no evidence it shifted the Tory ratings, what the ad did do was suddenly raise the profile of Saatchi & Saatchi – and Gordon Reece. The Labour Party machine was discomfited by the professionalism of it, although publicly its reaction was to complain that the Tories were selling soapflakes rather than policies. Behind the scenes, however, there was a wave of disquiet in the Labour camp. Edward Booth-Clibborn had been asked by Callaghan the previous May to organise the publicity for the Labour Party. He knew the work of Charles Saatchi well – he had been a fan of his from Charles's early days at Collett Dickenson Pearce in the 1960s. Booth-Clibborn was chairman of the Designers & Art Directors Association (D & AD), a charity set up to encourage high standards of visual communication. Each year, besides awarding prizes for the best ads, he published an annual – and for a dozen years ads in which Charles Saatchi had an involvement, either as copywriter or as head of the team which produced them, had been prominent in the annual.

In 1978 Booth-Clibborn headed a small team of volunteers from the advertising and academic worlds set up to control Labour's advertising and political broadcasts. On 4 April 1978 he sent Callaghan a memorandum, setting out his concern at the presence of Charles Saatchi in the opposing camp. 'Saatchi & Saatchi are not only London's fastest-growing and most successful agency in financial terms, they are also a force to be reckoned with in the execution of the work they undertake,' he concluded. Callaghan does not seem to have been over-impressed at the time, although later he may have changed his mind.

Tim Bell and his team were now hard at work. There was a considerable amount of research to be done, and a team went off to the USA to study what had been achieved there. Inside the agency they conducted a series of group discussions designed to identify what Bell calls 'the emotional attitudes which emerge when ordinary people discuss politics'. There were hours of discussion about finding the right tone, which had to be 'warm, confident, non-divisive – and exciting', and analysis of what all these adjectives actually meant. There was quantitative research and quality research, much talk about 'directional signals', 'target areas', how to attract women voters, skilled workers and much else.

Charles Saatchi may not have wanted to meet the client, but that did not mean he was uninvolved. Bell recalls: 'He was wonderful to work with; superb ideas were popping out all the time. It was a little bit like the early days of the agency when it was Charles, Maurice, Jeremy and me doing things. There were lots of other people helping now, but it was like the old team working together on a twenty-four-hour basis. It was wonderful.' One day Maurice said to Reece: 'Haven't you met Charles?' He took him across the corridor, and at last the two men met. Reece felt he had been signally honoured.

In the middle of it all Mrs Thatcher decided to honour her new agency with a visit. The whole team – with the exception of Charles – gathered in a ground-floor conference room to receive her, while Bell waited outside on the steps. First the security car drew up, then Thatcher's car. Bell ushered her out and into the building where she gazed around at the reception area hung with blow-ups of some of the Saatchi ads. Mrs Thatcher had developed a Jimmy-Carter-style habit of greeting people with 'Good morning, I'm Margaret Thatcher' and a proffered handshake, and she began working her way through the Saatchi reception area, with her 'good mornings' to each of them. A

rep from a newspaper on his way to the media department was flabber-
gasted to be suddenly confronted by her 'Good morning, I'm Margaret
Thatcher' greeting. Shakily he accepted her hand. She finally arrived
in the conference room. 'Good morning, I'm Margaret Thatcher,' she
greeted Jeremy Sinclair. 'Good morning, I'm Jeremy Sinclair,' was all
he could reply. From that moment on, Sinclair was a fan – and would
write some of his best ads for her.

Later, as they were leaving, Lord Thorneycroft gazed about him in
wonder at the display of cars parked in the Saatchi basement. The full
panoply of the brothers' favourite hobby was on show. Maurice's two
Mini-mokes were there, as well as some of the other cars they owned.
Other Saatchi executives, including Bell, had caught the bug too, and
they had found the brothers were generous when it came to rewarding
them. In between the Ferraris and the Aston Martins was a jeep which
Charles had driven in that morning. On the front was a large grid
which the chairman of the party paused at for a moment. 'Who drives
that?' he asked. Someone explained it belonged to Charles. Thorneycroft grunted. 'I didn't know you got many stray cows in Hampstead.'

The Saatchi team was now preparing what would be the most controversial ad they would ever make, and almost certainly their most notable
contribution towards Mrs Thatcher's election campaign. Reece was
well advanced on his plans for a summer advertising splash, designed
to unsettle Labour in the summer recess and to stem, or even reverse,
their rise in the polls. The Lib-Lab pact was falling apart and an
autumn election looked more and more odds-on. Thorneycroft was
against a campaign, insisting that no one would be around in the
summer, that it would be expensive and would serve no useful purpose.
Alastair McAlpine, unflappable as ever, promised Reece he would find
the money for it. Mrs Thatcher allowed Reece his head.

In June Tim Bell made his first presentation to Mrs Thatcher. Reece
had already seen the roughs of the poster ads that were planned, and
one of them in particular had caught his eye. It showed a dole queue
snaking out from an unemployment office and disappearing into the
distance. The title read: 'Labour isn't working.' Underneath, in much
smaller type, was: 'Britain's better off with the Tories.' That was the
ad Reece wanted.

'That's a wonderful ad,' he told Bell. 'Keep it for the last, put it at
the end.'

The presentation took place in the Opposition leader's room in the

House of Commons. Thatcher was never an easy person to present to, and Bell barely knew her. He took her through the poster ads they had prepared, then with a flourish produced 'Labour isn't working'. Thatcher gazed at it for a long time. 'Wonderful!' she said. It would be the poster they would go with in August.

Bell soon found it was not to be as simple as that. 'I had the most awful battle getting the party's approval,' he said later. 'The objection was that since few people would actually read the copy beneath the title the effect of including the name of the Labour Party in the title would be counter-productive. Yet, whatever the veracity of this argument, the poster will probably go down in history as one of the most effective political posters ever produced.'

When the ads appeared, government ministers hit the roof. Denis Healey emerged to complain bitterly about the tactics, and in the silly season the press gave the story front-page news coverage. It ran in the newspapers every day for a week, with photographs of the poster and attacks on it from Labour. 'The extraordinary thing is we didn't run it much,' says Reece. 'I think we only spent about £50,000 on it, it probably went up on only twenty sites, but it became the most famous poster in the country. The mileage we got out of it was incredible – so much so that it became a sort of strap-head for all stories about the campaign and the work of Saatchi & Saatchi.'

Healey came out with the revelation that the dole queue was not a real dole queue at all, but consisted of Saatchi employees. This caused a further storm. Saatchi's were able to deny it, creating yet further publicity. 'It was absolutely untrue,' says Bell. But they were not genuine unemployed either. 'The truth is that they were Young Conservatives from South Hendon.' Healey, in fact, had almost got it right: filming for a party political broadcast outside Charlotte Street had indeed used Saatchi employees. Healey had just got the wrong ad. Not that it mattered: Reece and Saatchi had achieved far more than they ever imagined. 'Healey made a great song and dance and it got shown on every television broadcast,' says Bell. 'Then it got shown on discussion programmes. It must have had £5 million-worth of free publicity.'

Although there were those in Central Office who would later claim that they had laid a careful trap for Labour and that it was all pre-planned, that is almost certainly a rationalisation. By running the ad in August, Reece certainly hoped to catch Labour off guard and unable to react properly, but he never reckoned on the huge over-reaction which took place. They had, however, already turned up an interesting precedent in their research: a book written by David Windlesham recorded the fact that Labour in 1959 had attacked Conservative Party advertising, done by Colman, Prentis & Varley, with adverse results. 'The angry reactions provoked in the Labour Party may have encouraged more people to look at them,' wrote Windlesham in his book, *Communications and Political Power*.

'I wish I could claim I knew this was going to happen, but we didn't,' says Bell. 'It was a bonus, but we learned from it.' When it came to the 1983 campaign Saatchi carefully designed a trap for Labour: a poster with the copyline 'Labour says he's black – Tories say he's British', which again caused Labour to attack them, winning free publicity and drawing attention to the ads.

But did it work? Many claimed so, and it may even have been a powerful influence on Callaghan. In early September all the polls showed the Conservatives ahead by between 2 and 7 per cent. The summer had not brought the swing-back in support to the government that had occurred in twelve out of the previous eighteen years. 'The government's failure to advance was attributed in part to the skill of the large-scale Conservative advertising campaign, "Labour isn't working", in August mounted by their advertising agents Saatchi & Saatchi,' wrote David Butler and Dennis Kavanagh in their book on the 1979 election.

When Parliament went into recess at the end of July 1978, some members who were not standing again were so convinced that an election would come in the autumn that they cleared their filing cabinets and gave farewell parties. It was thought that Callaghan would not be able to get a majority in the vote that always follows the Queen's Speech, the first business of Parliament when it resumed in the autumn. By the end of the recess, the first week of September, the Saatchi team had their whole campaign worked out.

It was here that the skills of Maurice came into their own. On strategic matters Bell deferred to him. So did Charles, whose skills were essentially on the creative side. 'Maurice is a brilliantly talented man at understanding communications strategies,' says Bell. 'He doesn't have great political flair. I would be very good at saying what the politicians thought, and how they thought it was going, and he would be very good at ignoring that, and saying, "Fine. Well, they don't know what they're talking about – now let's work out a good communications strategy." '

The strategy that emerged came under the slogan 'Time for a change', which they actually copied from the former Australian Labour prime minister Gough Whitlam, though that by itself was far from original: 'time for a change' has probably been used in one form or another in elections since Roman days.

Maurice now went much further. From the earliest days of the agency he and Charles had developed a technique for reducing new accounts to a simple logical flow, using the simplest of words and as few of them as possible. It was a technique much favoured by Michael Heseltine, who had influenced Maurice, and it greatly pleased Charles, with his short attention span and unwillingness to read long documents. Maurice produced a document setting out the combined thoughts of the team after hours of discussion and research; it covered a single sheet of paper. It started with the deceptively simple proposition that 'governments lose elections, oppositions don't win them', and that everything therefore had to be aimed at increasing the level of dissatisfaction, or in other words turning the original proposition around to one of 'oppositions win elections by ensuring that governments lose'.

'Thatcherism' was at that stage ill defined, and the Saatchi team spent hours trying to work out clearly what the message was to be. That too was carefully defined in Maurice's document: a Conservative vote would be a vote for freedom, choice, opportunity, prosperity. 'The notion was that if you asked people what a vote for the Tories means they would snap out with an answer which in some ways reflects these associations,' says Bell. 'We weren't talking about incomes policies, or tax cuts, or industrial-relations legislation or public expenditure. We were talking about the emotional meaning of a Conservative vote.'

Maurice explained to Gordon Reece that he didn't really know if he was writing it on behalf of the Conservatives, or because Saatchi's thought it was a good philosophy, or because Gordon or whoever else thought it was a good philosophy; but it was the best and most simple exposition they could devise of what they believed the Conservatives and Mrs Thatcher could and did stand for. Maurice remembers Reece reading it and exclaiming: 'Well, if you can convince people of that, that's it.'

Maurice waiting for someone to point out scornfully that he had misinterpreted the whole ethos of 'Thatcherism'. But nothing happened. 'Somehow the whole thing seemed to be accepted and it sailed through,' says one Saatchi man. Looking back later he now saw it as 'a very good exposition of what has now become known as Thatcherism'. That exposition became the basis on which the campaign was prepared.

It was around this time that Gordon Reece discovered how Alastair McAlpine intended to finance the summer advertising campaign. McAl-

pine went to see Maurice, and asked him how much the party owed
Saatchi & Saatchi. Maurice replied that the figure was up to about half
a million pounds.

'Phew,' said McAlpine. 'We haven't got that amount. Now, we're
entirely in your hands. We can pay you in a year's time. There won't
be any interest, of course.'

Saatchi was a big enough agency to carry it – just – but it made a
dent in that year's figures.

As the summer wore on, everyone waited on Jim Callaghan. When the
furore over the 'Labour isn't working' ad was at its height, Callaghan
was on his farm in Sussex helping with the harvest – and making up
his mind what to do. Should he go for an autumn election, or wait for
spring? He had promised to tell his cabinet colleagues of his decision
when they held their first meeting after the recess on 6 September, and
all through August he received advice from his whips and from other
leading members of the party, notably Michael Foot, who urged him
to forget about the autumn and wait until spring (he didn't have to call
an election until October of 1979, if he could muster a majority in
Parliament).

Although most of the advice he got favoured the spring, his own
Labour machine was gearing up for an election in late September or
early October. At Conservative Central Office and at Charlotte Street
there was even greater activity. Saatchi had to have a campaign ready
to go the instant Callaghan signalled the off – as everyone assumed he
would do in the first week of September. Was Callaghan influenced by
the Saatchi ads that summer? Reece for one was convinced he was.
Butler and Kavanagh indicate that, since the ad and the furore that
followed it affected the political climate, it was certainly a factor,
although not perhaps the vital one.

Callaghan later revealed that he took the decision in August to delay
until the spring of 1979, marking 5 April, the last day of the tax year,
as the likeliest date. A few days later, on 18 August, he invited himself
to tea at Denis Healey's house nearby. 'It was a lovely summer's day
and we sat in the garden while I told him what I had decided.' The
rest of the country was left guessing.

When Callaghan addressed the Congress of the TUC at Brighton
on 5 September the press, his own aides and certainly the Conservatives
still expected him to announce an autumn election. Instead he was
ambiguous, singing a little tune about leaving the bride waiting at the

David Puttnam (*right*) and Alan Parker (*above*) almost tempted Charles into a career as a film scriptwriter. They became friends at Collett Dickenson Pearce, where Charles first made his name, and moved to offices in the same building in Goodge Street in the late 1960s. Puttnam and Charles have remained close friends.

The brothers, Charles and
Maurice (*above*), in Maurice's
office in Charlotte Street where
they moved in 1976. This is
one of the few stock pictures
they supply of themselves –
they do not like either
photographers or reporters.

Doris Saatchi (*right*), whom
Charles married in 1973.
Together they built a collection
of contemporary art which is
regarded as the best of its kind
in the world. It is shown in their
own gallery in St John's Wood.
Charles and Doris are now
separated.

Josephine Hart (*left*), the Irish girl who first met Maurice at Haymarket in 1967. She became his second wife in October 1984 and they have a son, the first Saatchi grandson; she is now a major West End theatrical producer.

Maurice, pictured in 1972, is now the chairman of Saatchi & Saatchi plc, the biggest advertising business in the world. Charles has never had any other title than 'director'.

Ron Collins (*below*), one of the original Saatchi & Saatchi team; he only stayed a year, left without being paid for his shares and was a co-founder of Wight Collins Rutherford Scott.

Jennifer Laing (*bottom*) was tempted back to Saatchi with a red Ferrari.

Bill Muirhead (*top*), an Australian who became the first account executive; he is now chairman of the London agency.

Ken Gill (*middle*), chairman of Garland-Compton, played a central role in the Saatchi's first major takeover; he became chairman of the enlarged company, until Maurice finally took over from him in 1985.

James Gulliver (*above*) was asked by Gill to advise on Saatchi's takeover of Garland-Compton. He thought it was a bad idea – and sold his shareholding.

church, and leaving everyone still uncertain. 'I made a mistake in allowing the speculation to build up almost to a feverish crescendo without uttering a word to cool it,' he said later.

On 7 September Callaghan made a television broadcast and announced his decision: 'I shall not be calling an election at this time.' It was a surprise everywhere. In Conservative Central Office there was rejoicing: the political strategists there reckoned the Tories would lose in October but would win in the spring. There was, according to Butler and Kavanagh, 'some self-congratulation at Central Office among those who had sponsored the Saatchi & Saatchi advertising which perhaps had checked any adverse tide during August and September.' Reece remembers it as something more: 'there was wild cheering that you felt could be heard for miles around.'

At Charlotte Street there was no celebration. Jeremy Sinclair, working at his desk preparing another ad for the campaign, kept an eye on the TV set in the corner of the room. When Callaghan made his announcement, he threw his pen down in disgust, desperately deflated. Bell remembers being 'savagely depressed' and it was forty-eight hours before the team could pick itself up and get going again.

As events were to turn out, there is little doubt that Callaghan made a disastrous blunder in not going to the country in the autumn. Within a month the polls had swung back to favour Labour, and by November he was 5.5 points ahead. Thatcher herself has since voiced the view that she would probably have lost that autumn, and there was little confidence in Central Office that the Tories could pull it off. No one of course could have forecast the 'winter of discontent' that followed, with the unions humiliating the Callaghan government, and sweeping aside the incomes policy under which Callaghan had tried to hold wage settlements down to a maximum of 5 per cent. The dam broke when Ford made an offer in line with the government guidelines, its workers instantly went on strike and after three weeks settled at 15 per cent. When Callaghan sought powers to impose sanctions on Ford, the government was defeated by 285 votes to 283, although it won a vote of confidence the next day. Now settlement after settlement broke the 5 per cent guidelines. When striking technicians threatened to put the BBC off the air over Christmas, they received 15 per cent, bringing forth the bitter comment from a Callaghan aide: 'We sold our pay policy to have *The Sound of Music* on Christmas Day.'

The public sector, taking its lead from the BBC, now erupted. There were walkouts, militant picketing and violence by oil-tanker drivers, all of them in pursuit of wage claims the economy could not afford. In

Liverpool local government workers refused to bury the dead. In London three members of NUPE were dismissed for allegedly switching off hospital boilers in the middle of January, and local officials called a strike of the whole hospital. Local government manual workers put in a claim for 40 per cent. Violence flared on picket lines all over the country in the worst winter weather for years. Settlements in the private sector rose into double figures, sparking off a fresh wave of demand from hospital and other public sector workers. On 22 January over a million local government workers staged a day of action, the biggest one-day stoppage since the 1926 General Strike.

Callaghan himself made a further fateful error on 10 January at the height of the picketing and strikes when he returned from a world summit in Guadeloupe. Badly briefed and jet-lagged, he gave an impromptu press conference at the airport, where he said, 'I don't think that other people in the world would share the view that there is mounting chaos.' This was the statement that the press interpreted as 'Crisis? What crisis?', which Callaghan never actually said, but which became an unshakeable part of the myth. Mrs Thatcher immediately came forward with proposed reforms of the trade unions, which Saatchi's turned into a party political broadcast for 17 January.

As spring approached it became clear that Callaghan's gamble had misfired badly. It was only a matter of time before he was defeated in Parliament and he would not get the option to call an election when he wanted, an invaluable tool in the hands of any prime minister. The rate of inflation was beginning to rise again as the wage settlements came through, and Callaghan's own self-confidence had been shaken by the refusal of the unions to co-operate with a Labour government.

In the end it was the Scottish National Party which forced the issue by putting down their own vote of censure over the question of Scottish devolution. The Tories latched on to it, and on 28 March Callaghan was defeated by a single vote: 311 to 310. It was the first time since 1924, when the minority government of Ramsay MacDonald was outvoted, that a government had been defeated on an issue of confidence.

The Saatchi campaign, originally designed for an October election, had long been reshaped for a spring poll. Callaghan called a short campaign, which suited them perfectly. The Saatchi team moved to a separate office at the back of Charlotte Street. Here they had tight security and were well away from other clients and those not involved in the campaign. It was round-the-clock work. Bell had to attend a meeting at Central Office every night at 10 and again in the morning

at 7.30. Here the Tory campaign was planned under Lord Thorneycroft, with Alastair McAlpine (finance), Reece (publicity), Chris Patten
and Adam Ridley (research) and the two deputy chairmen, Janet Young
and Angus Maude. The day was a punishing one: all the newspapers
would be delivered at the team's homes, together with a digest of the
press, at two in the morning. They also got a video reel of the previous
day's television coverage which everyone looked at every morning at 6
o'clock. There would be a meeting at 7.30 and a press conference at
9. They would meet Mrs Thatcher at about 10 before she went off on
her day's tour. Then they would have the rest of the day to prepare
ads, get the print production done, buy the space in the newspapers
and put the party election broadcasts (PEBs) together. They would
meet again at 6 each evening, and there would be another meeting at
10.

This would be by far the easiest of the three campaigns that Saatchi
worked on for the Tories. In subsequent campaigns they were defending
a government which by 1983 had been in power for four years and, by
1987, for eight years. In 1979 Mrs Thatcher was the Opposition leader,
and the worst that could happen was that she could end up in opposition
again. There was little talk of majorities, as there was in the later two
elections: the main interest was to win, even by a handful of votes.

Those who worked on the campaign remember it with affection. 'It's
classically the way an account should be handled,' says one. 'You have
an account man who looks after the account – that was Tim. You have
a creative department, led by Charles and Jeremy – and Charles was
very involved, much more so than anyone thinks. And you have a wise
mind that you go to with everything that you're doing, and that was
Maurice. It was a terrific team effort, twenty-four-hours a day, seven
days a week, with three or four hours' sleep, often in the office.'

Reece came in every day and examined what they were doing. 'Do
you think that will work?' he would question. 'Okay – then let's do it.'
Reece and the Saatchi team developed a close working relationship
which was never repeated in later elections. 'Gordon understands
imagery,' says one of the Saatchi men. 'What we brought was the
concept of imagery, as opposed to words. Politicians live off words and
they don't think about imagery.' Bell and Reece continued to make use
of the lessons they had learned from the USA, not just on advertising
but on polling and campaign techniques, on one occasion organising a
youth rally, persuading pop stars and showbiz people to come along,
the first time that had been done in Britain.

'Gordon was sitting there saying: Give me more, more new ideas, let's do new things,' says Bell. 'And of course you can do that in opposition because you've no history. There was no point in discussing what was done in 1974 because the Tories had lost in 1974. And in 1970 there was a different leader and we were now in a different set of circumstances and could try new things.'

Reece and Thorneycroft did not entirely see eye to eye as the campaign wore on, but Bell hit it off instantly with the old Tory. He would often turn up in Thorneycroft's office with a stack of layouts and pile them on the floor at the side of the party chairman's desk. Then he would show them to him one at a time. 'You know, this reminds me of my daddy,' said Thorneycroft one day. 'He used to take me into the confectioner's and I'd look at a jar of boiled sweets and want one. And then my eyes would catch the glimmer of another jar of sweeties and I'd want them. And then there'd be another jar, and another. You sit there with your pile of sweeties under my desk, bringing them out one by one, and I want them all.'

Yet in the end, for all the energy, creative work, professionalism and new ideas, how much did the Saatchi campaign contribute to Mrs Thatcher's victory on 3 May 1979?

Of the five Conservative television broadcasts used in the election campaign itself the first four had been made before Callaghan was defeated in Parliament; there were another three that were never used at all. The final, fifth broadcast was videotaped and featured only Margaret Thatcher talking straight to camera. None approached the originality and effectiveness of the earlier broadcasts they had done, as both Bell and Reece later admitted. 'I'm convinced that the television work we did in the build-up was twice as effective as our work in the campaign itself,' wrote Bell a year later. The first broadcast of the campaign, a satirical film showing runners on a track, with the British weighed down hopelessly by weights labelled 'inflation' and 'taxes', went down badly with the party faithful in the country. Reece defended it on the grounds that it was aimed at the floating voter, but a number of the staff in Central Office thought it 'inappropriate'. The second was not much better: it used the 'What crisis?' theme (ignoring the fact that Callaghan had never said it), concentrating on the winter of discontent, with shots of rubbish in the streets, empty supermarkets, graves undug, hospitals picketed and so forth. Like the first, it was flippant and was not a success. Although the Labour broadcasts were made on a shoestring, and against a background of considerable in-fighting in Transport House, they were proving more effective. 'The Labour broadcasts judged the mood of the electorate better,' admitted

Bell. 'They were more serious; they were more to the point; they had more gravitas in them than our work. We recognised what was wrong, and as the campaign continued we changed the tonal quality of the work.'

According to Butler and Kavanagh, 'The sober style of the Labour broadcasts with their deliberate emphasis on statesmanship and "authority" contrasted sharply with the rather gimmicky style of the first two Conservative ones, and the audience appreciation figures for the Labour broadcasts (which cost only £50,000) were markedly higher than those for the Conservatives.'

The party's private polls on the broadcasts were at times dismaying. The third and fourth featured Lord Thorneycroft and Humphrey Atkins, on the grounds that they would provide 'style' – a theme that Saatchi had been developing in some of the pre-campaign broadcasts, one of which had been entirely devoted to a speech by Harold Macmillan to the Young Conservatives' annual conference, and which Tim Bell reckoned was one of the best speeches he had ever seen. Everyone was astonished to find that Lord Thorneycroft's broadcast was the highest rated of the whole campaign.

Yet somehow all five lacked the spark of the earlier efforts. Reece wasn't too worried. 'By that time they had won the war. There were some hiccups during the campaign, as there always are, but, yes, the party politicals weren't their best. They were very good indeed by comparison with a lot of others in the past, but they weren't up to the standard that we had come to expect.' The Saatchis had learned that making party politicals in 'peacetime' and making them during actual election campaigns can be very different. The electorate, they discovered, takes its elections seriously. It was a lesson they would not forget.

The posters and newspaper ads were more effective. 'Labour isn't working' was revived as 'Labour still isn't working', and Saatchi's had another poster, 'Cheer up! Labour can't hang on for ever', which had actually been prepared before the winter of discontent and was ideal for the new circumstances. There was no doubt that the Conservatives won the press and poster war, but then they spent much more too: £250,000 on posters to Labour's £112,000.

After the election there was much analysis to attempt to identify just how much the Saatchi advertising campaign had helped, but by then it no longer mattered. Even those who had worked on the Labour campaign, such as Tim Delaney (now of Leagas Delaney Advertising), warned that it was 'important for Labour Party officials to realise that what Saatchi & Saatchi have done for the Tories is not to sell them like soap-powder, but rather to produce the cohesion needed, first, to create a professional communications strategy and then, secondly, to make it work.' The Labour Party took some of those lessons to heart in later elections, particularly in 1987.

It was time for celebration. Mrs Thatcher held a party in 10 Downing Street for all those who had helped get her there. Maurice Saatchi, Jeremy Sinclair and Tim Bell all went. Charles Saatchi stayed away. He did not intend to be rude. He simply did not go to parties, unless they were given by a few very close friends; and he did not meet clients – even if it was the prime minister.

11

BELL: THE PARTING OF THE WAYS

One of Tim Bell's most prized possessions is a letter of thanks from Margaret Thatcher. He also has a photograph on his wall signed 'From Margaret, with love', given to him at the same time. For Bell they are visible symbols of the fact that he, more than anyone else in Saatchi & Saatchi, had been the man behind the advertising campaign which helped put her in Number 10.

The publicity attaching to the campaign boosted Bell's already rising career. In the London advertising world, and among the clients, Bell was seen as the man running the Saatchi business. It might still have carried the names of the brothers, but the agency in Charlotte Street was Tim Bell's shop, with Charles and Maurice seldom seen either by clients or by staff. With the takeover of Compton in 1975 he had moved his office to the ground floor of Charlotte Street, and from there he ran the agency. With the departure of Ron Rimmer, the nearest person he had to a rival for the key position of head of the agency was Ron Leagas, who was promoted to managing director of the agency in 1978, the same year that Bell was made chairman. Leagas, however, only lasted two years in that position. In 1980 he left to found his own agency and Bell took over as both chairman and managing director.

The distance between the ground floor and the sixth, where the brothers were, became something more than physical during these years. Bell was still sometimes referred to as 'the third brother', but now the phrase had a more plaintive sound to it. The Saatchis' eyes were more and more fixed on the USA, on acquisitions, on creating an international network. It was a much more strategic and financial role than that to which they had been used, and it was Martin Sorrell rather than Bell who joined them more and more in their private deliberations. Charles still watched over the agency like a hawk, pouncing on any creative work he didn't like, still shredding artwork not up to his standards; but Saatchi & Saatchi by the early 1980s had become a large business, and it required a lot of running. Bell, although he was reluctant to accept it, had not kept pace with the growth, and was further and further removed from the strategic thinking.

'Tim was up on the top floor, chatting, most days,' recalls Martin Sorrell. 'Like most people in the advertising business – probably most people in life – he was very insecure; he needed continual boosting and reassurance, massaging and reinforcement. The sixth floor was a wonderful working environment, with what I used to refer to as "corridor conversations", where things got done. But it could be very frustrating if you didn't happen to be in the corridor when the conversation took place.' Bell, working as hard as he was running the agency, could not always be in the corridor, although he did his best. 'There always was that difficulty in everyone's mind about the people on the sixth floor who were interested in the growth of Saatchi & Saatchi plc and the rest of the five floors which were interested in the agency,' says Nick Crean, then personal assistant to the brothers.

Bell had done an excellent job in putting the Saatchi business together under the one roof with that of Compton. He managed to keep most of the old Garland-Compton staff, almost all the business, and moulded two opposing cultures together. 'Tim really put that whole thing together brilliantly,' says Sorrell. 'He was very charismatic, and because of his personality and because he worked so hard I think he probably would have liked his name over the door.'

Bell made all the major presentations, gave the public speeches and represented the agency at all the prestige events. It was his name that appeared more and more in the trade press. Under Bell the agency put on more new business in 1978 and 1979 than any other in the industry's history, and with the election victory he was suddenly one of the top half-dozen advertising executives in Britain. 'He was a brilliant presenter, the best handler of business and a very good manager,' says one of the Saatchi men. 'He could sell anything, any message, any idea.' He could build relationships with clients that few could hope to achieve. Sorrell, even now from the top of his J. Walter Thompson empire, remembers Bell's abilities with a hint of awe. 'For somebody who is so extreme – I mean, if you're sitting in a room with him you don't get a word in edgeways – it is truly remarkable the relationships he builds, whether with the prime minister or whoever. He is very loquacious and people find that overpowering. But he's really aggressive, supportive . . . brilliant. I felt there was nobody who was as good as he was.'

There were danger signs in that too. Ken Gill was increasingly concerned at the toll Bell's work schedule was taking on his health. In a profile in the *Independent* in 1987, a former Bell colleague was quoted as saying: 'Tim's an obsessive. He's not moderate about anything. The joke at Saatchi's was that he rattled. There was a pill to go asleep, a vitamin pill in the morning, and so on. It's quite a dangerous personality to have.'

Bell's lifestyle was certainly more extravagant than that of the brothers. There are stories of a chauffeur waiting to take him the 200 yards down the road to the L'Etoile restaurant in Charlotte Street, where he would often dine with a cabinet minister, sitting in his favourite window seat, visible to anyone passing. To one interviewer, speaking of his Ferrari, he enthused: 'I work very long hours, and I like to drive to and from work in a lovely car being admired.' After the collapse of his marriage he and his girlfriend Virginia Hornbrook began to appear in the gossip columns. He was on a high. A profile in 1982 described him as 'the rollicking Saatchi frontman who, at Chequers weekends, shares snifters with Denis [Thatcher] and wisecracks with Maggie.'

He was capable of extraordinary, sweeping gestures which could win him the affection not just of the person involved but of everyone who knew him. For instance, when Jennifer Laing left to go to Leo Burnett, Bell was greatly disappointed. She had done well at Saatchi's, handling some of the biggest accounts, and was clearly heading for a top place in the agency at the time when she left. Two years later, when he heard she was moving on again, he invited her to lunch. Why not rejoin Saatchi, he suggested. She rejected the notion instantly; she would not be seen to creep back. But he persisted, talking about a new and enhanced role for her, a job of such seniority that no one could think she had crawled back with her tail between her legs. Finally she relented; but she wanted a symbol, something special, which would indicate to the world that it was Saatchi which had come to her, rather than the other way about. 'What do you want?' he asked. A car, she replied, 'a really flashy car'. Fine; but what sort?

Jennifer knew nothing about cars. In fact if the truth be told – and she didn't tell it over that lunch – she had not even driven since she passed her driving test at seventeen.

'A red one!' she said.

Bell pulled out a cigarette packet and wrote on it: 'Jen wants a flashy red car.'

She duly returned to Saatchi and a few months later, when she was sitting her in her office, someone appeared asking for her. He was delivering the new car she had ordered, he said. Laing went down, not knowing what to expect. Parked outside the Saatchi office was her new status symbol: a red Ferrari.

She had to get her brother to drive her home.

Bell treated the Saatchi business as his own, in the sense that he gave it everything he had. He was one of the first in and last to leave the Charlotte Street office, driven, he would say, by 'enthusiasm, terrific energy and a belief that life should be exciting'. He was intensely loyal to the brothers, insisting even years after that he owed his success to the Saatchis, 'who taught me to believe that all things are possible'.

To outsiders, he was the power at the agency, and, while a ripple of unease may have gone through Charlotte Street when Bell, in a TV interview, said that as far as he was concerned it was 'Saatchi, Saatchi & Bell', in reality it only seemed a matter of time before it was.

To the few who actually knew how it worked, however, the picture was different. From the beginning Charles Saatchi, largely by force of personality, had dominated Bell, and still did. They were nearly the same age, yet Charles was almost a father figure to Bell. They had frequent shouting matches and sometimes savage rows, but Charles invariably won, and it was always Bell who gave in afterwards. Yet for all that it was a close working relationship, with the brothers prepared to let Bell take the glory as their front-man.

Yet since 1984 the Saatchi brothers and Bell have not exchanged a single word, civil or otherwise. They will not even sit in the same restaurant, and in 1987 Maurice cancelled his attendance at a dinner party given for an old friend on his retirement when he heard Bell would be there.

What happened?

'It's a bit like asking somebody to explain what went wrong with a marriage,' says Bell.

Everyone has a different analysis, including the Saatchis, who nowadays tend to talk about Bell's personal problems at the time – his marriage broke up and he was drinking perhaps more than was good for him. Some believe the brothers had come to resent his power and, jealous of his popularity and reputation, decided to cut him off before he became a threat to their control. There were rumours of a cocaine problem, which Bell at the time did not deny but today insists were 'libels'. Others suggest that the Saatchi organisation simply outgrew him. 'He was much more at home in a small company where everybody knew everybody else,' says one executive who worked closely with him. 'The company was just getting too big, and they were having to bring in new management structures, finance people and all the rest. He was the "hands-on" man, running the agency on the ground floor at Charlotte Street, and they had already gone up to the sixth floor to think about the future.'

The truth is more complex than any of these individual reasons. The brothers today give no hint of ever having resented Bell – quite the opposite. Both brothers insist they decided early on they did not want to run the agency indefinitely, and wanted to move on to a more strategic role. Bell on the other hand loved running the agency – and was good at it. The brothers were delighted to let him get on with it. Bell, they acknowledge, was one of the reasons why Saatchi & Saatchi was so successful up to the time they bought Garland-Compton and then for several years afterwards. But there is another point cited by old Saatchi hands: Bell, they say, opposed all the major steps the brothers took. He was, initially at least, against the takeover of Garland-Compton; he was also against the Tory Party account and the acquisition in 1982 of the Compton business in New York. 'None of them were his ideas, and he needed constant reassurance and stroking; the brothers had to tell him how much they needed him and how great he was,' says the Saatchi man. The implication is that Bell wanted to remain the centre of the Saatchi universe and the major expansionary moves threatened that role. 'Charles and Maurice went to great pains not to diminish him in any way,' says the Saatchi man. 'But Tim developed a fear of not being a one-man band – everything had to be his idea, everything had to come from him, and everyone had to go around making him feel good.'

Bell worked harder and harder to retain his central role, but as the agency got bigger it was not possible for one man to do it. 'He simply couldn't be everywhere, but he kept trying,' says the Saatchi executive. 'Then a wonderful thing happened to him – the Tory Party account came along.'

Bell's initial opposition to it is put down to the fact that Gordon Reece had gone direct to the brothers rather than Tim Bell. But, once he started work on it, it was a new lease of life for him. For a year he rode a wave of euphoria during which he worked harder than ever. Political accounts, however, are not like others; they have huge highs, and then go dead for three or four years before the next election approaches. But Bell continued on a high – and this brought a new problem. 'From then on it wasn't possible to talk to him for more than a few minutes without Mrs Thatcher or another minister being mentioned,' says a Saatchi man. 'It got a bit tedious for us all, and it got tedious for the clients, who became fed up with the name-dropping.' The early Thatcher years were some of the hardest yet for British industry, as the new administration imposed tighter money controls which drove up both interest rates and sterling, at one stage prompting the Confederation of British Industry to threaten a 'bare-knuckled' fight with the government. It would be several years yet before British industry saw the benefits of the Thatcher revolution; in the early years they saw only the extra problems she brought. Her name was by no means universally welcome, but there are stories of Bell turning up to meet a major client and talking on and on about Thatcher. 'The Tory Party was the making and breaking of Tim Bell,' says a Saatchi man. 'After that, anything other than politics and advising the prime minister became boring for him.'

Soon the brothers were filling in the executive gaps he left with other men. Bell ostensibly was still the kingpin in the agency. But in reality he was already being edged aside.

In the two years after the 1979 election the relationship between Bell and the brothers bumped unevenly downhill. The crisis came to a head with the takeover, in March 1982, of the Compton business in New York. Bell had no role in it, did not participate in the negotiations or the planning – and, worse still, suddenly discovered that under the new structure he was reporting, not to the brothers, but to Milton Gossett, who was appointed head of the worldwide agency, which was a subsidiary of the main company. 'That was my job,' Bell later said, 'and they gave it to somebody else.'

Charles, according to Bell, attempted to reassure him, saying, 'Don't worry, he's going to retire in two years.' Six years later Gossett is still there. Ken Gill, in his role as chairman of the holding company and elder statesman, also tried to calm Bell. The older man was becoming increasingly concerned by what he could see as a widening rift between Bell and the brothers, and did what he could to head it off. For months he had been trying to defuse Bell's anger at the refusal of the brothers even to consider putting his name on the agency. 'Can you not see that the name Saatchi & Saatchi is a real power in itself? It's a most unusual name. It attracts attention. If you start fiddling with that you detract from it.' They had had to accept 'Garland-Compton' in the name of the agency, but it was always the intention to phase it out, and Gill was happy for it to drop away. 'What does it mean to have your name up there? It doesn't really matter, you know. You're having a great time, and, you have to admit it – you're the one who is being credited with the whole thing.' But Gill and the other senior Saatchi men could also see the problem from Bell's viewpoint too. 'Milt Gossett was bigger than he was in the organisation,' says one. 'And he couldn't stand it.'

With the takeover of Compton of New York, the Saatchis offered Bell something else: head of Saatchi & Saatchi Compton Worldwide. On paper it sounded good, but in practice Bell soon discovered that it was rather less than the name implied. 'Worldwide' in this context excluded the USA, where two-thirds of group profits were now coming from, and which was firmly run by Gossett; it also excluded the London agency he had run so successfully in the 1970s. 'I've ended up with the Third World,' he complained. In fact he had Europe, Australia and the Far East as well, and with Compton had come a substantial world-wide network which the Saatchis were already busily adding to with yet more acquisitions (Vander Biggelaar in Holland, Iroda in Ireland); but there was no disguising the fact that Bell, in the now much bigger corporation, was some way down the hierarchy.

For the first time since he had joined Saatchi twelve years before, Bell felt he had a real crisis. He had never considered leaving the brothers before, although he had plenty of offers: Bill Bernbach had even offered him $1 million to run his UK offshoot – 'he put the cheque in my hand,' Bell told a friend in wonderment later.

He was twenty-eight when he joined the brothers, and in the mean-time had seen his tiny shareholding become worth over £3 million. He had a large company house, a salary of over £100,000 a year, and he had found fame. Saatchi & Saatchi up to that point had seemed capable of giving him everything he wanted. But as part of the reshuffle his office had been moved to a different building, which further removed him from the brothers, and steadily his power slipped away.

For a time he tried to make the best of it. He made two tours of every Saatchi and Compton agency in the world including those for which he had no profit responsibility, ending up with a conference in Geneva, which is still a much talked-about event inside the company. David Frost spoke at the dinner, and Bell made a presentation of the Saatchi worldwide management philosophy and organisation, covering a worldwide media operation (now in place), a worldwide new business operation (also in place), and set out for the first time the Saatchi target of being one of the top ten agencies in every major country (also now achieved). 'Maurice and Charles were neither present nor involved and left the whole matter to Bell,' says a friend. He travelled to the USA at least once a month during 1982 and 1983, sometimes doing the round trip in a single day. Yet all the time the gulf between him and the brothers grew wider.

It was this which hurt Bell more than anything. In a curious way his relationship with the Saatchis, particularly with Charles, mattered to him more than money, status or prestige. Both Saatchis, again particularly Charles, are driven people, born entrepreneurs, prepared to take huge risks, relishing the gamble and the tension of pitting their wits against bigger opposition. It is perhaps part of their Iraqi-Jewish culture, increased by the natural urge of the immigrant to achieve. Bell, on the other hand, had a solid middle-class English background, and with his charm and good looks success came easy to him. In a sense, although he did not realise it until too late, he had come to rely on the Saatchis to motivate him.

The relationship was gradually withering when another event accelerated the process. Bell was at dinner one evening in late 1982 with John Perry, appointed by Lord King as public affairs director of British Airways in the run-up to privatisation, when Perry suddenly confided:

'You're getting the British Airways account.'

Bell was appalled. Not only did he know nothing of it, but he had been responsible for winning the rival British Caledonian account which Saatchi had made a success of with its 'we never forget you have a choice' ads. The agency could not run both – and Bell felt fiercely protective of BCal.

'That's fantastic,' he managed to say. 'I didn't even know we were talking to you.'

It would be Saatchi's most spectacular coup, an event which Bell knew would make the front pages not just of the trade press but of the national papers. Saatchi by that stage had a number of big and prestige accounts, but none of them would have quite the same high profile as British Airways. The airline under King was making major political and financial waves, and King deliberately kept it in the news as he fought a series of key battles, not just with the unions – he made over 20,000 workers redundant – but also with the government over complex issues such as the write-off of public debt and his air-route structure. A new advertising agency would be right at the heart of all that.

Perry explained that Saatchi had indeed done a pitch and had landed the account, one of the most important in the business. Bell remembers bluffing his way through dinner, trying to hide his deep sense of shock. The next morning he faced Charles. Was it true?

Charles, according to Bell, initially denied it; a week later Saatchi announced it had won the BA account.

'The trust broke down,' Bell later told a friend. 'In retrospect they never did trust me in the way I thought they did. I thought they had a certain relationship with me, and then I suddenly realised they never saw it that way. They never looked at it in the way I did.'

There was another incident which did not improve his relationship with the brothers, although it does not seem to have hurt him with Mrs Thatcher. He was at a birthday party for Kenny Everett, the television personality, at Chez Gerrard one evening, and began to expound about the prime minister and her family, telling a series of ribald anecdotes about Mrs Thatcher and referring to her son Mark as a 'twit'. What he hadn't noticed was that one of the people who had joined his table was a journalist from a magazine and he had switched on a tape recorder. His remarks appeared more or less verbatim. Bell apologised to her immediately, and she seems to have forgiven him equally rapidly.

In May 1983 Mrs Thatcher called another election, four years after her first victory, and once again Saatchi & Saatchi were in the front line. By this time Bell and the brothers were barely on speaking terms. But he would be the man leading the campaign for them – Mrs Thatcher expected, even demanded, that. Bell had his own special relationship with Mrs Thatcher and with Tory Central Office, and neither the brothers nor anyone else, other than perhaps Bell's assistant Michael Dobbs, had any close ties with the party.

Bell once again assembled his team and moved them to a little office in D'Arblay Street in Soho. This second Thatcher election was very different from the first. Now there had been four years of Thatcherism, and it was her record that was under scrutiny. In 1979 she was an untried and still largely unknown leader, and to some extent the big question mark had been: would Britain ever elect a woman as prime minister? By 1983 she was the dominant figure on the British political stage, towering over her own government and over an opposition which was in shambles. 'Thatcherism' and 'Thatcherite' had come to have a meaning, pejorative or reverential depending on your viewpoint, but there was a clear set of ideas and attitudes associated with her on which the election would be fought. The victory in the Falklands in 1982 had confirmed her image as a strong leader, the Iron Lady, but there were other clear aspects of her image which the public identified: her 'Victorian values', reducing the size of government, paying your own way, making Britain great again, and of course 'There is no alternative', or TINA, her oft-repeated refrain to justify many of the harsh measures adopted at that time.

Ranged against her was the charge that Mrs Thatcher had not been able to deliver on many of her election promises of 1979. Far from cutting government expenditure as a proportion of gross national product, she had actually expanded it from 41 to 44 per cent, largely because of the economic recession and the growing number of unemployed. Income tax had been cut in the first budget, but even so the tax burden had actually risen. State industries were still receiving large handouts, notably British Leyland, British Steel and the coal industry. The denationalisation programme had barely begun, and the Conservatives had taken only a few tottering steps down the road to Mrs Thatcher's cherished 'capital-owning democracy' where everyone would be share-owners and every family would own their own home. The one significantly visible achievement was a drop in inflation from over 20 per cent in the first Thatcher year to 5 per cent in 1983, the lowest level for ten years. But the unemployment rate was 13 per cent, and if one added that to the inflation rate to get what is called the 'misery index' it came to 18 per cent – a very high figure, and one which was causing governments around the world to be rejected by their electorates.

Yet by the spring of 1983 the early polls showed that there had been a major shift in the perception of the Thatcher government. A large proportion of the British electorate had begun to accept that economic change would be both a painful and a long process, but that it had to be done. There was considerable and growing support for denationalisation, a belief that the government had to beat inflation before unemployment, that lower inflation and pay rises did create more jobs (as Mrs Thatcher kept saying), and that government, both local and central, was too large. In other words, 'Thatcherism' was gaining ground, and various leaked cabinet documents showed the government still full of radical plans. If taxes and public expenditure had not yet been cut Mrs Thatcher still intended to do so, and there was a visible self-confidence among her ministers which communicated itself to the civil servants in Whitehall. Could that be translated into a second election victory?

There had been personnel changes in Central Office which were not to Saatchi's advantage. Gordon Reece was allowed back into Britain by Mrs Thatcher only after she had announced the election date – 'she was super-sensitive about the whole timing issue, and every time Gordon came back there would be stories about cigar smoke seen at

Heathrow airport, and an election in the offing,' says Michael Dobbs. Reece's role at Central Office had been split, with Chris Lawson in charge of marketing and Anthony Shrimsley in charge of communications. Reece found himself largely without a role, and Bell without a clear line of reporting.

Dobbs was destined to play a significant role not just in the 1983 campaign but in the 1987 one as well. A tall, rounded, freckle-faced man who looked younger than his thirty-four years, he was one of the more academically qualified people in Saatchi's, having taken a degree at Oxford and a PhD in the USA, after which he became a journalist in Boston for a few years. In the mid-1970s he returned to Britain and worked as researcher for Mrs Thatcher when she was leader of the Opposition. In that capacity he had come to know Bell well during the 1979 campaign, and after the election victory Bell offered him a job at Saatchi's. Dobbs remained active in the political arena, working as an adviser to Norman Tebbit, who was then rapidly emerging as one of the stars of the Thatcher government. Now, with the election campaign running, Dobbs was working for both Saatchi, which paid his salary, and for the Conservatives, a Saatchi client.

Although there was never any doubt in Central Office that Saatchi would play the same role it had in 1979, this time there was a determination to keep the campaign on a tighter rein, and cut back on expenditure. Saatchi was given a budget of £2.4 million, £150,000 of it for that year's local elections. The flippant ads of 1979 were remembered – there should be no more of those, Bell was told firmly. In January 1983, six months before the election, Bell made a presentation to Mrs Thatcher at Chequers over a weekend, setting out the central theme: 'We must capture the mood for change in outlook, while emphasising the need for continuity in direction.' In April the Saatchi team began work on anticipating how Labour might fight the campaign, and Bell worked out a plan for 'rubbishing' the Labour record on unemployment, an area on which they knew Labour would concentrate its attack.

In the event the campaign went well, but it had its ups and downs. For its first party election broadcast Saatchi prepared a ten-minute programme, only to discover that the party had booked five minutes only. In D'Arblay Street that night there was some hurried cutting. On another occasion, Saatchi planned to hire for a day a hospital ward in Tower Hamlets, in London's East End, to film a sequence about the government's caring attitude on health. To their considerable embarrassment, they discovered the hospital had actually been closed five months before. The most effective ad concentrated on the 1978-9 'winter of discontent', with pictures of angry picket lines, closed hospitals, closed-down industry and terrifying front-page headlines and a gloom-laden voice-over intoning: 'Do you remember . . .?'

Bell never had quite the relationship with the 1983 party chairman, Cecil Parkinson, as he did with Lord Thorneycroft. Parkinson, much younger and from an entirely different background from the aristocratic Thorneycroft, was much more conscious of how communciations and imagery worked, and involved himself more in the advertising. At the same time he was slightly nervous of the Saatchi reputation and, although he personally liked and respected Bell, he treated him without the same confidence that Thorneycroft had. Parkinson reported direct to the prime minister, so that Bell and the Saatchi team seldom talked with her – Bell reckons he may have seen her just three times during the campaign, once to present work to her at the beginning, once when the polls suddenly moved against the government and once near the end.

The Tories started the campaign 16 points ahead of Labour in the polls, so the central aim of the strategy was to keep it there. With just over a week to go there was the traditional 'wobble', when one rogue poll showed the gap suddenly narrowing. No other poll confirmed it, and right through the election the Tories kept the lead. The headlines tell the story: '17.5% LEAD FOR THE TORIES' (Daily Telegraph, 12 May), 'HEADING FOR A LANDSLIDE' (Daily Mail, 18 May), 'MRS T BY MILE SAY KEY VOTERS' (Sunday Express, 5 June) and 'THE LAST WORD – 16%' (London Standard on polling day, 9 June). Even so, that rogue poll was enough to send the party machine, including the prime minister, into a panic – and Saatchi back to the drawing-board. 'We had to find a strategy based on the same "Time for a change" line,' says Tim Bell. 'Our argument of course was that it wasn't time for a change. So how do we express that? Well, we couldn't say that we'd achieved all the things we wanted to, because we hadn't. So this great line was written: "Britain's on the right track – don't turn back".'

Bell describes some of the press ads done in that campaign as 'the greatest political ads that have ever been done in this country'. There were two in particular. The first compared the manifesto of the Communist Party with that of the Labour Party, showing them to be remarkably similar. The headline read, 'Like your manifesto, comrade', and was written by Charles Saatchi and Jeremy Sinclair. The other listed fifteen propositions along the lines 'I agree to have the value of my savings reduced immediately in accordance with Labour's wishes to devalue the pound', and invited the reader to agree or disagree by 'ticking the box'. Its authors were two other Saatchi men, Simon Dicketts and Fergus Flemming. Charles and Sinclair were as involved as ever in the creative work produced during the campaign, although as in 1979, Charles never went near a Tory politician if he could possibly avoid it.

Mrs Thatcher personally cancelled what the Saatchi camp regarded as its best work: three pages of ads set to go into the newspapers in the final few days of the campaign, setting out why the voter should not vote for either of the other parties and why they must vote Tory. Parkinson wanted to run them, and Bell and the Saatchis were desperate to do so, but by that stage the polls were back on track and it took no great foresight to see that short of a miracle, she was heading for a very big victory indeed. On polling day Mrs Thatcher increased her majority from a comfortable 43 to a crushing 144.

To the outside world, Saatchi & Saatchi had a good election, but all was not well with Tim Bell, and there were times in the campaign when he was far from well. Even then he had still managed to run it better than anyone else in the organisation was probably capable of. At one stage, Cecil Parkinson took Michael Dobbs aside to warn him about Bell's health. Dobbs passed the remarks back to the brothers.

From all accounts Charles Saatchi in particular was now getting very worried indeed by Bell. He told Maurice it was a problem that he would deal with, and he should leave it to him. Maurice willingly did, and Charles rang Bell almost daily. At first Charles was very sympathetic, encouraging him to seek treatment for his visibly declining health. Barry Day of McCann Erickson, who had run the advertising for the the Tories in the 1970 election, made a lunch appointment with Bell, and after waiting twenty minutes got a call to say his lunch guest was running late. Bell, he says, never appeared. Day mentioned it to Charles Saatchi, who apologised profusely, and added that regrettably it was now always happening: Tim had been overworking (Bell denies the story).

He could still win accounts: during 1983 he led the pitch for Mattel worldwide and got it; he also helped win the Gillette Europe account. He helped organise the worldwide British Airways launch with Bill Muirhead. But he was encountering other problems. In the late summer and autumn of 1983, he split up with his girlfriend Virginia Hornbrook, whom he had lived with for several years. She went back to Australia, and this crisis in his private life coincided with his final realisation that the breakdown with Charles was irreparable.

It was December 1983 when Bell and Charles Saatchi had their worst row yet. Bell finally nerved himself to ask for something he had wanted for years: could he join the holding company board? Many of his colleagues felt he should have been there long before, he argued, and it was traditional in the advertising industry for the stars to have their names attached to the agencies. But the Saatchis kept their board very tight. Even though it was a large public company, there were only five directors: the Saatchis, Kenneth Gill, the chairman, Martin Sorrell, the finance director, and the long-serving company secretary David Perring.

Charles was furious at the suggestion. 'You'll never, ever, go on the public company board,' he told Bell. No advertising people went on that board, he said. 'If they did, then every time we make an acquisition we'd have to put the person we bought on the public company board. It's just going to be Maurice and me and the money men.'

That conversation marked the end for Bell. 'It was a very hurtful conversation,' he said later. 'I just couldn't understand why he said it. I could understand him saying you can't go on now, or not for a couple of years, but to say what he said – "never, ever, on the board" – was a terrible thing to do.' (Later, after Bell left, others did go on the board, leaving Bell even more resentful.)

'I don't want to work here any more,' he told Charles. He hadn't decided what to do, and Charles initially made a strong effort to keep him, although in a very different role.

'Why don't you set up a public affairs consultancy? You're very good at that. We'll finance you. You can own 45 per cent or 50 per cent of it, or whatever you like. It will be yours and we'll own a chunk of it, and it'll be really good.'

That wasn't what Bell wanted. Later he would explain that he felt 'like you've been somebody's wife, and now you're told you can be the maid'.

He was still on Mrs Thatcher's special list, however, and that Christmas he was a guest at Chequers, a privilege given to a few close confidants and friends. In a quiet moment he told her of his row with Charles and his decision to leave. She too had worried about the decline in his health and suggested – as Charles had – that he take a break. He stayed at home in January 1984, persuaded Virginia to come back to him, then went on holiday to Kenya in February. He was back at work in March just as one of the biggest threats to Mrs Thatcher's rule began – a year-long miners strike. Bell offered his public relations consultancy services to the head of the National Coal Board, Ian MacGregor, who later acknowledged his 'able assistance' and 'great help' in beating the miners. But during this time Bell was a shadow of his old self, depressed and miserable. It was a bad time for him, and he was further and further removed from any power at Saatchi's.

Charles Saatchi thought he had his successor: for a few months he held talks with his old friend David Puttnam, who had just given up on his self-appointed task of changing the British film industry. 'The two brothers want to free themselves from the day-to-day affairs of the agency, and are looking for a leadership figure,' Puttnam was quoted as saying. How this would have gone down with Mrs Thatcher is an interesting point of speculation: Puttnam had been a Labour supporter and had changed to SDP. For a while he was enthusiastic about joining Saatchi, talking about his 'very definite ideas on advertising' and how it must change. Instead he went to Hollywood for an ill-fated job as head of Columbia Pictures.

In the autumn of 1984 Bell, still running the advisory business at Saatchi's, found himself working on Coal Board ads with his old friend Frank Lowe. Saatchi & Saatchi, because of its political connection, did not want the Coal Board account and so it went to Lowe Howard-Spink-Marschalk, an agency growing even faster than Saatchi & Saatchi (although a tenth the size). Lowe knew all about the fallout, not just from Bell but from Charles as well. The Saatchis had tried to buy Lowe's new agency six months after he started it, just as they had tried to take over CDP when he ran it, but had eventually abandoned their talks. Now Lowe, without telling Bell, rang Charles to enquire what he planned to do with Tim. Charles by that stage had no plans. Would Saatchi mind if he, Frank Lowe, made Bell an offer? Charles had no objection at all. Late in 1984 Lowe offered Bell what the Saatchis had refused him: equal status, his name on the door and a position on the board.

It was not a peaceful ending. Bell had to buy out his house at its 1985 price (many times what it had originally been bought for), buy out his large bonus and repay a loan to the company of £1 million. He had to sell £3 million worth of shares to do so, and he reckoned later it had cost him a net £1.5 million to leave. He was bitter about it, although Saatchi, as a public company, could not have done anything else. He still ended up with £2.5 million after paying off all his corporate debts. Charles also made him sign a contract under which he was paid a £24,000 a year retainer to be available to work on the Tory Party account for Saatchi & Saatchi on one more election, and forbidding him from taking the Tory Party account with him.

There was one final gesture which still rankles with Bell. His departure from Saatchi was a major news event for the trade press where every little thing that happened at Saatchi had been front page news for years. For fifteen years Charles Saatchi had been the biggest source of stories for *Campaign*, and now he wanted a favour. *Campaign* obliged – putting the story of Bell's departure on page 3.

Bell's natural good humour has since asserted itself, and he no longer seems to hate the Saatchis as much as he did, but he has not got over his hurt. 'I was just broken-hearted,' he said later. 'It seemed to me unnecessary. I don't know why they turned on me. I don't know why we came apart. I don't know why I got written out of the future. They've never been able to tell me.' For their part they felt a sense of guilt that they did not handle him better, that they had in effect grown bored with pandering to him. 'Tim should have had the guts to go out and start his own agency years before,' says a senior Saatchi man. 'He could have been a legendary advertising man. The Tory Party account was a golden age for him, and he was so extraordinarily gifted that he could have been an enormous figure today. If he hadn't screwed up in his last years, he could have taken half Saatchi's clients with him.'

A measure – perhaps the best objective one – of Bell's changed status in the industry was the number of Saatchi clients who followed him. When Frank Lowe left Collett Dickenson Pearce, nearly half the clients left with him. Bell had been the chairman and chief executive of Saatchi & Saatchi Compton, and the man dealing directly with the clients. He would find his feet again at Lowe Howard-Spink & Bell, but he took none of the Saatchi clients with him.

One feels that even after everything that has happened he would go back instantly, if only they asked. He is realistic enough to know they never will.

'Maybe they never liked me,' says Bell. 'Maybe that's what it is. Maybe they never, ever liked me.'

12

AND SO TO MADISON AVENUE

In 1954 Thomas Rosser Reeves, then head of the Ted Bates agency in New York, made what is generally regarded as the first real commercial advertisement for television. It is an advertisement which is instructive both of the Ted Bates style and of the thinking about advertising in Madison Avenue at that time. The 60-second spot showed hammers animatedly banging away at agonised skulls, and was an advertisement for Anacin, a headache remedy. It cost the client $8400 to produce, but Reeves boasted later that it 'made more money in seven years than *Gone with the Wind* did for David O. Selznick and MGM in a quarter of a century.'

The ad was to make Ted Bates the hottest agency in New York in the mid-1950s. Television had appeared and become the most powerful sales tool ever devised. Reeves, known as 'the blacksmith' for the way in which he hammered home a simple message with his repetitious ads, was the champion of an aggressive form of hard-selling advertising. The way of selling most effectively, Reeves decided, was to find in a product what he called its 'unique selling proposition', or USP, which made a claim for the product untouched by the competition.

Reeves was one of the giants of Madison Avenue of the 1950s and 1960s, commanding the heights that the Saatchi brothers could only dream of as they set out in the early 1980s in their quest for a major New York agency. Another giant was a Scotsman called David Ogilvy, today one of the legends of the industry, whose *Confessions of an Advertising Man* was required reading for young men entering the business when the Saatchis were starting out. His approach was more genteel than Reeves's: he once described the perfect advertising executive as combining the tenacity of a bulldog and the charm of a spaniel. He believed in scientific data and research, insisting that 'factual advertising outsells flatulent puffery'. Ogilvy was fascinated by salesmanship, and brought to the industry new marketing disciplines and a belief in the long-term image of the brand he advertised. 'Every advertisement is part of the long-term investment in the personality of the brand,' he wrote.

The son of a Gaelic-speaking Highlander, Ogilvy lived as a boy in Lewis Carroll's house in Surrey, went to several public schools, was expelled from Oxford and then became a salesman for Aga Cookers in Scotland. At the age of twenty-four he wrote *The Theory and Practice of Selling the Aga Cooker*: 'It does not cook the cook. It civilises life in the kitchen.' His life story, up to the point where he arrived, aged thirty-eight, on Madison Avenue, is an extraordinary one: he worked in the kitchens of the Hotel Majestic in Paris, and later went to the USA to work for Dr George Gallup. It was Gallup who had begun the new scientific methods of measuring radio audiences and newspaper and thus advertising readership at Young & Rubicam in 1932.

One of the chapters in Ogilvy's book starts: 'Fifteen years ago I was an obscure farmer in Pennsylvania. Today I preside over one of the best advertising agencies in the United States, with billings of over $55m a year.' Now *there* was a precedent for the Saatchis. And there was another: Ogilvy had originally been financed in his Madison Avenue venture by his elder brother Francis, then head of the agency Mather & Crowther. The Saatchis were thus not the first British brothers to tackle successfully the apparently closed and giant world of American advertising, colloquially but geographically incorrectly referred to as 'Madison Avenue', in the same way the British press will still be referred to as 'Fleet Street' long after the last newspaper has moved out.

In a short history of the Ogilvy, Benson and Mather agencies, written in 1975, Stanley Pigott observes: 'Francis Ogilvy fulfilled his vision. He had contrived, against all the odds, to start a British-owned advertising agency on the American advertising scene. He knew that his brother's genius would make it succeed.' Was there inspiration or at least encouragement there for the Saatchi brothers? Ironically, few advertising men would come to resent the Saatchis' move into New York more than the younger Ogilvy.

David Ogilvy in the 1960s and 1970s offered hope for many aspiring young advertising men. He pointed out that in 1937 Walter Chrysler gave the Plymouth account to Sterling Getchel, then only thirty-one; that in 1940 Ed Little awarded most of his Colgate account to a dark horse named Ted Bates, predecessor of Reeves and founder of the agency. And General Foods discovered Young & Rubicam when that agency, later the biggest in the world, was only a year old. There was nothing sacred about the pecking order of the Madison Avenue agencies. Ogilvy himself had proved that in about the same number of years it would take the Saatchis.

In fact it was neither Reeves nor Ogilvy who was the inspiration for the Charles Saatchi generation. That role went to a third giant of the day. If Reeves was the blacksmith of Madison Avenue, Bill Bernbach was the Picasso, the man who would lead the industry back into what became known as the 'creative revolution'. Again and again Charles Saatchi, Ross Cramer, Jeremy Sinclair, Ron Collins and so many other young creative men of the day refer to Bernbach as the most powerful influence on their formative years. Yet that influence was confined in Charles's case to the creative side; the agency he and his brother built after the first few years owed little or nothing to Bernbach, and perhaps more – although they would not welcome the thought – to Ogilvy. Ironically, in view of what was to occur later, the giant they owed nothing whatsoever to was Rosser Reeves; his work and his agency lay well outside their orbit.

Born in 1911 in the Bronx – his father was a designer of women's clothes – Bernbach was educated at various American public schools before studying English, music and philosophy at New York University. In the words of one biographer, he displayed 'the sort of easy eclecticism that allowed him later to range across a variety of disciplines in his advertising career'. Like so many others, he drifted into advertising by accident, and soon proved to be an inspired copywriter. By the late 1940s, however, Bernbach was increasingly disturbed by the research methods which dominated the business. In 1947 he wrote a memo to his boss which set out some of the themes he would espouse for the rest of his career: 'I'm worried that we're falling into a trap of bigness, that we're going to worship techniques instead of substance . . . I don't want scientists. I don't want people who do the right things. I want people who do inspiring things . . . Let us blaze new trails.'

In June 1949 Bernbach, then thirty-eight, set out to blaze his own new trail. With Ned Doyle (accounts) and Maxwell Dane (admin and finance) he created Doyle Dane Bernbach, hinting at their departure from the norm by including no comma or ampersand in the name. They had thirteen employees and $500,000 in billings, and their first office was on the top floor of 350 Madison Avenue, a floor and a half above the last elevator stop. Bernbach lived most of his life in an unfashionable part of town, travelling by subway, and claimed that he and his two partners probably did less entertaining than any agency in the business. 'We're just three guys who live very modestly and don't cater to clients [simply] because we need the money.'

In many ways he was the opposite of Charles Saatchi. Short and stocky, with bland features, mild blue eyes and greying blond hair, he was also sane, well balanced and uneccentric to the point of dullness. His hobbies included music, literature and the philosophy of Bertrand Russell, whom he often o ioted: 'Even in the most purely logical realms, it is insight that first arrives at what is new.'

Bernbach's era was about to dawn. By the 1950s the big American advertising agencies had expanded with the great consumer boom, of which they were an integral part – some even said its cause. They were regarded as fulfilling a vital economic function in the new 'Affluent Society' in an age when the deprivation of two decades of depression and war had given way to an enormous demand for products. America in the 1950s had virtually no unemployment, inflation was 1 per cent a year, and there was cheap and plentiful energy. As the nation's great factories mushroomed so the imperative was for consumers to consume – and for the advertiser to persuade them to do so. By the end of the decade the USA had 25 per cent of the world market share in manufacturing and, before the days of the Japanese, 95 per cent of US cars, steel and consumer electronics were made in its own factories. Madison Avenue became the background for films, plays and novels: Doris Day and Rock Hudson acted out their innocent romances in agency offices and Gregory Peck starred in *The Man in the Grey Flannel Suit.* Frederick Wakeman's book *The Hucksters* appeared in 1946 and painted the industry as unscrupulous and manipulative, but that did not disturb the public as much as Vance Packard's *The Hidden Persuaders* when it appeared in 1957, exposing the evils of the scientific methods widely used in the industry.

Bill Bernbach all this time had been making a new and different kind of advertisement, called the soft sell, which began to replace the brain-pounding repetition of the USP. Bernbach rejected the proposition, propounded by many large agencies, that 'once the selling proposition has been determined the job is done'. Research, in his view, perpetuated mediocrity and led to dullness. 'There are a lot of good technicians in advertising. They know all the rules . . . and they talk the best game. But there's one little rub. They forget that advertising is persuasion, and persuasion is not a science, but an art. Advertising is the art of persuasion.' He favoured what he called 'the intuitive flashes of inspiration that defied scientific investigation'.

In the post-Packard/Galbraith climate Bernbach became high fashion. He produced most of his best ads within a space of a few years. In 1959 he got the Volkswagen account, and 'like an earthquake broke new ground in every direction', in the words of one of his fans, the British advertising man David Abbott, who worked for him. VW was already selling 150,000 cars a year in the USA when Bernbach came along, but he considerably boosted that with a series of iconoclastic and daring ads. Bernbach capitalised on the obvious defects of the car, which was still closely associated in those days with Hitler's Germany. He poked fun at it with ads such as the one which showed a set of snow tracks on a desolate country road – with no car to be seen. The caption announced that there was finally a beautiful picture of a VW. On the screen came a VW being pulled by a tow truck and the caption read: 'A rare photo'. His ads talked about how 'our funny little engine sure can push our funny little car fast'. One ad, which broke new ground in the mid-1960s, just featured a line, roughly showing the ugly shape of the VW Beetle, and the caption 'How much longer can we hand you this line?' The trade paper *Advertising Age* later designated the VW ads the best campaign of the half-century. In a Britain being swept along by the satirical shows *That Was The Week That Was, Beyond the Fringe* and, later, *Monty Python's Flying Circus*, it is easy to see how such ads would appeal to creative young men like Charles Saatchi and Ross Cramer.

By the late 1960s some two dozen American agencies had gone public, little suspecting the hard times that lay around the corner. The early 1970s brought recession and a sharp downturn in consumer spending. After twenty-five years of unprecedented growth, the Affluent Society was suddenly over. Inflation and recession hit consumption hard, and the big manufacturers stopped spending on advertising. In 1971 many big agencies, including JWT, McCann, Young & Rubicam, Bates and BBDO, suffered large losses. The troubled agencies found themselves in a vicious downward spiral: the more their problems were signalled, the more clients withdrew. The more creative agencies in particular lost accounts, and were forced to move to a more conservative, marketing-orientated approach. Abruptly, the creative revolution, which had flourished for only a decade, died. A number of agencies that had gone public now bought back their own shares and went private again. Agencies sought marketing experts instead of creative talent, and David Ogilvy welcomed it. 'Today, thank God, we are back in business as salesmen instead of pretentious entertainers. The pendulum is swinging back our way.' In fact advertising was evolving rather than swinging wildly, and creative advertising, as Ogilvy himself was the first to admit, was still of prime importance to the industry.

The 1970s also saw a great wave of mergers among American agencies. Edward Ney took over at Y & R in November 1970 and proceeded, with an ambitious series of mergers, to build a company that surpassed JWT in size in the national billings. Its acquisition of

Marstellar in 1979 made it the leader in world billings too. Other agencies followed the same trend. Interpublic bought Campbell-Ewald, Ogilvy took Scali McCabe Sloves (the hottest new agency of the 1970s), while Wells Rich Greene bought Gardner. Bates absorbed Campbell-Mithun, and the three biggest public-relations firms were bought by Thompson, Y & R and Foote Cone & Belding.

By the end of the 1970s American advertising was back in boom times again. Soft sell had given way to hard sell, and the growth of corporate business favoured rational content in the ads. It didn't appeal to the creative men, and in 1977 *Advertising Age* announced that 'The industry is waiting for the next creative giant to shake us all up.' In 1980 *Advertising Age* again said that the industry was 'on the verge of a new creative revolution'.

So it was; but those changes were shaping up 3000 miles away. The Saatchis were ready for the new world.

The catalyst for the first major move by Saatchi & Saatchi into the US was the Cincinatti-based Procter & Gamble, for which over the years Saatchi had handled such products as Ariel and Fairy Snow soap-powders, Head & Shoulders shampoos, Pampers nappies and various others. Kenneth Gill had made P & G a promise in 1975, and had kept to it: they were going to benefit from the Saatchi/Compton deal. In Britain the Saatchis and P & G had got on well, and far from withdrawing its account P & G had given the agency new ones.

But P & G was not only Garland-Compton's biggest account; it was also the biggest account of Compton Advertising in New York. Milt Gossett began to worry about protecting it, feeling that the brothers' expansionary plans were sooner or later going to run it into trouble with the Cincinnati group – and that this was going to brush off on Compton in New York. There were rumours all over Adland in New York that the Saatchis were approaching one agency or another. They were true; the first talks in 1977 were with a food company which had acquired a medium-sized advertising agency which it wanted to sell and Sorrell led the negotiations which were coming to fruition when a better prospect loomed up: Daniel & Charles, a medium-sized agency, which Sorrell worked on for several months during 1978. Those talks too were making progress when one day Bob Gross of Geers Gross, hearing of the Saatchi interest in an American agency, rang up. He had a special relationship with the New York agency Cunningham & Walsh, which was another Proctor & Gamble agency, and he knew they were looking for a buyer. Sorrell immediately switched to this bigger and better prize and again the talks became both detailed and lengthy with Maurice and Sorrell now spending weeks in New York, keeping in touch with other prospects while pursuing this one.

It was painstaking and often frustrating work, but both Maurice and Sorrell were particularly well suited to it. Maurice's disciplined approach and Sorrell's exceptional financial grasp made them a formidable pair at the negotiating table. The brothers were intent on getting it right, making sure that this first step into New York was the right one. The takeover road to New York is littered with the bones of many past failures and the Saatchis were adamant they would not be among them. But the Cunningham & Walsh talks caused Milt Gossett some distress when the rumours filtered through to him at Compton – as inevitably they did. Aghast, he rang the Saatchi office in London: did no one there realise how hot Procter & Gamble were about spreading their business around a number of agencies? If they heard that Saatchi were going to take over another of their agencies, they would as likely as not remove *all* their accounts – from Compton in New York as well as from Saatchi & Saatchi Compton in London. It would be a disaster.

Maurice and Sorrell finally abandoned Cunningham & Walsh and chased another, even better, agency: Wells Rich Greene, founded by the legendary Mary Wells, one of the few successful women at the top of Madison Avenue agencies. Maurice and Sorrell went down to the South of France where she then had a villa on the Cap Ferrat, and again the talks went on for months. They too came to nothing. All this time they were talking to Compton in New York, but that never seemed a serious prospect, although the brothers would like it to have been. Then a better one appeared: Doyle Dane Bernbach. Sorrell had met a relative of Bill Bernbach, Neil Austrian, at business school and now contacted him to talk takeover. Tim Bell flew over and they all had dinner at La Cirque in New York. The deal was never seriously on, however. Bernbach did not want to sell and Maurice soon realised he didn't want to buy, even if he had been able to afford it. 'Bernbach struck me as a rather flaky outfit,' he reported back to Charles. The search went on.

Inside Compton the senior managers were as nervous as Gossett. The Saatchi reputation had grown enormously with the Tory Party account and the victory of Mrs Thatcher, and in the New York agency no one doubted their creativity. Gossett himself expressed his own worries to his directors. 'They're a couple of crazy guys, who won't stay by the conventions,' he said. 'They're brilliant, but they're crazy.' His team had worked well with them, and he had come to like both brothers, who often dropped in on him during their trips through New York. Maurice and his wife Gillian had spent weekends at Gossett's house, and he in turn had stayed with them. He had met Charles and Doris as well, and they had talked about art. Tim Bell had come over a number of times and they had made presentations together, notably one to Coca Cola. The relationship between the two agencies was working well, in a technical sense; but all that could be blown away by one ill-advised takeover which might benefit Saatchi & Saatchi but would not benefit Compton.

Gossett gradually began to put in place his own defence mechanisms. He talked to P & G and explained the position – just in case he was hit by a pre-emptive strike. Then he decided that either he had to increase his shareholding in Saatchi & Saatchi Compton and wrest back control, or he had to find another agency in London. Compton's shareholding was no longer in the parent but in the subsidiary Saatchi & Saatchi Compton, and Gossett had few levers. He broached the subject with Maurice, and the negotiations began. Gossett proposed increasing Compton's shareholding to 40 per cent. The negotiations were at times hectic, and the Compton side soon lost count of the number of times one side or the other stormed out. Finally, however, the Saatchis agreed: Compton could go up to 40 per cent. The papers were drawn up and everything was prepared for a meeting in Milt Gossett's office. Both brothers turned up for the signing. Then at the last moment Charles suddenly said, 'No, I don't want to do it', stood up and walked out, with Maurice close behind him.

It was Maurice who reopened negotiations. He rang Gossett one day in 1981 to make his proposition: 'Why don't you buy all of us?' Instead of buying 40 per cent, why didn't Compton buy 100 per cent of Saatchi & Saatchi? The brothers had been able to reverse their own agency into Compton in the UK with startlingly successful results six years before. Why not try it on a larger scale? That caused Gossett to begin thinking hard. Many of his senior management were of that post-war generation who were – as he was himself – moving towards retirement. 'Their relationship with the Saatchis was pretty similar to what they would be if they were Martians or people from the planet Saturn,' says a former Compton man. 'They had no idea how to deal with them. But Milt had an immediate and easy relationship with them, and he was incredibly impressed with their creative work. Compton's creative work was pretty poor then, and the Saatchi creative work was everything Compton's was not.'

Gossett, however, decided he was not keen on Maurice's proposal.

He believed he would never get his management to agree, and didn't think much of it himself. Even so, they started talks, and here Gossett had another eye-opener. Maurice began with one of his beautifully presented expositions on the Saatchi philosophy and his view of the industry. He showed how Saatchi had increased its earnings per share by an average of 30 per cent over the past five years, and its billings from £13.7 million in 1971 to a forecast £100 million in 1981. He outlined the need for advertising agencies to have international networks – he didn't have to remind anyone that McCann Erickson had used the Coca Cola account in Brazil as a lever to grab the US account too.

Compton, like many agencies, had no corporate plan as such. Gossett himself was a former creative man, and freely admitted he was not very good when it came to figures. The Saatchis seemed to have everything thought out years ahead. Gossett still didn't want to do the deal, but he decided he had better get moving with Compton before it was too late. He had his financial team draw up a plan for expansion, and Compton went on the acquisition trail, buying up Klemtner Advertising and Rumrill-Hoyt.

Then one day Maurice rang him with a suggestion: 'Why don't we buy all of *you*?' Gossett laughed uproariously. It was the most outrageous suggestion he had ever heard. 'You're crazy,' he said. Despite Saatchi's rapid growth, Compton was still twice its size, and had a much more established position. He would not even consider it. Yet when he had rung off he did, and the more he thought of it the more it made sense to him. The problem would be getting his senior managers to agree.

Meanwhile every week seemed to bring a new rumour that the Saatchis were in talks with someone or other. There was almost no one they could buy, it seemed to Gossett, which would not raise some conflict or other with P & G in particular. There was only one thing for it: he had to have his own agency in London.

More in desperation than anything else he travelled to London and bought Britain's seventeenth largest agency KMP, which had been started in 1964 with as big a splash as Saatchi, and by 1974 was actually fifth in the billings league. In the mid-1970s the company fell apart in the economic crisis of the time, lost £210,000 when one of its clients, Brentford Nylon, went bust, and was briefly owned by the Guinness brewing group. Then it went independent again – and now became part of Compton.

Having signed the deal, he called in on Charlotte Street to see his old friend and Saatchi chairman, Ken Gill. As a matter of courtesy, he told him about KMP. Gill, however, had something for Gossett. From his desk to took a letter which offered to buy the whole of Compton Advertising in New York. The Saatchis were not going to take no for an answer and were stepping up the pressure by pressing their bid formally.

Gossett was irritated. 'This is obviously a ploy,' he said. 'You knew I was going to going to tell you this afternoon we were buying a London agency. But you're not going to change my mind. We're still going to buy it.'

Back in New York, Gossett dropped the piece of paper containing the offer into a desk drawer and left it there for six months. He didn't even tell his management about it. Every so often one of them mentioned that he had heard that Milt had an important piece of paper, and that the word in London was they all should know what was on it. Gossett was still so annoyed that he refused even to get it out again.

Saatchi meanwhile had made a takeover, but not in the USA. The Saatchis were concentrating their efforts on New York, but some of the early feelers they had put out in London were coming to fruition. In 1978 there had been the lengthy negotiations with Charles's old firm, Collett Dickenson Pearce. Then in 1981 there was another opportunity which this time the Saatchis did not pass up. When John Bentley had bought, asset stripped and then sold Dorland Advertising a decade before, the buyer – for £850,000 – was Eric Garrott, who owned his own small ad agency. He combined the two agencies under the name of Garrott Dorland Crawford, and during the 1970s the agency did well. In 1981 Garrott was seriously ill, and with no heirs and no obvious successor he decided to sell. For patriotic reasons he refused to do so to the American agencies, including Compton, who were after him. Saatchi & Saatchi were quickly at hand. Dorland cost Saatchi over £7 million, £5.6m down and the rest based on turnover.

The Saatchis decided against merging with their existing agency – both businesses were too big for that. The Saatchi staff were still about 700 strong; Dorland's in its own right had over £50 million of billings, half Saatchi's size but its profit margins were only 1 per cent of billings against Saatchi's 3 per cent. Garrott lived long enough to see the deal through and to declare, 'This is a union of strength and a great day for British advertising' before dying on the operating table. The move meant that Saatchi & Saatchi had no challenger for the number one spot in Britain. JWT had fought back to make it level-pegging at £83 million of billings each in 1980, but could not match Saatchi-cum-Dorlands.

The Dorland bid was the first time Saatchi had made use of the

The 1979 election campaign: Tim Bell rehearses Margaret Thatcher on the roof of the building from where Saatchi ran the campaign. He became a fan – and she in turn insisted on him working on the account in later elections.

'Champagne-tippling Svengali': (Sir) Gordon Reece (*below*) is the public relations man who groomed Mrs Thatcher for power. He wanted an advertising agency to present her properly to the electorate – and hired Saatchi & Saatchi.

Lord Thorneycroft, the Conservative Party chairman, was much impressed by Bell – when finally he met him.

Giants of Madison Avenue:

Bill Bernbach (*below*) told Avis the best he could find to say about it was that it was the second largest and that its people were trying harder. His Volkswagen ads, which poked fun at the VW beetle, and his ads featuring black boys and Indians biting into rye bread with the caption 'You don't have to be Jewish to love Levy's', were among the best made in the USA in the 1960s. He was a guru to the new generation of advertising men, including Charles Saatchi.

David Ogilvy (*bottom*) is regarded as the doyen of advertising. A Scot, he worked in the Hotel Majestic, Paris, as a chef, sold Aga cookers in Scotland and started Ogilvy & Mather in New York in 1949 – the same year Bernbach founded Doyle Dane Bernbach. His *Confessions of an Advertising Man*, written in 1963, became a bestseller and is still compulsory reading for any young advertising executive.

New York agency chiefs taken over by Saatchi:

Milt Gossett (*top left*), chairman of Compton, initially proposed buying up Saatchi & Saatchi, then allowed the brothers to buy Compton in 1982, their leap into the big league.

Carl Spielvogel (*top right*) is a former journalist whose Backer & Spielvogel agency grew even faster than Saatchi & Saatchi before he sold in 1986. He is now the chairman and chief executive officer of Backer Spielvogel Bates Worldwide, created from agencies taken over by the Saatchis in New York, including Ted Bates.

Ed Wax (*bottom left*) is an ex-Compton man who was persuaded to rejoin in 1982 by Milt Gossett and Maurice Saatchi. He now runs Saatchi & Saatchi OFS Compton in New York, the biggest agency in the group.

Bob Jacoby (*bottom right*) got $110m for his shares in Ted Bates – and another $5m for wrongful dismissal after they fired him. The ensuing battle at Bates, dubbed 'MacBates' in the New York trade press, when they lost a series of accounts and received a large quantity of bad publicity, gave the brothers the worst time of their corporate careers.

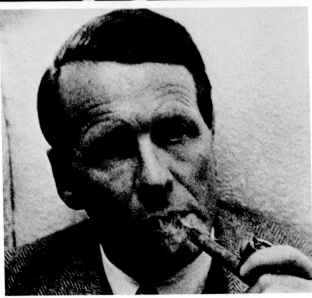

Anthony Simonds-Gooding (*below*) was chief executive of Whitbread when Maurice Saatchi 'climbed in my window with a rose between his teeth' and persuaded him to become the head of the communications division. He arrived just as the Saatchis set out on a takeover blitz in New York, and spent the next year trying to sort out the chaos left from the 'MacBates' affair. He left in the autumn of 1987 to run British Satellite Broadcasting.

Victor Millar (*right*) was one of the two senior worldwide managing partners of Arthur Andersen, the world's largest management consultancy, when the Saatchis hired him at a reputed $1 million a year to spearhead the drive into consultancy. When Simonds-Gooding left, he took over responsibility for communications too.

stock-market. The idea was that they would place £1.5 million-worth of shares in the market, then pass the cash to the Dorland management. It turned out to be a sobering experience. The Saatchi stockbrokers, Phillips & Drew, one of the biggest in London, were very nervous about it, and not at all sure it would go. Maurice and Martin Sorrell drove into the City to address the Phillips & Drew sales-force before the markets opened. 'They were all white-faced and worried about it,' recalls Sorrell. But the placing went well, and Maurice made a note to use it again. It would become the standard method of financing takeover bids.

During this time there was no contact between Gossett and his team in New York and the Saatchi team in London. Compton now had its own London operation and didn't need Saatchi, although it still of course had its 20 per cent stake in the Saatchi agency. Maurice Saatchi was still doing his rounds of the New York agencies, patiently explaining what his plans were, sometimes getting some way down the road, sometimes getting the door slammed. No one treated him with contempt: the Saatchis' creative reputation went before him. Everyone in the New York ad business knew about the pregnant man and the 'Labour isn't working' ads. That of course didn't mean he had anything to offer them in New York, but it gave him a hearing in most places, and the persuasive and earnest Maurice could accomplish a lot with that.

It was a lonely furrow. He usually went alone, or with Sorrell, sometimes presenting his case to a packed boardroom. Charles never went at all. Ken Gill was still keen to revive negotiations with his old friends at Compton, and kept urging that they be reopened.

After about six months of silence, Gossett rang Maurice. 'This is ridiculous,' he said. 'We have the international networks, we have the accounts, we have a wonderful opportunity to be together, and we can learn a lot from you.' The talks were on again. Gossett, however, was not going to rush into it. He put his chief financial officer, Bob Huntingdon, in charge of the negotiations, knowing full well that Huntingdon was opposed to the merger, so that if they could work something out it would be a good deal for Compton. David Perring wrote to Gossett asking him 'how much would it take' for the Compton board. Gossett picked a figure, and he and Maurice began their talks. The Compton side soon learned to respect the young brother's detailed grasp of the financial detail and his ability to deliver instant decisions without reference to anyone. Charles never appeared, but as always was fully in the picture and driving from behind. He never wanted to be bothered with detail. It was, as always, a question of 'Do it'.

Except that they almost didn't do it. There was to be a crucial meeting in New York where the final details would be thrashed out, and for this Charles accompanied Maurice. In some ways it was almost a re-run of the original Compton bid in the UK. One of the last details to be settled was the name of the merged company. After long negotiation Gossett had accepted, as Gill had, that the Saatchi name came first. But how many Saatchis? At a previous meeting he had agreed the name would be Saatchi Compton. Now Charles, who had said very little, suddenly spoke.

'I hate to do this to you, but we need both Saatchis in the name.'

Gossett stared at him a moment. 'Well, screw that, that's the last straw.' It was his turn to storm out. The talks were off again.

This time, however, Gossett's irritation lasted only a matter of weeks. If the agency had just been called 'Saatchi', it would never have been so distinctive. It was that second 'Saatchi' which gave it its special effect, as Charles had known it would all those years before. Gossett gave in: he would settle for the two Saatchis coming first in the name.

It was a big deal for Saatchi, many times bigger than anything they had touched so far. Compton was twice their size. They would need to find $30 million immediately and another $24.8 million paid over five years, again on their 'earn out' formula. Once again Maurice and Martin Sorrell paraded into the City early in the morning, this time to get away a rights issue of some £26 million. It was a turning point for the brothers. At that stage they owned 36 per cent of the company. The issue they were about to make would reduce their holding to 18 per cent. They both hated doing it. Sorrell laid it out for them the night before. 'Are you prepared to own 18 per cent of Saatchi & Saatchi plus Compton, or 36 per cent of Saatchi on its own?' It was Charles, very nervous, who gave him his answeer: 'Do it.' Gossett, with 10 per cent of the Compton business, would become a rich man, and another 100 of the staff also got handsome payouts.

In dollar terms, Saatchi's billings that year were running at about $350 million. Compton's were $650 million. So the combined group would have billings of around $1 billion a year. Overnight Saatchi had become the thirteenth biggest agency in the USA, the ninth biggest worldwide, and, with the addition of KMP, which it now acquired with Compton, was even more impregnable in London. The deal was formally announced on the 15 March 1982, and *Campaign*, for the only time in its history, brought out a special issue on the following Monday to mark the occasion.

13

GLOBALISATION

Maurice Saatchi's reading list is catholic; on his desk at any given time one may find a tidy heap of economic journals, analysts' reports on half a dozen different industries, or the latest Tom Wolfe or Scott Turow novel. The visitor, politely remarking on any of these, will receive an enthusiastic summary, followed by a copy of the book or photocopy of the article delivered to their office a few days later. Both brothers like to share their enthusiasms, so that, if Charles has seen a film or a West End or Broadway show that he likes, everybody *must* go and see it too. If Maurice has found a new novel or writer, then everyone has to read the book. It is, perhaps, a gesture of bridge-building, of reaching out, the nearest the brothers get to letting the outsider glimpse their inner selves. They don't share their private lives with colleagues or business friends, not because of any overpowering desire for privacy, but simply because they genuinely find it difficult. Charles finds it hard to sustain a conversation of any length with anyone he hasn't known for years, and who is therefore unattuned to his shorthand way of communicating. He and Maurice don't need to say much to each other; they wander in and out of each other's offices all day and talk constantly on the phone or in the car driving to meetings together. Involving others in a book or a film that has caught their interest provides a tiny opening in the curtain.

In addition, both brothers, Maurice less so than Charles, have low boredom thresholds. If something does not interest them they will not do it. Having done something once, they are not very interested in doing it again. Each successive stage of Saatchi & Saatchi had to have some element which caught their imagination and made it more than the – for them – straightforward progression of a company up the profits ladder. They set out to make money, certainly; but that came remarkably easily, and after a few years was not enough. Charles wanted to show that a 'hot-shop' agency could grow and become the biggest in the land; several years before that happened both brothers had already mentally discounted it and were looking beyond. In the late 1970s they could both get enormous intellectual satisfaction in watching the ease with which the agency pulled in new accounts and in seeing the men they had hired as youngsters take on, and beat, the biggest names of the day – with not very much input from the brothers. Helping Mrs Thatcher win the 1979 election had given them as big a thrill as anything, not so much because of what it meant politically but because it posed a technical challenge to their professional skills and to the organisation they had created. Their name and reputation had become closely associated with the new Tories, so winning meant a great deal. And the fame it gave them allowed them to do even more, take on things they could not have attempted. Buying a big New York agency, never before done by a foreigner, was yet another challenge which engaged their interest, and their imagination could work overtime on seeing the enormous possibilities, then solving the difficulties. Each stage of their progress had to have a philosophical justification, often discovered retrospectively, but growth for the Saatchis was never the simple affair it is for many corporate predators. There would be a consistent strand through that philosophy, and through their growth, but many times the brothers had little idea where that strand was leading them. That too was part of the thrill, the excitement of making a leap and discovering that the ladder was indeed where they hoped it would be, and that they were safely halfway up it already.

It is possible to be highly sceptical about their philosophical utterings, dismissing them as no more than whitewash for a ruthless and single-minded preoccupation with size, power and self-satisfaction. Indeed, much of what the brothers would claim as their philosophy does not, on first glance at least, justify such a high-blown term.

It is worth looking again at the 1987 Harvard Business School study of Saatchi and Saatchi, which has a section headed 'Philosophy'. As the company grew, says the study, so the brothers lowered their profile 'to minimise the company's apparent dependence on themselves . . . operating management had been delegated to a number of experienced . . . executives.' That is fairly straightforward; the Saatchis say that they have consistently, and from the earliest days, tried to work themselves out of a job. Thus, within a couple of years, Maurice had turned over the whole machine of getting new business, which he started with his Rolladex, to others; Charles stopped writing many of the ads within the first couple of years, and Tim Bell took over first the presentations, then the running of the agency. Martin Sorrell took on the financial affairs of the group, and also its relationship with the City and the bankers and stockbrokers. It all made the brothers more distant and added to their mystique, but in terms of building a large-scale business it was a perfectly sensible thing to do.

But is it true? Is it really why they did it? It is probably nearer the truth to say that the Saatchis made a management virtue of their own thirst for new challenges; by the time they merged with Compton in London, they had no interest in running an agency any more, so they never did it – they gave it to Tim Bell, and probably congratulated themselves on their cleverness in motivating someone who would do it as well as he could to work so hard for them. Their devolvement of power and delegation of responsibility are good textbook stuff, which the Harvard Business School teaches its pupils; but it also happened to be the only way in which the Saatchis could keep themselves interested in the business.

Typically, having discovered that it both worked and suited them, the Saatchis soon began encouraging their own executives to think in that way. Maurice, interviewing people for senior roles, would tell them that one of the things he wanted them to do was 'work yourself out of a job' as soon as possible, thus freeing executives for even bigger and better things.

The next paragraph in the Harvard's case-study analysis of the Saatchi philosophy makes more sweeping claims. 'The twin elements underpinning Saatchi & Saatchi's strategy,' it says, 'were a belief that being large was important, but being the number one, two or three in the industry was vital; and that markets were defined globally.'

The Saatchis undoubtedly always had a belief that 'being large was important', as shown by their cheeky offers to the other agencies from their earliest days. They had no interest in being a 'creative hot-shop' a moment longer than they needed to be; they instinctively yearned after size and prestige, and their instinct was supported by their experiences in the early days when they could not get near the big accounts because they themselves were too small. They also wanted to be the number one – Charles told everyone, both inside and outside, that it was where they were heading. But that was so more because Charles wanted to prove something to the world than for any commercial reason. Think of their delight, therefore, when they did find a philosophical reason for it. Ted Bates, in conjunction with Harvard, undertook a study which produced what it called the 'Law of Dominance'. Simply stated, it contends that unless you are in the top three companies in an

industry you are nowhere, or, as Bates put it: 'One, two, three or out.'
The Saatchis refined this slightly to read:

1 One is wonderful
2 Two can be terrific
3 Three is threatened
4 Four is fatal.

The Law of Dominance was supported by a number of statistical
analyses of the Harvard data bases, all of them showing the importance
of market share in determining profitability. It seriously questioned
whether, in the long run, firms outside the top three could be consistently profitable in any international industry. It was an argument in
favour of 'power of scale', which meant that the bigger firm could
attract and keep better talent, could take bigger risks, could invest in
research and development, could establish a worldwide information
system and could also benefit from economies of scale.

The second element of Saatchi strategy was, according to the Harvard
study, a belief 'that markets were defined globally'. In 1982, when they
signed the Compton New York deal, the Saatchis had never heard the
word 'global' used in this way. At an early stage they perceived the
need to be international, and had opened offices in Paris, Brussels,
Frankfurt and other major European cities in the mid-1970s, putting
the name Saatchi & Saatchi on the door, hiring someone to run them
and waiting for the business to come along. They had not seen it as
symptomatic of any great seminal movement taking place in world
markets but as a practical solution to the demands of their clients which
they were otherwise unable to satisfy. They soon retreated from their
European venture, realising the advertising world did not work in that
way. No one wanted a Europe-wide agency, particularly as tiny a one
as they were offering; it had to be worldwide to be of any value to the
client. It was one of their more humiliating failures.

Over the next few years the need for a large and well-organised
international network was borne in on them again and again. Saatchi's
found they would not get on to the shortlist for a new client because
only the multinational agencies were included. That was bad enough;
but then they began losing business. Maurice remembers one big client
coming to him and saying: 'Well, I think you're great, and you're
marvellous people, but the decision has been taken back in America
that we're going to have a chain. I'm very sorry, it's very unfair, you're
the best people, but you'll just have to go.'

With Compton, Saatchi did acquire an international network, and was now able to offer a worldwide service. But the brothers, like most people in the industry, had never seriously thought about why an international network was so necessary – they had simply reacted to the pressure from clients to put one in place. They had bought a big New York agency because they had seen, ahead of most of the pack, the direction in which their big clients such as Procter & Gamble were going. They had tried to create their own international network, and failed. So they had bought one. Now they were to find an intellectual justification for this move too.

On Maurice Saatchi's regular reading list is the *Harvard Business Review*, a highbrow economic publication which contains many articles by leading academics. Maurice never went to Harvard, and it is one of his few regrets that he did not take a few years off after the London School of Economics to study outside Britain. In the middle of 1983 an article in the *Review* caught his attention and as he read it Maurice became more and more enthralled. It was called 'The globalization of markets' and was written by Theodore (Ted) Levitt, a professor of business administration and head of the marketing area of the Harvard Business School. Its subheading read: 'Companies must learn to operate as if the world were one large market – ignoring superficial regional and national differences.'

Levitt had been making the same points for several years, but as Maurice read it for the first time that day Levitt's analysis struck him as exactly fitting the circumstances of his own company. Here for the first time was an answer to the 'why' – Levitt was explaining precisely what the brothers and most big agency chiefs had found out by trial and error. Levitt's thesis was essentially this: the big multinational companies of the day were finding that their old markets were becoming saturated. New markets, on the other hand, were more and more difficult to find; and, if they had to customise their products to suit the new markets, the extra sales were not worth the candle. They had been so caught up in trying to anticipate what these new markets would want that they had become befuddled and could no longer see the forest because of the trees.

Another, and wiser, group of companies were taking a different approach. They regarded the whole world as the same market; they sold the same advanced, standardised, functional and reliable product everywhere. Thus, explained Levitt, in Brazil thousands swarmed daily 'from pre-industrial Bahian darkness into exploding coastal cities' and installed the latest television sets in corrugated huts; or made sacrificial offerings of fruit and fresh-killed chicken to Macumban spirits 'next to battered Volkswagens'. In Nigeria's civil war, the soldiers listened to transistor radios and drank the very same Coca Cola that teenagers did in America. 'Corporations geared to this new reality benefit from enormous economies of scale in production, distribution, marketing and management. By translating these benefits into reduced world prices, they can decimate competitors that still live in the disabling grip of old assumptions about how the world works.'

Levitt insisted that national and regional preferences were gone; last year's models could no longer be sold in the Third World, because no matter how poor they were the developing countries wanted the latest. And they wanted them at the same price the multinationals charged in their home markets. 'The globalization of markets is at hand. With that, the multinational commercial world nears its end, and so does the multinational corporation.' The multinational and the global company were not the same thing, said Levitt. The first operated in a number of countries and adjusted its policies to each – at a high cost. The global corporation sold the same thing everywhere.

Economists had been making a similar point long before Levitt. Peter Drucker's *Age of Discontinuity*, published in 1969, had a chapter called 'From international to world economy', which argued that the world was rapidly moving to become one large market-place for products other than Coca Cola – the Volkswagen, for instance – and that the wants of affluent consumers were pretty much the same whether they were American, French or Russian. Levitt took the argument several stages further, particularly in his assertion about the death of the multinational. The article that Maurice Saatchi read that day ended on a warning note:

> The global company will shape the vectors of technology and globalization into its great strategic fecundity. It will systematically push these vectors toward their own convergence, offering everyone simultaneously high-quality, more or less standardized products at optimally low prices, thereby achieving for itself vastly expanded markets and profits. Companies that do not adapt to the new global realities will become victims of those that do.

For Maurice, it was a revelatory message – and one he could use to his advantage. Procter & Gamble, he now realised, had been a global company for years, and had long learned the lessons Levitt set out. So were other Compton clients, all of them demanding that their advertising agencies keep pace with them. The world was going in that direction and Saatchi & Saatchi had been pulled along with it. Now it must get ahead. Levitt had little to say about the advertising industry in this article (Maurice didn't know it, but Peter Drucker, in a book *Management: Tasks, Responsibilities, Practices,* published in 1973, had hinted that such a trend was developing for the advertising business, as had various others), but his theories fitted the industry so neatly that they seemed to be tailor-made. Maurice decided to fly at once to Harvard and talk to Levitt, and place globalisation at the heart of the Saatchi doctrine.

Levitt warmed to Saatchi's enthusiasm, but Maurice was not the only advertising man to beat a path to his door that year. Another big New York agency, Foote Cone & Belding, struck first. Its annual report that year featured an article entitled 'Global markets, global advertisers, global agencies – the wave of the future'. Its author was the same Ted Levitt. The New York agencies were not going to allow the Saatchis to hijack their gurus without a fight.

In that Foote Cone & Belding article Professor Levitt applied his theories along the precise lines that Maurice Saatchi would have wanted. 'A powerful new challenge and opportunity faces advertisers and advertising agencies,' he wrote, 'with results even more profound than the great transformation for which Albert Lasker, the founder of modern advertising, is justifiably credited. Suddenly, commerce throughout the world is getting radically different. Competition has become intensely global.'

Advertising, he went on, had played a remarkably small role in this so far, although the trend had in fact been brought about by communications: by the jumbo-jet, 'digitized and transistorized telecommunications', containerised shipping and so forth. 'What was once known to, and available for, only the affluent and the leisure classes is now becoming known and accessible to impoverished masses everywhere.'

Levitt in this article suggested that the advertising industry should do more than respond to the global needs of their clients: they should actually lead the way. 'Most important is the necessity for advertising agencies to help their clients to see how the world is changing.' He elaborated on the Coca Cola example, pointing out that Coke was not always a mass-market, transnational, low-cost product, and nor did it grow into one by slow self-propulsion: it was created 'by imagination in the design of its strategies and the implacability of its executions. The resulting economies of scale and consequent profitability are obvious.'

The advertising industry, said Levitt, had to get in step with the new world, and turn its multinational clients into global competitors. He

ended by quoting from W. B. Yeats's poem 'The Second Coming':
'Things fall apart; the centre cannot hold'; adding that 'nothing could
be more true regarding the old abnormalities of world commerce.
The phrase "passionate intensity" with which Yeats ends the stanza is
appropriate to the way we must rethink competition in "The Republic
of Technology".'

What Levitt failed to mention is that Yeats in that poem, forecasting
a world of anarchy, said: 'The best lack all conviction, while the worst /
Are full of passionate intensity.' Did Levitt intend to imply that the
rethinking should now be done by the 'worst'? And who did he mean?
One wonders if the Foote Cone & Belding directors had ever read
Yeats – or if they realised that the same poem ends:

> And what rough beast, its hour come round at last,
> Slouches towards Bethlehem to be born?

So there were others in the advertising industry alongside, and perhaps
even ahead of, the Saatchis in their thinking about the direction of the
industry in 1983. There were many who were ahead in their execution
of it. The worldwide Compton network that Saatchi now owned was
not a good one, certainly nowhere near as good as half a dozen of the
top New York agencies. The Saatchis knew that, but it didn't bother
them. They could make it good – by beefing it up, by making more
acquisitions and by using it properly for some of the major new
accounts. The first real test of the international network would be the
British Airways account.

March 1983. In a small studio in the Saatchi & Saatchi headquarters
in Charlotte Street a small group waits for the lights to go down. One
is a square, heftily built man, now past middle age, but whose jutting
jaw and vast, squat hands convey an impression of considerable forceful-
ness. He sits in the front row, in the centre, for this show is in his
honour: Sir John King, appointed by Mrs Thatcher to take the near-
bankrupt airline British Airways out of state ownership and into private
hands, has put Saatchi & Saatchi at the centre of his marketing strategy.
A great deal hangs on the ads he is about to see.

Beside him sits Maurice Saatchi, his tall, thin figure and his youthful-
ness – he is nearly thirty years younger than King – contrasting with
King's powerful stockiness. Bill Muirhead, the Saatchi executive put in

charge of the BA account, holds the floor, and the assembled group of BA executives and Saatchi men listen attentively as he makes his presentation.

This is to be no ordinary campaign, but will, it is claimed, break new ground. It is to be one of the few totally worldwide brand advertising drives ever attempted, and is probably the most co-ordinated, broad-scale, international marketing push ever mounted by a British company. Television sets in the United States, Canada, Australia and Britain will carry the same ad on the same day. Some twenty-five other countries, ranging from the Gulf States, Egypt, Hong Kong and South Africa, to India, Thailand . . . everywhere that has a developed commercial tele-vision network and a few passengers who might fly British Airways will see it shortly afterwards. It will cost £25 million worldwide in the first year, not an enormous figure by the standards of Procter & Gamble, but huge for an airline.

Saatchi has latched on to a key statistic: British Airways can boast that it flies more people to more places than any other airline in the world, a function of its inheritance of routes to the old British empire and its base in the international centre of London. In contrast to the United States, there are not many profitable domestic routes around Britain; the big US carriers carry more passengers than BA, but no one carried more *international* passengers – or to more places. BA flies to seventy destinations around the world, and only Air France comes anywhere near that number. BA clocks up 130,728 international aircraft departures a year; Air France is second with 116,700.

Saatchi converts this into the slogan: 'The World's Favourite Airline'.

There is another statistic Saatchi can make use of: British Airways carries more people across the Atlantic than live on Manhattan (1.2million). The first ad shown by Muirhead reflects this. It is a dramatic science-fiction piece of film, designed to illustrate BA's domi-nance of the toughest route of all, the North Atlantic. A dog on a night-time stroll with its master stops, whimpers and looks up; a housewife in a quilted housecoat peers skyward from her doorway; the music builds up as a dark shape passes overhead. Then the scene shifts to air traffic control. 'Roger, Manhattan, continue to 2000 feet,' says a controller. As crowds emerge from a Tudor-style village to gaze upwards, Manhattan Island, its lights blazing, its major buildings recog-nisable, appears on the flight-path for Heathrow. A voice-over, shaking the sinister sci-fi mood, suddenly booms: 'Every year, British Airways flies more people across the Atlantic than the entire population of Manhattan.'

The special effects have been done by the same team which worked on *Superman*, *2001 – A Space Odyssey* and *Star Wars*, and is straight out of the Spielberg genre of the day, with music and effects similar to those of the feature film *Close Encounters*. The director is Richard Loncrane, who has just finished filming *The Missionary*. The group are shown other, less dramatic ads, each of them ending with a film star (Joan Collins, Omar Sharif, Peter O'Toole) checking in at British Airways.

As the lights finally lift, King leads the chorus of approval. He loves the Manhattan ad. 'The dog is great,' he says. 'It was a great idea to have the dog.' King has seen roughs of the ad before and even scripts, but this is the first time he has seen the finished product.

I was one of the small audience in the studio that night, invited by King to see it with him. He was anxious about the impact it would make, and despite his apparent self-confidence was feeling under pressure. Maurice Saatchi and several of his team accompanied us to dinner, where King and his chief executive Colin Marshall talked about the importance of these ads for British Airways.

King explained that the Manhattan ad, which he had personally approved in the planning stage, was intended for another purpose than persuading the public to use his airline. 'I wanted an ad that would cause the staff to look up,' he explained. 'That's what the man does who is exercising his dog. I want them all to look up and say, "My God, did we really do that?" '

King at the time was at a low point in his task of turning BA around, and getting it into shape for a stock market flotation. In his first year he had shown losses of over £300 million, and discovered that on manning levels BA was the least efficient in the world. Its reputation and image were low, and morale in the company was even lower, particularly after he had axed 23,000 jobs.

King was one of the very few Saatchi clients who had met Charles, and had become – and would remain – close to Maurice. He was not the average head of a company, but a powerful political figure, a self-made millionaire from humble beginnings who became a Thatcher favourite in the early 1980s, and who knew his way around Whitehall and the Houses of Parliament even better than did Tim Bell. When he took over BA one of the first things he did was precisely what Robert Townsend advises in his famous book *Up the Organisation*: 'Fire the whole advertising department and your old agency. Then go get the best news agency you can. And concentrate your efforts on making it fun for them to create candid, effective advertising for you.'

King had not read Townsend but his thinking was along the same lines. Foote Cone & Belding had held the British Airways account for thirty-six years, had coined the highly successful slogans 'Fly the flag' and 'We take more care of you', and assumed it would hold it for the same period again. Its work was good, and BA had been happy with it. But there was another reason for King's deciding to make the move. 'When I became chairman of the airline I had the problem of getting people to understand I was there and would actually see it through.' Foote Cone & Belding were used to dealing with marketing men, and King felt he was not getting through to them – or they to him. Two or three times he sent messages asking them to come and see him, but they had never dealt with an airline chairman before and were reluctant to do so now. FCB's chief executive in London, Bill Barry, met King twice, the first time when King told him he was scrapping BA's cheap fares policy and going for maximum profit per head; and on a second occasion when King came along to a presentation at the FCB office. 'King told us our TV ads for British Airways were brilliant,' Barry said later. 'But he was unhappy about two of our press ads.' As King was leaving he turned to Barry and remarked, 'You have made it very difficult for me to see what other agencies can do, but I cannot promise you that I will not go on looking.'

Barry needed to understand King and his task at British Airways to have any comprehension of what was going through his mind at this stage. King wanted a high-profile, morale-boosting campaign which would be talked about well outside the industry, which would lift the visibility of BA and of himself. He was in the political arena, fighting round after round with government ministers and officials as he tried to get them to write off debts, guarantee his routes and support him in the battles he was having with the unions and the workforce. Foote Cone & Belding, he decided, was producing good ads; but he wanted something more.

He unburdened this problem on a friend, a young art gallery owner, Bernard Jacobson, one day. King at the time knew nothing about the advertising industry, about the relationship between clients and agencies, and never thought how much of a stir it would make if he moved. Jacobson knew the Saatchis from boyhood days and Charles often dropped into his gallery, which he encouraged him to set up, to give advice.

'Do you know Saatchi & Saatchi?' he asked. King didn't, although he had heard of them in recent weeks. 'They're very good,' said Jacobson. Would he like to meet them?

A few weeks later King and Jacobson had dinner with Charles and Maurice at the Mirabelle, one of the best restaurants in London. It is a sign of the importance of the account that Charles agreed to be there; although King did not know it, it would be the only time they would meet – 'I've never seen him since!' The evening went well; King has a wry sense of humour and a keen political sense, and he warmed to these two bright young men, who responded. 'We talked about the media, we talked about advertising and of course we talked about my problems. They said they could come up with a programme which could do what I wanted, so I made the change.'

Saatchi had two airline accounts at the time, British Caledonian and KLM, and even with Maurice's highly tuned new business machine and Saatchi's parallel agencies there was no avoiding a conflict. However, it was not often an account as big and prestigious as BA approaches you – and even rarer when the approach is from the chairman personally.

Some weeks later Saatchi made a pitch to BA; they were the only agency asked to do so other than Foote Cone. Maurice personally handled it, developing a rapport with King that would develop into warm friendship over the years. The announcement went out in September 1982, making the front pages of most of the national papers. At Foote Cone & Belding, Bill Barry was furious. Not only was BA a visible and important account, it was also worth over £20 million a year, and losing it would mean redundancies as well as lost prestige. It would be a savage blow to his agency, all the worse because it was undeserved. He fired off an angry letter to King, complaining he had been given no explanation. To the press he stormed: 'I would dearly love to know the reason. Saatchi & Saatchi have strong political connections, and Sir John was appointed by the prime minister. Here is a political pay-off.'

King insists he never even spoke to Mrs Thatcher about it. 'I didn't know at that stage that you couldn't change your advertising agent. I thought you could do that the way you changed your newspaper if you wanted to.' He would never, he says, even if he had thought of it, have taken it up with the prime minister, even though the government still owned the airline, and she was his ultimate boss. 'It was a purely management matter, and as a matter of principle I would not have taken it up with her.'

There is other evidence to suggest the move was not politically inspired. For a start, the only Saatchi person with the ear of the prime minister was Tim Bell, and he, of course, played no part in getting the BA account. Maurice had not seen Thatcher for several years, and

Charles had never spoken to her. It is possible she might have encouraged King off her own bat to plump for Saatchi, but she knew as little about the advertising world as he did.

There were other factors in favour of Saatchi. First of all its reputation, deserved or not, was higher than that of any other agency in London. Second, it was British. Third, it had the ability to handle the account worldwide. No other British agency had ever been able to deliver such an advertising network. Now Saatchi could – and BA was its first new client gained as a result.

That week's *Campaign* set the tone. 'It is no exaggeration to say that the whole world of advertising will be scrutinising the new British Airways campaign . . . in an attempt to predict the impact it will have on the perception of the airline and, therefore, on its performance in the market-place.'

The British Airways ads, when they appeared in New York, had an immediate impact on Saatchi's reputation. They were the first television ads made in Charlotte Street that the Americans had seen. King was even more delighted with the response as the whole press took them up, both in Britain and the USA. He went to New York that week to find that 'People were being interviewed on the streets in America and being asked, "Have you seen that British Airways ad?" and they were saying, "Yes, it's fantastic." It really caused a stir. It won a series of awards too and it's in the Museum of Modern Art in America.' The Saatchis, King said reflectively five years later, delivered what they had promised; 'Our people started looking up again.'

There were also many critics of the Manhattan ad, and of the campaign that followed, which never achieved a standard approaching that of the first ad. But it happened to hit the American market just as things were changing – caused, among other things, by the arrival of video recorders and the remote control device for the television set. 'Suddenly people didn't have to get up any more and cross the room to change from a bad commercial. All they had to do was move their thumb a quarter of an inch,' says the head of one of the big New York agencies. 'So the time was right for outstanding creative work like the British Airways Manhattan ad – work that totally transfixed the individual and broke every rule of American advertising, like you mention the product in the first ten seconds, repeat it four times, and so on. All that stuff went out the window.'

Compton was not the ideal agency to respond to the change, and the Saatchis soon began to become nervous about it. Some of the clients were getting unhappy – including Procter & Gamble and Jeep.

Compton's profit margins were also perilously low by Saatchi's – and even the industry's – standards. Something had to be done. Changes had to be made in management – a tricky affair, given the position of Milt Gossett, whom nobody wanted to lose.

The man they chose was Ed Wax. A tall, thin, lugubrious man, with a bushy moustache, Wax is the son of immigrant working-class parents, and grew up in Lynn, Massachussetts. He took a chemical engineering degree at Northeastern University in Boston, then went to work for Du Pont. He was twenty-seven when he decided to move into advertising and marketing. However, of the 200 companies to whom he applied, only a handful replied and only Compton offered him a job. He took it, and stayed for fourteen years. Then, in 1977, frustrated by Compton's staid advertising, Wax moved on, this time to a small agency called Richard K. Manoff, which by a curious coincidence was bought by the British agency Geers Gross. By 1981 he had moved on again, this time to Wells Rich Greene. It was there he got a call from his old agency Compton: would he be interested in heading up their European operation? The idea, he was told, was that if he did a good job there he would be brought back after a couple of years to take over the agency in New York. Compton was a private business, owned largely by the management, and Wax had been offered a chunk of stock. He was just about to accept when on 17 March 1982 he got another call: Saatchi & Saatchi had bought Compton, thus killing any chance, or so Wax thought, of his accumulating any capital. 'The boat's gone and I was too slow,' he told a friend.

Wax was no stranger to the Saatchis. He was a senior director at Compton when Gossett first brought Maurice over in about 1977, and the long round of negotiations that would take over five years to complete had begun. He was at Wells Rich Greene when the Saatchis made their abortive bid in 1980. He was impressed with what he had seen, and assumed that the Saatchi influence must push Compton into doing more creative work.

He rang Maurice, had a long chat, and at the end of it Maurice offered him the same job he had already been considering in Europe. 'You have the opportunity to get to know us, to re-establish your reputation with Procter & Gamble, and I'm sure at some point Milt would welcome you back to New York to help run the agency.' The plan was for him to spend three years in London, and then head back to New York to take effective charge of Compton.

In the event, things moved faster than that. The brothers were hearing rumblings from the clients. Wax was known in New York, and knew the business there; he also had an outside perspective which would help.

Wax took the job in June, moved to London in August, and primarily looked after Procter & Gamble in Europe. But within a few months Gossett told him they wanted him to return to the New York office.

Back in New York, Wax found there was trouble with a couple of the bigger accounts; he managed to save them, but he was only just in time. Wax was careful not to be seen as what he called a 'Redcoat Benedict Arnold',[1] and went to elaborate trouble to explain that he was not 'the Saatchi boy here to Saatchi-ize'. He liked the Saatchi style, but not *that* much. There were far more clients happy with Compton than there were unhappy ones, and as much a fan as he was of British advertising he would only adopt some of the better ideas.

Wax, with his experience of both London and New York, likes to compare the two different advertising styles. Asked in December 1986 by the magazine *Across the Board* why American advertising was beginning to look more and more British, Wax replied: 'Don't forget, not all British advertising is terrific. There is a lot of crap over there too. But their best has been far superior to anything seen in the United States.' But *why*, pressed the interviewer, are the British better? 'They aren't,' said Wax. 'But they've developed graphics, sound, camera work and production values in such a way that they can be funny and still get the message across.' On the other hand, he went on, the British had no choice. 'They *had* to make their commercials better, because in the UK they have fewer commercial breaks during programmes than we do. They tend to bank large groups of commercials into each break, which means there is a lot of time for viewers to go to the toilet or leave for a beer or sandwich.'

Wax took back to New York with him some of the British ideas of getting 'wit and charm' into his commercials, and he was determined to make them more entertaining. The British Airways ad arrived just at the right time for him, but he began to change the creative output of Compton, he emphasises, because he could see the changes taking place in US advertising. Charles and Maurice Saatchi had little or nothing to do with it.

The changes at Compton were just one of the many decisions for the

---

[1] Benedict Arnold (1741–1801) was an American soldier who became a traitor for the British after being reprimanded by George Washington.

Saatchis as they pursued the Levitt doctrine with growing enthusiasm. All the energies they had channelled into developing the agency in London back in the early 1970s were now focused on expanding it in New York. Compton was a step, but there had to be more.

Their planning at this time was meticulous and impressive – and as bold as ever. Maurice was still doing his rounds, talking to the big agencies, carefully laying the groundwork for another bid. Compton had taken five years of on-and-off negotiation, but it had been worth it. He went back again and again to the same agencies, refusing to accept that he could not tie up a deal. In June 1983 he landed one: McCaffrey & McCall, a medium-sized New York agency, was bought for $10 million down, and another $10 million to be 'earned out' against profits over three years. It was all right; but he was after much, much bigger things.

In September 1983 the Saatchis made another of their leaps. They would get a listing for their shares in Wall Street, becoming only the third British company (after BP and Tricentrol) to do so, and raise some new cash at the same time with a share placing. It was only an over-the-counter listing, not a full stock market quotation, but Saatchi & Saatchi had to go all the way through the rigorous requirements of the Securities and Exchange Commission. In October Maurice took a team to the USA to begin a roadshow which would take in New York, Chicago, Los Angeles, San Francisco and Boston. Only a week behind them, on board Concorde and on a similar circuit, was John Harvey-Jones, the chairman of ICI, and soon many other British companies would be joining in with the same idea. The British invasion of the USA, which would gather pace and transfer owner-ship of many of America's most prestige assets, from Jacuzzi whirl-pools to Brooks Brothers menswear, into British ownership, was under way.

The meeting with analysts in Chicago was typical of the others. At noon on Thursday, 27 October 1983, the Cadillacs and limousines delivered the last of the investment analysts for their date on the 66th floor of the 110-storey Sears Tower, the highest building in the world. Maurice was flanked by Martin Sorrell and Saatchi's corporate develop-ment director, Simon Mellor. A man from the sponsoring bank, Morgan Stanley, a leading house on Wall Street, made a brief speech:

'Ladies and gentlemen, let me introduce Saatchi & Saatchi, by a wide margin the world's most successful advertising agency.'

By what criteria he made that judgement he didn't elaborate, but Maurice didn't object as he took the stage. He had his presentation finely tuned by now: he and his brother had founded the business in 1970; today they were the eighth largest in the world. They had an impressive client list: American Motors, Avis, British Airways, Black & Decker, Du Pont ... and so on. Biggest in Britain, biggest in Europe, tenth largest in the US, earnings growth averaging 34 per cent a year over the past five years ... it all came out with the help of charts and graphs. The American audience had heard of Saatchi in connection with the election of Margaret Thatcher, but they did not know any of this. Maurice then gave them his little lecture on Levitt and globalis- ation, a speech he and Levitt would give as a double act so often that the myth soon developed that the Saatchis were the first to discover Levitt. 'This global trend is something that Saatchi has been working on for years. We have a head start, and are geared for it,' said Maurice.

The issue duly went ahead, and did a number of things for Saatchi. First, it gave them money – they now had some £40 million with which to make acquisitions; second, it gave them American listed shares which could be used to reward and tie in senior American executives; and third, it gave them a much higher profile in the American financial world, a factor which would become increasingly crucial as they continued their takeover activities. Their shares were now monitored by the small group of specialist media analysts in the Wall Street houses. A few months later the *Wall Street Journal*'s 'Heard on the Street' column began a piece: 'Analysts are recommending advertising agency stocks even though the sector has been sluggish of late.' It ended by pointing out that Saatchi & Saatchi was selling at twenty-seven times earnings, 'a multiple reminiscent of the days when agencies were glamor stocks'. That rating, it went on, reflected Saatchi's status as a 'hot' agency, and quoted one analyst, Mary Vandeventer of Widmann, Blee saying that maybe some of the British glamour would rub off on Amer- ican agency stocks as Saatchi became better known in the USA. 'Well, maybe,' echoed Heard laconically.

Morgan Stanley were prepared to recommend the shares, as were Paine Webber, another leading Wall Street house involved in the issue, and a third house, Wertheim, which had no involvement in the issue, was soon recommending the shares too because of the 'dynamic outlook'.

As 1984 progressed the brothers were widening their field beyond advertising. They bought two more companies, Yankelovich, Skeely & White and McBer & Co, both market research specialists. They bought an agency in Australia, Gough Waterhouse, the first British agency to do so. There were more buys in Dublin and Scotland. Then, at the

end of 1984, came the biggest takeover yet: $100 million plus another
$25 million of 'earn out' for the American-based Hay Group, a leading
international firm of management consultants, with ninety-four offices
in twenty-seven countries. In many ways this was one of the most
important bids they made, making them the first advertising company
to branch seriously into consultancy. A new phase in the Saatchi story
had begun.

It was becoming an almost unstoppable advance. Many newspaper
articles at the time have the same first sentence. 'There is no stopping
Saatchi & Saatchi'. It was an onslaught never before seen in the advertising industry, and even the biggest groups on Wall Street began to
become nervous. The clients worried about it too, particularly when
they heard the rumours, and Milt Gossett and Ed Wax were continually
having to deal with questions about conflicts of interest. When they
passed these on to the brothers, they were ignored. The Saatchis were
on a roll, and were not going to turn back until they had accomplished
the target of being the biggest advertising business in the world. Each
bid took them closer, but even at this stage less than one per cent of
the world's advertising passed through their hands.

In 1985 they talked and negotiated incessantly, yet ended the year
having bought no more advertising agencies in the USA. They came
close, but somehow never made the final breakthrough. On their
burgeoning consultancy and other businesses, however, it was a
different matter – in 1985 they acquired companies outside advertising
at a rate of one a month. The series of bids they had made in advertising
was now replaced by a bigger string of bids aimed at widening the
services they offered: Hay was followed by nine takeover bids, giving
the group a major position in everything from direct marketing and
corporate design, to sales promotions, public relations and conferences.
Most were in the USA, but there were three advertising bids outside
the USA too: in Hong Kong, in Canada and in Britain.

It was a monstrous, mind-boggling pace, but the markets loved it.
The share price rose, even though Saatchi was now issuing new stock
almost monthly. More importantly, the company was getting so big and
so widely spread that they needed senior professional help to manage
it. As they had done when they employed Martin Sorrell, they went to
a head-hunter. And that was how Anthony Simonds-Gooding, chief
executive of the Whitbread brewery company, came to join them.

On the day in June 1985 when it was announced that Simonds-Gooding was leaving Whitbread the brewer's shares fell sharply, knocking £45 million off its market value. Simonds-Gooding was forty-seven, and had some advertising experience, both directly and indirectly. He had begun with a short spell at Lintas, where he had worked alongside Frank Lowe, who handled the £11 million a year Whitbread advertising account. In 1973 he joined Whitbread, one of the more conservative members of what the City liked to call 'the beerage' – the group of British brewing families who dominated the industry – and for the last three years had been its top executive. Born in Ireland, Simonds-Gooding was a heavily built, English public-school educated man, of considerable wit and charm, who took a keen interest in advertising, particularly Whitbread's own.

When the Saatchis approached him he had no intention of leaving – he had, after all, one of the best jobs in Britain. But he is a restless man who could not envisage the thought of working through to retirement at Whitbread doing the same job year after year. None the less he would not have moved had Maurice not, as Simonds-Gooding often told him, 'come through my window with a rose between your teeth'. The head-hunter effected an introduction, and Maurice followed up. Simonds-Gooding would later refer in almost awed tones to the persuasive power of Maurice Saatchi, and that day he saw it at its best. Maurice complimented him on the 'wonderful job' he had done at Whitbread, then went on to point out that, having done it, there was not much else to do. On the other hand, Saatchi & Saatchi was reorganising itself after a blitz of acquisitions. Maurice himself was taking over from Gill as chairman, but 'we really need someone like you' to put the whole thing together. 'We've made lots of acquisitions, but we've only just started, particularly in the USA. We need a person of your calibre to administer and run the business and get it into some sort of order. So far we haven't done much with all the acquisitions, but there are enormous opportunities.' Why didn't Simonds-Gooding join? Wouldn't it be very exciting?

The two had several more talks before Simonds-Gooding made up his mind: he would take the plunge. His official title was chairman and chief executive of Saatchi & Saatchi Communications, which included all the advertising companies worldwide, public relations, design, direct marketing and sales promotion. The fledgling management consultancy side would be in a separate division with its own Simonds-Gooding-type figure, both of them reporting to Maurice.

His first day is a vivid example of how the Saatchi operation can function. He had been subjected, as he said to a friend, to 'all the love and seduction of Maurice', and persuaded to abandon his lovely office and his comfortable, cared-for lifestyle at Whitbread. On that first morning at Saatchi, early in September 1985, Simonds-Gooding came down to earth. He was given Tim Bell's final office in Maple Street, behind the Saatchi building, known in the organisation as 'Bell's last stand'. It was a dark and dingy place, in a semi-basement, looking out on to a small enclosed yard at the back in which Simonds-Gooding remembers thinking, 'We should all have blue denims and shuffle around at lunchtime in this sort of windswept courtyard. It was awful.' There was a desk, two chairs and a telephone; no files, no systems, no secretary even, no one to welcome him or to tell him what to do, no handover, no introduction. But there *was* something else: masses of flowers, roses everywhere, and a card saying:

'Welcome Anthony. Over to you. Love, Charles and Maurice.'

They had both gone on holiday for two weeks.

Simonds-Gooding was aware that he was treading in tricky waters at Saatchi. The men and women who ran the advertising agencies, Roy Warman, Terry Bannister, Bill Muirhead, Jennifer Laing and Jack Rubins in London, and Milt Gossett and Ed Wax in New York, now reported to him, not to the brothers. For the first time in the history of the company there was a filter between the advertising personnel and Charles and Maurice, and the old hands in particular were going to resent it. Even Jeremy Sinclair, who played chess with Charles every lunchtime and who was a powerful figure in the agency, theoretically reported through the new head of communications.

The power in the organisation was on the sixth floor at Charlotte Street. Simonds-Gooding wasn't even in that building, let alone on that floor – which was overcrowded, with no room for a new office.

How to start in those circumstances? Simonds-Gooding soon discovered that the Saatchi principle was to let you make your own way. First he got an agency to get him a secretary. Then he sent a telex to Milt Gossett saying he was coming over to New York and he would like Gossett to brief him on the situation there. Gossett, clearly resentful of the new man, telexed back to say he could fit him in for half an hour over lunch the week after next. Simonds-Gooding angrily replied, stating clearly that he was coming for four weeks, and that he wanted to see every single manager in the American organisation, and could he arrange that for him as soon as possible. Gossett got the message.

There was still nothing for Simonds-Gooding to do in his dreary little office. 'At least when you join Whitbread you're given a book, *The Green Jackets* by Arthur Bryant, and *Brewers since 1703*,' he remarked later. On the second day his phone rang. 'Hello, Simonds-Gooding,' he said, with some relief.

Back came a thick Australian accent. 'Thank Christ I've got some fucker at last. It's Cliff Cobbett here, ringing from Melbourne. All my creative staff's walked out, and I wonder what authority I've got because the creative director's coming back from holiday and I want to sack him. Is that okay?'

'Well, Cliff, it's very nice to talk to you,' began Simonds-Gooding, 'but I've only been here two days, and it's a bit difficult . . .'

'Ah – well, I've only been here for two days too,' said the Australian.

Finally, Simonds-Gooding gave him some instructions: 'Do as you see fit,' he said, and put the phone down. He later learned that Cobbett, the head of one of the Saatchi agencies in Australia, duly sacked the creative director, who was instantly hired by a sister Saatchi company at a higher salary. Simonds-Gooding found it baffling – and bizarre. Where was the clear philosophy about globalisation, benefits of scale and all the rest of it? Obviously there was a lot of air in the system, a lot of organisation to be done. He departed on a tour of the Middle East, visiting all the Saatchi subsidiaries there, before travelling on to the USA.

In September 1985 when he joined, Saatchi & Saatchi had 4000 employees. Within a year it would have 14,000, most of them reporting to him. The bid activity so far was merely a prelude to the biggest bids ever seen in the advertising industry, bids which would send shock waves through the whole American advertising industry and force a series of mega-mergers that would help change its shape for ever. 1986 was to be the year of the mega-merger – and the year Saatchi climbed to first place.

14

L'EMPEREUR JACOBY

Robert E. Jacoby is a short man – 5 foot 4½ inches – Napoleonic, cigar-smoking, elfin featured, with a penchant for military heroes (Rommel and Patton). Jacoby ruled the Ted Bates advertising agency autocratically but unimaginatively. He was an advertising man who tends to rouse strong feelings, either of dislike or of admiration, more or less it seems in equal quantities. He gained a *cum laude* economics degree from Princeton, worked as an economic analyst for the Shell Oil company, and on his good days was at least the match of Maurice Saatchi in analysing the problems of a client – or in forecasting the direction in which the advertising industry was going.

Ted Bates had traditionally had a strong chairman. Bates himself was a young vice-president at Benton & Bowles who was given the Colgate Palmolive account to handle. He complained to the Colgate chairman that he found it impossible to get his ideas through to the top management – so, with the toothpaste-maker's backing, he set off on his own. Bates had a very simple view of advertising: that every advertisement should offer an unusual or 'unique' benefit to the consumer. His copywriter, Rosser Reeves, would later spread the gospel in a book, *Reality in Advertising*, which became required reading for all aspiring ad men in the 1960s, and for several decades the American public tuned on to 'It's not just a job, it's an adventure', Bates's campaign for the US navy; or 'Melts in your mouth – not your hand', the campaign for Mars', M & Ms; or 'Get a piece of the Rock' for Prudential.

Jacoby became president of Bates in 1971 and three years later, in 1974, the year its founder died, its third chief executive. The agency now began the most explosive growth period of its history, and by 1985, after a series of acquisitions not far short of the Saatchis' record, Jacoby headed the third largest agency in the world. As he trawled Madison

Avenue for new acquisitions Maurice Saatchi often came across the footprints of Jacoby who had been there before him. In ten years Jacoby made seven acquisitions, bringing into Bates agencies such as William Esty, Campbell-Mithun, AC & R, Cole & Weber, Diner/Hauser/Bates, Sawdon & Bess and McDonald & Little. Jacoby was a workaholic, putting in eighteen-hour days, meeting clients at weekends, spending hours every week in aeroplanes. Bates's skills at 'hard sell' advertising had left the agency with a strong list of packaged-goods clients but few 'image' accounts, and through the 1980s Jacoby was determined to change the balance. In 1982 he hired Mike Becker from Young & Rubicam, then spent $5 million to bring in eighty new staff to beef up the creative department.

Jacoby, now in his late fifties, had seen other trends too. He had been an early adherent of the new doctrine of global markets, probably getting there before the Saatchis, but with less publicity. Bates's worldwide network was certainly far superior to the Compton one. Client conflicts increasingly blocked the way of further takeovers in the USA, so in 1985 Jacoby turned his sights even more intensely on the rest of the world. He bought a 51 per cent stake in Scholz & Friends, based in Hamburg, and announced he was looking in France, Britain and Canada 'where we are not at a ranking commensurate with our total'.

There may have been other reasons for these bids, however. Winston Fletcher, chairman of the British end of Bates, saw a different image from the one presented to the world by Jacoby. He had observed from the inside, he said in an article in *Campaign* in April 1988, the organisation in New York 'reshuffled with the regularity of a poker deck' by Jacoby, whom he described as 'Stalinesque but without the compassion'. Each reshuffle 'promised to be the dawn of a bright new era' which never dawned. Fletcher's analysis of Bates is an interesting one in view of the brothers' thinking at this time – and the message they were trying to get across to Jacoby. He says that Bates's USP philosophy was so deeply embedded it could not be shaken out and was hurting the agency around the world. Bates had been left behind by the changes in the industry in the 1970s and 1980s: 'a new generation of consumers had arrived, young men and women who had grown up with television. They had learned to decode sophisticated advertising messages ... they wanted to be entertained and amused while being sold to.' Bates continued to 'peddle its muscle-bound USP philosophy' and began to lose its market share, a fact which had 'been obfuscated by some spectacular acquisitions'. The agency had always been highly profitable and had, said Fletcher, 'built up a piggy bank with which to fund its growth', which it now achieved through acquisitions rather than winning new clients. But its 'continuing commitment to an outdated and constricting advertising philosophy was a prescription for long-term disaster'. This is a sentiment which uncannily echoes what Maurice Saatchi was preaching to Jacoby, and what other people inside Bates had also come to realise. 'By the mid-eighties,' wrote Fletcher, 'you hardly needed a doctorate in management studies to deduce that Bates was in severe danger of becoming an agency with a great past but no future. I have no doubt whatsoever that the key Bates shareholders in New York reached exactly that conclusion.'

Ted Bates had believed in spreading the equity of the business throughout the executives, but now five senior men, including Jacoby himself, were approaching retirement age. To buy them out would cost at least $150 million, and Jacoby became increasingly convinced that, given what was happening in the industry, a private company could not raise the capital needed to survive and compete. He seriously investigated the possibility of seeking a quotation for Bates's shares, but there was another option which could solve all his problems at once. Fletcher was right in his interpretation. 'I'm going to sell this company within two years,' Jacoby told a meeting of his senior executives in Hawaii in March 1986, 'and I don't give a damn what anybody says about it.'

Bates had not eluded the Saatchi acquisition pitch, but for a variety of reasons it never seemed a starter. Every time Milt Gossett heard rumours that Maurice might be talking to Jacoby he would get on the phone to plead with him to lay off – Compton clients such as Procter & Gamble would simply not accept the conflict with the Bates clients. There were times when other Compton executives found Gossett with his head in his hands, muttering, 'Oh God, what are they up to now?' Sometimes the brothers consulted him about their plans; most often they didn't. The company had taken a floor in the General Motors building in Manhattan, and Andrew Woods, a young merchant banker who had been hired from County Bank, Martin Sorrell's old friends, had set up shop there, combing the market for potential acquisitions, vetting the lists that Maurice continually thrust at him and holding round after round of talks with potential target companies.

Irrespective of what the Saatchis were up to, Madison Avenue was starting to heave with the biggest eruption of merger mania in its history. The takeover wave of the 1980s which had restructured and changed much of industrial America had reached the world of advertising. Few agencies would come through it unscathed.

Gossett did not know it, but the Saatchis were planning their biggest deal yet, one that would cause Gossett, Ed Wax and their team huge agonies and considerable problems. Ted Bates was a definite runner.

The first meeting between the Saatchis and Robert Jacoby in the spring of 1985 to discuss the takeover set the scene for what would prove to be eighteen months of on/off discussion, some acrimony and not a little humour. Maurice persuaded Jacoby that a marriage of their two companies was at least worth seriously talking about, and Jacoby, intrigued by the Saatchi reputation and by the speed at which they seemed to be climbing the ladder, agreed.

They met in London on one of Jacoby's visits there in search of acquisitions. Maurice began with one of his immaculately delivered perorations on the shape and direction of the industry, on how Saatchi had developed and how it saw global markets. The three biggest advertisers in the world, Procter & Gamble, Philip Morris/General Foods and R. J. Reynolds, had all been involved in 'mega-mergers' themselves in the past couple of years, as indeed had almost every company in the *Fortune* 500, the list, published by the business magazine *Fortune*, which measures the biggest companies in the USA. Contrary to the accepted view, the big advertisers were not in any strong moral position to preach against mergers or takeovers in the advertising world. They were the ones who were pushing for greater size and international networks in their advertising agencies, and that could not easily be achieved without further concentration in the industry. In five years the proportion of world advertising expenditure which went through the big eight or nine multinational agencies had risen from 14 to 20 per cent, which still made it a fragmented industry by any other standards. The big clients were increasingly seeing surveys showing them that 60 per cent of companies were centralising their advertising management, and that 75 per cent of advertisers would prefer one global agency to handle their advertising for them. In the future there would just be three or four 'mega global' agencies, and if you were in that group – and it didn't really matter if you were number one, two or three – you could look forward to a secure future, because these trends, now they had taken root, were not going to go into reverse. Large global companies were never going to go back to working with non-global agencies – that period of history was over – but if you were in the top three global agencies the prizes were enormous. The shift to them was gathering momentum and would carry them forward for the next twenty years; there were twenty years of growth built in just by being in that big league. As for advertising expenditure, in 1986 it was running at $160 billion a year. So the prize was not only very considerable but also very secure.

Saatchi was also anticipating other trends: advertising was just one industry, and clients wanted more. They wanted services such as direct marketing, sales promotion, corporate design, public relations and management consultancy; global markets in advertising were just one thing. Thus the company that could offer, under the one roof, all the services a big company needed right around the world was going to be ahead of the game. Saatchi had the resources and the organisation to ensure it was in that position – and a very few companies would dominate that business. Saatchi & Saatchi had announced its intention of getting a 10 per cent share of the world advertising market – and no one now had even got 5 per cent – and 10 per cent of the world markets in consulting, market research and public relations, and that was an achievable target.

On the other hand, if you are not in the top three, what future did you face? A world in which your clients were saying: well, have you really got what it takes? Aren't you a bit of a marginal player in all this?

Jacoby listened in silence, smoking his cigar, raising his eyebrows occasionally at one of Maurice's more ambitious statements, waiting for this carefully prepared and persuasively delivered speech to end. Bates, Maurice went on, had a number of choices. They could say to themselves that they would be one of the surviving mega-agencies, and go out and make some acquisitions of their own, then carry on as they were. They had, the Saatchis had discovered, already talked to a number of investment banks about the possibility of going public. That obviously was one route towards achieving such a goal. Or they could join with another agency that was, whatever happened, going to be one of the top three. By merging with Saatchi, Bates would make the combined group the biggest in the world, so its place in the sun would be assured.

There was a silence when he finished. Then, according to one former Saatchi man, Jacoby removed his cigar from his mouth and spoke, almost for the first time.

'That's very good, Maurice. Now tell me about the dough.'

This first set of negotiations would last over a year, with the papers whizzing to and fro over the transatlantic fax and by special messenger. Jacoby passed the job of dealing with the Saatchis to John A. Hoyne, his quietly spoken, silver-haired, international agency chief. When the rumours on Madison Avenue that year identified Bates as a takeover target – and the word was around – most experts put a price of

$200–$300 million on it. Jacoby, however, wanted $500 million – and he was not interested in one of Maurice's classic 'earn out' deals, developed and perfected by Martin Sorrell, whereby the target received an initial payment with the rest spread over five or ten years, depending on its performance. Jacoby wanted it all up front – or there was no deal. Bates, with its high levels of profitability, was too good to walk away from, however much Jacoby irritated them. The Saatchis, unable to land any of the other big companies they were chasing, began to weaken, but still hoped to work out a deal that suited them as well as Bates.

Just before Christmas 1985, Jacoby went to London again, with John Hoyne, expecting to sign the contract that would formalise the negotiations which had painstakingly moved forward through the summer and autumn. They met the Saatchi team in a London hotel suite. Again Maurice began, not with a peroration this time, but along the lines of 'Since we talked last we've been thinking a little bit more about the concept and the price and . . .' He was not going to meet Jacoby's price, nor his terms for all the money up front. He had another proposal, but it was not what Jacoby wanted to hear. The American listened impatiently for a few minutes, then said abruptly, 'Excuse me, we need to confer', and left the room, followed by Hoyne. Twenty minutes passed while the Saatchi team nervously waited, until finally Hoyne appeared again, this time on his own.

'Could I have Mr Jacoby's coat?' he asked.

Jacoby had gone, furious that the Saatchis had moved their ground. There were other offers on the table back home, and he returned to New York to see if he could tie up something better, or perhaps even persuade the Saatchis to meet his price – up front. 'It was a marvellous tactic by Jacoby,' says a former Saatchi executive. 'We didn't know what pressures he had back home, or what offers he had, but we had read the rumours about McCann's and others. If he was trying to screw more money out of us it was a very effective way of doing it.'

The story leaked to the American trade press. Jacoby denied it, but the Saatchis admitted it. In January *Adweek* quoted an unnamed Saatchi executive as saying: 'There have been meetings. . . . This isn't something the Saatchis will walk away from – even if they're struggling to make a deal.'

In the light of what happened later there is an interesting paragraph in this *Adweek* story. It quotes a Bates executive as saying, 'It could be Jacoby wants more cash than stock from Saatchis', seen by the reporter as a reference to 'the agency's reported $250–300 million price tag'.

The trade press contains a number of other references to prices within this range, which is roughly where Saatchi's valuations put Bates at this time. Jacoby, however, was playing a deeper game, and still believed he could get $500 million for Bates, a price even its good profit record could not justify.

Saatchi entered 1986 with the big prize still elusive. There were plenty of balls in the air, and sooner or later one would be caught. But which? With Bates no longer high on the list – although it was not crossed off – it was time to revive another old favourite: Doyle Dane Bernbach. Bill Bernbach's once great agency would definitely not emerge as one of Maurice's Big Three. It was losing clients, had no proper international network and was clearly going to be taken over. The industry hummed with rumours and stories, reflected in an issue of the *Gallagher Report*, a confidential newsletter in the advertising and marketing industries, which in April 1986 stated that the head of Doyle Dane Bernbach, Barry Loughrane, was 'beating the bushes' in his attempt to find a marriage partner for his $1.7 billion (billings) agency. He had approached the chairman of Needham Harper Worldwide, Keith Reinhard, in mid-March 'with a bid to reinforce Needham thrust'.

Anthony Simonds-Gooding was told by Maurice to get into the bidding for Bernbach and see if it could not be retrieved before it was too late. Simonds-Gooding knew he was starting well behind several other bidders, but, urged on by the brothers, made an appointment to see Loughrane anyway. Saatchi & Saatchi, he told him, was prepared to make an offer in cash which he hoped would at least match, and probably better, what Loughrane had on the table. Loughrane had set up a board meeting to consider the various offers, and Simonds-Gooding now offered to come and address it. He had an offer in his pocket, which he planned to pull out, hoping that would tempt the directors away from some of the more nebulous proposals in front of them. The Bernbach directors, however, did not want Saatchi. 'Martin Sorrell had made a run on behalf of the Saatchis several years before, and there had been some bad feeling over that,' said a Doyle Dane director afterwards. 'So we were sort of anti. BBDO and Needham were fellow Americans, and closer.'

Early in May 1986 the BBDO chairman Allen Rosenshine announced the first of the season's mega-mergers: BBDO, the sixth largest US agency, Needham Harper (number 16) and Doyle Dane Bernbach (number 12) would get together to form an agency with billings of $5 billion – and at least a dozen potential account conflicts. BBDO itself had the $225-million-a-year Chrysler account, while Doyle Dane had the $120 million Volkswagen account. BBDO's $100 million Pillsbury business compared with Doyle Dane's $35 million Nabisco cereal billings. Augie Busch, the head of the giant brewery Anheuser-Busch, withdrew his $50 million Stroh brewing account. However, Rosenshine had achieved at least one objective. As he said: 'We are the biggest – but maybe only for ten minutes.'

The pace of mergers on Madison Avenue was now frenetic. The American Association of Advertising Agencies listed eight mergers in 1984, nineteen in 1985 and eleven in the first four months of 1986. Rosenshine's new holding company, Omnicom, to some extent copied the concept pioneered by Interpublic, the McCann Erickson holding company, which had merged three agency networks under one holding company a decade before. Now there were rumours that more agencies were doing the same thing. Everybody, it seemed, was either taking over or being taken over. There were dark hints about the Saatchis, seen, even after the Bates talks broke down, as the most predatory of all. 'It's hard to say where a company like Saatchi, with such deep pockets, will strike next,' *Time* magazine quoted Abott Jones, president of the Chicago-based Foote Cone & Belding, as saying in its issue of 12 May. It was equally hard to see where any one of a dozen agencies was going to end up; and the Saatchis at that moment had no clearer an idea than anyone else who they might take over.

They did at least have some possibilities – and some successes. While pursuing both Bates and Bernbach they had kept open other talks, and some of them, caught up by the merger mania, came to fruition. In the early months of 1986 Saatchi made two acquisitions of New York advertising agencies, neither of them ranked in the mega-league but still significant additions to the Saatchi & Saatchi empire. The first, in February 1986, was Dancer Fitzgerald Sample, the thirteenth largest agency in the USA, with $876 million of billings. It was another Procter & Gamble house, with a reputation for good creative work, and a talented staff led by Stu Upson. It had taken some time and effort to persuade P & G's chairman John Smale to agree the sale, and Milt Gossett had to be at his most persuasive. Maurice argued that the whole concept was to create a second international advertising group, merging Dorland in London with Dancer Fitzgerald to form a parallel network to the Saatchi & Saatchi Compton one. It was an idea the brothers had been working on for some time as a way around the irritating client-conflict problem. The deal had first been mooted in 1984, and at that stage Smale had killed it. Dancer had around $60 million of P & G business and if he refused to allow too much of his business under the same roof then even the Saatchis at that point were not prepared to push it. Later it would be different.

The deal was a major boost for Jack Rubins, the head of Dorland in London, who since 1981 had run his agency inside the Saatchi empire, keeping its operations – and clients – separate. The new DFS Dorland Worldwide was a fancy name for what was only the sixteenth biggest network, a long way from the 'one, two or three' often quoted by Maurice, but it was another step along the way, and gave Saatchi's some more of the world's top advertisers: Nabisco, Toyota and Wendy's. It cost Saatchi's $75 million.

The Dancer takeover is significant for an additional reason: suddenly the American advertising industry seemed much less impregnable to British takeovers than they had in the past. True, Compton had been taken over, but for a number of years that had seemed an anomaly, a special situation which had come about because of the relationship which Compton had with Saatchi in London. Dancer Fitzgerald in contrast was a straight purchase. *Campaign*, in an editorial, said the significance of the bid was that 'the dominance of American agencies is no longer unchallengeable. The great networks built up before and after the war by the US pioneers are perceptibly running out of steam as competition becomes fiercer and the generation which created them moves gradually aside.' Even the great Doyle Dane Bernbach, it reported, was up for sale.

Campaign ended on a ringing note: 'Is there a world role for other British agencies in this changing scene? None is likely to succeed on quite the scale that Saatchi has, for no other outfit has spent the time and energy (or, arguably, has the required business flair) in gathering itself for the transatlantic leap; but there is clearly room for more partnerships in which it is not necessarily the Americans who will have the final word.'

Campaign had spotted an interesting trend. Martin Sorrell had by this time left the brothers to set up on his own, and he for one began to look closely at what was happening in the American advertising world – would there be a chair for him when the music stopped? It was only now, four years after the Saatchis went to New York, that other British agencies began to think that perhaps they could do the same, that there was nothing written that said the new global agencies had to start in New York or Chicago and then spread to Europe and the Far East. It could go the other way too.

In April 1986 the brothers caused another crop of stories with first sentences such as 'There is no stopping the Saatchi brothers' and 'The ambitions of the Saatchi brothers know no bounds'. They had bought another agency, bigger than Dancer, but still no giant: Backer & Spielvogel was the twenty-third biggest agency in the USA, with revenues of $500 million. Founded only eight years before, it boasted the fastest growth rate in the business, faster even than the Saatchi agency in Charlotte Street. Its addition took Saatchi to within a single bid of being in first place: it had billings of $3.4 billion against Young & Rubicam's $3.6 billion. (Rosenshine's Omnicom merger was still a fortnight away.) Backer & Spielvogel was run by a man who would later become important to the Saatchis: Carl Spielvogel. Spielvogel was actually one of the original architects of the Interpublic giant when he had been assistant to another legend of the industry, Marion Harper.

Born in Brooklyn, the son of a raw-fur processor, Spielvogel was once an advertising columnist for the *New York Times*; he had spent twenty years with Interpublic, the parent company of McCann Erickson, working his way up to vice-chairman, before striking out on his own with five other McCann executives. His own agency was regarded as something of a creative hot-shop, just as the Saatchis had been a decade earlier. It had startled Madison Avenue when it pulled in the entire $85 million Miller beer account two months after its inception, and had forged close links with a small number of major clients who were well pleased with its service – up to a point. Backer & Spielvogel in the mid-1980s was a victim of exactly the circumstances that Maurice had described to Jacoby. The six partners who had left McCann had boasted of their independence and had no intention of selling, until three events occurred. First, their client NCR decided it wanted to develop internationally, and Spielvogel was forced to put together a patchwork of independent agencies to accommodate it, in London going to Martin Boase of Boase Massimi Pollitt, carefully avoiding Saatchi because of its position in New York. Then another major client, Philip Morris, took over General Foods, and suddenly there were another five agencies in the PM family, all of them far bigger than little Backer & Spielvogel. The biggest blow was the third: the Miller High Life and Lowenbrau accounts went to J. Walter Thompson. 'The loss of Miller sobered us,' said Spielvogel. 'We realised that you need a critical mass of stability to sleep easy at night. For a long time we knew we had to sell. Miller's loss made us realise we should sell sooner rather than later.'

Backer & Spielvogel was an attractive agency, with excellent growth and potential – if someone could supply the global network. Saatchi was by no means the only agency Speilvogel talked to; in those months on Madison Avenue everyone seemed to be talking to everyone else. He had talks with Don Johnston of JWT, with Bill Phillips of Ogilvy and with others.

When Spielvogel first met the Saatchis it was about something else entirely. He is a man deeply involved in *pro bono publico* works – a trustee of Mount Sinai Medical Center, a member of the Municipal Art Society's board and chairman of the Committee on the Public Interest which helped save New York from bankruptcy. He is also head of the business committee of the Metropolitan Museum of Art, and it was in that capacity that he called on Charles Saatchi, the great art collector rather than the great advertising man. He persuaded Charles to join his business committee at the Met, and the contact, once made, continued.

It was Maurice who one day in the spring of 1986 told Spielvogel that the Bates deal was off: he could not agree terms with Jacoby. That news was all over Madison Avenue in any case. So was the word that Backer & Spielvogel was seeking a home. Maurice offered him one. 'We'd be prepared to run you independently at all times. You want access to international facilities; we'll provide that. You want access to direct marketing and promotion; we'll provide that too.' All the areas where Spielvogel knew his agency was losing out could be filled in by Saatchi.

Compared with many of the other negotiations the purchase of Backer & Spielvogel was a relatively straightforward one. Maurice and Spielvogel did most of the negotiating themselves, and Spielvogel, seventeen years older, soon realised that the innocent-looking Maurice was an astute and experienced negotiator. Several times the talks broke down, but finally they had a deal, and Spielvogel went off to tell his clients about it before finally signing. Unlike Jacoby, Spielvogel had agreed to the Saatchi 'earn out' formula; he and his six partners were paid $56 million down, the rest to be earned over six years.

It was announced in April to an industry now seething with rumour and proposed deals. By then, unknown to Spielvogel, the Bates talks were on again.

The first week in May 1986 witnessed impossible, absurd rumours in the industry. Ogilvy & Mather was to team up with Interpublic to form a colossus which would outdo everybody; JWT and Young & Rubicam were to merge. Bates was linked with BBDO – or with any of another half-dozen agencies. Some rumours had some factual basis, since most companies at this stage were talking to at least one other agency. Several, like Bates, were doing the rounds, negotiating the Saatchi price higher and higher. Some talks even ended in deals: Foote Cone & Belding took over Leber Katz of New York, the Omnnicom trio got together, and in London Lowe Howard-Spink & Bell (now including Tim Bell) bought the privately owned Allen Brady & Marsh, while Wight Collins Rutherford Scott, which houses a number of former Saatchi men, joined forces with FCO.

Meanwhile Robert Jacoby quietly let it be known that he favoured a deal with Interpublic. At Compton, Gossett, staying closely in touch with the big clients, particularly Procter & Gamble in Cincinnatti, was relieved to hear it – he kept passing on messages to the brothers that P & G would undoubtedly remove some accounts if the brothers were so foolish as to buy Bates. Bates had Colgate Palmolive, the big rival to P & G, and the Cincinnatti company had indicated clearly it would not stand for it. Gossett had been brought up to believe that no one ever dared buck P & G, and he was highly nervous about the outcome. 'Don't do it,' he pleaded. The brothers decided to ignore him – they would make their peace with P & G later. The whole issue of client conflict was up in the air in the merger hothouse, and either they would run Bates as an independent agency, in the same way they were offering to run Backer & Spielvogel, or they would merge it with Backer to complete the second global network under their umbrella. They were once again taking a bold jump into the unknown – and loving the thrill of it.

In April John Hoyne, Jacoby's number two, sent out messages that Bates was interested in a deal with Saatchi – but with no earn-out, and at a price of $450 million, $150 million more than Saatchi had offered six months before. Maurice finally rang Jacoby. They were interested, he said. The Saatchi merger team under Andrew Woods looked at their figures again. Bates would cost them more than twice as much as they had spent on all the thirty-seven acquisitions they had made in their whole existence. The war-chest was empty. To pay for Backer & Spielvogel they were committed to a rights issue. It was finally decided to raise all the money in one go: a £406 million rights issue, one of the biggest the London stock market had ever seen, only topped by Lord Hanson and Sir Gordon White when they raised over £500 million to pay for SCM Corp, the old Smith-Corona typewriter company. If the Bates bid still fell through, Saatchi would use the money for something else. The issue of shares brought the market value of Saatchi above the £1 billion mark for the first time (and the brothers' stake below 5 per cent) – where it would stay only briefly. In value terms at least, if not yet in billings, it was the biggest advertising business the world had ever seen.

The final deal took less than a week to negotiate. There was in fact little room for negotiation; Jacoby set his price, and his terms, and Saatchi agreed to meet them. Shrewd as they were in the area of negotiation, the Saatchis had never come up against a Bob Jacoby before; he knew exactly what the Saatchis wanted to do, knew the options open to them and saw, as the windows of opportunity closed, that they needed Bates – or they risked being shut out of Maurice's 'one, two or three'. Bates would make them number one, and would give them that security for the next twenty years that they wanted so badly. They should pay a premium for it. Jacoby himself would receive $70 million from the deal, and a further $40 million for his voting shares in the agency, which everyone had assumed had little or no monetary value – $110 million in all, much more than anyone had made in the entire history of the industry. It would make him richer than the brothers. It was also agreed that he would still be in charge, with a five-year contract paying him $1 million a year – which was also more than the brothers were paid.

In the final weeks before the deal was announced Jacoby allowed thirty staff members, many of them low-level ones, to buy more than 1000 shares each in Bates, thus making some of them millionaires. Those not included grumbled furiously, but Jacoby pointed out that he had helped the people who 'got to me first'. There was widespread gossip in the agency that one beneficiary was a woman friend, but Jacoby has repeatedly denied it.

The deal, when it was finally announced, had been so well signposted that it was not a surprise; but it was still a major story. This was partly because of its size, partly because of the names – the Saatchis and Bates were both well known beyond Madison Avenue – but mostly because it brought to a head the concern growing throughout the industry and beyond at the enormous rush of mergers and takeovers. On the morning the bid was announced (12 May 1986) the *Wall Street Journal* quoted Jacoby as already making plans to expand his about-to-be-expanded group. 'We have a list of 30 possible acquisitions world-wide. But the opportunities aren't good, because it's been picked over to a fare-thee-well. There's nothing of quality.' The next day's *New York Post*, which carried a picture of Jacoby, huge cigar in hand, at his

27th-floor office on 1515 Broadway, reported: 'Wall Street analysts, who had been slow to turn their eyes uptown at what was once thought of as a flaky business, are now recommending that institutions invest their funds in the largest agencies.'

If that had been true a few months before, it no longer was. The rumblings from Cincinnatti were reverberating through the country – Procter & Gamble had said it would punish Saatchi if it took over Bates. Now it could not back down, even if it wanted to. Other clients were less than happy too. The Saatchis, it was reported, had gone too far. Milt Gossett was said to be in despair.

Jacoby was widely quoted as defending the bid on the grounds that agencies without global capacity 'can't go it alone', but that message was not appreciated on Wall Street. 'This fetish for bigness. . . is beside the point. It's big for big's sake,' said Alan Gottesman, an advertising analyst at L. F. Rothschild, Unterberg Towbin. 'When was the last time you encountered synergism, except in a crossword puzzle?' Roy Grace, who had just left Doyle Dane Bernbach as executive creative director because of that agency's chase for 'this imponderable size, this mindless size without meaning', was critical too. 'Advertising is really a personal service, and the bigger it gets, the more impersonal it becomes. It's not like manufacturing sausages.'

These criticisms were directed, at least in these early days, as much at Rosenshine and the merger he had put together under a new holding company, Omnicom, as it was at Saatchi. However, there was a special edge to the Saatchi criticisms which soon began to assert itself. 'Our industry is going through fundamental changes and consolidation,' said John Bernbach, president of Doyle Dane Bernbach International, who had observed the Saatchis at work when he was in London, 'and the changed environment is due entirely [to the Saatchis]. We are all living in the environment they created.'

Given what was happening in every other American industry at that time, this is a considerable overstatement. Sooner or later merger fever had to arrive on Madison Avenue, and even the Saatchis' most ardent critics, including Ogilvy & Mather (itself the product of a series of mergers and acquisitions) would not remain immune. Did Boone Pickens change the environment of the oil industry? Or Rupert Murdoch and Ted Turner the media industry? Or Carl Icahn the airline industry? Perhaps; but a historian with a longer perspective might argue that these men, and the other predators of the day – Jimmy Goldsmith, Lord Hanson, Irwin Jacobs, Ron Perelman – were only pawns in a much longer game of restructuring, where the forces for change were present and irresistible, and that the Saatchis were simply the most visible element in that change. Put another way, if the Saatchis had never ventured out of Golden Square would American advertising – and therefore world advertising – be any different from what it is today? We have already seen how the Saatchis were not the first to discover Ted Levitt – and even Levitt was not the first to discover globalisation. They did not invent the forces which were driving the business into bigger and bigger units; they did not create the retreat of the American multinationals, or the fall in the US dollar which resulted in foreign companies sweeping into the United States and taking over many of the companies which had come to symbolise Americanisation to the outside world, leading *Time Magazine* to lament, in November 1987, 'suddenly, the US seems to have become a country for sale, a huge shopping mart in which foreigners are energetically filling up their carts.'

The Saatchis were certainly in the forefront in identifying some of these forces, and in using them for their own special purposes. What they succeeded in doing was *persuading* the world that they had invented globalisation. They were not even the first British agency to buy into America: Geers Gross had done it in January 1978, and another British business, Lopex, bought a minority stake in Warwick Welsh & Miller, a New York agency a few years later. It is possible to argue too that Ogilvy & Mather was originally a British invasion of Madison Avenue.

Again it is the perception that matters – the Saatchis rewrote the history, not deliberately perhaps, but simply by allowing people to persuade themselves that that's how it was.

They also did something more – they contributed to a general undermining of confidence of the New York agencies in their own creative product. 'We've grown up in awe of American advertising,' said Maurice Saatchi in 1982. 'It's been our mother's milk. But now it's generally accepted that British advertising is the best in the world, and we'd like to wave the flag a little.' It wasn't at all generally accepted then – or even later. Television advertising had developed differently in Britain for a variety of reasons: for a start it was a decade later, so could learn from American mistakes; it grew up on better technology than that to which American business had been accustomed; and because British commercial television groups the ads together in less frequent interruptions to programmes, as Ed Wax said, it was forced to be more entertaining to catch the attention of its audience.

When the Saatchis arrived in New York they came as the flag-carrier for a whole school of 'British advertising'. And it worked, at least limitedly. Like it or loathe it, Saatchi & Saatchi today has a reputation in New York as a 'creative agency'. Ask anyone what they like about its ads, and they will remember three: the pregnant man, 'Labour isn't working' and the Manhattan landing sequence for British Airways. Saatchi has gone on winning as many prizes as ever for its creative work, and with Charles and Jeremy Sinclair watching over it, it produces some fine work. But did it have great new creative lessons to teach the Americans? Ed Wax at Compton would dispute that; Stu Upson at Dancer would probably resent it; and Carl Spielvogel would definitely reject it. For their part the Saatchis were clever enough to know their own limitations; even had they wanted to, they could never impose their own creative ideas on the big New York agencies they acquired. It simply wouldn't work.

For better or worse in May 1986 they had taken over Ted Bates, with Bob Jacoby and all. They had achieved the objective Charles had set years before: they were bigger than anyone else. No one, not JWT or Ogilvy or anyone else in the world, would ever look down on them again. True, the Saatchis had long since ceased to care about that aspect of it and were focusing several stages ahead; but they could still allow themselves a few hours of celebration – before beginning to sort out the problems they had created for themselves. Many of these they had anticipated, but nothing could have prepared them for the difficulties that lay ahead.

15

MACBATES

'After sealing their latest deal, [the Saatchis] sent champagne to Bates executives,' reported *Business Week* on 26 May 1986. 'If all goes well, that may be the last they hear from Maurice and Charles Saatchi.' The magazine was commenting on the Saatchi way of running its subsidiaries, allowing them autonomy and considerable freedom. It quoted Michael Wahl, chairman of the Howard Marlboro sales promotion company of New York, bought for $14 million in 1985: 'Their style is not to become involved unless there's a problem.'

But there *would* be problems at Bates – perhaps the worst the Saatchis had encountered in their business career. It would not be many months before the celebrations over getting to that first place changed to anger and bitterness. Within a year Charles Saatchi would be complaining about the 'pain' that the deal was putting the brothers through, and wondering plaintively whether it would ever end. If everything had gone right for the Saatchis to that point, the next eighteen months were a time when they suddenly went wrong.

The first fallout from the Bates deal was the Saatchi share price. For eleven years it had risen rapidly, taking the Saatchi fortune with it, so that by April 1986, on the eve of the Bates takeover, the value of the brothers' holding, listed in their joint names in the accounts, was £35 million. By the autumn that had fallen by more than £12 million, and a year after that, after the 19 October crash in 1987, had more than halved. Bates was by no means the only cause of that fall; but that deal marked the high point, only touched fleetingly again, for the share price – and in many ways that was the height of the Saatchi magic too. As Anthony Simonds-Gooding began the task of producing some order from the mass of companies that had been acquired, he turned to Charles to say:

'You know, you're not a real company until you've gone through adversity and then come out the other side. You've had such a gilded life, you don't know what it's like until you've felt pain.'

Charles glowered, but later turned it into a joke, firing it back at Simonds-Gooding. Every time there was a new bit of bad news, he would come in the next morning and say: 'Have we had enough pain yet? Are we big boys now?'

The task facing the company was immense. Bates was the thirty-eighth successful takeover by the Saatchis since they began, a fast enough rate averaged over sixteen years. However, some of those years had seen no bids at all: the first bid came in 1973 when they had been in business three years, there was nothing in 1976 or 1977 after they absorbed Compton-Garland, and even in 1978 and 1979 the only bids were Hall's in Edinburgh for £2 million and O'Kennedy Brindley in Dublin for £250,000. 1980 was again blank and 1981 was the year of the Dorland's deal which cost £7.1 million. It was from the moment they took over Compton in the USA that the acceleration began: three bids in 1982, two the following year, then seven in 1984, twelve in 1985 and now three considerable agencies in the first five months of 1986. Add to this the fact that Bates itself was every bit as predatory as Saatchi, that its billings at the time of the merger were almost dollar for dollar equal to Saatchi worldwide, and that there was no love lost between the heads of the different agencies, and one has some idea of the problems now faced. The atmosphere after the rush of mega-bids became antagonistic both inside the industry and among some of the clients, and that spread to Wall Street and to the press. Martin Sorrell had been the person most active in keeping open the lines of communication to the Wall Street analysts, but he was gone, and in these months his absence was felt. Greg M. Ostroff, an analyst in the Wall Street house Goldman Sachs, had followed Saatchi for several years and put a lot of his clients in the stock. Now some of the pain spread to him too.

At six o'clock in the morning I would get up and sleepwalk to the front door, pick up the *New York Times* and turn straight to the advertising column. Anything nasty that had happened to Saatchi was put in a box. If I saw a box my heart would start palpitating; I would get to the office, call London which did all the trading, find out what was going on, write something up, and try to get on with the rest of my work. If there wasn't a box I'd go back to sleep, then come in and have a normal day. The trade press, which had given so much coverage to the Saatchis since they arrived in New York, was really gunning for these guys, and giving them their come-uppance. I mean, the first eight pages of *Adweek* and *Ad Age* each week were filled up for a six-month period with Saatchi stories: who's gonna leave, who's worried about getting merged, and what clients are gonna storm out. Stuff like that.

Charlie Crane of Pru Bache, another major Wall Street house, also watched the change of status with concern for his investors.

The speed with which they had grown their business in the early 1980s did manage to turn a few heads. And the vehemence with which they claimed they were going to be number one in such a short period of time was one which was met initially with scepticism. After they got going and really started rolling in these acquisitions, people started thinking: 'Maybe they can do it, let's buy the stock, and drive up the share price in anticipation of their succeeding; if anybody can do it, they probably can.' I suppose now [this was January 1988] that many of the financial decisions are ultimately questionable in hindsight. If indeed investors bought the concept that they would be number one, and bought into the shares on that basis, what do you do when they achieve that goal? What's next? What can you do when you're already at the top of the heap? Create a new heap? Probably – that's what they are trying to do with the consulting arm. And what then? A third heap?

Saatchi & Saatchi had until this point plenty of fans both on Wall Street and in the City of London. Crane comments:

One of the things they deserve an awful lot of credit for is positioning their company as one worthy of a high rating on their stock. They convinced the City that the agency business was one of the few true growth industries for UK investors. And they persuaded quite a few people over here too, on a different basis. The agency business in the States was a fairly mature one, with some growth left, but it was no Silicon Valley. In Britain and on the Continent it was a growth business, and in the States they could grow fast too by acquisitions, then make them perform a little bit better – which is what they did, greatly improving the margins of Compton for instance. It was a good line to pitch to the financial community and they pitched it well. They learned first and foremost that it wasn't a bad thing to hype your own story, and their connections with the trade press are the stuff of legend.

Crane and other Wall Street analysts who came to follow Saatchi after the Compton deal all made money for their clients on the share price rise, and Crane observes:

They really did succeed in improving Compton. Not so much through devastating head-count reductions, although there were certainly cutbacks. It was through watching where the money flowed, making sure it flowed at the right pace and through the right hands. What I saw was not only a change in the financial strength of what had been a longstanding satisfactory agency but I also saw the introduction of a new creative spirit there. The quality of the product that emanated from Compton was higher, more daring, as if the staff had been released from their financial worries and were prepared to be freer spirits.

All of this had driven up the Saatchi price and given them an image no advertising business had ever had – often by choice. Most big agencies in New York were run by advertising rather than financial people. David Ogilvy could boast, 'I cannot read a balance sheet, work a computer, ski, sail, play golf or paint. But when it comes to creative advertising, *Advertising Age* says I am the "creative King".' The Saatchis *could* read a balance sheet, particularly Maurice, and from the beginning had a clear understanding of the financial aspects of what they were doing. They had used the stock market to finance their growth in a way that no other agency anywhere in the world had even thought of. Greg Ostroff again:

> One of the problems in covering agencies as an analyst is that they're run by agency people. They don't run these businesses as businesses should be run. The Saatchis were unique in that. They had, up to the time of Bates, been going along well, courting the financial community, raising capital, buying businesses and using rigid financial management techniques on those businesses to get the proper margin out of them, and making these acquisitions pay for themselves. I guess that on Madison Avenue in general, from a purist's point of view, that was not looked on with favour.

It wasn't. David Ogilvy, in a new edition of his *Confessions* published in 1987, showed how he hated this element. In a clear reference to the Saatchis, he wrote that one of the major problems facing the industry was 'the emergence of megalomaniacs whose mind-set is more financial than creative. They are building empires by buying up other agencies, to the consternation of their clients. They have never heard of the South Sea Bubble.'

That view could be heard all along Madison Avenue in the summer and autumn of 1986. The Saatchis had taken one step too far. Their latest leap had not landed them on the next building, and they were in trouble, said the gossip. And if it hadn't been for the damage they were seen to be doing to the entire American advertising industry there would have been an unrestrained air of *Schadenfreude*. Bob Jacoby was not widely popular, and had become even less popular when it was realised how much money the Saatchis had paid him. For anyone in the advertising industry to get $110 million was regarded as disgraceful;

for Jacoby to get it was almost obscene. It was clients' money, it was argued, and if advertising agencies were so hugely profitable maybe the clients were paying too much. 'There was clearly an attitude of waiting with bated breath for these guys finally to make a mistake,' says Ostroff. 'Then every dog would have its day.'

In the months after the Bates takeover it seemed to the Saatchis that the dogs of Madison Avenue were indeed having their day – and the cats of Wall Street and the City of London too.

The weekend of the Bates bid I found Maurice in his office in Charlotte Street looking relaxed and contemplative. I still have my notes of that conversation and in the light of events since it is interesting to look back on that meeting. The brothers clearly were not anticipating any problems. Maurice had received a phone call at 3 am the previous night from Bob Jacoby to tell him that everything had been worked out with the lawyers, and the deal was done. He had also received a large cake, sent to 'Charles, Maurice and the boys' from Sir John (now Lord) King, as a celebratory gift from one of their favourite clients. That morning he ran through the wider arguments that he had at his finger-tips: the need for size, the impact of the big mergers among the major clients which were driving agencies into still larger units, the fact that Saatchi & Saatchi was well short of its stated target of having 10 per cent of the world advertising market, and even further away from the target of 10 per cent of the other markets they had identified – consult-ancy, research and public relations, plus all the ancillary services that revolved around these. But at least Saatchi & Saatchi now had a critical mass which would guarantee its position for some years to come. He expounded on the relationship with Procter & Gamble, which had been so important for them, basically because P & G were in the forefront in developing globally, and Saatchi had been able to observe it and learn from it. Just that week P & G had appointed a Pampers brand general manager for Europe, running the whole of Europe as a single market. Managements were being aligned across regional boundaries – in every industry.

Maurice was not interested in talking about Bates; that deal was done, and he wanted to go on. One of the key aspects of it was that they were the market leader, so that people would no longer laugh when they talked about achieving market leadership in the much bigger and faster-growing markets of consultancy and research. The combined groups would be world leaders in direct marketing too, so that the

Bates acquisition accomplished two targets while making the others look more achievable. It would take some time, but it should be in place by the end of the century. It had taken sixteen years to do what they had done, and probably would take an equal amount to achieve the rest. By that stage he and Charles would be . . . He paused to work out their exact ages then.

'A couple of old buffers,' I interjected helpfully.

Maurice roared with laughter. 'Exactly. A couple of old buffers sitting under a palm tree in the Bahamas!'

Clearly he did not mean it, because in the next breath he was talking about motivation, the desire, as strong as ever in both of them, to get the job done, and the excitement of *doing*, of putting it all together. Sheer size, he said, gave them no particular pleasure; what did excite them both was translating their concepts and ideas into practice, combining size with dynamism in a way few companies could achieve – keeping people motivated.

He had read a new book that had inspired him, which showed how many good companies were run along what the author called the 'tight/loose principle'. It described Saatchi & Saatchi perfectly, he felt – a combination of loose controls in terms of allowing the individual companies their autonomy, and tightness in terms of financial control. This was the system that Simonds-Gooding was installing throughout the enlarged communications part of the group, and that was how it would be run around the world.

Meanwhile on the other side of the Atlantic Bob Jacoby was enjoying the success of his deal. On 22 May 1986 he held a meeting of Bates stockholders, complete with slides. The agency's book value, he showed, was $390 a share (analysts put it at much less than that). Jacoby then showed another slide displaying the price that Saatchi had paid: $853.02 a share. There was a spontaneous burst of applause. Jacoby might not be a hero on Madison Avenue, but he had done well for his fellow stockholders.

It was another few weeks before the full implications of the deal began to come through. That same month Bernard Gallagher sent out a gloomy view to clients of his private newsletter, the *Gallagher Report*. The current mega-merger movement among ad agencies, said the report, was the 'most significant development in advertising in 20 years', but there would be a major fallout over the next three to five years. Many of the deals were highly leveraged (Saatchi's, financed by a share placing, was not), and had been 'fuelled by deal-makers', timed to cash in on the merger mentality which was sweeping through the industry and beyond. The interests of the clients had been forgotten, and there was no indication of improved services or increased efficiencies. The super-agency concept, it added, was viable only if it was conceived with the interests of the client paramount to the financial rewards of the principals involved. He forecast the reversal of the globalisation trend and the return of the 'boutique' era of the 1960s with the birth of a whole new group of agencies led by a new generation of Bill Bernbachs and Mary Wells.

Indeed, as the Saatchis would soon discover, all was far from well. Forrest Mars, head of Mars Inc., soon let it be known he personally was disturbed by the Bates takeover. The Mars account was worth $100 million a year in billings to Bates; now Forrest Mars himself ordered a review of the entire Mars $200-million-a-year advertising budget. Worse was to follow. Colgate Palmolive withdrew $80 million and the Warner-Lambert Company, Bates's biggest domestic client with annual billings of $68million, indicated it was about to move too.

In June Robert Jacoby was elected chairman of the American Association of Advertising Agencies, the industry's trade group. He found his peers in that organisation highly critical of his sale to Saatchi, but at first shrugged it off. 'They're just jealous,' he said to his wife. Only there seemed more to it than that. When the Saatchis heard the rumours about Warner-Lambert, a major rival to Procter & Gamble, Jacoby is said to have assured them the account was on 'solid ground'. The Warner-Lambert president, Melvin R. Goodes, took a different line. When he learned of the takeover his first question was: 'How much does Jacoby make out of it?' When he was told it was over $100 million he was appalled. 'What is Procter & Gamble going to do about this?' was his second question. Others wanted to know the answer to that question too. Goodes didn't wait to find out. In June he sacked Bates as his advertising agency.

Procter & Gamble meanwhile had no intention of letting the deal pass without showing the Saatchi brothers the full weight of its anger. Milt Gossett was the man who had to field most anger, as P & G had always been his special account. For him the Bates acquisition was a bitter blow. The brothers, he said, should never have done it. He had visited them several times in London to try to dissuade them, and listened as they in turn inveighed against Bob Jacoby, who they said was really taking them to the cleaners. 'Bates is everything that you say you don't want,' argued Gossett. 'You are buying the antithesis of what this company ought to be. We have a reputation of being creative before anything else. Well, Bates is not very creative.' The brothers calmly told him they would change all that, and he shouldn't worry about it; but Gossett did, particularly when P & G warned him of what they would do if the brothers insisted on going through with the takeover.

Gossett urged Maurice to travel to Cincinnatti, see John Smale, the head of P & G, tell him and the man in charge of P & G's huge advertising budget, Robert V. Goldstein, what he intended to do – and fall back on their mercy. The brothers were against that. They loved to have P & G on their books, but they would not kowtow to any client.

There was pride on both sides. Smale had let the world know of his disapproval, and he could scarcely back off now, even if he wanted to. On 16 June the *Gallagher Report*, in its terse shorthand style, had another key mention of Saatchi. Smale, it said, had reined in the brothers, and told 'the boys to call halt to ad agency acquisition spree (primarily P & G houses) or face client defections. . . . Maurice takes to road to appease clients.'

Maurice had indeed at last taken to the road. Charles, of course, had never been to Cincinnatti, but he urged Maurice to make the trip now. He knew how well liked Maurice was within Procter & Gamble and it was clear to him, as it was to Maurice, that only a personal visit could head off serious trouble.

In June Maurice flew to New York, collected Milt Gossett and Simonds-Gooding, who had now more or less based himself in New York, and together they flew on to Cincinnatti, one hour and 50 minutes flying time from New York, for a meeting with Smale and what seemed to be half the senior executives of P & G.

Maurice's charm did not let them down. Simonds-Gooding was continually astonished by Maurice's ability to get on with people, but even by those standards this trip was a revelation to him. In Cincinnatti he found Maurice something of a celebrity among the P & G wives: 'Someone would always invite us back to their place for dinner, and all the others would come round, and there would be half a dozen top P & G men and their wives, all old enough to be Maurice's parents, and the wives sort of treated him like a little son. "Well, Maurice, what have you been up to? You've been naughty again, we hear, and caused a lot of trouble, and you really shouldn't do this." They adored Maurice, and he loved it.'

Gossett was also a calming influence in Cincinnatti, and he had done his best to keep things on an even keel. Nothing, however, could easily cool the anger of Smale and his colleagues. Procter & Gamble prides itself on being the most professional marketing company in the world – almost a university of the subject. It has systems which have been developed, refined and added to over decades. It is the biggest advertiser in the USA, spending $819 million in 1986, just ahead of Philip Morris with $815 million, and a long way ahead of the numbers three and four, R. J. Reynolds and General Motors, both around $450 million. It has developed tight systems for controlling its advertising expenditure, measuring its effectiveness and its ability to create the all-important brand image. Possibly no company in the world works as closely with its advertising agencies as P & G does. From Cincinnatti executives boast they are in daily contact with every one of them and agency executives are required to visit Cincinnatti every so often for what the industry calls 'indoctrination' sessions. An agency with a P & G account has to work within very close confines but in return receives big rewards – and loyalty. P & G does not lightly change its agencies – the magazine *Marketing Week* worked out that on average P & G's agencies (largely Leo Burnett; Grey; Wells Rich Greene; D'Arcy Masius Benton & Bowles – and of course Saatchi & Saatchi Compton) have been working for it for thirty-seven years. It is big and powerful enough to set strict limits on what other clients its chosen agencies should have – and it hated their being broken. Never in its history had the conventions been flouted as flagrantly as the Saatchis had now done.

The meeting the first morning was a stiff one, but went better than the Saatchi people could reasonably have expected. Saatchi would not get off completely – P & G would withdraw its $6 million Encaprin account from Dancer Fitzgerald (now renamed DFS Dorland World-wide) – but that was only a light slap. There was also a severe warning that P & G was not happy and that it would watch events, particularly at Bates, with keen interest. Fond as it was of Compton and Saatchi, it would not hesitate to protect its products.

Maurice continued his tour of the USA, desperately trying to stop further defections. He visited Mars in McLean, Virginia, just outside Washington, for another uncomfortable meeting. In Minneapolis he had a tough session with Art Schultze, the president of the grocery products division of General Mills, who was reported to be taking a hard line over $125 million of billings at DFS Dorland Worldwide, plus another $50 million of spending at another Saatchi shop, Campbell-Mithun. Simonds-Gooding seemed to be living on a plane, dashing from one account to another, in between trying to pull together the threads of his vastly expanded operation.

The losses went on. On 23 June Gallagher reported further trouble: Bates was about to lose some General Foods business. 'Reason: Bates "compromised" cardinal principle of GF agencies (must retain flexibility in coffee ad efforts).' Bates handled Maxim and Mellow Roast coffees, as well as Oscar Meyer and Louis Rich meats; but at Compton the Saatchi group handled Folgers and High Point, two P & G brands.

Week by week the account losses mounted, with rumours of much more. The Bates takeover was not actually consummated until 6 August, three months after it was announced, and by then the stream of losses was considerable, most of them at Bates. RJR Nabisco pulled out $96 million of billings, Michelob another $38 million, Ralston $12 million and McDonald's $8 million. Backer & Spielvogel lost some clients too, and so did the other Saatchi agencies: ABC dropped McCaffrey & McCall, and Helene Curtis dropped DFS Dorland. By mid-August the account losses came to $359 million, almost all from Bates – and more were on the way. Early in September Gallagher reported that Saatchi was taking a hard line with General Mills chairman Brewster Atwater: 'offer to resign $170 million in GM business. Reason: Atwater adamant over elimination of client conflicts.' There had been some gains too – Bates had won a $48 million Xerox account and RJR Nabisco, dropping $96 million of billings from Bates, had given DFS Dorland $32 million. Even so, the net loss that summer was considerable.

By early September the Saatchi price was hitting new lows for the year, and the brothers' equanimity had long faded. Much of their anger was directed at Jacoby, who they felt had not done enough to stop the fallout. It seemed to be a never-ending spiral of account losses, which damaged morale and their reputation, leading to still further losses – and then to redundancies. All over Madison Avenue agencies, particularly those involved in the mega-mergers, were laying off people, creating further bitterness.

The scene was set for the most damaging blow yet – something which was probably inevitable from the beginning but which the Saatchis had not foreseen: war with Bob Jacoby.

The departure of Jacoby from Ted Bates was actually not of the Saatchis' making, at least not directly. The brothers and their head of communications, Tony Simonds-Gooding, found themselves propelled into it because of a boardroom battle between Jacoby and two members of his own staff, Larry Light and Donald M. Zuckert. Light, forty-six, was a Montreal-born intellectual who had cultivated in particular Forrest E. Mars, the domineering head of Mars Inc., makers of Kal Kan pet foods, Uncle Ben's rice and seven of the world's bestselling chocolate bars. According to the *New York Times*, 'the superdedicated Mars appreciated both Light's strategic repositioning of Snickers candy bars as an adult snack and Light's ability to bring himself to tears in evocative paeans to Milky Ways and the American consumer.' The legendarily frugal billionaire was also said to approve Light's unpretentiousness. 'Larry wears the same blue suit every day and his buttons are always popping,' a Bates executive was quoted as saying. 'To Forrest he's a man of the people.'

Zuckert was fifty-three, an overweight, heavily built man whom Jacoby had promoted in 1983 to president of Bates New York – the number two in the organisation. The two men had not got on, with Jacoby accusing Zuckert of not being tough enough and Zuckert complaining he was being picked on. Jacoby, he said, would 'cut you to ribbons with a very sharp tongue'. On another occasion he declared, 'Bob believed in personal conflict and fear.'

Zuckert and Light were now to feature at the centre of a tragic drama that *Advertising Age*, in a neat Shakespearean allusion, called 'MacBates', and which capped for the brothers what had already been the worst summer of their careers.

On the night before the Bates deal was signed, Light refused to agree to his new employment contract, thus threatening the sale. He demanded promotion to the role occupied by John Hoyne, who had negotiated the Saatchi deal: president of Bates International. Hoyne had served Jacoby well throughout the deal, but faced with the collapse of the Saatchi talks once again the chairman gave in. He suspected that right through 1986 Zuckert and Light, neither of them close to him any more, were meeting at weekends to discuss how they could advance their careers inside the agency, and later accused them of plotting to take away accounts, including Mars. Both men denied it.

Simonds-Gooding spent most of that summer, when he wasn't trying to put his finger in the dyke, working out how to reorganise his vast communications empire. He controlled 14,000 people in four agencies. Bates could stand on its own as a global network inside the Saatchi stable, with access to all the various special companies Saatchi owned: Siegel & Gale (corporate design), Clancy Shulman and Rowland (PR), Howard Marlboro (sales promotion) and so on. What of the others: Saatchi & Saatchi Compton, the first agency they owned in the USA, Dancer Fitzgerald Sample, already merged with Dorland but scarcely a global agency, and Backer & Spielvogel? There were all sorts of client conflicts and staffing problems, as he juggled the various possibilities.

In August he outlined some of his thoughts to Jacoby, whose analytical mind he had come to admire. 'You are obviously the key player in this, and I look to you as an ally. I am an Englishman, and I don't know this market. I need your support.' Simonds-Gooding had probably said something very similar to Gossett, to Stu Upson and Carl Spielvogel, but he was, as any good manager would be, anxious to take everyone along with him. Jacoby seemed perfectly willing to oblige. 'You paid the money, and you tell me what you want, and we'll do it. I'll tell you if it's wrong, but if you want it we'll do it.' Simonds-Gooding had heard of Jacoby's reputation as something of a tyrant – the trade press liked to caricature him as Napoleon because of his size, his autocratic air and his love for military figures – but invariably found him pleasant and amusing company. In those months before Bates officially became Saatchi's he had a series of detailed and constructive discussions with Jacoby, each time more impressed with his grasp of the business and his thoughts on how the different agencies could be run. Whatever else might be said of him, the American was a professional to his fingertips.

At Bates, some of the others saw a different and much less co-operative Jacoby. 'Here was a guy who had the hammer and sold the hammer, and once you sell the hammer you can't swing it any more,' said Don Zuckert. 'Someone here said that once Bob sold the agency he couldn't accept the fact that he was a hired hand.'

Simonds-Gooding, however, reported back to the brothers that Jacoby seemed much maligned, and that Napoleon seemed to be on their side after all. 'I'm having no problems with him. He's absolutely delightful.'

'Well, you know why that is, don't you?' said Charles. 'He's got about $100 million of our money in his wallet. Cash!'

On 7 August Jacoby wrote to both Maurice and Simonds-Gooding to say he wanted to make some management changes. Zuckert, he said, had done a good job for him but he was now tired out. 'Zuckert is a housekeeper and I would have changed his role whether you bought us or not,' he wrote. He proposed to promote a new man he had hired in 1985: John H. Nichols, a forty-nine-year-old Texan, whom he had brought in from the Chicago agency Leo Burnett and put in charge of getting new business. He also wanted to promote John Hoyne, who would become Jacoby's number two, which would mean that Larry Light reported to Hoyne rather than to Jacoby. This would, he explained, free Jacoby to help Simonds-Gooding, now spending more and more time in New York, with the great affairs of state with which he was having to deal. The Saatchi executives were non-committal – the message went back that Jacoby should obviously run the company the way he thought fit, but everything was about to be reorganised and the new roles might not fit the organisation. They suggested he wait until Simonds-Gooding had got an overall structure clear in his mind before doing anything. However, the brothers were keen to show Jacoby how much they appreciated him. 'We have not come across anyone quite as dynamic and determined as you have been,' wrote Maurice in a letter dated 19 August 1986. 'It is a new experience for us and a very pleasant one.' It would not be pleasant for long.

Early in September Simonds-Gooding, after a brief time back in London, set off again for New York on a week's programme to see all four top Saatchi executives: Stu Upson, head of DFS Dorland, Carl Spielvogel of Backer & Spielvogel, Gossett at Saatchi & Saatchi Compton and Jacoby at Bates. He made the same speech to each one: they were his four top people and he trusted them. They had to help him find a way of pulling all the businesses into an organisation which would work and benefit the whole company – and benefit each of them individually too. Everyone must gain out of it. He was, he said, giving each of the four the same information, and he wanted them to confer, then he would come back in a week and they would get down to the serious business of thinking where they should go from there.

Jacoby that morning was less responsive than he had been. Simonds-Gooding spent two hours with him going over his rough plans. As he was leaving, Jacoby said: 'You know that organisational thing I was talking about – involving Zuckert and Light? I'd like to do that now.'

Simonds-Gooding hesitated – he didn't know any of the four people involved, and couldn't assess it. 'I'll ask you two questions,' he said. 'Will it militate against any of these manoeuvres?'

The answer was no.

'Will it cause any disruption?'

'Zuckert will be happier than a pig in shit,' said Jacoby. 'He has $22 million, and he can go and think how to spend it, and he'll do administration. Nichols is very good. Larry Light is pleased to have a solid finance man to help with the business. And of course I will then be free to help you with your dream and make it happen.'

Simonds-Gooding agreed, and set off on his rounds. That evening, Wednesday, 3 September 1986, Jacoby scribbled a note to Zuckert in pencil, gave one further memo to his secretary, and left for a camping holiday in Colorado – out of reach of everyone except his secretary, who kept this fact to herself. 'There was a saying in Bates that among Jacoby's interests were booze, money, women and revenge. And this was revenge. The deal was over and he was going to put one on Light and Zuckert,' says a former executive. The next morning when Zuckert and Light appeared there was consternation. Light discovered that Hoyne was now senior to him, while Bates executives recall hearing an outburst of shouting from Zuckert's office. The memo told him he had been replaced as New York president by Nichols.

That day Simonds-Gooding was passing by the Bates office in Broadway, still doing his rounds. He needed a lavatory, and suddenly decided he might as well avail himself of a Saatchi facility. He went up to the executive floor and as he was standing at the urinal he suddenly found Zuckert beside him.

The Bates executive was still angry. 'You might want to look at this,' he said, waving a bit of paper. 'It's going to cost you two or three million dollars.'

Simonds-Gooding assumed it must be litigation of some sort. 'I don't want to talk about it here. Let's go to your office.'

When he opened up the paper he found it contained an announcement of the management changes together with photographs of Nichols and Hoyne and Jacoby's pencilled note to Zuckert. There was also a copy of Zuckert's reply, telling him of his extreme anger at the way he was being treated after twenty years working for him, that his contract had been broken, and that he demanded to be reinstated in full. Zuckert had also sent a note to the staff along the lines of 'You will have been as surprised as me to learn . . .' – which gave the others some hint of his distress at the move.

Zuckert then gave Simonds-Gooding a long and unflattering lecture on Jacoby, and the problems in store for Saatchi. 'You didn't think properly about this, you didn't do due diligence,' he said, pointing his finger accusingly at the Saatchi executive. Saatchi, according to Zuckert, had brought the problems on itself by underestimating Jacoby, whose last-minute granting of Bates stock 'received notoriety that whipped through the halls like crazy'. He also told Simonds-Gooding that Jacoby was drinking excessively, something which Jacoby later denied to the *New York Times*, which quoted him as saying: 'I had to drink to be successful in the advertising business. But I don't think you would find anybody who ever saw me drunk and nonfunctional.'

The Englishman was exhausted after flying the Atlantic and his round of meetings, and sat there completely impassively. Even Zuckert was impressed by his calm. Finally Simonds-Gooding said he would see Hoyne, who was at that moment the most senior person present in the agency.

'Fine,' said Zuckert. 'You do that. This is all public knowledge now.

There's nothing that I've said which is off the record. I'm giving it to you as a board member.'

Simonds-Gooding then went to Hoyne's office, where Hoyne tried to be reassuring. 'Don't worry about it. Relax, it will all pass. If you want me to see Larry, I'll see Larry.'

By the time Simonds-Gooding arrived at Milt Gossett's office for his next appointment, he discovered the news was out. Gossett greeted him with, 'Have you heard about Bates? It's all over the street.'

That afternoon Greg Ostroff had a phone call from one of his investors at his office in Goldman Sachs. 'We hear Bob Jacoby's disappeared.' That was dramatic news, of great significance to the Saatchi share price. Ostroff rang a contact at Bates. Yes, she said, Jacoby was not there.

'Did you fire him, or did he quit?'

'Well, neither,' said the friend.

'Then where is he?'

There was a pause.

'Well – we don't know!'

Jacoby could not be contacted – he was said to be on a farm without a phone. There was much talk of sending a helicopter to find him, but in the evidence later presented at his case for unfair dismissal it turned out he was in daily contact with his secretary. The story began hitting the press, and there were waves of complaint from clients. Without Jacoby, Zuckert and Light were able to rally a large number of Bates staff behind them; and advertising executives know how to apply pressure on their masters: do it through the clients.

A few days later Maurice Saatchi had a call from Forrest Mars. It was terse and to the point. Jacoby learned of the call at his arbitration hearing, and according to his version it went thus: 'My good friend Larry Light doesn't like what Jacoby's done, and I don't like it when Larry is unhappy. Fix it.' Mars put the phone down. From Cincinnatti came angry growls from Saatchi's biggest client, Procter & Gamble. This was getting too much. Clients had received a circular letter from Jacoby setting out the changes, and they resented that. 'Who are these guys?' asked one client. 'I don't know Hoyne or Nichols from a hole in the ground.'

On the Monday morning Greg Ostroff rang up his friend at Bates again. The rumours over the weekend had made many of his investors in Saatchi & Saatchi very nervous, and he was looking for information to evaluate the changes. Just what was going on? 'Listen, it's Monday morning, and he's not around. You guys are telling me that you didn't fire him, and he didn't quit. Well, he's surely pissed off.'

On 10 September, the Procter & Gamble volcano which had been rumbling in increasing anger at Saatchi's all summer finally erupted. P & G would not let Saatchi's off lightly this time. It decided to withdraw $85-million-worth of its foods business from Saatchi & Saatchi Compton New York. Out went the Crisco Oil and Duncan Hines business from Compton, while DFS Dorland lost Luv's diapers and Bounty paper towels. P&G typically was prepared to limit the damage. Greg Ostroff that day sent a note to investors saying, 'We have spoken to P & G, who report that this does not reflect on the quality of the advertising from Saatchi's agencies but that because of their strict no-conflict policy these moves were necessary. Saatchi retains P & G's soaps and detergents business and remains Procter's lead agency worldwide.' None the less it was the most savage blow yet, and convinced the brothers they had to take drastic action immediately. They could not risk losing the Mars account, which would almost certainly go if Light left. And Light would not stay if Jacoby did.

Simonds-Gooding finally made contact with Jacoby on the evening of 10 September when Jacoby arrived in Lake Tahoe, Nevada, for the American Association of Advertising Agencies western region convention. The brothers told Simonds-Gooding what they wanted him to do with Bates: merge it as rapidly as possible with one of the others. The instructions were passed on by Charles, who dealt with Simonds-Gooding almost daily. 'Perm any combination you want – but do it fast,' he told him. Charles originally preferred to put Bates under the Compton umbrella in the hope it would help with the Procter & Gamble problems, but Simonds-Gooding soon decided whom he wanted in charge of it: it had to be Spielvogel. In the cabinet of New York advertising executives he was trying to put together, he found that Spielvogel was the only one the others 'would bend the knee to'. Charles, in his gloomier moments, prompted Simonds-Gooding to go a stage further, and do a 'big bang': merge Bates with both Compton and Backer & Spielvogel, to create one huge Saatchi & Saatchi business worldwide, run by Spielvogel, and build a Saatchi brand name that would be even greater than that of Young & Rubicam or Ogilvy. That would have been a dramatic – and probably foolhardy – leap, but the brothers say they saw it only as their 'doomsday scenario' to be carried through only if the account losses became cataclysmic. Simonds-Gooding, however, found himself working on just that scenario for several months.

When Simonds-Gooding talked to Jacoby in Lake Tahoe he came straight to his central point. 'I want to meet you to discuss the merger of Bates,' he said. Even the tough Jacoby had not expected this. His contract, he protested, stipulated that he should run an independent Bates for five years. The Saatchi executive was no longer interested in that. Saatchi owned Bates and it was going to make whatever changes it wanted. Jacoby could not go on running Bates, not with the present turmoil. He would have to stand aside from the agency, work for Simonds-Gooding directly in the public company Saatchi & Saatchi and help him put the agencies together, a job, argued the Saatchi executive, which was very important, and which still gave Jacoby credibility and responsibility. The one role he could not go back to was the chairmanship of Bates – that was over. Further, Simonds-Gooding was reversing the decisions about Zuckert and Light. Nichols and Hoyne, Jacoby's two favourites, would be demoted again.

Jacoby would not move easily. He had no interest in the job Simonds-Gooding was offering him. Disdainfully, he ordered his portrait to be taken down off the wall on the twenty-seventh floor, and sent Saatchi a $3,000 cheque for it, saying he wanted it for his daughter. Then he went off to Washington for another advertising convention, leaving the Bates staff to stare at the empty space on the wall.

That Friday Simonds-Gooding called the Bates board together – twenty-eight of them, even without Jacoby. He was abrupt and to the point. Jacoby would be shifted, would continue in a different role in the Saatchi organisation, but would not be running Bates. Zuckert was taking over as chief executive officer. They must all act to stem the loss of clients, and to restore morale. Jacoby, according to the *New York Times* account, got the news later that day when Steven W. Colford, *Advertising Age*'s Washington bureau chief, interrupted him at the AAAA conference. 'Did you know you'd been fired?' When Jacoby got back to New York that night on the eastern shuttle, his driver, meeting him at La Guardia, confirmed that Zuckert was now the chief executive officer.

Jacoby of course had not been fired. He was still being paid $1 million a year and he continued to go into the office; but his power was gone, and he could not take seriously the job that Simonds-Gooding intended for him. He and Zuckert had booked a skiing holiday together over Christmas, but they avoided each other in the corridor. The rumours continued: Jacoby was said to be about to be investigated by the Securities and Exchange Commission (which was total fantasy), while stories of the big stock gifts he had made on the eve of the Saatchi bid became more and more racy – and absurd.

On 22 September the knowledgeable Gallagher newsletter reported that Jacoby had given 'the thumbs down' on the offer as assistant to Simonds-Gooding. He had been 'shown door in biggest executive purge in ad agency history'. However, the return of Larry Light had defused the Mars time bomb – that account at least was safe for the present.

In fact Jacoby stood it until 21 October when he finally quit and sued Saatchi's for breach of contract. He won his case – getting another $5 million to add to the $110 million he had already made. It was this money which now, as much as anything else, became the focus for the industry's wrath. 'Everyone knows that Bob Jacoby got enough money to compete with the Sheik of Araby,' said Leonard S. Matthews, president of the AAAA (Jacoby had to resign as chairman of the AAAA when he left Bates). 'We may stand today looking more like hucksters than when Frederick Wakeman wrote the book twenty-five years ago.'

From the head of Young & Rubicam, Ed Ney, came an even more damaging remark that is still quoted around New York: 'I thought this particular merger was an unfortunate occurrence, because I never saw anything said about we're doing this to give better service to the clients. The reason it wasn't said is it couldn't be said. What was said was we're the biggest. In the consumer service business that's just nonsense.'

Zuckert, whose first action was to fire John Nichols, hit back, but he was very much on the defensive. 'Clearly I wish this had never happened. It would have been a lot easier to do a Douglas MacArthur and just fade away. Clearly, we must be the major new business target of every agency in town. On the one hand they're saying this is bad for the industry and then they're giving all these stories to the press about how awful mega-mergers are. I wish Ed Ney would put us in Y & R's profit-sharing plan. We've given them half of their new business this year.'

From Wall Street came the view that the ruckus had been damaging for the whole level of investment interest in the advertising sector. 'In the short run, it will contribute to all the old fears that investors have about ad agencies,' said Charlie Crane of Prudential-Bache: 'that the assets do go down with the elevators, and that this is not all that stable a business.'

As the crisis deepened, so the pressure put on Simonds-Gooding by Charles to find a solution increased. Through September and into October Simonds-Gooding pressed ahead at full speed with the concept of the Great Merger. He knew the chances were against it, but he believed – wrongly, according to the brothers – that it was what Charles and Maurice wanted him to do. It was to be textbook stuff: everything would be grouped under the Saatchi & Saatchi brand name, including the consulting group – one huge and unified Saatchi & Saatchi brand applying to everything right around the world. Taken region by region, Saatchi was not number one everywhere, but if there was just one business, in the same way there was one Young & Rubicam, the brand would be a clear world leader. 'It was a wonderfully manic concept that appealed to Charles,' says a former Saatchi executive.

Only it could never work – and it didn't. Simonds-Gooding was exhausted and his strategic thinking was flawed. In London the brothers had taken such a battering they were not thinking with their usual coolness. It might have been possible to do it organisationally, with the goodwill of the New York agency heads; but the clients simply would not accept it.

At Compton, Gossett and Wax reluctantly went along with it, although they didn't like it. 'It was just hell for them, this concept,' says a former Saatchi man. But the two men had begun to realise that in the drive towards globalisation even Saatchi & Saatchi Compton was not big enough on its own, and needed more of the Saatchi pieces to keep them ahead. Don Zuckert raised no objections, although Bates would in effect disappear, particularly if Spielvogel was running the whole thing. 'With Jacoby gone, Bates is like a headless chicken,' Simonds-Gooding told the brothers in London.

Once again it was Smale in Cincinnatti who put his foot down, killing any faint hope of Simonds-Gooding's 'big bang'. Gossett and Wax, the two men least enthusiastic about Charles's dream, were sent out to P & G to sell them the concept. They came back, as one executive put it, 'with their tails between their legs'. Procter would have nothing to do with it. Their dislike of Bates as an agency was such that they would not let it near any part of their account. They also pointed out that if the three agencies were combined all over the world, every Saatchi office in America, Australia, Britain and elsewhere was going to be turned upside-down. They were not prepared to accept the damage this would have on the handling of their own business. 'They said: "Forget it," ' Gossett reported back. 'They said, if you're going to put these three agencies together, they're off. The whole account. It's not on.'

Simonds-Gooding was back at square one. He had made no progress in merging Bates with any of the other Saatchi agencies, and abruptly the brothers changed tack. They would not merge anything, but would leave them all as they were – separate, autonomous units running inside the Saatchi & Saatchi holding company. The defections were now slowing, new business was coming in, the shares were bouncing back well in the continuing bull market and actually ended the year more or less where they started. They would get on with building the other divisions of the group and leave what they called 'migraine city' alone for a while.

It was Simonds-Gooding who early in 1987 argued that this route would not work either. Over the autumn they had pulled back in new business more or less what had been lost, although the new accounts did not have quite the same quality. The point was, however, that the growth had gone: the whole motive behind taking over these agencies was to produce an accelerated growth-rate for the company, and after a year of standstill they were 20 per cent behind where they should be. In the meantime the executives of Compton had urged Wax to consider a merger of the agency, and asked him to work out what agencies they could merge with.

Simonds-Gooding flew back to London to present the situation to Charles and Maurice. 'We have a real problem, and doing nothing will not solve it. Nobody understands what we are about. We have Backer & Spielvogel sitting there, a big agency. We have Bates, still a headless chicken with endless client defections post-Jacoby. We have DFS Dorland which we pretend is a third world network but it's not. Compton in New York has lost the P & G business and is bleeding. DFS are complaining that they too have lost Procter business and a lot of Cadbury's because we now have Mars, and none of it has anything to do with them; they're not winning the pitches they used to.'

He proposed going back to New York and working out a complete new structure for all the agencies. He would talk to the clients, to the agency executives, to everyone who could contribute to the debate. Then he would come back with a plan and put it to the full board. Simonds-Gooding had been at the group long enough to know that Saatchi & Saatchi did not have full board meetings as other companies did – Charles was constitutionally incapable of sitting through a full meeting, and no one at Saatchi had ever seen him do it. However, this was an issue that Simonds-Gooding thought was so important it would have to be considered by everyone, and he would need the complete backing of the directors to put it into effect.

The brothers were not enthusiastic about the option that Simonds-Gooding now recommended: one of 'manageable units'. However, they would go along with it. But 'speed it up' they urged him. He flew back to New York.

*

One morning in January 1987 Carl Spielvogel was in his office in 1140 West Street when Simonds-Gooding came through on the phone. Could he come and see him? He had something important to say. Spielvogel was intrigued. He had watched with some concern as the Saatchi share price had collapsed in the summer, clients had defected, and attacks were made in the press – at one stage Simonds-Gooding, tracked to his hotel, had resorted to putting a paper bag over his face. Spielvogel had been slightly detached from it, but none the less it had brushed off on him too. He hated the controversy into which he had unwittingly put himself and what one Saatchi executive called the 'noise, noise, noise' of the critics. Charles Peebler of Bozell Jacobs Kenyon & Eckhardt labelled the mega-merger trend an advertising version of Chernobyl where the fallout could damage the whole industry – a remark directed straight at Saatchi and those, including Spielvogel, who had sold their businesses to it.

When Simonds-Gooding turned up, Spielvogel thought he looked tired and drawn. The days when the English executive could sit in Tim Bell's old office with nothing to do had long disappeared. Now he had given up the 'big bang' plan and was about to propose something else. He sat on Spielvogel's couch and began: 'I'd like you to consider something. I'd like you to consider taking over Bates.'

Spielvogel was startled; he had never even thought about it. However, when he did, he reckoned it was not at all a bad idea. Backer & Spielvogel had a reputation as a creative agency and Bates did not. It made sense to do it that way around. He became an enthusiastic supporter as Simonds-Gooding outlined the rest of his plan.

It would take months of extraordinarily delicate and painful negotiation, during which time the brothers left him alone, but from the spring onwards Simonds-Gooding began putting his changes into effect, merging some of the smaller agencies, including McCaffrey & McCall with Rumrill-Royt, and a three-way AC & R/DHB & Bess.

It was June 1987 before Simonds-Gooding finally put the first major stage of his plan into effect. Dancer Fitzgerald would be merged with Saatchi & Saatchi Compton to form a new agency called Saatchi & Saatchi Worldwide, with its major North American subsidiary called Saatchi & Saatchi DFS Compton Inc. Its combined annual billings would be $2.3 billion and it would have ninety-eight offices in fifty-four countries. Dorland was left out of it, becoming again a stand-alone London agency, the attempt at creating a Third World network having ended. Jack Rubins departed in disgust. One part of the empire now had some order to it.

What about Bates? Simonds-Gooding had put into effect his plan for this troubled agency too. On 15 July, after months of rumour, manoeuvring, denials and changes of course, the announcement was made: Backer & Spielvogel would merge with Bates. Significantly Carl Spielvogel would be the chairman, and the name of his agency came first in the new title, Backer Spielvogel Bates Worldwide. Billings were $2.7 billion, and the agency had 104 offices in forty-six countries. Zuckert was to be chief operating officer (he has since left), but there was no doubt in anyone's mind whose agency this was: the fifty-eight-year-old Spielvogel had emerged on top, and his creative reputation, it was hoped, would set a new tone for Bates. 'The wind is at our backs,' said Spielvogel that day. 'Let's spread our wings and run with it.'

The rest of Simonds-Gooding's plan for the empire was complex, but equally practical. He had soon learned that within the Saatchi organisation the Charlotte Street agency, although now only a subsidiary of a subsidiary, was still 'the holy grail'; it had, he told the brothers, a 'bunker mentality', although in effect the philosophy and the driving force for the whole group came from there. If the philosophy were to be injected into other parts of the group, he had to bring the Charlotte Street management much more to the fore. Roy Warman and Terry Bannister found themselves elevated to running a new international division, a reward for the way in which they had successfully replaced Tim Bell, and Bill Muirhead moved up to become chairman of the agency.

There were still other bits to be sorted out. A number of the smaller agencies were lifted out of these two agencies altogether: Campbell-Mithun, William Esty, AC & R/DHB & Bess and Stern Walters/Earle Ludgin reported direct to the Saatchi parent.

By the autumn of 1987 the agency side of Saatchi & Saatchi was relatively calm and the new networks were settling down well. It was then that the man who had done so much of the work at Saatchi revealed he had decided to leave.

Simonds-Gooding had been head-hunted as early as May 1987, just as he was putting the finishing touches to the mergers of the agencies. 'I was absolutely hell-bent on finishing the task,' he says. 'The adrenalin was really flowing, and I was going to do it or die – literally die – in the attempt.' As the pressure eased, he gradually came to realise that what he was doing was not sustainable, and that his personal life had gone by the board. His wife had gone with him to New York, but he had seen little of his children, and the pressure had been extraordinary. Once the organisation was in place his job was essentially done. The agencies would have to run themselves.

He had come both to admire and like the brothers a great deal, but he realised that they saw his role in a different light. He would always be the man they sent in to clean up the mess their big bold leaps created. He was now offered an exciting new job – to head British Satellite Broadcasting, a private-sector consortium which planned to put a satellite in orbit over Britain, and offer viewers three new television channels. It was an entirely new business which offered an entirely different form of challenge.

The brothers were gracious about letting him go. Perhaps they felt he had no real future role in their organisation either, although Charles awkwardly offered his thanks for Simonds-Gooding's success in sorting out the problems in New York. He stayed through the summer for the announcements of the mergers, then left quietly in October, when there was a lull in the publicity and the controversy that seemed to follow Saatchi & Saatchi.

As for Jacoby, he linked up with his old mates Hoyne and Light again to make two takeover bids. The former Saatchi finance director Martin Sorrell beat them for control of J. Walter Thompson in yet another bold British move into Madison Avenue, then Hoyne and Jacoby bought a stake in Ogilvy & Mather, but sold out again when they discovered the O & M board wanted nothing to do with them. Jacoby ruminated on his defeat for months afterwards at his sprawling ranch-house in Saddle River, New Jersey, and planned a comeback.

'It would be fun to have something that would get me closer to knocking off the Saatchis,' he said. 'It's easy to do because I can see these guys are amateurs.'

The brothers, however, had for the moment put New York to the back of their minds. There were more pressing problems back home in London.

16

ENTER JOSEPHINE HART

The takeover of Ted Bates and of the other agencies in the United States may not have gone according to plan – not by a long way – but by the time the new structure was in place the analysts in the City of London and on Wall Street had grudgingly come to accept that Saatchi had probably, overall, got it right. For the year ended September 1986, which included only a few months of Bates, profits rose 73 per cent to £70 million. Much of that increase was accounted for by acquisition; but the bottom-line figure, the one the analysts look at most closely, showed that earnings per share were up 21 per cent, dividends rose 20 per cent and profit margins, at 15.8 per cent among the highest in the industry, were up 18 per cent. Saatchi & Saatchi, whatever its problems, was still a financial success.

The following year, 1987, was the year of the big reorganisation of the agencies, the year when all those account losses and Charles's 'pain' should show through in the accounts. Yet profits rose another 77 per cent to £124 million, a figure beyond the dreams of any company in the history of the advertising industry. Again both earnings per share and dividends per share rose by more than 20 per cent. Financially the brothers remained as surefooted as ever. From the end of 1986 there was a renewed flow of recommendations from the stockbrokers and analysts who followed the advertising sector. In December, Emma H. Hill, an analyst at Schroder Wertheim, the New York investment house, told her clients that Saatchi 'remains our primary recommendation'. It had, she said, 'been one of the most eventful years (to date) in Saatchi's dynamic history', but she reckoned that its management 'had distinguished itself in two regards – first its vision and second its financial discipline'. County Securities USA, a New York subsidiary of NatWest Bank, made the shares a strong buy, and elaborated on this to say that its recommendation was both 'quantitatively and conceptually based'. The 'quantitative' aspect was, of course, the profit record and prospects – which looked good. 'The conceptual part of our recommendation is that Saatchi is becoming the prototype of the communications/business service company of the future.' Saatchi was the only agency stock listed in Paine Webber's 'attractive' list that December; and there were several others who thought the same. Time would prove the analysts wrong, at least for the next couple of years. The shares had bounced back, but were again under-performing the rest of the bull market and did not rise above their pre-Bates peak. However, as 1987 progressed and the shape of the new agencies was clearly identified, the perception of the Bates purchase changed. Yes, it was agreed, Saatchi had paid a high price, and, yes, Jacoby had done well for himself and for Bates's other stockholders. On the other hand, Saatchi was now so well positioned with its two parallel world networks, and good people at the top of each one, that it had probably been worth it.

Back in London the brothers moved offices in early 1987, leaving the premises in Charlotte Street, which were bursting at the seams and which they had extended into the adjoining buildings. Ever since the takeover of Compton New York in 1982, Charlotte Street had essentially been the home of a satellite agency. From that moment Saatchi & Saatchi had become a holding company, and as acquisition followed acquisition the need for a separate headquarters became more and more apparent. The takeover of a small advertising agency and public-relations business, Grandfield Rork Collins, brought with it a short-term lease on that same building in Lower Regent Street where they had moved in 1974. The brothers went to look at it and discovered a top floor that was used only for storage. Maurice poked a ceiling and found a large skylight. There was another one at the other end. This was the place for them. They had the top (sixth) floor done up, the skylights uncovered, and moved into the brightest and airiest offices they had ever had, the brothers as usual opposite each other, separated only by a small lobby. Simonds-Gooding moved with them.

The new offices provided space to display more of the Saatchi art collection. Charles and Doris had by now opened their own art gallery in St John's Wood, in North London, but big as it was it could contain less than a fifth of the rapidly growing collection. In any case, the public company, Saatchi & Saatchi plc, owned around 20 per cent of the art, so it rightfully belonged in its corridors and offices. It was not to everyone's taste, of course, but no one complained to Charles.

A dozen years had passed since they had last occupied that Regent Street building, and it had seen changes in their private lives as well

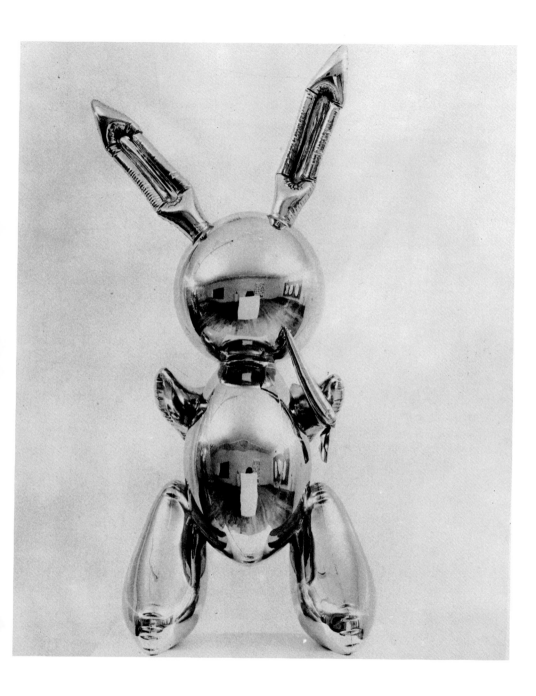

One of the centrepieces of a Saatchi exhibition, NY ART NOW, which featured some of Charles and Doris Saatchi's collection of East Village artists. The stainless steel rabbit is by Jeff Koons, a Saatchi favourite, better known for his vacuum cleaners in glass cases or basket balls suspended in water.

Election 1983

Cecil Parkinson (*below right*), Party chairman, never had the same relationship with Tim Bell as Thorneycroft did in 1979; but he delivered Mrs Thatcher her second victory.

Tim Bell (*right*), pictured appreciating the initiative of a young man seeking a job in advertising, was once seen as the 'third brother'. He joked that he was in fact the 'ampersand' in Saatchi & Saatchi. By 1983 he and the brothers were falling out.

Michael Dobbs worked in Mrs Thatcher's private office before the 1979 election, but she didn't offer him a job in Downing Street. In 1983 he worked as assistant to Tim Bell and in the 1987 election, as chief of staff in Conservative Central Office, he was at the centre of the battle between Norman Tebbit, Lord Young and the three advertising agencies, all claiming credit for Mrs Thatcher's victory. Now Director of Communications at Saatchi.

Election 1987

Norman Tebbit (*below*), once seen as heir apparent to Mrs Thatcher, was at a low point when this picture was taken in the Tory Party chairman's office in August 1986. The next day the Prime Minister rang him to make it up.

The slickness with which the Labour Party presented its leader, Neil Kinnock, in the first party election broadcast of the campaign, caught the Tories – and Saatchi – by surprise. But it was not translated into votes.

Lord Young (*bottom*) met secretly with Tim Bell and other 'exiles' who advised Thatcher during the campaign. He was not a Saatchi fan. The brothers resigned the Tory Party account after the election.

Martin Sorrell (*top left*) learned much from the brothers. He jumped from being finance director of Saatchi & Saatchi to staging a dramatic $560m bid for J. Walter Thompson, the 'university of advertising'. When the brothers decided to become bankers, Maurice first went to see Sir Peter Middleton in the Treasury (*top right*). He was noncommittal.

Midland Bank chairman Sir Kit MacMahon (*bottom left*) rocked Maurice: 'What would you do if we had to write off another £1 billion?'

David Davies, chief executive of Hill Samuel (*bottom right*), was impressed with Maurice's plans for banking; only the fall in the Saatchi share price prevented a deal.

as in the company. The brothers themselves had probably changed very little; physically they were both still trim with no suggestion of paunchiness or grey hair, and despite their wealth and fame neither had lost any of his shyness. Charles might have been more reclusive, but he was far from a Howard Hughes: he still played snooker, cards and chess with the same group of friends; he kept in close contact with the people who interested him – he talks most days on the telephone to David Puttnam, for example – and had made a wide number of new acquaintances in the art world. Doris's interest in contemporary art had brought a new dimension to his life, one which had become as important to him as the advertising business. Just as Maurice had come to know the lobby of every major advertising agency in New York, so Charles knew most of the Greenwich Village galleries. Both brothers went at least once a week to see their parents, who were ageing gracefully, and Nathan and Daisy remained a constant in both their lives.

Yet changes there had been, more for Maurice than for Charles. Maurice's marriage to Gillian Osband had originally seemed the ideal match; they had known each other since childhood and had grown up together in the same North London Jewish community. Neither brother had ever lacked for girlfriends before their marriage, but of all the girls they took home Gillian must have seemed the most suitable to their parents. Tall, with a mass of red hair, and a considerable sense of humour, Gillian had plenty of admirers. Wealthy in her own right, she continued to be independent of Maurice after they were married, working both as a children's book editor and then as a writer, and keeping her own name; and Maurice seems to have encouraged her to do so. Colleagues remember her at the Bologna Children's Book Fair, the big event of the season, where 'she stopped hearts and turned heads with her mini-skirts and her fluffy angora sweaters'. She created a considerable reputation for herself in the children's book world with her own special style of book. 'The archetypal Gillian book is full of jokes and activities,' says a colleague. 'She puts it all together herself, maps out the ideas – hundreds of ideas – and really keys it into children.'

They moved to a house in a secluded estate called the Vale of Health in Hampstead. It was a very private, very expensive bit of real estate. It was a large two-storey, villa-style house, set behind an 8-foot wall. The grounds were so spacious they gave the impression of countryside. One friend described it as 'one of the most beautiful houses I've been in', although it was not to everyone's taste. There was a garage big enough to house some of Maurice's cars (although most of them were in the basement garage at the company) and room enough in the house for his collection of old trains and toys. Gillian was a highly social person, with a wide range of friends and contacts, and loved to entertain – people from the publishing world, from the film industry, from the field of music and elsewhere. To the outside world they seemed an idyllically happy couple – which they were for the first eight or nine years. But Maurice's closest friends had been aware since the early 1980s that all was not well with the marriage.

The brothers have always had the ability to compartmentalise their lives. For instance, Tim Bell, in all the years he worked with Charles Saatchi, had never been to his house, and nor had many of the others. Similarly Maurice, although friendly and charming to clients and colleagues, still retained a reserve which few penetrated. Unlike Bell, neither brother had the slightest interest in playing the 'friend of Margaret Thatcher' card, and they stayed well away from the cocktail party circuit haunted by the politicians and City men. Nor did they mix their private lives with their business lives. Neither Doris nor Gillian was to be seen much about the office, although Doris did turn up from time to time to take Charles off to a new exhibition or a West End show. Doris, more than Gillian, was willing to play the director's wife when it was required, taking some trouble over such tasks as buying Christmas presents for the staff. 'Maurice would personally go off on Christmas Eve and buy people strange presents – bars of exotic soap or something like that – and he would wrap them up or put them in an envelope in his office and come out, be slightly embarrassed, and say, "Happy Christmas", and run off again,' says Nick Crean. With Charles and Doris, Christmas presents were something of an event. Doris usually organised them, and they came, says one former staff member, 'unbelievably beautifully wrapped with ribbons all over them, from Tiffany's or somewhere like that'. The odder the present, the more fun Charles had in presenting it. 'One present they gave me was a silver key to wind up my toothpaste,' says Nick Crean. 'It was the sort of present that Doris thought was amusing to give. And Charles laughed and said, "I bet you can't guess what it is." Which I couldn't. It was another little game to him.'

Gillian and Doris Saatchi had little in common. Doris was ten years older, and, despite all the years she had lived and worked in London, she remained an American immigrant in a foreign country. Ask her friends what they think about her and they say, 'She's very *American*', as if that were enough to describe her. They seem to mean a person who never merged herself into her adopted country but retained some of the elements the British tend to classify as *American*: chatty but cool, given to much more obvious analysis of her friends and acquaintances, with fewer inhibitions – and, of course, an American accent. She had majored in French and minored in English, at Smith College, and then went to the Sorbonne in Paris. It was there she became interested in art for the first time, studying French art up to the impressionists. Back in New York and later London, she switched on to Minimal New York art when most of her fellow-countrymen despised it. She wrote free-lance articles for a number of publications, including *The World of Interiors*, *Artscribe* and *Architectural Review* and was for a time the London editor of *House and Garden*. One profile describes her as 'blonde, figure kept trim by twice-weekly visits to Dreas Reyneke, bodybuilder to the famous. Mousy or glamorous, depending on who is doing the talking. Typical transatlantic laid-back-but-tough-as-hell image. Keen socialiser.'

Gillian lived her own life, keeping her distance from the Saatchi office and staff. Neither wife had any children, and Daisy complained that none of her four sons had yet made her a grandmother.

Both marriages eventually broke up, Maurice's several years before Charles's. Maurice first met Josephine Hart, a tall, attractive Irish woman who was another of Lindsay Masters's success stories, when he joined Haymarket in 1967. She was working one day in the advertising department when some of the other girls mentioned the new arrival in the building. Since he was going to be involved in the same magazine, *Campaign* – Maurice in a more junior capacity – and because the girls described him as 'young, appealing and attractive', she went down to see him. Maurice was twenty-one but seemed even younger, and Josephine was twenty-five. She reported back to the other girls that he was 'not my type at all'. However, soon they were working side by side and became friends as well as colleagues. Romance between them would wait another ten years.

Josephine came from a very different background from Maurice's – or from Gillian Osband's. She was brought up in a typically close Irish Catholic family; her father owned a garage in Mullingar, an unlovely town on the edge of the great bog that makes up much of the centre of Ireland. She went to a Catholic boarding-school, which may not have taught her much about life outside the convent walls, but gave her an excellent literary education. Her father, like many Irishmen of his generation, loved poetry and recited to his children endlessly; Josephine from her early years knew by heart most of Goldsmith's *Deserted Village* and much else. English, however, was the only subject she learned in that language – her maths, Latin, history and even French were taught in Gaelic, which under the Irish education system gained her five extra percentage points in national examinations. Her great love, besides English literature, was acting, and she won prizes in competitions all over Ireland, reciting her prepared pieces to judges from RADA and other British drama schools. One woman, awarding her first prize, said, 'This girl breaks all the rules – magnificently.' She was the eldest of a family of five, but in her last year at school a brother and a sister died in separate incidents and she returned home to look after her devastated parents. For four years life effectively stopped for Josephine; she got a job locally and stayed with her family until they were well enough to cope again. Then, when she was twenty-two, she went to London, hoping for a career on the stage. She worked in a bank in the daytime and in the evening went to drama classes at Guildhall. But eventually she decided the stage was not for her, and she took a fairly mundane job at the Thomson Organisation, working in that same Gray's Inn Road building where the Saatchi brothers six years later watched their full-page ad come off the *Sunday Times* presses. It was there she learned the simple skills of selling classified advertisements and she excelled at it. From childhood she had an exceptional memory, and she now discovered she was a good organiser too. When she finally arrived at *Campaign* in the late 1960s, both Lindsay Masters and Michael Heseltine said she was far better trained – and skilled – than anyone they had ever had in that area.

Masters appointed her assistant classified advertising manager for the new magazine, but was aware she would outgrow it. 'She took charge very quickly,' says Masters. 'She was clearly better than the man who was her boss and within a few months she had taken over.' Haymarket had never produced a weekly magazine before which contained actual news, nor had it ever sold classified advertising. Josephine soon showed them how to do it. 'She was quite brilliant at it,' says Masters, not easily impressed by ad salesmen. 'I had a little thing with her that for every page she sold extra she could have an extra salesman. Finally I had to say, "That's enough", because she had so many. She was the best organiser and motivator and trainer of salespeople that I've come across.' Heseltine echoes that. 'She was an extraordinarily polished and sophisticated trainer. And I can remember how thrilled we were to have her.' The early mastheads of *Campaign* feature Josephine Hart as classified advertising manager and Maurice Saatchi as business development manager -- and often an article or two about Charles Saatchi.

In 1970 Maurice confided to her his plans for setting up an agency with his brother, and she asked him what he would call it. 'We're thinking about Saatchi & Saatchi,' he replied. Josephine, along with everyone else at Haymarket, thought he would do well whatever he did. She still remembers a discussion around the lunch-table just after Maurice left, when one Haymarket director remarked that the Saatchi brother 'had effortless superiority'. She knew him well enough to agree.

Josephine stayed fifteen years with Haymarket, ending up on the board; while there she married Paul Buckley, a Haymarket director who had also started as a personal assistant to Heseltine. The Buckleys and Maurice and Gillian Saatchi often made up a foursome in the evening, and spent weekends together. Josephine by now had a son, but her marriage, like Maurice's, was beginning to go wrong. Maurice gradually became more and interested in the Irish girl who laughed her warm, rich laugh at his dry, witty remarks, and whose mind seemed to work on a similar level to his. Her passion for the theatre had grown with the years, and, although his approach to it was on a less exalted level than hers, he shared it. She was less successful with her attempts to kindle his interest in poetry, but he accompanied her to poetry readings, another of her passions. Poetry had played little part in Maurice's life, and although he tried he never acquired anything approaching Josephine's love of it. After some years he could respond to Eliot and to the Irish poets that Josephine thrust at him, but he is not a person to be found in a corner reading a book of poetry. Not that it mattered to their blossoming relationship. Above all he found Josephine fun – and she found him funny. 'I've always found him the funniest man I've ever met,' she told friends. 'He's just such a funny man all the time – he has such a quick wit.'

In 1984 their separate divorces came through and in October Maurice and Josephine married. It was a very different event from Maurice's first ceremony. This time it was in a register office. Maurice, like Charles, was marrying outside the Jewish religion. To some extent Nathan and Daisy had become resigned to a world that had changed since they first arrived in Britain; London's once tight Jewish community was declining in numbers as more and more Jews married outside. None the less there can be few greater shocks to a Jewish mother than an Irish Catholic, and a divorced one at that. Josephine, however, was welcomed into the family, and Daisy and Nathan warmed to her even more when in 1985 she produced another son, Edward – the first Saatchi grandchild. 'The grandparents were in heaven,' says a friend. 'You've never seen anything like it.' (Gillian remarried too, and now lives on a farm in Wales, where she is a full-time – and successful – children's author.)

Maurice now had not only a son but a stepson, Adam, aged eight in 1985. He proved an attentive father to them both. 'He's very good with children,' says a friend, 'and it's been a surprise to him how much he enjoys it. None of the other boys was terribly interested in children.'

They were now living in Bruton Street, in London's West End, and Maurice spent hours redesigning and then overseeing the work on their home. They lived briefly in Brompton Square, but Maurice increasingly was only happy in a house he could redesign to suit his own eye, and it became a growing interest to him. His visual sense contrasted totally with Charles's; the elder Saatchi likes clean, starkly bare space around him, and his houses tend to be not very different from his minimal art. Visitors get the feeling that even a coat casually draped over a chair would spoil the visual effect; children would destroy it. Maurice's taste produced a much more peaceful, family effect – a delight for children. Adam told his mother there was a nice surprise round every corner in a Maurice house.

The property that gives him most pleasure is a house near Staplefield in Sussex called Old Hall, which he bought in the mid-1980s. He and Josephine began to go house-hunting at the weekends and were driving past when they saw it. 'That's it,' said Maurice, without hesitation. It was a mock-Tudor red-brick house, with its own keep, complete with weathervane and narrow arrowslit windows, ivy-clad castellated walls and a small amount of land. He bought it, and began a major reconstruction not only of the house but more particularly of the garden. Within a year, Maurice had made himself an expert on English gardens; he bought every book he could find on them, and toured Kent and Sussex studying the great gardens created by past enthusiasts. At weekends in the summer he would leave work early on Friday evenings, collect Josephine and the children, and drive to Sussex, where he instantly began wandering the garden and fields, sketching his plans. He bought the farm next door, and soon the bulldozers were in, clearing whole fields to be replaced by lakes and waterways. Josephine joked that if he kept on that way visitors would have to come in by boat. He built a huge Kew Gardens-style conservatory where he keeps semi-tropical plants. Around the house he designed a more intimate garden, along the lines of Vita Sackville-West's Sissinghurst, with its own separate 'rooms' for different colours and different seasons. When he decided on a rose garden, Josephine found him earnestly studying a pile of books on roses before he even began; he knew the Latin name of every one of them. One visitor commented that visiting the Saatchis in June was like something out of *A Midsummer Night's Dream*.

He went to work with even greater interest than he had on his London houses. Maurice never uses interior designers, but works out the architectural drawings and even the fabrics himself. Josephine briefly resented the fact that Maurice took it all upon himself – Doris, for instance, was in charge of interior design in Charles's household until they broke up – but she was soon boasting to friends about his 'marvellous eye'.

They bought a house in the South of France too, at Cap Ferrat, which was semi-derelict and had not been lived in for years. It suited Maurice perfectly, with its little jetty by the sea, its own small beach and the views out over the Mediterranean, full of boats and windsurfers all summer long. It is also within easy reach of Nice airport and thus accessible at weekends. He and Josephine enjoyed doing it up, making themselves a bedroom on the top floor, with a view out over the bay, and a large living area on the ground floor. It is not as grand a house as many in the area, but they love it. Maurice even developed an interest in boats; he bought a Riva Aquarama, a 24-foot heavy mahogany speedboat, the Rolls-Royce of its class, and uses it most days he is there, motoring around the coast to moor at a little bay and swim and sunbathe. Several times he scared himself and Josephine while out in the boat, finding themselves caught up in sudden changes of weather. He had never had a boat before, and had not discovered the sea until he was into his thirties. His early scares did not deter him and he soon learnt to handle the boat with much of the same confidence with which he drives his cars.

As Doris had sparked Charles's interest in art, so Josephine persuaded Maurice to become a West End angel, financing some of her plays. But, although he dutifully attended poetry readings given by some of the best actors in London, his business training made him start toying with another idea. Josephine was the only woman on the Haymarket board and was regarded as a considerable success there, but then she was given her own magazine, *Engineering Today*, to run – and it failed. It was the opportunity Maurice had been waiting for. He had listened for years to her talk about the stage and was well aware it was her first love. She enjoyed publishing, and she was good at it, but her heart was elsewhere. He had often told her the belief he and Charles held to: 'If you want something badly enough, you'll get it. But you have to really want it.' She refined it to 'If you have the will *and the vision* to do something, then you'll do it.' She had never got over

the death of her brother and sister, and she told Maurice she felt she
had once had the vision to become an actress – but she had lost the
will to pursue it. Now it was too late.

But with the closure of *Engineering Today* Maurice urged her to set
up her own theatre management company committed to presenting new
writing in the West End. 'This is something you have wanted to do for
years. You've walked away from it for too long. Now do it!' Josephine
had co-produced a number of plays, including *State of Affairs* at the
Duchess Theatre in 1985, and in 1986 she set up Josephine Hart
Productions. She had left it late in life to go into the theatre profession,
so to make up for it she was determined to produce only new plays 'I
can be proud of'. She was determined to be commercial as well, but
that was not her major objective – nor Maurice's. Within months of
starting up, she and her partners were receiving up to twenty playscripts
a week, and she was besieged with requests to be co-producer of a
large number of productions. She created rather than picked the plays
she wanted to do, buying the rights to a new book on Oscar Wilde, for
instance, then persuading a writer to turn it into a play. Curiously it
was Maurice who came up with one of the five plays she was working
on in the summer of 1988 – a stage version of Iris Murdoch's novel
The Black Prince. Josephine had been a Murdoch fan most of her life
and immediately picked up the phone and rang her. 'I'm absolutely in
love with this novel,' she said. 'Maurice and I have talked about how
we could do it.' She had lunch with the Dublin-born novelist, who could
scarcely have resisted her enthusiasm. Josephine wanted to produce *The
Black Prince*, she explained, because she saw at the centre of it 'a
marvellous harsh moral imperative'. The book's narrator and hero,
Bradley Pearson, an elderly writer with a 'block', goes to prison for a
crime he never committed. But he could not escape moral responsibility
for the final violent catastrophe. 'I just want to hear some of those lines
on the stage,' she told Murdoch. In the spring of 1988 she began
serious work on putting it on.

Maurice was supportive in other ways too. Josephine soon found that
one of the most difficult aspects of producing stage plays is getting the
right actors together at once. Maurice became deeply involved in the
casting, making suggestions to her and urging her to wait, get it right,
only go for the best. She in turn was deeply grateful to him; he had,
she said, been responsible for getting her back to something she had
always dreamed of, something she had been forced to give up in her
teens.

She was impressed with other Maurice virtues, notably his extraordinary self-discipline. From his earliest years, Maurice had always been able to organise and marshal his schoolwork very effectively. His brother David noted that at an early stage, and at LSE Professor Cohen remarked on how prepared he always was, never flustered or caught out, always using his time to maximum effect. Lindsay Masters commented on his control and discipline, and at Saatchi it became one of the principal factors enabling him to translate the big bold strokes into effective action. He practised this self-discipline in his private life too, planning his activities on the basis that he had time and energy for all the things he enjoyed doing. Both brothers firmly believed that they must get maximum satisfaction and pleasure from both work and play, and organised themselves to that effect.

Josephine was aware Maurice was intelligent, but gradually realised that his self-deprecating air and complete lack of boastfulness hid a keener brain than even close friends were aware of. Someone told her that he had an IQ of 165, and it took her five years of constant questioning to get him to admit it. When he eventually did, she believed it. Long before they were married he confided to her his dreams and ambitions, often still laughed at in the outside world – but steadily being translated into reality. He and Charles had a *Star Wars* joke – 'To boldly go where no man had ever been before' – but behind it was a grim determination to push past barriers and achieve goals not achieved before in their industry. Maurice, at least as much as Charles, was deadly serious about being the biggest and the best, and Josephine watched keenly their relentless way of pushing on past the difficulties. Yet in all the years she knew him she never once saw the slightest hint of insecurity or hesitation in him, or in Charles, whom she knew much less well. From the start they both knew where they wanted to go and were utterly determined to get there. As she would say, 'They had the vision – and the will.'

The Bates and Jacoby affairs might have caused the brothers professional anguish but it never disturbed the pattern of their lives or caused them to take their eye off the other interests of the group. Just as the Tim Bell affair had been handled by Charles, so the post-Bates problems fell to him too, and it was to him that Simonds-Gooding continually reported. Charles was very protective of his younger brother when it came to problems with personnel, but also reckoned Maurice's time was far better spent working out his longer-term strategies than dealing with individual difficulties.

Even as they grew larger, the brothers hated to see anyone go. Time and time again, they had solved a personnel problem by what they called 'building around it', hiring other people to fill in the gaps left by an executive who had turned to drink or drugs (which occasionally happened in the advertising world). Mike Johnson, for instance, had played a significant part in the early days as the financial man, but when the business grew away from him the brothers left him there and brought in Martin Sorrell above him. Similarly they had built whole teams around Bell when he had his personal problems. When friends came to them for advice on how to deal with a particular management problem, they gave them the same message: 'Build around it.' Often it was bad management advice, and meant crossed lines of responsibility and confusion. But they preferred that to a sacking. If a person became disruptive, they would find an office for him somewhere outside the building and often he would eventually drift away.

Tim Mellors, now creative director at McCormick Publicis in London, posed a very different problem to that of Johnson or Bell. He cites how the Saatchis and Jeremy Sinclair helped pull him back from the depths of drug-taking, drink, a marriage bust-up, bankruptcy and a mental breakdown. Sinclair hired him, he stopped drinking, won a series of awards and even worked on some of the Tory Party ads. 'Then I foundered and got into trouble with drink again and the agency backed me. I went into a clinic and stopped drinking, and haven't taken any drugs or drink since. I think only in Saatchi's could that happen. They were fantastic to me. Charlie said, "Go in there and it doesn't matter how long it takes".' There are other instances of this side of their character, as unknown to the outside world as some of the less attractive character traits exposed in this book.

There is a tendency to classify successful businessmen, probably more than any other category of human being in our society, as unidimensional. The myth is that they get to the top by single-minded drive and ruthlessness which shut out more human impulses. Typically successful businessmen have no interest in the arts, even though they are to be seen at Covent Garden, the New York Met or Glyndebourne; they have loyal but dull company wives, read only balance sheets and financial reports and live only for their companies, which in turn pay for all the perks they do not appreciate. In practice it is impossible to find a successful entrepreneur who fits the stereotype. Entrepreneurs are as varied and multidimensional as any other category of human being – in fact probably more so, since they can afford to indulge whims and interests that others cannot. But even by these standards the

Saatchis are very different and do not fit into any preconceived concept either of self-made millionaires or of advertising men. They could be as ruthless as anyone in chase of a goal; Charles could throw his angry tantrums and Maurice dream up schemes to make them still more millions. Yet they remained as human as anyone, with all the accompanying failings and strengths.

The events of 1987 would expose all their vulnerability and test their nerve even more than the Bates affair had done.

17

ELECTION OF '87

As 1987 opened, the Saatchis were keenly aware of the major challenge that faced them that year. Although her five-year term was not up until June 1988, Mrs Thatcher was almost certain to call an election in either the spring or the autumn. The polls suggested she was heading for her third victory in a row, but there were other factors clouding the horizon for Saatchi & Saatchi. Although they still paid Tim Bell a retainer for his services, they had decided they would not use him in the election. It would be the first time they handled the account without him. By itself this caused them no special worries. Maurice and Jeremy Sinclair would become more involved in presentations, and they decided John Sharkey, a bright, imaginative account manager, but without the same personal charm and manner as Bell, would be the account man. But with or without Bell there were enough signs already to suggest the campaign of '87 was going to be a fraught one.

The circumstances leading up to the election were anything but auspicious. In 1983 Mrs Thatcher had a close working relationship with her party chairman, Cecil Parkinson, which helped that campaign go relatively smoothly. In September 1985 the prime minister moved Norman Tebbit into the job, replacing John Selwyn Gummer, who was seen as a lightweight, and certainly not a man to run an election campaign. Mrs Thatcher had several reasons for this particular move. One was a positive one, in that she respected and liked Tebbit, and felt that he, above all her other cabinet colleagues, was the man with the best political skills for handling a campaign which she hoped would see her into the history books as the longest-serving prime minister of the century. Another reason was that she was aware that Tebbit was not entirely well, still suffering the after-effects of injuries from an IRA bomb planted in the Grand Hotel in Brighton during the Conservative Party conference in 1984 which had left his wife, Margaret, permanently paralysed. Although he had returned to his cabinet role as Secretary of State for Trade and Industry, Tebbit was said by his colleagues not to be the same man, more touchy and short-tempered than before, and unable to work the long hours that he had once relished.

On the eve of the Brighton bomb Tebbit had emerged as the clear number two in the cabinet, seen by the press and the party as Thatcher's potential successor. True, potential successors to Thatcher came and went at speed, but Tebbit was an ideologically committed – some even said fanatical – Thatcherite, a free-market thinker who had been one of the small group of Tory MPs who had urged the case for monetarism, privatisation and the general 'rolling back of the state frontiers' before Thatcher was elected leader in 1975. He had risen rapidly from trade minister in 1979, a non-cabinet role, to senior cabinet minister in 1983, and now party chairman.

Within a few months of putting him into Central Office the relationship was under strain. For a start, Tebbit was even less well than he pretended, suffering considerable pain from a wound in his thigh which stubbornly refused to accept skin grafts. He was also deeply upset by the injuries to his wife and the simple practical difficulties it raised for both of them: 24-hour-a-day nursing, special lifts and all the other facilities needed for a quadraplegic. There were emotional moments when they appeared in public together, Tebbit pushing the wheelchair, while his wife Margaret could do no more than smile, unable even to move a hand to wipe away her tears.

There was another factor too: Tebbit was a superb politician, a man who relished the cut and thrust of parliamentary debate. But he was not a natural administrator – and the job at Central Office was essentially administrative, making a professional organisation from what was an amateurish, poorly run machine. Parkinson had been a manager before he became a politician, and had been good at it, but even he had found Central Office difficult and had left it without ever getting much order into it. Under Gummer it had become demoralised as well as disorganised. Tebbit's friends argue that his lack of administrative skills was greatly exaggerated, and that his proposals for reforms, like those of previous party chairmen, were continually vetoed: Mrs Thatcher did not want a powerful chairman with a highly professional machine of his own because it posed a potential threat to her. 'Central Office had delivered two good election results for her and was on the way to delivering a third,' says one staffer. 'Norman led the recovery in the polls, but she never gave him much credit for it.'

The improvement in the polls, however, only came later, and there were some black moments for Thatcher before the Tories could begin to approach the election campaign with any confidence. No prime minister had been elected three times in succession in British history. Mrs Thatcher was the first woman prime minister; now she was after more records still. At the end of 1985, however, she suddenly found herself in deep trouble over Westland, the helicopter firm, which divided her cabinet between those who supported a partial bid by the American Sikorski group and those led by the Defence Secretary, Michael Heseltine, who favoured a European solution for the near-bankrupt company. The row cost her two cabinet ministers, Heseltine and Tebbit's successor at the DTI, Leon Brittan, and much credibility. As she prepared for a crucial debate on the morning of 15 January 1986 she confided to a close colleague that it was quite possible she would no longer be prime minister by that evening. In the event the Opposition leader, Neil Kinnock, fluffed his chance and she survived; but during those crucial weeks she felt that Tebbit was against her, siding with Heseltine, denying her his support when she needed it most. In fact he was not against her, but he did not side with her either. He saw his role as the healer and bridge-builder, and desperately urged Heseltine to stay in the government, fearing the damage his departure would do to the party and its re-election hopes. He thought he had succeeded, until Heseltine abruptly got to his feet in the middle of a cabinet meeting and walked out, leaving behind a stunned prime minister. The next day, with the government crisis at its height, Tebbit went into hospital for another operation on his thigh. For the next month, as Mrs Thatcher plunged into the worst crisis of her premiership, the man who should have been her closest ally was out of action. Mrs Thatcher visited him several times, and they talked on the phone, but the rift between them was widening.

It was while Tebbit was in hospital that the position of Saatchi & Saatchi as the Conservative Party's advertising agency was suddenly challenged. The government's ratings in the polls had dropped sharply as the Westland affair and Heseltine's resignation took their toll. The Tories were neck-and-neck with Labour up to Christmas 1985, but in January Labour opened up a five-point lead – 38 per cent to 33 per cent in the *Sunday Times* MORI polls. Some polls even showed the Tories slipping to third place, behind both Labour and the SDP/Liberal Alliance. The Tories were suddenly in trouble.

Mrs Thatcher, unwilling to accept the blame for the party's low ratings, looked for someone else to shoulder it. She complained to her colleagues that there was no initiative coming out of Conservative

Central Office to reverse the trend. Recent Saatchi work, she said, lacked 'edge', and she had begun to feel that the agency had grown so big that it no longer cared about re-electing the Tory Party. In 1979 Saatchi had been a smaller, hungry agency, her argument ran. Now it was a huge international business it had lost its creative vitality. At Saatchi there was puzzlement when these comments filtered back; the agency had done almost nothing for the Tories for months – it had been a dead period on the campaigning front. But most observers agreed with her that Central Office was not performing as it should.

The prime minister had never had the same relationship with Saatchi since Tim Bell left, and continued to find fault with it. During the early part of 1986 she complained the agency had become 'too gimmicky', and that the advertising done by Labour, which had learned much from earlier Saatchi campaigns, was often better. Again the Saatchi camp was taken aback: what ads was she talking about? There had only been a couple of party political broadcasts, and they had been a response to Tebbit's request that with an election still probably two years away they should do 'something adventurous'. It had been an experiment only – surely she was aware of that?

Thatcher was at a low point in her fortunes when on 15 February 1986 she held a meeting of her political advisers at Chequers. Sir Ronald Miller, one of her most trusted confidants and speech-writers, was there, as was Geoffrey Tucker, a veteran of many election campaigns and the man who had been responsible for Tory advertising back in 1959. Tucker was a consultant by then, working for Young & Rubicam. That weekend Tucker offered the agency's help: a detailed statistical analysis of the government's ratings, its public standing on a series of issues and policies and some suggestions on how Mrs Thatcher could effect a recovery. It was the type of work Mrs Thatcher would normally have expected to come out of Central Office and Saatchi & Saatchi – and indeed such work was available. Tucker, however, was offering something different. Y & R had developed a sophisticated system for looking at the electorate in a different way, and several cabinet ministers, including Lord Young and Lord Whitelaw, had been impressed enough to persuade the prime minister to see it. It had originally been offered in 1984 to Central Office by Tucker and Ed Ney, the head of Young & Rubicam Worldwide, who had advised Ronald Reagan in 1980 and 1984, and was occasionally used by them, but Tebbit and his staff were unimpressed by it. 'It didn't conflict with anything we were doing,' said a Central Office man later. 'We just weren't convinced of it.' Now it was being offered to the boss herself.

The Y & R method was an adaptation of fairly standard US 'psycho-graphic' research on what is called 'values and lifestyles'; Y & R called it 'cross-cultural consumer characteristics', or CCCC, and it was based on the premise that consumers (or voters) hold similar attitudes the world over, and can be divided worldwide into nine categories. Y & R developed its research in great secrecy over ten years, surrounding it with considerable mystique. 'It has given us some unique personal insights into attitudes to pressing social issues such as drug abuse,' said John Banks, Y & R's forty-one-year-old chairman in London. 'It gives us an edge over our competitors.' CCCC replaced the conventional A, B and C categories with more sophisticated groupings, the main one, making up 40 per cent of the population, being 'belongers': patriotic, home-loving, family men and women with a sense of duty, which was the group that had voted in Mrs Thatcher twice already.

When John Banks showed his breakdown of the British voter to Mrs Thatcher she was immediately taken by it. It did not necessarily present a more cheerful picture than the Saatchi findings at the time, but it did appear to offer both an explanation for Mrs Thatcher's low ratings and possible solutions. It also argued, perhaps crucially, that Mrs Thatcher was a strength for her party, and that without her the Tories would lose.

That weekend in Chequers Tucker gave the prime minister the latest Y & R analysis, and she agreed she would continue to hold these secret meetings where he could provide her with a separate view to that coming from Central Office and Saatchi. She had further sessions in March and April, each time without telling Tebbit. Then on Sunday, 13 April 1986, Mrs Thatcher for the first time turned her full attention on Saatchi & Saatchi. The brothers at the time were moving into the final stages in their negotiations with Bob Jacoby at Bates, and tying up Backer & Spielvogel. Heading the Saatchi team, as the replacement for Tim Bell on the account, was John Sharkey, although as the election approached the account would increasingly be handled by Maurice himself and Jeremy Sinclair.

The meeting with Saatchi's too was at Chequers, where Mrs That-cher preferred to handle party political briefings, as opposed to Downing Street, where the week was fully occupied with affairs of state. Around the table sat Mrs Thatcher's senior ministers: Lord Whitelaw, deputy prime minister and leader of the Lords, Nigel Lawson, the chancellor of the exchequer; Lord Young, employment minister; John Wakeham, chief whip; and Stephen Sherbourne from her private staff at Number 10, who now works with Tim Bell. Tebbit was there too in his capacity both as cabinet minister and as party chairman. They made up most of her so-called A-team, or Strategy Group.

At centre stage that day would be the man who would play a significant role in the Saatchi story over the following eighteen months: Michael Dobbs. Dobbs, with his relaxed, slightly hesitant manner, was still in his thirties. He had worked for a while as a journalist in America, on the *Boston Globe*, then returned to Britain in 1975 to work at Central Office just as Mrs Thatcher took over as leader of the Opposition. For two years Dobbs was in the research department at Central Office, then seconded to the private office of Mrs Thatcher, helping to prepare material for prime minister's question time and for major parliamentary debates. He continued in this role for another two years, then to his disappointment Mrs Thatcher did not offer him a job in Downing Street after the 1979 election. Dobbs, although regarded by his colleagues as one of the brightest young men in the Tory Party at that stage, reluctantly had to accept that something was wrong in the chemistry between them. Just as Mrs Thatcher loved to have Tim Bell and Gordon Reece around her, so she seemed to dislike Dobbs.

Bell had met him a number of times during the 1979 campaign and offered him a job as his assistant. So Dobbs went to Saatchi. Encouraged by Bell, he retained his interest in politics and acted as adviser to Norman Tebbit, helping him first at the Department of Employment and later at Trade and Industry. When Tebbit took over as party chairman, he persuaded Dobbs to join him as chief of staff, and Dobbs willingly accepted. Tebbit wanted to make him joint deputy chairman, alongside the novelist Jeffrey Archer, but Thatcher refused to allow it and he had to settle for chief of staff. Saatchi agreed to second him to the party, although there was no guarantee he could return to Saatchi.

The Saatchi team had been working on the Chequers meeting for three months, aided by a research programme called 'Life in Britain' which it had used successfully in the 1983 campaign. It was the result of detailed market research and analysis, and contained some bad news for Mrs Thatcher. Sharkey for Saatchi and Dobbs for Central Office, using videos and boards, presented their findings, which showed that much had altered since the 1983 election. The message in 1983 had been clear and positive, but now the public message given off by the Tories was confused. A majority of the public wanted 'Calvinism', a word the researchers used to mean a return to the work ethic and self-sufficiency, but that was no longer clearly associated with the Tories. Both Dobbs and Sharkey were careful not to personalise Thatcher's image and her role in the decline of public support, but she still interpreted it personally, believing that what they were saying to her was that she was now seen as extreme, but with no sense of direction or purpose and incapable of handling the major problems faced by the country: unemployment, education, the health service. Afterwards Dobbs ruefully reported back to his staff: 'We went in there knowing what we wanted to say and came out thinking we had told it too well.'

One piece of research, presented by Dobbs, went down particularly badly: it showed that on three of the qualities of leadership – strength, confidence and intelligence – Mrs Thatcher rated highly; but on 'forward-looking' she was below the other leaders. That was the low point of what was a highly uncomfortable day. Perhaps Tim Bell, with his special rapport with Thatcher and his humorous asides, might have got away more lightly, but Thatcher that day did not want any more bad news, and certainly not from Dobbs and Sharkey – or from Tebbit. At each point the researchers made she intervened to snap, 'Yes, we know that already', and by lunchtime the meeting had gone well off track. In the afternoon it got worse, and when they finally broke for tea at four the men from Central Office and from Saatchi felt like wet rags. It was the day that would go down in legend as the first time Mrs Thatcher heard the phrase 'TBW' ('That Bloody Woman'), which was not used by either Dobbs or Sharkey but which was widely whispered behind her back.

The rumours of that awful day at Chequers soon spread. They became worse for Saatchi when the news that Mrs Thatcher had been seeing Young & Rubicam leaked. Now, it was said, Saatchi & Saatchi was to lose the Tory Party account, a move that had minimal commercial significance but would be damaging for its reputation, particularly when it was just recovering from the trauma of New York. In fact there was never a serious possibility that Y & R would replace Saatchi as the Tory Party's agency. For a start, it is American-owned, and that almost certainly ruled it out; second, it did not, on principle, go in for political advertising – some months earlier a couple of its executives in Austria had helped Kurt Waldheim with his campaign for the presidency, and had been told by the agency to do it in their own time; third, Mrs Thatcher knew she could not get rid of Saatchi, even if she had wanted to, without a major confrontation with Tebbit, who bluntly indicated that they reported to him in his capacity as party chairman, not to the Prime Minister, and if they went he would have to go too since his whole position would have been compromised. After losing two cabinet ministers so quickly Mrs Thatcher had no intention of losing a third.

*

Charles and Maurice had thought seriously about resigning the Tory Party account on several occasions, each time following the election victories. After 1979 it seemed unlikely they could ever achieve the same triumphant publicity again and that everything that followed would therefore be an anticlimax. Why not go while on the crest of the wave? After the 1983 election that consideration seemed even more pertinent, particularly as the rift between the brothers and Tim Bell had steadily widened. Again they decided to stay with it. 'The time never seemed to be right to resign the account, although we always wanted to,' says one Saatchi man.

From the summer of 1986 stories that they were about to be sacked began to appear, and the Tory Party account switched from being a business winner to a liability. Somehow the future of Saatchi & Saatchi as the Tory Party agency was inextricably caught up in the break in the relationship between Thatcher and Tebbit. At one point Dobbs wrote to Tebbit, offering to resign from Central Office if the chairman thought that might remove one of the areas of 'angst'; Tebbit said no.

At the height of their estrangement, when the press and the political world were openly speculating on Tebbit's political future, I spent several hours with the Tory Party chairman, preparing a *Sunday Times* 'Focus' article on the conflict between Thatcher and Tebbit. Tebbit was about to depart the next day for France for a holiday with his wife, a tricky job which required special planes and ambulances. He was just moving homes in London, accommodating his wife in a Belgrave house lent to him by the Duke of Westminster and fitted with lifts, widened doors and special lavatories. Unlike many of his cabinet colleagues, Tebbit was not a rich man (he had been an airline pilot before entering politics) and could not have afforded it himself. But his wife needed 24-hour-a-day treatment, and he was finding the long night hours, which he insisted on covering himself, exhausting. Normally thin, he was now cadaverous, his face grey and wan. He had spent the morning putting up curtains, moving furniture and generally trying to make the house liveable in for his wife. Although no stranger to battles and controversy, being at odds with his own prime minister, the person to whom he had devoted so much emotional energy, was deeply upsetting for him.

That morning he sat in the chairman's office at Central Office under a photograph of Mrs Thatcher and carefully sifted the truth as he saw it from the gossip of recent months. He did not blame Mrs Thatcher, even by inference, although he was hurt by a number of incidents, notably at her decision to allow American F111s to use British bases to bomb Libya without telling him. He had also been irritated by stories that Mrs Thatcher was to bring back Cecil Parkinson to counter him.

He had no idea what his political future might be, but indicated he was willing to do whatever the prime minister asked him, including step down. He would still be loyal, still work hard for her, whatever *she* did. 'He is probably her stoutest and truest supporter,' a leading Tory told me that day. 'And it's not on the basis of trying to get to power either. He really believes in her, even now.'

Her attitude to him had clearly been coloured by her continued low rating in the polls. In April the Conservatives lost a by-election in Fulham and saw a majority of 15,325 in West Derbyshire cut to a mere 100. Two months later the Tories dropped to third place in another by-election in Newcastle under Lyme. They were trounced in that year's local elections, losing 789 seats and gaining just 62. As things grew worse, so Thatcher blamed Tebbit. Tebbit himself was philo-sophical. 'When you lose by-elections you start asking questions of the chairman of the party and the party machine. Nobody looks in the mirror.' That was limited consolation.

The day after I saw Tebbit, 9 August, Mrs Thatcher rang him, the first time they had talked for weeks. She was as concerned as he was by the press reports of the growing rift and the gossip that was whirling around them. She was about to leave for Cornwall for her annual holiday, and Tebbit put back his French trip for a day as they talked on for twenty minutes. She had no intention of removing him as party chairman – she very much wanted him to stay on. She was sorry they had not been seeing more of each other, and wanted to put that right from now on. She accepted his assurances of loyalty, and the conversation, leaked by Downing Street to the press that afternoon, settled any immediate suggestion that Saatchi would be fired. They were safe, at least while Tebbit was chairman – which meant until the next election.

Saatchi had been an innocent party in the Thatcher–Tebbit fallout, unable to intervene but feeling the backwash. The Tory Party rumours coincided with the beginnings of the account losses from Bates, and the fall in the share price throughout that summer did little for Saatchi's image back home either. It was yet more pain for Charles.

Just before Christmas 1986 her party headquarters presented Mrs Thatcher with a blue ring-binder file. Known internally as 'the blue book', it went a good deal further than previous early campaign plans.

Saatchi & Saatchi had submitted its proposals and they were incorporated into the 100-page strategy document by Dobbs, who pulled the plan together. Only half a dozen copies were made, carefully numbered and recorded: this was to be the blueprint for the election campaign and must not leak. It set out in elaborate detail the results of the research done so far, and what the party officials believed it meant for another campaign. The manifesto 'should be an essay on the future as well as a detailed political programme', it recommended. The theme Thatcher should adopt was 'The next step forward', which had already been used at the last party conference. There was also a section (fairly accurate, as events were to prove) on Labour's strategy, with recommendations on how it could be countered – the Tories, for instance, were seen to be vulnerable on health, education and pensions and these should be brought up and dealt with early in the campaign. Defence and taxation would be the big issues for the Conservatives to concentrate on, it said, adding that inflation and trade-union reform 'are underrated by the electorate because they are no longer high-profile issues'. It firmly rejected the suggestion, then gathering support, that Thatcher should soften her image. 'While your personal campaign should emphasise being in touch with ordinary people, we believe you should play to your strengths, which above all are *leadership, strength and experience*.'

In view of what later occurred in the campaign itself, this document has gained in significance. It laid out a strategy to which the Tories, after a wide and damaging wobble, effectively returned in the final week. It spotted many of Labour's strengths – Kinnock's image, it said, would 'doubtless be professionally presented' and his campaign would 'emphasise his youth and family image and engage in "razzmatazz" rather than detailed policies'. The Labour leader must be put on the defensive, and kept there, by concentration on defence, tax, trade-union reform and Labour's long list of extremist party candidates. 'We must put as much personal pressure as possible on Mr Kinnock,' said the document, reflecting Tebbit's view, which was to prove wrong, that the inexperienced Kinnock could be pressured into a series of calamitous mistakes in a campaign.

There was even a recommendation that, in view of the brief panic which had set in a week before polling day in 1983, Thatcher should allow herself 'thinking time' in her programme, rather than drive herself – and everybody else – at the frantic pace she had set in the last two campaigns.

On 8 January 1987 a small group of party officials gathered at the house of Lord (Alastair) McAlpine in Great College Street, just a few

hundred yards from Conservative Central Office. No one from Saatchi
was there. It was the first real campaign preparation meeting, called by
Tebbit to go over the 'blue book' with Thatcher. It started at ten in
the morning and finished at four in the afternoon; Thatcher suggested
copious amendments and additions, but basically accepted the strategic
plan. By the end of the day, everyone present believed a campaign
strategy had been decided on. 'Had we followed what we agreed that
day, we would have had a much more successful campaign than we
did,' said one official later.

Once a year Jeremy Sinclair takes himself off for a week entirely by
himself, just to think about life in general. During that week he protects
his privacy fiercely – even his wife and Charles Saatchi know better
than to disturb him. He reads no newspapers, watches no news and
tries not to answer the telephone. In April 1987 Maurice broke the
golden rule and tracked him down in Oxfordshire. It was a year after
that last uncomfortable meeting with the prime minister at Chequers,
and there was considerable speculation that Thatcher was about to call
a June election – which meant she would make an announcement during
the next fortnight. 'We're summoned to Downing Street,' Maurice told
Sinclair. 'And they've asked for *you*.' Sinclair had not seen Thatcher
since the last campaign, and then only briefly. 'I thought she would
have forgotten who I was,' he told Maurice; clearly she had not.

Back in London, Sinclair and Maurice got themselves ready; they
wanted no repeat of the previous year's débâcle, and were determined
to impress her with their readiness. But what did she want from them?
A full presentation of the ads they had ready? They checked with an
aide. Was she expecting a full presentation? Should they bring all their
ads down? 'No,' said the aide. 'Just come.' Both men were wily enough
to know how Thatcher liked to catch people off guard, and they decided
they would compromise: they would not bring the ads, but they would
take their presentation with its charts and strategy laid out in portable
form, so they had something to show her should she change her mind
and ask. Norman Tebbit, who was to accompany them to Downing
Street, had already been through the presentation and approved it, and
they were confident she would like it too.

Once again it was not a comfortable session. As she entered the
room Mrs Thatcher began, 'Well, what have you got for me?', and
looked around for the ads she clearly seemed to expect. At that point
they were very pleased indeed they had brought the presentation, which

Maurice now began to show her. Its theme was how she could increase her already huge majority. Thatcher was incredulous – how could she possibly do that? 'At least that's a challenge,' said Maurice. 'You aim high.' The next idea went down just as badly. They wanted to tell the public that socialism was an idea whose time had gone, that it had served its purpose and that even the Chinese and the Russians were beginning to turn their back on it. Her own recent trip to the Soviet Union, hailed by everyone as a great success, fitted in well with this theme, showing support for *glasnost* and how the Russians were tailoring their system. Most people acknowledged that socialism had also done something for Britain, Maurice told her, but the concepts of state ownership, trade-union power, high taxation and an over-protective welfare state were ideas of the past. The next campaign should show that, however the Labour Party put it, they were essentially dressing up an old idea. The future lay with Thatcherism.

Mrs Thatcher hated it. She refused to accept that socialism *ever* had anything to offer, and for Saatchi to suggest it now brought a withering blast from her. She did not want anything at all along those lines; they must start again. Within twenty minutes, Maurice and Sinclair began to be glad they had not brought any ads, feeling that whatever they showed her in her current mood would be shredded. In their book on the 1987 election David Butler and Dennis Kavanagh wrote: 'Mrs Thatcher praised the copy which attacked the other parties but expressed dissatisfaction that there was not more positive material on the government's achievements. She asked that advertising work should maintain a balance of two-thirds positive to one-third negative copy. The advertisers were not convinced, but complied.' This is something of an understatement. Maurice and Sinclair were not only 'not convinced', they were appalled – and tried vainly to fight back. They made little headway.

Thatcher then brought up the subject of Tim Bell. Why wasn't he working on the account? She understood he was available, and Saatchi had him on contract to advise on this election; she had expected to see him, she said. The Saatchi team had the impression she had been briefed already on their position on Bell, but she still made a plea for him. Maurice, however, was firm; Saatchi would not be using Bell during the campaign, he told her. Other people had been phased in to do what he once did, the company had moved on since he left and it would be too disruptive to use him now. But Thatcher did not easily let the subject go. 'It was Maurice's refusal to second Bell to the 1987 campaign which soured her relationship with the Saatchis,' said one close observer later. In truth the relationship had already gone sour, but that day it went sourer still.

For three hours they batted around ideas, with Mrs Thatcher both critical and quarrelsome. Out on the street afterwards Sinclair was furious. 'For this they dragged me back from holiday!' he exclaimed, before going back to his seclusion. Unknown to the Saatchi team, another little drama was taking place at that very moment back in Downing Street. Thatcher had asked Tebbit to stay behind for a very private word. Colleagues would later remark that from this half-hour session the previously grim and brooding Tebbit emerged smiling and relaxed, and to everyone's astonishment would remain so through the next months, despite the fact that Thatcher had moved Lord Young into a central role in the election planning, potentially cutting across the job of the party chairman. The assumption was that Tebbit had been offered a new cabinet role after the election.

In fact the opposite was true. Tebbit had been nurturing a secret for nine months which he had told to only a very few close friends. He had decided that, for the present at least, he would retire to the backbenches, maybe make some money in industry, and spend more time with his wife. He had been told by the doctors that 90 per cent of her recovery would take place in the first two years; he could expect little after that. Two and a half years had passed since the bombing – and miraculously she was still improving. Tebbit, always secretive, kept his hopes to himself, but he had been hugely cheered by the fact that first she could move one arm enough to feed herself and then, when the doctors finally got her upright, she could even take a couple of steps, held up by four nurses and with special supports. She suddenly wanted to go out more – to the theatre, to see her grandchildren and to visit friends; and she wanted her husband to go with her. In a sense his problem would have been easier if she had stayed fully quadraplegic – it wouldn't have mattered how much time he spent with her, since she would never have got better. Now that there was a chance she would make more progress he could not endanger it.

That day he told Mrs Thatcher he would not accept a cabinet post after the election. Contrary to the views at the time – most comment suggested she wanted to get rid of him – she was deeply disappointed, trying hard to get him to change his mind. In the end she decided to have another go after the election when perhaps his thinking might be different.

Having got that off his chest, Tebbit brooded no more. Suddenly he was his old cheerful, genial, witty self, accepting Young's role with apparent pleasure and getting on with the business of the campaign. On 1 May, a week after that awkward visit, the Saatchi team was back with the 'more positive' approach requested, and by the weekend of 2–3 May Thatcher had approved a campaign package, including the first party election broadcast. Everything was in place and the momentum building towards a June election was unstoppable. Butler and Kavanagh reckon that Thatcher may have allowed expectations to go so far that she lost control of the timing. She finally made her decision over the weekend of 9–10 May at Chequers after a long round of meetings with her ministers and advisers. There was no one from Saatchi present; but there *was* someone else, whose presence was kept secret from the others, and whose invitation to the house that weekend, had the brothers known it, would have caused them as much anger and irritation as the loss of another major Bates account.

Tim Bell and his fiancée Virginia Hornbrook arrived at Chequers at 6.30 pm on the evening of Saturday, 9 May. They were ushered briskly into a downstairs study, where they waited for half an hour. Upstairs Thatcher was working on the Conservative Party manifesto, with a group which included Tebbit and Professor Brian Griffiths, the head of her policy unit at Downing Street. At seven o'clock Mrs Thatcher finally went down to greet her visitors, apologising to Bell for having to keep him 'hidden'; she did not want Tebbit, or anyone other than a few trusted advisers, to know that Bell was there.

That evening there was a dinner party given in honour of Denis Thatcher, who was to be seventy-two the next day. Mr Thatcher, however, was late – he was at the annual Rugby sevens finals at Twickenham, and arrived not only late but happy. Mrs Thatcher didn't mind; the dinner party provided an excuse for her to get together with Tim Bell. Most of the evening was taken up with a discussion of the coming election. The press expected the prime minister to visit the Queen on Monday and formally set the election process in motion, and she had already made up her mind to do so. Bell had seen her several times since leaving Saatchi, usually at receptions, but this was the first time he had the chance to give her his advice in detail.

Mrs Thatcher took out a notepad and wrote at length while Bell expounded on how she should present herself, on the tone of the campaign she should run and on the whole question of communications. They talked for hours, running through the television programmes on which Bell thought she should concentrate, how to handle the press, and much else besides – advice, in effect, she had grown to expect from Bell in his role at Saatchi & Saatchi.

For several reasons, Mrs Thatcher wanted to keep Bell's presence at Chequers a secret. First, Tebbit had already told her he did not want Bell to work on the campaign; the *Mirror* group newspapers were said to be preparing a story on him which would be potentially damaging. Second, Bell had had a peripheral involvement with Guinness in its bid for Distillers, which was boiling up into the financial scandal of the decade, and she did not want any of that mud to stick to her (Saatchi had an involvement with the previous Guinness bid, for Bell's whisky group, but was on the James Gulliver side in the Distillers battle). Third, she knew the terms of his contract with Saatchi's and wanted no trouble from that camp either.

The next day, when Lord Young, who was in on the secret, asked her in the presence of other ministers about her conversation with Bell the previous night, she instantly shushed him, saying, 'No one here must know about that!'

Bell, however, was already busy working for her, proposing a video which would include most of the senior members of the cabinet talking about their achievements, which would be given to all Tory Party candidates and to the press as a means of explaining policy clearly. Thatcher that day gave her enthusiastic go-ahead and the filming took place around the corner from Conservative Central Office, at the house of Alastair McAlpine. When Tebbit arrived to do his bit a few days later Bell quietly absented himself. A major part of the promotional work was thus being done for the Tories without any input from Saatchi. That had not happened since the agency was appointed.

On 11 May Mrs Thatcher called an election for 11 June, and as the campaign opened the Tories were ahead in the polls with 42 per cent against Labour's 32 per cent and the Alliance's 23 per cent, and, barring a catastrophic campaign or a series of monumental gaffes, there seemed no way Thatcher could lose. However, the Saatchi team adopted a different line. At that first meeting they pointed out that 'our lead is only a fragile six months old' and that in each of the two previous election campaigns the Tories had fallen back seven percentage points. 'A repeat this time will mean a hung parliament.' There was no margin for error.

The original campaign recommended by Tebbit and Dobbs in the 'blue book' and accepted by Thatcher was soon going astray. The plan at the outset was based on protecting the lead in the polls, a policy which the Saatchi camp retrospectively called the 'brickwall' strategy. The Tories should start later, let Labour and the Alliance make the running in the early stages, then when the voters were becoming bored come in with everything they'd got. The Saatchi papers outlined the strategy for the final week, which included what they called their 'sucker punch', when they would launch the biggest media blitz ever seen, giving '88 per cent of the adult population 14 opportunities to see the Conservative message'. Later there was some argument, as there was about almost every aspect of this campaign, about when this part of the strategy was conceived, but the 'blue book' supports the view that it was policy at the outset, even if that policy was soon being disregarded. There was more along the same lines: let Kinnock become over-exposed, hold the prime minister back, and attack Labour on its defence policies and its vulnerability to its 'loony left' element.

Very little was to go according to the plan. Mrs Thatcher started the campaign in measured enough style, but within days had strayed into her first mistake. In her first major television interview she waxed euphoric, talking evangelically about the tasks still to be done which would take her through a third term and even into a fourth.

'Yes,' she told the BBC's political editor John Cole, 'I hope to go on and on.' Over the next few days her opponents had much fun with this, adding a few 'ons' of their own so that she was now said to be 'going on – and on – and *on*' for ever. In contrast Neil Kinnock set off at a cracking pace, and was showing no signs of slowing down. Worried MPs were soon ringing Tebbit to plead with him to get going, and bring Thatcher, who after that first gaffe had been almost invisible, centre stage. By the end of the second week waves of unease were beginning to spread through Central Office. Had they left it too late after all? In the opening days there had been jokes in the Saatchi camp about how Labour had 'troughed too soon', but attitudes soon changed as Kinnock picked up momentum and the Tory campaign, when it was finally launched a week later, sputtered uncertainly. The Labour Party used the film director, Hugh Hudson, whose *Chariots of Fire* had won a series of Oscars, to present Kinnock in the first party election broad-cast, and it was a polished and professional job which broke new ground in British TV political history. It ignored party policy and didn't even mention the general election. It was solely about Neil Kinnock, the man, the leader, his origins, marriage, family and oratory; there were a string of tributes from Labour veterans and the famous phrase, later plagiarised by Joe Biden in the 1987 US presidential race: that he was the first Kinnock 'in a thousand generations' to get to university because his forebears had no platform 'upon which they could stand'. It ended with no ringing evocative cry to vote Labour – just the one word: 'Kinnock' against the background of the Houses of Parliament.

The Labour Party for the first time was out-Saatchiing Saatchi – or at least that was how it was perceived; and it seemed to be working. Saatchi's first party election broadcast concentrated on the twin themes of patriotism and Britain's economic resurgence during the Thatcher years. It was sensible stuff – but created little effect. The unease began to grow in the Tory ranks. Who would have expected this of Labour? And where was the Tory – and Saatchi – response?

Thatcher's advisers that weekend found her tired and depressed with her own performance and that of the party so far. Her daughter Carol, trying to put new life into her, was confronted by a prime minister who suddenly felt she could well lose the election. It was a mood not unknown to those who had seen her through previous elections, although totally unsuspected by those who saw her confident television appearances and campaign speeches. Tim Bell was certainly familiar with it; and it was he and Lord Young who now came to her to show her the way out. According to Rodney Tyler in his book *Campaign*, Bell's presentation to her that weekend in Downing Street was a *tour de force* 'in that it managed to convey to the prime minister what was wrong, while at the same time keeping her more or less focused on the prize in store once it had been put right'. Bell had been impressed with the Hudson broadcast, and told her so. He also pointed out, much to her indignation, that Labour at that point were winning the campaign, although they had still not dented the Tory lead in the polls, which remained at 12 per cent. At one point Bell, after relating a series of unpalatable details to her, snapped: 'It's no good surrounding yourself with people who tell you that everything's fine – that way you'll miss the boat, prime minister.' He urged a change of strategy, a break with the Saatchi/Central Office campaign. The Tories must attack, go for Labour's policies, revive the theme with which she had originally started the campaign, with an attack on Labour's 'iceberg manifesto – one-tenth visible, the rest beneath the surface'. Without realising it, he was urging a return to many of the points agreed in the 'blue book'.

From that day on Bell would play a significant yet still highly secret part in the campaign. By telephone Gordon Reece (now Sir Gordon) also contributed advice and succour; he had been hired as public-relations adviser by the Guinness chief executive Ernest Saunders in his Distillers bid, and although he never got close enough to tender any advice to Guinness it was decided he should stay clear of Downing Street in case the stigma spread. Cecil Parkinson, who was still out of government because of his affair with his former secretary Sara Keays, was also one of Thatcher's unofficial advisers. The fact that this small group, who called themselves 'the exiles', had the ear of Mrs Thatcher caused both distress and concern at Central Office – particularly when, as now happened, the prime minister demanded a change of strategy. When Bell's involvement became known to Charles Saatchi, he boiled with rage but knew he could do nothing about it: the Saatchis had no one who could compete for the prime minister's favours. They had forfeited that position back in 1979 and there was no recovering now.

For Saatchi third time round there was little of the excitement and exhilaration which had characterised the first two campaigns. Their advertising, once such a talking-point, continued to draw more criticism than praise. To some extent this was a reflection of the clumsy machinery which existed. The Saatchi campaign team had blocked off a floor in the Regent Street building and the brothers had committed more resources, in the shape of more people, than they had in either of the other two campaigns; but there was an awkward chain of reporting to the client, with Sharkey and his team roughing out the ads, running them past Charles and Jeremy Sinclair, then taking them to Tebbit and Lord Young, who finally showed them to Thatcher.

The early posters in particular came in for considerable flak in the party itself, although Tebbit and the Central Office officials were pleased with them: the first featured three dogs, with a British bulldog towering over a German alsatian and a French poodle to emphasise how much stronger Britain's economy was than that of its opposition. Then there were three red books, with the titles: 'Young, Gay and Proud', 'Police: Out of School!' and 'The Playbook for Kids about Sex' under the headline: 'IS THIS LABOUR'S IDEA OF A COMPREHENSIVE EDUCATION?' The most memorable poster in the first week was the simple slogan 'Don't undo eight years' work in three seconds – vote Conservative.' Saatchi, despite the success of some of the television ads, gave the impression they were labouring – and Mrs Thatcher conveyed her view that she was unhappy with them.

At the beginning of the third week Kinnock made his first serious fumble, and the Tory Party and Saatchi machines clicked into gear at last. It was David Frost who prompted it. Arriving at the TV-AM studios at 7.15 on the morning of Sunday, 24 May, Frost was looking forward to interviewing the chief guest on his programme that morning: Neil Kinnock. Frost had worked on his line of questioning all week, and had stayed up most of the night reading the early editions of the Sunday papers in preparation to confront Kinnock on a number of themes, but particularly on defence. Kinnock set off on his well-rehearsed anti-nuclear policy, arguing, as he had done many times before, that the use of nuclear weapons meant genocide and national destruction. What would happen, asked Frost, if a non-nuclear Britain were confronted by a nuclear-armed enemy? Would it not be either unfair battle or surrender? 'In those circumstances,' said Kinnock, 'the choice is exterminating everything you stand for . . . or using the resources that you have got to make any occupation untenable.' Kinnock left the studio, unaware of the significance of what he had said. The Tories were slow off the mark too – no one in the high command saw the Frost programme that morning. It was only later in the day that a researcher, going through the transcripts, came across it. He rushed down to Tebbit who exclaimed: 'We've struck gold!'

Within minutes Saatchi & Saatchi was working on a poster ad to take advantage of it. Sharkey's team, with Jeremy Sinclair and Charles watching over them from a slight distance, soon got it: a British soldier, unarmed, and with his hands held aloft as though he were surrendering. The caption read: 'Labour's policy on arms'. An actor and a soldier's battledress were quickly found, but it was a bank holiday, and the fancy-dress shops that could normally be relied on were closed. Nowhere could Saatchi find a soldier's helmet. It was decided they had better shoot him in a beret, but it had nothing like the same visual impact. Finally, someone found the real thing, it was suitably draped in camouflage netting, and the ad was shot. It would be the best of the campaign.

Abruptly the tone and direction of the Tory response shifted. They had been about to concentrate on the economy and the 'loony left'; Saatchi's were now ordered to shelve that and work on defence. Tebbit was pushed into the attack, making use of his considerable political skills instead of his less-sure organisational ones. Thatcher too appeared more, attacking Labour's defence policy. At her first rally of the campaign at Newport that Tuesday she said Labour would leave Britain helpless and 'the present Labour leader admits as much.' The Tory campaign had finally come alive.

From that point on it should have been plain sailing. The fact that it was not was to mark the decline of Saatchi & Saatchi as advertising agents to the Tory Party.

Before the election campaign began Lord (Alastair) McAlpine, the Tory Party treasurer, put a little squiggle against the date Thursday, 4 June, on the calendar on his office wall. What did it mean, someone asked? That, forecast McAlpine, would be 'wobble day'; in every election campaign there was one day when a rogue poll and a couple of misfortunes combined to spread panic through the ranks. It was usually a week before the election, so he had picked that Thursday. Other battle-hardened people at Central Office had seen it all happen too. Tebbit's secretary, who had worked for Thorneycroft in 1979 and Parkinson in 1983, kept a little notice on her wall showing the six phases of a general election, starting at enthusiasm, and working its way through disillusionment, panic, search for the guilty, punishment for the wicked and, finally, praise and honours for the non-participants. The party was about to hit phase three: panic.

McAlpine's forecast date for the wobble was spot on. Two days before it, on the Tuesday night, a poll done for BBC *Newsnight* by Vincent Hanna, a journalist not renowned for his sympathies to the Thatcher government, began the rot. It showed that Labour had closed up dramatically on the Tories and were only 2.5 points behind. The following day rumours began to circulate through the City that the next day's Gallup poll in the *Daily Telegraph* would be even more disastrous. Share prices fell sharply. Dobbs got word of the poll that night: the Tories had fallen to 40.5 per cent, their lowest yet, and Labour had risen to 36 per cent. The gap had halved in a week. When people were asked about the quality of the two campaigns, Kinnock scored 39 per cent to Thatcher's 23 per cent, a 16-point lead. The figures, if translated into actual votes, threatened a hung parliament and the biggest election upset since Labour defeated Winston Churchill in 1945.

When Tebbit heard the news he was unperturbed. All other polls showed the Tory lead steady and he considered both the Gallup and the BBC polls were suspect. But the BBC poll produced a savage row between Lord Young and Dobbs, the worst of the campaign. Dobbs produced an analysis of previous Hanna polls to support his contention that the BBC reporter should be ignored and arguing that 'you do not change strategy on the back of one rogue poll'. Young argued otherwise, insisting that here was evidence that the campaign so far had been a poor one and had to be pulled around quickly.

When the news reached Downing Street the reaction was seismic. Mrs Thatcher's depression had been exacerbated by a series of late nights, a ferocious schedule and her continued frustrations at what she saw as the increasing problems into which the campaign was running. The target for much of her wrath over the next 24 hours would be Saatchi.

Thatcher was suffering from bad toothache. She had started the campaign with an infection in one of her teeth and it had grown worse; she dared not take time off to have it properly seen to. That Wednesday night she was in pain, and those who were unfortunate enough to see her during this time all testify to her savage anger and whiplash tongue.

Jeremy Sinclair went to Downing Street that evening with what he hoped would be the final party election broadcast. It consisted of cuttings from her best speeches: to the Conservative conference, incorporating brief reminders of the Falklands spirit and the Brighton bomb, and to other audiences, building up to a climax almost drowned out by the stirring music of 'I Vow To Thee, My Country'. There was room for a five-minute talk to camera from her, yet to be filmed, which would bring out the main themes of freedom, peace and the economy, to be put over in her softest and most persuasive tone. Thatcher at first was far from convinced and the others in the room were noncommittal, awaiting her reaction. Gradually Sinclair talked her round. At 8.30 she left to go to the dentist, and Sinclair went home, telling Maurice, 'We've made a sale', adspeak for 'The client likes the ad'. Early the next morning he went to Paris for a meeting.

'Wobbly Thursday', as it became generally known, began with Mrs Thatcher arriving at Central Office at 8.30 am for her regular morning briefing with Tebbit and other senior Tory staff. She refused to take any comfort from Tebbit's efforts to minimise the morning's poll. Lord Young and the group of so-called 'exiles', including Bell and Gordon Reece, had fed her misgivings the night before after she had seen Sinclair. She now demanded major changes in the way in which the campaign was being run, with Tebbit to do much less of the television work and some of the younger ministers to be used more. The day continued to produce bad news. First Kinnock upstaged her by producing the case of a ten-year-old boy who had been waiting fifteen months for a hole-in-the heart operation; then a few minutes later, at her morning press conference, Mrs Thatcher was trapped into her worst mistake of the campaign, stating that she paid for her own private medical insurance 'to enable me to go into hospital on the day I want, at the time I want and with the doctor I want'. That might be fine for her, said the Opposition, but what about all the millions, like little Martin Burgess, the hole-in-the-heart boy, who couldn't pay for the same privilege?

Thatcher's full fury was unleashed a few minutes later when she again sat down with her advisers. No one escaped, not even Lord Young. Sinclair may have jumped the gun in believing she had accepted the party election broadcast the night before, because now she announced she did not want it and must have something else. She wanted some fresh ideas by the time she was back from a tour in the Midlands that afternoon. Worse was to follow. She gestured at the proofs of the Saatchi ads that lined the walls and verbally shredded them. Lord Whitelaw defended the one of the soldier with his arms raised, and she was forced to agree. The others she said were terrible. When she asked to see the Saatchi advertising for the weekend press, Dobbs was again sent for. John Wakeham went to fetch him, but the ads had not yet arrived from Saatchi. They were on the way, he explained lamely, but Wakeham, fearing another Thatcher blast, refused to go back in without Dobbs. Sharkey and his team, Dobbs explained to the assembled group, were working on the theme of choice, comparing the Tory record with what Labour offered. To some extent both Saatchi's and the Tory tacticians had been caught off guard by the speed at which the Alliance campaign fell apart within the first week; but the 'blue book' had correctly anticipated that Kinnock would campaign well (although not as well as he did), and that in the final week the battle would be a two-horse race, rather than the three-horse one so loved by the pundits. Now Tebbit urged a return to the original 'blue book' strategy with an elaboration of the opening ad of the campaign, 'Don't undo eight years' work in three seconds.'

Sinclair, in Paris, knew nothing of all this. Midway through the morning, he suddenly had doubts about his own broadcast. Had he sold Thatcher the wrong one? He decided it was worth investing some money to make sure; he rang Sharkey. 'John, you know that broadcast I sold the prime minister last night? I want you to do some research on it. Would you do it now?' Sharkey was puzzled. 'Don't worry about it,' Sinclair told him. 'Just get the research done.' Research of the kind Sinclair was requesting is not uncommon in the advertising industry. It consists of showing the ad to carefully selected audiences around the country, getting their reaction and then analysing it – in effect a form of polling. The results would take a couple of days to come through. When it did, it allayed all of Sinclair's doubts; the broadcast was a very effective one.

Before she finally left for the Midlands (a tour that also went badly) Thatcher ordered new newspaper and poster ads for the final week. She wanted something more positive and hard-hitting than anything she had seen so far, ads which stressed the Tory success and Labour's failure. To some extent she was repeating the message with which Bell had left her, but she was also reacting from her own frustrations at her recent mistake on health and her fears over the polls. That afternoon's meeting was yet another unpleasant one, and at one stage Lord Young is said to have wheeled upon Tebbit, who until that point he had been treating with great care and diffidence, to say that he had not devoted eight years to the Tory Party to go down with a sinking ship.

Meanwhile Tim Bell, in his office in Knightsbridge, had two calls in quick succession. The first was from Young to tell him of the prime minister's demand for a change of advertising. The second was from Downing Street, summoning him to a meeting to discuss the final week's party election broadcast at 3.30. The prime minister, it was explained, had thrown out the Saatchi one, and she wanted ideas for a new one. Furthermore, Jeremy Sinclair was in Paris, so he could come to Number 10 openly – no one wanted a confrontation between the two men. It would be the first time in the campaign that Bell would enter through the front door rather than sneak in the back – 'past the dustbins', as he referred to it. It must be a real crisis, he reasoned. But from that point on any real attempt to keep Bell's presence a secret was abandoned.

Just before lunch a fresh set of rumours reached the City: a new poll by Marplan for the next day's *Guardian* would actually show Labour ahead by two points. Share prices crashed – notably those of Saatchi & Saatchi, which was seen as a big loser if Thatcher went out – and panic began to spread through the Tory ranks. What was going wrong? Tebbit was heard quoting Kipling:

> If you can keep your head while all about you
> Are losing theirs and blaming it on you,
> If you can trust yourself when all men doubt you,
> But make allowance for their doubting too . . .

He couldn't quite remember the final words, but it was the sentiment that mattered: 'You'll be a Man, my son.'

At the Knightsbridge office of Lowe Howard-Spink & Bell, Tim Bell and his chairman Frank Lowe worked through lunch on ideas that Bell had been thinking about for some days. They did so voluntarily – neither got paid by the party. They prepared eight or nine lines of attack, revolving around a slogan for the final week, one they thought would appeal to Thatcher's desire to be positive, and to hit at Labour: 'Britain is a success again. Don't let Labour ruin it', which was a version of the slogan used by the Tories back in 1959, 'Life's better with the Tories. Don't let Labour ruin it.' The agency's art director, Alan Waldie, hastily drew them up on boards and Bell left for Downing Street.

Young chaired the meeting to discuss the final week's party election broadcast (PEB). By the time Sinclair got back, an entire new broadcast was to be made and Saatchi's were working on a new script presenting a more 'caring' Mrs Thatcher, showing how the Tories really did 'care' for people – the precise strategy the 'blue book' had rejected.

At the same time as the PEB strategy session was taking place in Number 10, another meeting was taking place in Downing Street. The Young & Rubicam men had arrived an hour earlier at the offices of John Wakeham, the chief whip, whose office was two doors away at 12 Downing Street. Geoffrey Tucker had contacted Lord Whitelaw the previous day, Wednesday, to say that Y & R had prepared an analysis of the trends in the campaign and he would like to show it to him. It was not a cheerful paper for the Tories. The trend, it warned, was 'now dangerous'. Y & R advised a change of strategy which should 'centre all' on Thatcher herself and repitch the campaign in the final week along the line: 'We have not been through all this together for nothing. Don't let Labour throw it all away.' On 'Wobbly Thursday', Tucker and Y & R's London chairman John Banks outlined their findings to Wakeham and Whitelaw, causing the gloom to become even deeper. It was a detailed and well-presented analyis, backed by fieldwork and complete with charts. In just three weeks, it showed, the Tory ratings in the polls had fallen from 48 per cent to 42 per cent; Labour had increased from 27 per cent to 35 per cent. Y & R's 'mainstreamers', a big middle-class category, were shifting in droves to Labour, which was winning their hearts rather than their minds. 'Lost mainstreamers believe Kinnock – emotionally. They believe he can control the party. . . . Labour have stolen the mainstreamer high-ground hearts and minds. They have undermined Tory fiscal success and are seen as "caring" for mainstreamers.' There was much more along the same lines. By the time the presentation was over, Wakeham, deeply depressed, decided the message was important enough to go to Number 10, and took the Y & R men across.

The PEB meeting ended at five, and as Bell came out he tackled Lord Young. He had these ads he would like to show him. Would he like to see them? Young said he would, very much – preferably before Mrs Thatcher got back. An aide, Howell James, was dispatched to Bell's office to fetch the ads, and Young and Stephen Sherbourne, Thatcher's political secretary, studied them. They were, decided Young, much more in line with what Thatcher wanted; they were getting somewhere.

When the prime minister arrived back from her Midlands tour, Young intercepted her on the stairs and drew her into the room where the Bell/Lowe ads had been set up on the bookshelves. She liked them. They were direct and to the point. She was particularly pleased by one which stated: 'The Conservatives are spending three times as much on the Health Service as the last Labour Government. The only government to reduce spending on health was the last Labour Government.'

The prime minister, however, was under a new pressure: she was due to be interviewed by David Dimbleby on the *This Week* programme, one of the most important appearances of the campaign. She needed to prepare. Saatchi's were standing by ready to bring their material over. She had no time to see it, and in the end left it to Young to handle, on the basis that, whoever did what, these were the sort of ads she wanted.

There are various and conflicting versions of what happened next. Maurice Saatchi and John Sharkey arrived at Number 10 at 6.30; Tebbit was stuck in traffic and arrived some minutes later. Maurice wanted to see the prime minister but she was preparing for her TV interview, and he and Sharkey had to wait. When Tebbit arrived Young told him Thatcher wanted to run the Bell ads. After some harsh words, they both looked through the new Saatchi ads, rejecting several, but agreeing that a number of the others had picked up the theme insisted on by Thatcher that morning – and which were not very different from what Y & R were urging, or what Bell had recommended for that final week. In truth, it did not take a genius to work out the message the Tories needed to hammer home. All over Fleet Street and at countless dinner parties others were arriving at very similar conclusions.

Maurice was furious when Tebbit showed him the Bell ads. There was no way, he said, he was going to make those – the Saatchi ads made similar points and were much more professional. They were still talking when Young, who had stayed behind upstairs, stuck his head round the door. He had just heard the news of the Marplan poll: the Tories were not behind at all. They were still 10 points ahead. The pressure was off. Thatcher left for her interview, smiling. Maurice left soon after, having seen Mrs Thatcher for a few minutes only; he was still irritated with Bell's intervention, and what he saw as some odd behaviour on the part of his client. The prime minister had not given in on her demand that Bell's ads be used – she wanted Saatchi to rework them. She also wanted a new party election broadcast.

The Tory Party was breaking every rule in the book about client/agency relationships. Robert Townsend in his *Up the Organisation* gave as his moral for dealing with advertising agencies: 'Don't hire a master to paint you a masterpiece and then assign a roomful of schoolboy artists to look over his shoulder and suggest improvements.' Tim Bell and Frank Lowe could never be called 'schoolboy artists' – they are both among the most professional in the business – but their mere

6 PHASES OF AN ELECTION

I ENTHUSIASM

II DISILLUSIONMENT

III PANIC

IV SEARCH FOR THE GUILTY

V PUNISHMENT OF THE
   INNOCENT

VI PRAISE & HONOURS FOR
   THE NON-PARTICIPANTS

From the wall of the office of Norman Tebbit's secretary during the 1987 campaign

presence on the scene, double-guessing the Saatchi ads, makes Townsend's point.

The next day a new set of rumours spread, first through Whitehall
and then into the City and Fleet Street: Saatchi & Saatchi had been
sacked after a huge row with the prime minister. All sides denied it,
but there was no denying the conflict that was taking place. Jeremy
Sinclair did his best to gloss matters over when one newspaper
approached him. 'Mrs Thatcher's meeting with Maurice had an effect,'
he admitted. 'It had everyone jumping up and down. But we remained
in charge of the account.' Lord Young insisted, 'Our relations with
Saatchi are as before. We are quite happy with the way things are
going.' Neither he nor Tebbit had any intention of downgrading the
agency's role, he added.

Sinclair meanwhile decided he would not give up on his party election
broadcast. The research done by Sharkey's team was even better than
he hoped; the broadcast had been highly effective with the audience
which viewed it. He called Lord Young. Could they discuss the broadcast Thatcher had thrown out? Had Young himself seen it? Young
agreed to come and look at it, and when he arrived Sinclair began with
a classic advertising man's pitch – show the research before the client
sees the ad. By the time Sinclair had taken him through the audience
reaction, Young was intrigued. The broadcast itself left him in two
minds: he had given the instruction to get rid of this ad, yet when he
saw it, and the supporting research, it was too good to lose. At the end
he made up his mind. 'This must go ahead. I don't care what reason
it was decided not to have it, it must go ahead.' But how to convince
Thatcher?

It was Young who came up with the idea of using Gordon Reece,
who went round to see the broadcast the next morning, to persuade
Thatcher to change her mind. Again Sinclair started with the research
and followed with the broadcast itself, and Reece, like Young, was
impressed. That day Reece and Young showed it again to Thatcher,
who was this time in a more relaxed mood. Denis Thatcher was also
in the room and the consensus was favourable. Sinclair got his broadcast
reinstated, and it would end the Tory Party campaign.

That weekend's press ran ads of a more controversial nature: the
results of the combined efforts of Bell and Saatchi – and goodness
knows who else – were placed at a cost of some £2 million. It was the
biggest press advertising campaign in British history. Bell's line, 'Britain
is a success again – don't let Labour ruin it', came out as 'Britain is
great again – don't let Labour wreck it'. Some of the ads bore more

than a passing resemblance to the work produced by Bell, but this again may be because similar minds had arrived at the same conclusion. 'We were given three sets of ads to make that day,' said Sharkey wearily at the end of the week. 'We ended up making the one we intended to all along.'

As for the Young & Rubicam work, its proposed remedies to pull back the 'mainstreamers' were at first incorporated into a draft Thatcher speech; when the Marplan poll came through they were ripped out again. By the weekend all the polls were showing the Tories with a 10–12 point lead, with the Alliance dropping right back.

On 11 June that was how it ended – where in fact it had started before all the campaigning, all the battles and infighting. The Tories started 12 points ahead in the polls and they finished that way. Mrs Thatcher was back in Downing Street with a majority of 101, and the Saatchi brothers were left to brood on their future as advertising agents to a difficult client. At the low point of the campaign, Saatchi's were blamed for all that was wrong, and the brothers hated it. 'The Tory Party went from being the best client in the world to being the most difficult over a space of eight years,' said a former Saatchi man later. It was a big shift from the days back in 1979 when the Saatchis stood acclaimed by Tories and reviled by the Opposition as the agency which had ushered in Thatcherism. Perhaps it was time to move on.

18

LET'S BUY A BANK

The election campaign of 1987 may have ended on 11 June, but the battle between Tim Bell and the brothers did not. Once more the Saatchis found themselves making front-page headlines day after day, this time in a way which left them far from happy. The election itself had been bad enough, with the criticism of the lacklustre Conservative Party campaign focusing particularly on the Saatchi ads. For the Conservative leadership to be asked by the press about Saatchi being sacked in mid-campaign was humiliating. And for the Tories – and Tim Bell – to interfere with their carefully crafted work was intolerable. One senior Tory was quoted as saying sympathetically, 'If the advertising is not up to scratch, then that is a reflection not on the agency but on the client.' The Saatchis in their more bitter moments might have felt that too, but this was a matter too delicate for them ever to talk about in such a way. The key factor they had to accept was that Mrs Thatcher had no confidence in them as her party's agency, and in those circumstances there was not much point in going on. They had always contended that they treated the Tory Party account just like any other, but that was never entirely true, simply because it was *not* like any other. It was high-profile stuff, with instant feedback and a unique level of analysis from all sides. It could be very exciting, but it could also ruin the agency's morale when the going got rough. It was worth little in terms of direct reimbursement, yet the controversy over it sharply affected the Saatchi share price and its financial image.

All this made the celebrations of the Tory victory a subdued affair in the Saatchi camp. Analysing their own ads, they could not see how they could have done better, even if many outsiders could. I had a long post-mortem with Maurice, Sharkey and Dobbs in Tebbit's office on the day after the election, when all three defended the ads they had done and the campaign they had worked out. They would never criticise a client, but they were more grim-faced than I had seen them. It had not been a happy experience. The shares recovered 30p to 600p on the day after the election, but the rumours that Saatchi & Saatchi and the Tories would soon part had not gone away.

On the Saturday after the election *The Times* devoted the top of its front page and most of the back page to a story headed 'How Project Blue rescued the Tory campaign', an account of how Young & Rubicam had purportedly stepped in to replace Saatchi and save Mrs Thatcher from electoral defeat. It infuriated Bell and the Saatchis, who both claimed it bore no resemblance to what had happened. That weekend there was more of it. 'The future of Saatchi as the Tory party's agents would now appear to be in the balance,' said the *Observer* (14 June 1987). 'Speculation had it last week that a parting was nigh.'

Saturday was the day Mrs Thatcher was due to announce her round of cabinet changes; the fact that Tebbit had made up his mind to leave had been a closely kept secret before the election but had now leaked, and this was widely expected to be his final day. Mrs Thatcher had spent three hours with him on election day, and when she could not move him she put Lord Whitelaw on to him, but Tebbit remained adamant; he was going. By nightfall he would be out of government.

I went to see him in his rooms at the Cabinet Office that Saturday morning. It was a strange scene. In other circumstances there should have been an almost carnival atmosphere. It was a beautiful midsummer day in London, and all the windows overlooking Horse Guards Parade were open. From below, the swelling, uplifting music of the annual Trooping the Colour contrasted oddly with the sombre, wake-like atmosphere in the offices. There were wives and children gathered with the husbands who had worked through the past frenetic month with Tebbit, now come to watch the Queen. Margaret Tebbit sat at a window in her wheelchair, with perhaps the best view of anyone in the square of the ceremony below. There was drink and food, and from adjoining offices the sound of other parties uninhibitedly enjoying one of the privileges of government. Here even the children knew that something was amiss, and they talked in the same hushed tones as the adults.

I found Tebbit himself sitting at his desk in another room, his head down, redrafting a letter. He apologised when he saw me. Could I go through to the others? He was, he said, writing to the prime minister. I didn't have to ask why. Although it would not be officially announced for some hours, Tebbit was working on his letter of resignation. By the following day this fine suite of offices and all the trappings and privileges that went with the position of the Chancellor of the Duchy of Lancaster would be someone else's.

It was another factor moving against the Saatchis. Tebbit still retained his position as chairman of the party and therefore, nominally at least, was in charge of appointing its advertising agents; but even that role was looking increasingly vulnerable and the wisdom among the political pundits and in the party hierarchy was that Tebbit would leave Central Office within six months. Lord Young had gained in power and stature right through the campaign in his role as chief executive of Central Office and also as head of the secret kitchen cabinet at Number 10. Now Mrs Thatcher moved him from Employment Secretary to Secretary of State for Trade and Industry, the role once occupied by Tebbit. There were strong rumours that Young would also take over as chairman of the party, but that move was killed by strong opposition from the rest of the cabinet, and Young had to retreat later in the autumn. Saatchi was losing a powerful friend in the cabinet with Tebbit, and found it hard to look on Young's rise with enthusiasm. He had hardly shown himself a Saatchi supporter during the election, and he had far too close a friendship with Bell for their liking.

Tebbit, however, had not lost his zest for a battle. That weekend he went in to bat on behalf of his advertising agency. At a press conference he hit out at some of the wilder speculation about who had, or had not, written those ads. 'There were two or three battles going on during the general election,' he said. One was 'the battle between an American advertising agency' – which Tebbit delicately refused to name but which everyone present knew was Young & Rubicam – 'who were sore at Saatchi's success and who thought the best way to get back at them was to make a pitch at the account which was the most prestigious account they had – the Conservative Party.' He went on: 'After they failed [to get the Tory Party account] quite clearly they set out to say that it was Saatchi's campaign that lost us the election. Since we won, they started again and said it had nothing to do with them [Saatchi]. They were saying it was their agency behind the scenes. That is the big bad world of business.'

That speech helped the Saatchi price again when the market opened on Monday. That morning, however, the ire of the brothers had been increased by another press item. The *Daily Mail* diarist Nigel Dempster joined in. On Sunday Dempster had been phoned by Frank Lowe, an old friend of his. Tim Bell's considerable efforts on Mrs Thatcher's behalf, Lowe complained, were being ignored. The success at the end of the campaign was not due to Saatchi, nor was it due to Young &

Rubicam. The slogan 'Britain is great again. Don't let Labour wreck it' was a Tim Bell/Frank Lowe creation. Dempster duly obliged the next day with a lead item in his well-read and influential diary: 'Privately Mrs Thatcher is congratulating Tim Bell' for her victory, said Dempster.

Lowe, in contrast to his partner Bell, was no enemy of the Saatchis. On the contrary he was – and is – one of Charles's closest friends; they regularly play poker together and have similar ideas on the world of advertising, and both resented finding themselves on opposite sides in this public way. As a fresh row erupted, Lowe discovered he had got himself into a minefield from which it was not going to be easy to extricate himself. He blamed Bell for it, as did the Saatchis. For his part Bell had his good humour stretched that weekend as he found himself caught up in an increasingly messy situation which he also felt was not of his making. And it seemed to be escalating by the hour.

That evening the BBC *Panorama* programme, recapping the events of the election, reported that on 'Wobbly Thursday', 4 June, Mrs Thatcher 'had effectively dispensed with Saatchi & Saatchi and handed her campaign over to advisers from another agency'. Maurice and Charles were incensed. Saatchi may not have finished the campaign in good shape, but they had finished it still writing – or rewriting – ads for the Tory Party, and there had been no sacking. The BBC was over the line.

It was time to hit back. The Saatchis, as Tim Bell avers, are good friends but bitter enemies. Brian Basham, a leading public-relations consultant in the City and a man who had acted for them for many years – but refused to be taken over by them despite offers which were larger each year as Basham's business prospered – was brought in to plan a counter-campaign. So were the lawyers. The brothers went into a huddle. Maurice and Charles wrote out a statement which Basham issued to the press. They had not been sacked, but were still employed by the Tory Party, it said. Young & Rubicam's much-talked-about special research techniques with their 'mainstreamers' and 'belongers' were, said the press release, 'completely useless' in the election. Both Y & R and Bell's agency were indulging in a 'campaign of disinfor-mation'. Central Office issued a supporting statement saying that the *Panorama* reference was a 'total fabrication' and that the agency was 'at no time fired, nor did the question of firing arise'.

In the days that followed the heat suddenly turned off the Saatchis and on to Lowe Howard-Spink & Bell. There were rumours that Bell and Frank Lowe had fallen out, that key people were leaving, and that the tabloids were about to publish damaging allegations about Bell's personal life. Bell accused the Saatchis and Basham of spreading the rumours, and the Saatchis denied it. By mid-week it had got out of hand. In the City of 1987, a year after Big Bang when the markets had been deregulated, there were dealers who specialised in just such rumours, and it soon turned into a classic bear raid. On Wednesday the shares of Lowe Howard-Spink & Bell crashed 62p, wiping £12 million off the value of the company. The story of the share fall was on the front pages of most of the quality papers the next day, linking it to the row over the campaign ads. It was not funny for Frank Lowe. 'I regret ever writing those ads now,' said Lowe later. 'I never should have got the agency involved.'

Nor was it funny for the prime minister. Sir Gordon Reece called her on Wednesday. She was seething. 'It really is unseemly,' she said. 'I've just won an election by 100 seats, and all anyone can talk about is which advertising agency wrote which ad in the campaign.' Couldn't Gordon do something? 'You know the Saatchis, and Tim Bell and Frank Lowe and all the others. Can't you stop it, Gordon?' Reece agreed it was absurd, and would do what he could to 'knock a few heads together'.

Both sides felt the other was to blame. The Saatchis were bitter about Bell's interference, while Bell accused the Saatchis of hijacking his ads and presenting them as their own. The stories of the row were being picked up in New York, in Canada, Australia and everywhere else the Saatchis were known, and they were damaging both them and Lowe's company, but neither side could let it alone, particularly the Saatchis. Bell must be made to back down.

Downing Street was getting alarmed by the growing clamour. That day calls went out to Tebbit, Lord Young, Lord Whitelaw and others to see what they could do to 'cool it'. Meanwhile both sides were already briefing journalists for what promised to be yet another round at the weekend. Lowe, Bell and their finance director, Julian Seymour, went to the offices of Peter Carter-Ruck, a solicitor who specialises in libel, to talk about bringing proceedings against the Saatchis.

In the event a peacemaker appeared in the unlikely person of Lord Hanson, chairman of the giant conglomerate Hanson Trust. The saying about Hanson was that he loved 'Mrs Thatcher, free enterprise and the United States – in no particular order'. He did not like the damage this public squabble was doing to two of those three loves; and he was in a position to intervene to stop it.

Hanson had just completed his biggest-ever flurry of takeover bids, pushing his company to number 48 on the *Fortune* 500 list in the USA, and the fifth biggest in Britain. He now owned the Imperial Group, Britain's biggest cigarette company, which were major clients of Saatchi & Saatchi, while Lowe Howard-Spink & Bell also had a number of Hanson accounts.

Hanson called Lowe on Friday morning and suggested he come to see him. Lowe walked across from his own office in Bowater House to the 1960s office block on Hyde Park Corner, overlooking the gardens of Buckingham Palace, where Hanson had his headquarters. The Saatchis, still furious with the rumours about them, didn't want peace talks. They were intent on getting their side of the story fully heard, establishing beyond all reasonable doubt that the advertisements used during the election had come from their team and their copywriters and artists, not Bell, Lowe, Young & Rubicam or anyone else.

Hanson is a persuasive, calm, intelligent man who found Lowe only too willing to make peace. He could, he agreed, silence Tim Bell. But how to persuade the Saatchis to desist? The battle was damaging the shares of both companies.

Hanson placed a call through to Maurice Saatchi, and when he came on told him he had Frank Lowe in the office, listening on the conference phone. Lowe, he said, was keen to resolve this silly matter between them, and Hanson thought it must stop too, if only to protect the prime minister, whose election victory should not be sullied in this way. What did it matter who had written those ads? What did matter was that Thatcher had won. Now, could there be peace?

Both Maurice and Charles spoke on the phone. They were reluctant to drop it there, but could scarcely cross Hanson so blatantly. They finally agreed to a truce.

Later that morning an extraordinary press release was issued under the heading 'ALL SMILES AT LOWE AND SAATCHI'. Both sides, it said, wished to end the rift. Frank Lowe formally congratulated Saatchi 'on their great success with the Tory election campaign' and Saatchi thanked Lowe for his 'valuable contribution'.

The press the next day missed the key point of the statement: Saatchi thanked Lowe for *his* contribution. Surely the contribution from the agency Lowe Howard-Spink & Bell owed something to Tim Bell? Yet there was no mention of Bell in the press release. Lowe later insisted this was because the Saatchis would not have agreed to Bell's name appearing in a joint statement. 'They really seemed to hate him,' he said. The Saatchi camp, on the other hand, told a different story. Lowe had been embarrassed by Bell's behaviour and it was he who insisted his name was not mentioned. Bell, wisely perhaps, stayed mum (but later vehemently denied the Saatchi version of the press release).

The battle of the election advertising was over, at least for a time. The Saatchis settled their libel case against the BBC for a grudging retraction and a modest £1000 paid to charity. The BBC had been tempted to fight, but was still recovering from another bruising battle with the Conservative Party which had cost it £500,000, savagely damaged publicity and cost the director-general his job. It didn't help that the reporter, Michael Cockerill, was the same reporter in both cases. Saatchi issued a statement claiming victory, but at the BBC the message given to reporters was interpreted by *The Times* the next morning as 'collapse of stout Saatchi'. A BBC executive was quoted as saying: 'With all the Tebbit pressure on the BBC there has been a certain loss of nerve. Once we would have fought a thing like this on principle but now we would rather wriggle out of it quietly.' The BBC version, although not correct, had not been a million miles from the truth.

For Saatchi's, it was time for more serious business ventures. In New York the merging of the agencies into Simonds-Gooding's carefully worked-out structures was almost complete. The global gospel may have had holes in it, but it was holding together reasonably well as the brothers moved rapidly on, impatiently putting behind them the nuisances of people complaining about conflicts of interest, size, demotions and even redundancies – over 1000 people had been let go from the agencies taken over in the USA.

Other problems too kept emerging: the British pharmaceutical group Beecham sued them in the USA over what it claimed was an absurdly optimistic projection made by the Saatchi market research subsidiary, Yankelovich Clancy Shulman. The firm had claimed that by spending $18 million on promoting a new washing powder Beecham would get a 45–52 per cent market share. Beecham had duly spent the money, through a Saatchi agency, and got only 25 per cent at the peak. Their share soon lapsed back to between 15 and 20 per cent. It was not a good advertisement for the powers of the multi-service approach. But in the overall picture it was a tiny sideshow.

Back in London there were still other ventures. The brothers decided to back a new satellite TV channel led by their old friend Michael Green of Carlton Communications. If they could get it off the ground it would be a rival to British Satellite Broadcasting, the consortium which the previous year won the franchise for British direct broadcasting by satellite, and which would soon be headed by the formidable Tony Simonds-Gooding who, if nothing else, had learned a great deal in his two years at Saatchi. It would be their first venture directly into the world of the media, and they had some powerful partners: Dixon, the retail chain, and the two London TV companies Thames Television and London Weekend Television. And there were a few further acquisitions: a litigation support company in California and a sales promotion company, filling out the multi-service profile.

They wanted to move on to the next phase, one they had been considering in a vague way but which they now wanted pulled off the back-boiler and activated. It was time to move into financial services; time, in short, to buy a bank.

Although the company now employed over 14,000 people around the world the management structure was so designed that little of the day-to-day load fell on the brothers. In their sixth-floor offices they could plan their bold gestures and keep the adrenaline flowing. The financial services plan was in the hands of the City merchant bankers, Kleinwort Benson, but Maurice had asked Michael Dobbs, who had left Conservative Central Office and rejoined Saatchi, to co-ordinate it on the company front.

Saatchi & Saatchi had changed a great deal in the two years that Dobbs had been away. Bill Muirhead was chairman of the agency, and Paul Bainsfair and John Sharkey were joint managing directors. Jeremy Sinclair, Roy Warman and Terry Bannister had all been promoted to the international division, and Jennifer Laing, wooed back with the red Ferrari by Bell, was on the point of leaving again, this time to join a small agency where she felt she would welcome the challenge of building it up. Dobbs was given an office in the new Regent Street building, a floor below the spacious rooms occupied by the brothers, and Charles and Maurice briefed him at length on their plan to buy a bank.

As a prelude to the move they had commissioned a study of the financial service industry from Touche Ross, one of the big seven accounting firms. They had both become enthusiastic about the logic of it all, Charles in his typical straight-to-the-heart analysis picturing it as an industry almost identical in structure and diversity to advertising as it had been in the 1970s. No bank, however big, had a large market share. Both brothers had seen uncanny echoes of their own thoughts – and those of Ted Levitt – on the subject of globalisation. The financial columns were full of articles discussing the global-versus-niche argument taking place throughout the banking world as technology and deregulation had turned financial markets into one large international market-place. London's Big Bang, the equivalent of Wall Street's May Day a decade before, had brought the biggest changes in the financial services industry the City of London had ever seen. Americans, Japanese and Europeans had swept in to take positions in the securities markets, and all but a tiny handful of London's once proud stockbroking and jobbing houses had surrendered their independence, swallowed up in the financial combines which insisted that to survive in the new world you had either to have the capacity – and the capital – to distribute securities around the world or to look for a specialised niche to make your profit.

To the brothers it was irresistible. The Saatchis had persuaded many, including themselves, that they had discovered the concept of globalisation, at least in so far as putting it into practice in a service industry was concerned. Now everyone was jumping on the bandwagon. In a matter of weeks the trauma of the election had been forgotten. Here was a new challenge, many times bigger even than the Bates deal. By widening their field of activity beyond advertising and on to consulting, marketing, sales promotion, corporate image, public relations, design and the other areas, they had increased the size of the market they were operating in – and intended to have a 10 per cent share of – from the $40 billion a year of advertising expenditure to a market four times that size. By 1990 they estimated the consulting market alone would be worth $230 billion. Their management consultancy business ranked twelfth in the world, but acquisitions already well advanced would shoot them up the league before long, and by the early 1990s they planned to have as much revenue from that area as they had from advertising. There were other areas, such as specialist computer-based research for the legal industry, where they now ranked first.

Saatchi & Saatchi was not just an advertising agency; not even a communications company. It was a 'multi-service' company. This would be their approach to the financial services industry, which would widen the horizons much, much more. Dobbs was already drafting the argument they would deploy. 'Saatchi has brought together leading companies in the management service fields, each with independent objectives but common standards of excellence and cultural values,' he wrote. 'Its aim is to provide clients with a professional range, quality and co-ordination of services that allows them to pursue their goals effectively.' There was more along these lines, material which would later make City bankers look away, muttering, 'What's this got to do with Mexican debt?' But Maurice was pleased with it.

Now was the time to settle on the target. The professional adviser on the deal was David Clementi, a merchant banker in the corporate finance department of Kleinwort Benson, who was busily organising the resources they would need. The British banking market was in turmoil, with no less than five banks 'in play' in the sense that someone had announced a share stake or an actual bid for them, and it was only a matter of time before they were taken over.

Of these one stood out above the others: Midland Bank, once, thirty years before, the biggest in the world, now not even in the top twenty after its disastrous takeover – and disposal – of the Crocker Bank of California, which had run into major problems over South American debt. Midland that summer had cleaned itself up, making a provision of over £1 billion against its loans to Third World countries, and at the same time selling two British subsidiary banks, Clydesdale and Northern. Its balance sheet suddenly looked much healthier, but Sir Kit McMahon, the chairman and a former deputy governor of the Bank of England, privately warned his board of something else: while Midland was burdened with its bad Third World debt, no predator would dare bid for it. Before the provisions, it had, in effect, the perfect 'poison pill', something so unpalatable that no one would swallow it. That was now gone, and the world could see that Midland had a long-term future. That made it very vulnerable. 'Once we do this,' said McMahon, 'we will become interesting. We will be a bank that is still weak but is showing that it is prepared to do something and is now, in ratio terms, tolerable.'

Someone else saw it in the same light. Within three days of Midland's major announcement, Lord Hanson began buying shares. Early in September speculation heightened around it when Hanson let it be known he now owned between 5 and 7 per cent. It was, he said, just 'an investment'. McMahon went to see him, and Hanson assured him his intentions were 'friendly'. The City was sceptical but McMahon thought otherwise. Hanson, he reckoned, had done the same calculation he had; he had recognised the key moment when Midland had moved out of its troubles to the vulnerable period before the benefits of the reorganisation being carried through by McMahon had come through. Someone, Hanson reasoned, would make a bid; and when they did he wanted a slice of the action. McMahon believed Hanson was a 'punter' rather than a serious bidder, he reported back to his board. He might push the price up higher and be a 'destabiliser', but the Midland chairman thought Hanson's objective was to put the bank 'in play', persuading another bidder to come in. He was right: taking over an industrial company held no terrors for Hanson; taking over a clearing bank was another matter, and even he shied away from it, knowing he would almost certainly not get away with it, even if he wanted to. There were too many regulators and vested interests to make it worth even attempting it. He had bought the shares as a speculation.

If Midland would have been an enormous leap for Hanson, whose company was capitalised at more than £6 billion, it was an even bigger leap for the Saatchis, valued on the stock market at less than £1 billion. But then Garland-Compton had also been a huge leap a dozen years before, and so had the big bids in the USA. The brothers were never afraid to try. If they did the planning right, this would be no more difficult, they reasoned. But would the sums work?

David Clementi calculated that they would. Midland was capitalised on the stock market at £2 billion. To win it, Saatchi needed to offer more than the current share price: so it would cost nearly £3 billion. There would have to be a capital injection as well, for them to have any hope both of gaining the support of the Midland board and also of turning it back into a world-class bank. Clementi estimated that would have to be another £1 billion – so £4 billion in all. Could Saatchi raise that? Clementi emerged a few days later with the answer: it could. He had made tentative arrangements for £3 billion of new Saatchi shares to be underwritten, plus a standby facility of another £1 billion. The City was awash with cash, Saatchi's credit stood high and there was no problem raising money to buy an organisation as distinguished as the Midland, which still had huge assets and an excellent income stream from its domestic operations. Midland was a serious runner. Even if their attempt failed it would serve notice on the world that Saatchi was ready for its biggest ever move, and was far more than just an advertising agency.

Maurice had been greatly impressed with a piece in the *Economist* that summer which mentioned the 'commonly agreed view that the money industry will have room only for, at best, 25 global financial intermediaries'. On the basis of what was happening in other industries, most of these would be Japanese or American. Why shouldn't there be another British one?

After the election Charles in particular wanted to regain the impetus of the business, and that, he felt, required the biggest, boldest move yet, something even those who thought they knew Saatchi could never envisage. Midland would do that. Midland and its sister clearing banks, Barclays, NatWest and Lloyds, were something more than just companies: they were almost national institutions, a species as protected as the golden eagle.

However, just at that particular time there was a window, one which might never open again. The Bank of England, guardian of the banking sector, had allowed a number of bids in recent months. A new Banking Act was about to come into force which meant the Bank of England could limit any shareholding to 15 per cent, and could decide that anyone who dared to go above that without its approval was not a 'fit and proper person' to control a bank. Although the Bank of England's powers would be retrospective, a number of bidders felt the time was ripe to move. Saatchi should launch quickly.

Maurice's first call was to an old Saatchi friend, Sir Donald Barron, a former Midland Bank chairman, and now a semi-retired City figure, whom the brothers had known for years. Maurice met him a few days later, and explained to an astonished Barron what they proposed to do. Would Barron with his Midland connections act as an intermediary? Barron liked Maurice, but was reluctant to get caught in the middle of a bid for his old bank. For a start, he thought a bid was a bad idea, and told Maurice so. Secondly, he was a member of the bank supervisory board of the Bank of England, with responsibility for monitoring Britain's banking community, and this bid was bound to come before that board. He would not help the Saatchis in this bid, but he proffered some advice: they must approach the Bank of England, and also the Treasury, before they did anything else.

Maurice took the advice, and a few days later found himself in the Whitehall office of Sir Peter Middleton, the Treasury's permanent secretary, who listened politely as the younger Saatchi outlined a well-rehearsed and reasoned summary of Saatchi's case for being allowed into the City's inner circle. Midland still had 15 per cent of the UK domestic market, but that in turn was only 5 per cent of the world banking market, so in global terms it was not large. It was too small to compete with the big players, and even retreating into a 'niche' role was no answer: competitor banks with access to the world markets would sweep it aside there too. In the City it had closed down its equity-market-making side, Greenwell's, a casualty of Big Bang.

Middleton, an ascetic fifty-six-year-old unorthodox civil servant much respected both by his chancellor, Nigel Lawson, and by Mrs Thatcher, listened with polite but noncommittal interest as Maurice talked for about twenty minutes, interjecting keenly when Maurice mentioned that in the past year the number of British-owned 'market-makers' in UK government securities had shrunk from thirteen to ten out of a total of twenty-seven. That touched on the Treasury, as Maurice had known it would. 'I wasn't aware of that,' Middleton said.

A few days later Maurice was in the Bank of England for a similar conversation with George Blunden, the deputy governor, and Rodney Galpin, the Bank of England director in charge of the banking sector. They were also polite but noncommittal, careful to play it absolutely straight. They would give neither the Bank's approval nor its disapproval to Saatchi, but suggested it was time Maurice talked direct to the Midland. Much would depend on their attitude. The Bank of England did not want a hostile takeover battle, and would be unlikely to approve the Saatchi move if it could not get an agreed bid. They also formally pointed out that their powers under the new Banking Act to prevent anyone going above a 15 per cent shareholding would be retrospective. The brothers already knew that without Midland approval their bid was going nowhere, but the warnings were beginning to get heavy.

Seeking that approval was the obvious next move, and Maurice had his presentation all typed up, ready to present to the Midland. The man he would meet at Midland was no ordinary bank chairman. McMahon is an Australian who started his career as an English don before joining the Bank of England, where at one stage he was strongly tipped as the next governor. But he had never been a favourite of Mrs Thatcher and finally left the Bank to join Midland, where he had taken the major but necessary decisions to retrench. After two years of his management Midland might have been smaller but it was rapidly coming out of its problems.

McMahon already knew what the Saatchis intended before he made his approach. The Bank of England had told Maurice it was its duty to inform the Midland, and an official made a phone call to an astonished McMahon. The Bank of England's position, said the official, was that the Midland's attitude to a Saatchi bid was 'an overwehelming consider-ation' and that had been made clear to Mr Saatchi.

The Midland chairman had already decided he would not support a Saatchi bid before he had even met Maurice, but he still felt he must see him when Maurice rang for an appointment. The name Saatchi & Saatchi was so closely associated with the Thatcher government that McMahon was by no means certain what forces Maurice could muster against him. Nor did he want the brothers to be able to say, as he confided to a colleague, that 'this stick-in-the-mud can't do lateral thinking'. He also had to be careful not to give the impression that Midland was for sale, which could easily happen if he had a series of meetings with Maurice and his advisers. He made his own battle plans: one meeting with the Saatchi chairman, just the two of them, hear what he had to say, put it to a board meeting which by chance happened to be scheduled two days later, get their unanimous backing (which he was certain he would do) and call off any further negotiations. He must end it cleanly and quickly.

On Wednesday, 9 September, Maurice travelled into the City. His car drew up outside the splendid portals of Midland's headquarters in Poultry, just a stone's throw from the Bank of England. Instead of entering the elegant banking hall, one of the finest in Britain, he took a small lift to the right of the entrance hall and ascended four floors. The flunkeys were waiting as he stepped out, and a few minutes later he was sitting opposite McMahon. Both men, who had not met before, were courteous and elaborately polite, and no outsider would have guessed from their tones the keen intellectual battle that was going on.

Maurice began his pitch cautiously and carefully, building his case brick upon brick. McMahon was not unfamiliar with the globalisation arguments, and embraced them himself as enthusiastically as most, so that part was fine. Much of what Maurice said was neither surprising nor disagreeable to the Midland chief. The £1 billion of new capital made the banker catch his breath – it was certainly tempting for a bank desperately short of capital and having trouble raising it anywhere else (McMahon later got most of what he needed when the Hongkong & Shanghai Banking Corporation bought a stake in Midland). So was Maurice's assurance that the Saatchis wanted him, Kit McMahon, to continue running the Midland, and that they proposed no redundancies. This was more interesting than he thought. He listened attentively to the full exposition, already, in varied form, given to the Treasury and to the Bank of England; much of it made sense, and he could see some attractions in what Maurice proposed.

But he had some objections too – major ones. 'You know, we depend for a great deal of business on a lot of people who don't want us to be livened up or made more exciting. Our lifeblood is our deposit base, which comes from Swiss bankers and other very conservative people; we depend on the interbank market, and, as far as they're concerned, the duller we are the better. If that deposit base goes, everything goes.' That was why, he went on, Midland was different from all the other businesses the Saatchis were in. 'We can't get out of that part of our business. We can diversify away from it, but that's basically what we are.' He repeated this argument several times, not certain that Maurice understood the complex nature of a deposit base, how important and vulnerable it was. He made other points too: 'My managers and customers would not find it easy to understand why they were part of an advertising agency.' NatWest and the other clearers he reckoned would have great fun with an advertising campaign built around that. He found Maurice responsive and well prepared on the broader arguments but not so certain on the more detailed ones. Maurice did not know where the Midland's deposits came from or how the treasury function worked, and was ignorant about other banking matters.

McMahon then delivered what he believed to be his clincher. 'What happens when things go to pot in Latin America and you have to put up another billion?' Maurice visibly started. 'I thought you'd taken care of that,' he muttered. McMahon was astonished. Maurice, he felt, obviously knew a lot about controlling the risk in his own business; but he had not thought through the type of risk that banks encountered. Midland had certainly provided £1 billion against bad Latin American debt; but if the situation deteriorated again it might have to provide another slug of reserves. After two hours Maurice left, still clinging to a hope that he could persuade McMahon to join him, but uncomfortably aware of the deep waters he had entered. Despite all his preparation, he had been out-argued by a man who knew as much about international banking and globalisation as anyone in the world. Saatchi would never even get close to landing Midland.

On Friday, 11 September, McMahon briefed his board. They reacted in precisely the manner he had predicted. Becoming part of a worldwide advertising agency, however broadly based and go-ahead, would not do anything for Midland's problems. It needed a tie-up with another international bank, and they were already talking to several. The answer was no.

Maurice, desperately disappointed, tried to set up another meeting with McMahon. The Midland chairman had enjoyed the talk, but decided that if they met again rumours would start and be misinterpreted. He declined. The brothers had to accept defeat on the Midland front.

Even before the final decision had come through from McMahon's office, the brothers were already focusing on target number two. On the morning of Friday, 11 September, Sir Robert Clark, chairman of Hill Samuel, had a phone call. His secretary passed him the message. Maurice Saatchi, chairman of Saatchi & Saatchi, wanted to see him as a matter of urgency. Could he possibly have an appointment that afternoon? Clark, irritated, told his secretary to pass back a message that Hill Samuel was quite happy with its arrangements for advertising and public relations, and he didn't think they had anything to talk about.

The news of the abortive bid for Midland had not yet leaked and Clark, together with David Davies, Hill Samuel's chief executive, were in meetings attempting to resolve some pressing problems of their own. Hill Samuel was one of London's larger merchant banks, which like every other group in the City was going through the same strategic thinking process as Midland: whether to go 'global' or 'niche'. They had chosen 'global' and held months of detailed talks with the Union Bank of Switzerland, so much against the views of the chief executive, Christopher Castleman, that he had resigned. Then out of the blue the Union Bank pulled out, leaving Hill Samuel feeling foolish and exposed. Further catastrophe struck when they were forced to fire the heads of the corporate finance side whom they discovered were negotiating to sell off a whole division of the bank without even telling the main board. In the first week of September, when the Saatchi approach came, Hill Samuel was spending all its time trying to find a way out of its problems. Clark did not want to be bothered with advertising proposals.

Half an hour later Davies got a call, this time from David Clementi at Kleinwort. He was speaking, he said, on behalf of his client Saatchi & Saatchi, whose chairman wanted to come and talk, not about advertising, but about taking the bank over. 'There was pandemonium for a few hours,' says one Hill Samuel man. Clementi and Kleinwort Benson indicated it was a serious bid, and Davies knew Clementi well enough to know he meant it.

At four that afternoon Maurice appeared, on his own. He was escorted into Davies's office, since it was the chief executive rather than the chairman who would handle the matter. Davies had Clark with him, but no one else. Unknown to Davies, Maurice already knew all about him. He had asked a head-hunter to find him a man to run the financial services venture for him. High on the list was Davies, who had recently returned to London after three years in Hong Kong sorting out the problems of Hong Kong Land.

That afternoon Davies was booked on a flight to Dublin, where he intended spending the weekend at his house in Wicklow. He missed two planes, as he listened fascinated to Maurice spelling out the case for a merger with Saatchi. Davies, he understood, wanted to keep Hill Samuel together rather than break it up, which most solutions now proposed would have done. Fine, Saatchi wanted that too. Maurice said he wanted to keep all the management. He was offering to open

doors for Hill Samuel around the world: Saatchi had 150 offices in
forty countries and a client base of 10,000 corporate customers. It
worked with 280 of the Fortune 500 and 300 of Europe's biggest
companies.

There was a clincher: Hill Samuel needed an injection of capital.
Saatchi was prepared to put in £200 million, which would double its
existing capital.

When Davies finally caught his plane to Ireland he didn't see how
he or his colleagues could say no. Every objection raised had been
countered. Only the price had not been settled, and on that score too
he was reasonably happy: Maurice assured him Saatchi would pay a
'substantial' premium, and when Davies pointed out that in banking
parlance 'substantial' meant 20 per cent Maurice nodded agreement.

Over the next few days Davies talked to all his senior management
colleagues. Most opposition to accepting Saatchi's bid came from John
Chiene, a Scottish stockbroker who had built up Wood Mackenzie into
one of the most respected stockbrokers in London as well as Edinburgh.
A year earlier, as part of the City's Big Bang, Wood Mackenzie had
been taken over by Hill Samuel, and Chiene in turn took charge of the
enlarged group's securities business. Chiene was dismissive of Saatchi,
arguing they had no place in the world of banking and financial securities markets.

However, by Monday Chiene had come round. That afternoon
Davies reported to his chairman. The management was in favour, he
told him. He had checked with Clementi at Kleinwort and had established that the premium on the share price would indeed be 'substantial', so that part of it looked good too. It seemed a wonderful way out
of Hill Samuel's difficulties.

'Well, if the management thinks it's okay, we'd better put it to the
board,' said Clark. He arranged a meeting for Wednesday, when
Maurice Saatchi would again appear to present his bid formally.

Outside in the City, events were moving against Saatchi. The controversy during the election campaign and the open battle with Tim Bell
afterwards had done them more damage than they realised. So too had
reports that they were losing clients, and that they were not able to
manage the huge group they had created. Worst of all, the news of the
abortive Midland deal leaked that weekend, and the City hated it. The
Financial Times commented that it was a move which would not 'strike
terror in the boardrooms of American Express, Citibank and Nomura',
three of the biggest international banking houses, and added that it
'smacked of a firm which had run out of ideas'. The *Economist* said that

no one in the City believed that 'the firm which polished Mrs Thatcher's image can add much glamour to the Brazilian debt business'. The word 'megalomania' was to be heard in the City that week, and Saatchi, it was said, was being 'carried away by its own self-importance'. The Midland Bank deal was roundly condemned everywhere as the most ill-judged deal the brothers had ever dreamt of – a criticism which even their friends would later come to agree with.

As the storm broke, Saatchi shares fell sharply, reducing the value of the offer it could make to Hill Samuel, which was still a secret. When Maurice redid his sums before going to the boardroom, they were no longer looking so good. When he got to Hill Samuel he was able to offer the 'substantial' premium on the share price: 750p, well above the current market price. That was fine. What about a cash alternative, asked Davies. Normally bidders make offers in two forms: in their own shares, which would have meant, in this case, shareholders in Hill Samuel exchanging their shares for those of Saatchi & Saatchi, a paper-for-paper offer; and a cash offer, or 'cash alternative', which is usually around 5 per cent below the paper offer.

Because of the fall in his share price Maurice was not able to raise the cash he needed without future damage to Saatchi's profits. The best he could manage was 640p, an 18 per cent discount on his paper offer. Hill Samuel shares stood at 660p, and its assets were probably worth, if the company were broken up, around 850p. The board knew that if they accepted the offer two of their biggest shareholders, the Australians Kerry Packer and Larry Adler, would instantly make a higher cash bid and dismember the company.

They could not accept. There would be no Saatchi move into financial services – at least not for some time. A month later Hill Samuel was taken over by Trustee Savings Bank, much to Davies's relief. He, at least, has little doubt how near he was to joining the Saatchi empire. 'If they had made their move just a couple of months earlier when their shares were high it would have worked out very well. It would have suited us perfectly.'

On 21 October 1987 Maurice Saatchi wrote to Margaret Thatcher. It was a letter that marked the end of an era, both for Saatchi & Saatchi and for the Conservative Party which Thatcher had ruled over since 1975.

The previous week, on the night of 16 October, a freak hurricane had swept the south of England bringing devastation to the garden at

Old Hall. He spent the weekend mournfully examining the 200-year-old oaks and beeches which had been uprooted, but within hours had the bulldozers at work, tearing out the roots and replanting new trees. After the man-made setbacks he had suffered, Maurice was not going to be put off by a mere act of nature.

On Monday, 19 October, the stock market suffered the biggest one-day crash in its history, and Saatchi shares fell by a third in a period of 24 hours. It was no consolation that every other share went down too; or that if the Hill Samuel deal had gone ahead they would now have had an £800 million rights issue in the market, placed at twice the current price. They were much more concerned that Saatchi's ability to grow by takeover, financed through share placings on the market, was being severely blunted. But even that could not be allowed to stand in the way of tidying up one of the loose ends. Maurice carefully composed his letter.

'Dear Prime Minister,' he began formally. She had always been 'kind enough', he reminded her, to take a close interest in the development of Saatchi & Saatchi 'and the success we have enjoyed in recent years'. Now the company was widening its range of activities – it would become involved in direct satellite broadcasting (in opposition to Simonds-Gooding) and in financial services, both fields heavily regulated by government, and thus potential areas of conflict with the Tory Party account. The advertising business was also operating for more and more government departments. 'We are conscious that this might open the company, public authorities and ministers to misrepresentation,' he added, and the commercial links between Saatchi and the Conservative Party could 'only complicate the task of all concerned'. Saatchi was therefore 'with the greatest regret' resigning the account. It had worked for the party for a decade, seen Mrs Thatcher through three election victories, and also 'benefited from your revolution in enterprise' – profits had grown from under £2 million to £125 million in those ten years. 'Charles and I remain deeply committed to you and your cause, and shall remain your most enthusiastic supporters,' he concluded.

Mrs Thatcher sent back a courteous reply. Maurice had addressed his letter to 10 Downing Street, the official residence of the prime minister rather than the leader of the Conservative Party. But this was party business, not an affair of state, and she observed the correct protocol when she wrote back on Conservative Central Office notepaper. She shared Maurice's regret, was grateful for their efforts and enthusiasm, which she would never forget, and wished Saatchi & Saatchi 'every success in the years ahead'.

It was over at last – an association which had had a dramatic impact on the business and personal lives of Charles and Maurice Saatchi, and which also had some importance for Thatcher and her party, particularly in the first election campaign. No other account could ever have the same impact on the agency again; and probably no other agency would have such an effect on party politics in Britain.

19

FALL OF THE UNIVERSITY OF ADVERTISING

The brothers now entered one of the very few times in their careers when they decided the best thing to do was consolidate – a word scarcely in their vocabulary. From New York came pleas from Milt Gossett and Carl Spielvogel to 'do nothing' for a while and let the businesses there sort themselves out in a time of relative tranquillity; the Midland Bank and Hill Samuel bids had both astonished and dismayed their followers in the investment community and in the post-crash atmosphere much reassurance was needed. From now on the bid for Midland would be dismissed as an aberration, almost as something which never happened. 'We are not interested in buying an investment bank,' Andrew Woods, newly appointed group deputy chairman, told *Management Today* from New York in April 1988, 'even though there are investment banking activities, such as human resources, which interest us.' Jeremy Sinclair was even more dismissive. The Midland affair, he told the magazine, had been blown out of all proportion. 'We were not interested in High Street banking. It was unfortunate that it came out as a major change of strategy.' Saatchi, he added, now had no 'great aspirations' in financial services.

By that stage, he meant it. The investment community, however, would not forget so easily. 'Their ill-fated and ill-timed announcement of their move into financial services was probably the most glaring example of poor strategy on their part that we've seen,' says Charlie Crane of PruBache. 'It must have crossed the minds of so many clients to think: Here's this company, which is supposed to be an expert marketer and disseminator of information and presenter of an image, and then they bungle their own PR in this way. How can they do that? And I think that is a legitimate gripe.'

Unlike the advertising world, which thought the Saatchis had gone out of their minds, Crane and other Wall Street analysts could see some sense in the Hill Samuel deal as a business opportunity in its own right. The bid for Midland, however, defeats them, not least because if it had gone through all the advertising analysts would, in the words of Greg Ostroff of Goldman Sachs, 'have turned the stock over to the bank analysts'. Saatchi & Saatchi would have ceased to be an advertising company with financial ambitions and become instead a bank with advertising interests. What would the analysts have told the clients they had persuaded to invest in Saatchi in the first place? 'I'd have said, I don't know what they're trying to prove but it beats the hell out of me,' says Ostroff. 'If you want to own a bank, I would have told them, stick with the shares. If you want to own an advertising agency, I've got a couple of better investments for you. The communications in the company were so convoluted, so directionless, that I had no clue as to what was happening until they finally went for Hill Samuel.'

Gradually the analysts resumed their old interest in Saatchi, but it would be some time before a bruised Charlie Crane would get back to recommending the shares as a buy again. The analysts' renewed interest in the shares reflected more the fact that after the savage fall they represented good value, rather than the old positive view that this was a great growth company. The stock market glamour had rubbed off. 'We pushed our luck very hard for years in the City and Wall Street,' says a senior Saatchi man. 'Now the luck's turned against us. They don't realise what a good deal Bates is for us.'

On Madison Avenue – or what corresponds to it in terms of where the New York industry is now based – the Saatchis, mega-mergers and British takeovers remained the main topics of conversation whenever advertising men got together for months afterwards. So much had changed in a year, and Saatchi was seen as the catalyst. The criticism of the price Saatchi had paid for Bates, and the argument about advertising people making too much money from the merger boom, was further fuelled when Saatchi took two-page spreads to advertise its seventeen-year unbroken record of rising profits. Now it was accused of making *too* much money – clients' money. The matter continued to nag at Bob Jacoby, who felt the criticisms were aimed at him personally and he must have a final word on it. On 18 January 1988, from his Saddle River house in New Jersey, Jacoby issued a 617-word statement under the headline: 'Did I make too much money?'

It is a curious statement, repetitive and bitter, directed more at his former peers in the big agencies than at the Saatchis, whom he now in effect cited as allies. He accused the rival agency bosses of being 'little people' who 'relished my bloody firing from Bates'. None of them, he said, had called him since he left, although these same people 'used to call me for personal favours every day when I was CEO at Bates'. The jealousy of these same men and their wives when they heard of his $110 million fortune 'was disgusting'.

There had been much talk, said Jacoby, that the $507.4 million paid by Saatchi for Bates (the Saatchis always insisted it was $450 million) 'caused a groundswell of indignation on the part of clients and has led to a rush to cut agency compensation'. He had stayed clear of the debate, he went on, because 'the ruckus was being raised mostly by self-serving hypocrites at ad agencies'. He pointed out that the chief executives who were most vociferous in condemning mergers were those who had bought and sold agencies themselves. Their criticisms he would disregard. 'But the emotional issue with clients persists. Clients consider their agencies to be servants and have for many years. When your servant gets rich and you don't, the blood boils.' He and John Hoyne, he went on, had negotiated with Maurice Saatchi for two years and convinced him Ted Bates was worth $507.4 million. 'Of course it was worth $507.4 million: a year later JWT was sold for $566 million even though it barely made a profit. This just shows that Hoyne and I are good negotiators and that Maurice Saatchi is smart.'

This wasn't what he had said just a few weeks earlier to the *New York Times* when he accused the brothers of being 'amateurs'. But now he brought in Maurice in defence of his own argument. Several times in the statement Jacoby came back to the 'emotional issue' with clients, which he defined as 'Why should all those agency people get rich, and, particularly, why should Jacoby get $110 million?' This had been raised by 'some client types' but his answer was very simple: 'I must be smarter than they are.'

Nor was it clients' money 'we were getting'. The money paid by the Saatchis belonged to UK stockholders (there were a few American stockholders in there too, but Jacoby ignored them). 'Then our clients said, "Yes, but they wouldn't have paid all that money if Bates wasn't making a lot of money, and that was our money." These clients don't understand that the Saatchis didn't care what Bates's profit was. They just wanted to be the biggest agency in the world. We knew that, we capitalised on that, and we made the Bates shareholders – and there were a lot of Bates shareholders – a lot of money.'

In the middle of his statement, Jacoby made some good points. 'The main issue clients must understand is that agencies must run themselves as businesses. They have obligations to their own shareholders, not just to the client. It amuses me to read that Ogilvy discovered recently that "profit margins" are important. We at Bates knew that twenty years ago. Agency managers had not been good businessmen, before Bates sold to the Saatchis and woke up every agency president.'

Bates was indeed a highly profitable agency, with profit margins around twice the average; that part of Jacoby's statement is certainly right. But had he been responsible for waking up the other presidents by selling out to the Saatchis? Some at least had been awake before, although some were still sleepy. McCann Erickson had created the first advertising holding company in 1960, and there had been another wave of mergers in the 1970s when the top US agencies sought to maintain their status as the biggest. Maurice had been doing his rounds for most of the 1980s, and in the last two years had intensively lobbied just about every advertising house worth the effort. There may have been some who did not get the message before the spring of 1986, but the mega-merger phase had made every agency boss the world over think about his organisation and position in the industry. The Saatchi-style thoughts on globalisation, which came some years after JWT, Interpublic, Ogilvy and others were already building global networks, were now familiar stuff.

Even after all that, however, there were big New York agencies still available to a hungry predator long after Jacoby had shuffled off the stage. In the summer of 1987 Madison Avenue saw a classic example of Saatchi training and philosophy in action as the greatest name in the business – indeed one of the great corporate symbols of America – was carried off in one of the most spectacular takeover coups the corporate world has ever seen. Martin Sorrell took over J. Walter Thompson.

The Saatchis watched Sorrell's hostile bid for the company generally regarded as 'the university of advertising' with a mixture of emotions. On the one hand they were proud that a protégé of theirs, even one they no longer nurtured much affection for, should attempt such a daring bid. On the other hand they still had a lingering regret that they themselves had never managed to take over JWT, which had loomed so large in their careers from the beginning. As Maurice had trawled Madison Avenue before doing the Bates deal, the brothers had crossed JWT off their lists only to put it back there, and think again, a few weeks later. Its reputation for looking after clients and producing good ads was unrivalled; but its profits were desperately low. Several times Maurice had spent hours with Don Johnston, the fifty-nine-year-old head of JWT, but there was no way that Saatchi & Saatchi could ever take over the business because of the many conflicts of interest – even if JWT had been willing to sell to Saatchi which it was not. Procter & Gamble would not stand for it (JWT works for its arch-rival, Unilever), nor would several of the other leading accounts, and there was no fit with the Saatchi group. None the less it nagged at Charles.

JWT was vulnerable to a takeover bidder – that much was clear. Then in January 1987, six months after Saatchi had completed its Bates deal, a bizarre management conflict at JWT suddenly put it 'in play' (the Wall Street jargon which denotes that a company is actively in the bid arena). Joe O'Donnell, the forty-four-year-old head of the main agency, approached Johnston and told him, among other things, that he had lost the confidence of the JWT people. For years O'Donnell had been a protégé of Johnston's, carefully schooled and promoted to the point where he was the heir apparent. Now O'Donnell, who had previously met five of JWT's outside directors to make the same sugges-tion, told Johnston that profits were now so bad that he should turn over control to him straight away. He and some of his colleagues were putting together a management buy-out, and they planned to take charge now. Johnston, shocked by the disloyalty, instantly fired O'Don-nell and his ally Jack Peters. He had no intention of going, he announced. But the damage had been done; it was only a matter of time before somebody made a bid for JWT.

For a while it looked as if the somebody might be Bob Jacoby and his old Bates team of Hoyne and Nichols. They were rumoured to be buying shares. Salomon Brothers, the big Wall Street house, were big buyers. The Saatchis took another longing look but wisely decided it was not for them. Venture capital groups all over Wall Street were approached by long-serving JWT men with plans for management buy-outs.

Martin Sorrell had been watching JWT closely since the previous August when one of his Wall Street analyst friends, appalled by JWT's poor performance, took him along to meet a former JWT executive. Now, with Johnston in big trouble, and rumours of client defections, Sorrell decided to have a go. Sorrell had a vehicle to hand ready for just such a bid. In the spring of 1985, while still working at Saatchi, he had bought a stake in a tiny company called Wire & Plastic Products, or WPP. Based in Kent, it made supermarket baskets and was valued at a minuscule £1.4 million; it was no more than a 'shell', a company with a stockmarket quotation into which he planned to inject other businesses. He then went to Maurice to tell him about it, expecting an explosion. Instead Maurice pulled out a copy of the *Financial Times* and said, 'Gosh, we were thinking about doing something similar – taking a stake in a public company and developing it.' Although he did not formally step down as finance director until 17 March, 1986, from that moment on Sorrell began disengaging himself from Saatchi. The brothers bought a stake in WPP, but they gradually accepted there was a conflict and they would not be able to hold Sorrell. 'I wanted to do my own thing in my own time,' says Sorrell. Emotionally the brothers found it difficult to cope with his leaving but after a year they gave in. Says Sorrell, 'The finance director had a stake in another company; and, there was the question of what the long term was going to be.'

Sorrell stayed long enough to ensure he had a good successor, but relations between him and the brothers were not good at the end. At one stage there had been talk that he, rather than Bell, was really 'the third brother', but his role was never that. Charles and Maurice acknowledge him as a first-class finance director and all who worked with him support that view; but they also point out that he was not quite the innovative and creative corporate genius he would later be given credit for being, at least not at Saatchi. Ken Gill remembers Sorrell watching Maurice and 'soaking it all in like a sponge'. Sorrell refined and perfected the Saatchi systems for forecasting cash flow, but it was Maurice who originally installed them (today they are so sophisticated that on a £9 billion turnover in 1987 the projection was less than a half per cent out). Sorrell himself acknowledges how much he learned from Maurice, but his personal qualities were also significant. The Saatchis would later argue that their history is to have the right person for each different stage of their development, but that implies that the organisation outgrew people like Bell and Sorrell. That suggestion is possibly unfair to Bell; it is certainly unfair to Sorrell, who could handle the big capital-raising operations in the City and the analysts on Wall Street probably better than Maurice. The *Wall Street Journal* would later write about the securities analysts 'who have been infatuated with Mr Sorrell', which is not a compliment anyone ever paid the brothers. He might not have had the charm of Maurice, but he could communicate better than either of the brothers with the financial community, and others would note that after his departure the Saatchi share performance was never the same (although that would probably have happened with or without Sorrell).

In two years after striking out on his own in 1985 Sorrell made fifteen takeover bids and took the market value of his WPP Group to £134 million which was still far short of JWT. The company, he says, although constantly voted the 'best agency' by *Advertising Age*, had always disappointed the Wall Street analysts and disenchanted both them and the institutional investors. Creatively, in both New York and London (where it was back at either number one or number two, depending on which table you believed – although if all the Saatchi businesses, including Dorland, were added together there was no contest), JWT was staging a revival; but, financially, its margins were disappearing. In the final quarter of 1986 JWT began losing money and it opened up 1987 with another loss – and its boardroom row. Johnston foiled the buy-out arrangements of O'Donnell, Peters and half a dozen other executives, but JWT's chances of remaining independent were nil. 'Low profit margins and management upheaval put JWT Group in play,' said *Advertising Age*.

There was one deciding factor as far as Sorrell was concerned. Burger King, one of JWT's biggest and most prestige accounts, put its account up for review, and it was clear to Sorrell that JWT was going to lose it. From a peak of $40.50 in March 1986, the JWT share price fell to $27.

Sorrell began raising the finance. By coincidence he used some of the same financial team who had put together the money for the £2.7 billion bid for Distillers made by his old mentor, James Gulliver: Rupert Faure-Walker and Ian MacIntosh at Samuel Montagu, and the stockbrokers Panmure Gordon. In New York they brought in Bruce Wasserstein and his team at First Boston, at that stage probably the hottest mergers and acquisitions team in the business. Sorrell had worked out early on that he couldn't afford to pay the expenses of the bid unless he could make a profit from JWT shares, which he would expect to rise after the bid was announced. Quietly he began buying a stake, and then made his first gentle approach to Johnston. It was rudely rebuffed, Johnston sending back a message that he did not even consider it was worth talking about. Soon Sorrell realised he was going to have to do what Saatchi had never done: go hostile.

On 12 June 1987 he did, at $45 a share, and a fortnight later raised his offer to $50.50 contingent on the deal being agreed. There was a couple of weeks of frantic deal-making while JWT sought out various 'white knights' in a last-minute attempt to get backing to go private: Jacoby was still in the offing and talking about backing a management buy-out group with $10 million, and there were others who expressed interest too. But it was all too late; Sorrell had timed his approach well and no one could get their act together to make a serious challenge. His offer was a full one, and not easily turned down – and Johnston knew it. Finally, after a flurry of threatened legal suits, at 9.30 am on 26 June at the offices of Sullivan & Cromwell, JWT's New York law firm, the two sides signed a 'definitive agreement'. The lawsuits were dropped and Sorrell agreed not to bring back O'Donnell or Peters to JWT unless the JWT management agreed they should. (Peters was already – and still is – a consultant to WPP.) Sorrell had won, and the world's third largest agency, a name that symbolised the heart of American business to outsiders, had fallen to the British.

Where were the brothers during this time? There were all sorts of suspicions that they stood right behind their old finance director. 'Saatchi owns 7 per cent of WPP, and some observers believe this investment was designed to keep Mr Sorrell from doing what he's doing – becoming a competitor in the ad agency arena,' wrote *Advertising Age* on 29 June. 'Other industry observers believe Mr Sorrell is acting as a "front man" for the Saatchis.' It was nonsense, of course – as soon became apparent when the Saatchis sold their shares for a profit of £4 million. Sorrell had not needed them; he had done it on his own.

The brothers would later observe that Sorrell had broken all the rules they had taught him and with which they had carefully moved into New York. 'Maybe you don't need to woo people for years and sign them up with long-term contracts,' Charles remarked to Maurice. 'Maybe we didn't have to put all the work we did into our US acquisitions. Maybe we should just have done what Martin did.' He did not mean it, of course. The Saatchis have never made a hostile takeover bid; even if they had to wait several years, pay a higher price or even lose a good deal, they have always either made an agreement with the management or walked away. The reason is a purely practical one. Advertising is a 'people business', where hostile bids are anathema; by getting an agreed deal with Compton and even with Bates, they were able to tie up the senior managers on long-term contracts, and keep most of the people they wanted. With Bates they had been forced to rush and had abandoned one of their cardinal rules: the 'earn out' deal whereby the Bates management would only have received a portion of their buy-out – and had come to regret it bitterly. But on the whole they had kept most of the senior staff.

Now they watched with keen interest to see how Sorrell would fare. Within weeks their forecasts were being confirmed. JWT lost some of its biggest clients, including Burger King (which would have gone anyway) PepsiCo's Slice brand, and Sears Roebuck's Discover card. Goodyear, the tyre company, withdrew its account in disgust at the British takeover – it had recently fended off a bid from Sir James

Goldsmith and had developed a strong sense of xenophobia which Sorrell now caught the brunt of. Ford withdrew its European business, and before the tide turned JWT had lost $450 million of billings and had gained $330 million. The effect on the company, already reeling from the events leading up to the takeover, was dramatic. Losing so many accounts so quickly had caused 'a shock wave', said a former employee, Pamela Maythenyi. 'It's never good for morale and never good for an agency to have your concentration divided.' By the end of the year 200 people at JWT had been laid off and morale had plummeted. One employee was quoted in the *Wall Street Journal* as saying 'There's a bunker mentality taking hold.' WPP's shares more than halved in the October crash, dropping the value of the company to £147 million – less than half the $566 million paid for JWT.

Sorrell, however, was far from written off in the Wall Street community, where his reputation still stood him in good stead. 'Here is a company,' said Greg Ostroff, 'which was top of the charts for service and account handling and bottom of the charts for profits. The key question is: can Martin change this entire culture?' The view seemed to be that he could and Sorrell was doing his best. He replaced Johnston with Burton Manning, the former chief executive of JWT's US operation who had left two years before, in a move widely hailed as a sensible one; he confirmed three other chief executives, Robert Dilenschneider (head of the PR side, Hill & Knowlton), Dick Lord (head of the specialist agency Lord Geller Federico Einstein) and Frank Stanton (head of the MRB market research organisation) in their existing roles. For the rest he went slowly, carrying out what he called a 'mild reorganisation', which abolished the old JWT structure under which advertising men had been imposed on non-advertising businesses; now the divisions reported direct to WPP.

In March 1988 Sorrell announced profits of £14.1 million, £1 million better even than his analyst fans had expected, and showed that despite the account losses JWT's revenues were up 8.5 per cent. 'Things have bottomed out and are starting to rebuild,' said Emma Hill, an analyst at Wertheim Schroder, who was among Sorrell's leading Wall Street admirers. Within a matter of days, however, the worst problems yet arrived: the Lord Geller senior team, including Dick Lord, departed to set up their own rival business. Lord Geller, although a small agency, was vitally important for JWT's image; it was regarded as one of the most creative in the industry, and nurtured one client in particular, IBM, which accounted for half its revenues. There were strong rumours that IBM would pull out, with devastating results for the JWT subsidiary. 'Without IBM, this agency would close,' said an account executive gloomily. In June 1988 IBM formally announced its account was up for review.

At the time of writing the jury is still out on Sorrell's JWT takeover, but inevitably the doubts about it have brushed off on the Saatchis. Sorrell argues that his Madison Avenue buy has got far better brand names, a far better corporate culture and was much better value than Bates. The Saatchis, on the other hand, say that they are through their bad period while Sorrell is still in the middle of his. The Lord Geller controversy heightened further the anti-merger sentiment, and particularly the anti-British-takeover feeling, in the industry. The JWT takeover was seen as even more of a purely financial deal than anything the Saatchis had done, although Sorrell soon showed that he was not interested in 'stripping' the company but in running it as a profitable and well-balanced agency. Sorrell has so far focused on the immediate problem of raising the JWT profit margins back to the industry average – as a first step.

Oddly enough, while the brothers watched every detail of Sorrell's manoeuvres with fascination, in Washington their own man seemed wholly disinterested. The *New York Times* interviewed Victor Millar, head of both the advertising agencies and the management consultancy business, in the middle of the Lord Geller dispute and asked him what he thought about it. Millar 'said he was unaware of it', the paper reported with some astonishment. Millar, it surmised, was 'clearly detached from the world of advertising. In fact his appointment [as head of communications at Saatchi] seemed so incongruous there were rumours that it was temporary.'

The Saatchis have high hopes for Millar, detached or not. On him rest their plans for doing to the consulting industry what they have done in advertising. Simonds-Gooding had brought order to the great splurge of takeovers, and by the time the Lord Geller issue surfaced Millar could afford to leave the advertising industry to others to worry about. 'Victor Millar has one of the best track records and one of the best strategic brains of anyone in the business service sector,' said Michael Dobbs, acting as a Saatchi spokesman when the *New York Times* rang for a reaction to what it perceived as Millar's *faux pas*. 'We already had the best advertising brains.'

Born in California in 1935, Millar (pronounced Mill-ar) joined Arthur Andersen straight out of graduate school as an accountant. He transferred to the consulting side in San Francisco, then moved rapidly up through the ranks to become senior managing director at the top of

Andersen's worldwide consultancy practice, which he helped propel into the position of the world's biggest management consultancy, a business which Maurice coveted. In 1983 he took charge of all Andersen's practices, including accountancy, audit and tax, and was second-in-command to the worldwide chief executive Duane Kullberg. In January 1987 he joined Saatchi, where he is said to be paid $1 million a year.

Saatchi had moved seriously into the business of consulting with the takeover of Hay in 1984, but the brothers had not been able to devote much time to it. Millar, based in Washington, was charged with making Saatchi as big in consulting as it was in advertising – a formidable task. In his 1987 chairman's statement Maurice spelled this out in finer detail. In Britain between 1980 and 1987, he said, advertising expenditure grew by 126 per cent, twice as fast as 'real' investment in the economy as a whole. In the same period management consultancy fees grew by 443 per cent. Companies, he argued, were investing in 'knowhow' at a far faster rate than they were in machinery, buildings or other tangible assets. It was a process which could only speed up; by 1990 Saatchi estimated the total consulting market would be worth $230 billion worldwide, and Saatchi, with its Hay subsidiary, had only a tiny fraction of it.

Maurice now talks about his ideal conglomerate being a combination of Saatchi's advertising skills, the consulting business of McKinsey, the accounting skills of Arthur Andersen and the financial clout of Goldman Sachs. He can mention those latter names with confidence because none of them is for sale, but it gives a clear enough idea of the size of the mountain still to be climbed. But to advance towards the summit the Saatchis need to be able to raise money for more bids. And after the Bates, Midland and 1987 election rows the stock market rating does not allow it. 'The City and Wall Street are no longer in love with us,' says a senior Saatchi man, 'and it may take some time to get that right.'

In the meantime the cash flow from the advertising agencies has allowed Millar to begin a series of small-to-medium-sized takeovers in the consulting field. The collapse in the share price has removed the possibility of a single great stroke in the arena, but the existing businesses are expanding again. The advertising divisions are back on course.

Ask the brothers whether they regret taking over Bates because of all the fallout and the reply is an emphatic no. In terms of total world billings, Young & Rubicam with $4.9 billion ranked number one advertising agency in the world in 1987. But close behind it were the two Saatchi agencies, Saatchi & Saatchi DFS with $4.6 billion and Backer Spielvogel Bates with $4.1 billion. Taken together, the two Saatchi agencies added up to nearly $9 billion of billings – well ahead of Young & Rubicam. 'If you've got two of the top five agencies in the world you will always do well, just so long as you put some decent people into place and mind the accounts,' says a Saatchi man. 'And Charles and Maurice have always been pretty good at finding, motivating and keeping good people – and at minding the accounts. So really they don't have to concern themselves too much with advertising. That's all in place now and in good shape.'

None the less there is every sign that Charles in particular will continue to concern himself with advertising. In Britain in the spring of 1988 figures published by the *Media Register* for the year to March 1988 showed that its Charlotte Street-based agency, Saatchi & Saatchi Advertising, still seesawing with JWT for first place in 1987, had moved clearly into top place with the biggest increase in new business ever seen by an agency in Britain. Behind it was a new agency created by merging Ted Bates with Dorland, which jumped into second place above JWT. And still a third Saatchi agency, KHBB, boasted third place in the new business league. That was a jubilant moment for the brothers, giving them an unprecedented position in the market which psychologically still mattered most to them.

They could also boast of something else. As *Campaign* remarked in February 1988, 'Saatchi's dominated most awards ceremonies' during the previous year, although both Collett Dickenson Pearce and Boase Massimi Pollitt were not too far behind. At the 1987 Cannes Festival, the big prize-giving event of the year, Saatchi's international network won more awards than any other agency in the world. In the last five years *Campaign* estimated that Saatchi had won 12.6 per cent of the principal European awards for creativity, more than any other group. It led the field for two of the five years and was in second place for the other three. The bigger they got, the harder they worked at keeping their creative image. Jeremy Sinclair, who had been responsible for so much of the good creative material produced by the agency over the years, had now moved into an even more senior role at Regent Street – joint deputy chairman of the group – which the brothers hoped would spread some of the Saatchi culture through the empire, and also help the City image. Behind him he left a creative department over 100 strong at Charlotte Street with no fewer than four creative directors to run it.

To Charles in particular, but also to Sinclair, new business and

awards for creativity have lost none of their importance. In the early
days they associated 'small' with 'good' in the creative sense – and big
meant bad. How could they marry the two as they got larger? 'When
we started the big agencies, the Thompsons and Masiuses, didn't get
an award from one end of the year to the other,' says a Saatchi man.
'One of the enormous achievements of Saatchi is that the bigger we've
got, the more awards we've won. We've defied gravity.' Others would
say that by single-mindedly chasing awards, of which there are so many
in the advertising industry, any agency could do well, and that awards
by themselves mean little. They meant something to Charles, however,
and if the new business kept coming in at the rate it was in the spring
of 1988 he was happy.

Early in February 1988 Vic Millar in Washington rang Maurice in
London. He was still sorting out the various non-advertising companies
acquired with Bates and the others, and there were a couple that just
did not fit with the Saatchi culture. He wanted to sell one. The brothers
were appalled. For seventeen years they had bought companies; they
had never sold one. 'You can't imagine the agony that went on,' said a
Saatchi man. Maurice could see the logic in what Millar was urging
but, as Charles remarked to him, 'being a seller is not something we
relate to'. On the other hand they were paying Millar $1 million a year
to take decisions like that, and they would not stand in his way.

Millar is familiar with the Saatchi philosophy he is required to follow.
Maurice has set out to get it across with the same intensity he used to
persuade the City to upgrade the Saatchi share-rating all those years
ago, or to push the theories of Ted Levitt into the public domain. Again
and again he repeats his 'supermarket' theme, one which the advertising
world will hear again and again over the next few years. 'I would
compare our position today with retail supermarkets in the 1950s and
1960s. In those distant days each extension of the type of product to
be sold in supermarkets was met with controversy.' But in the future, he
claims, people will no longer question his company's offering corporate
finance and pensions alongside advertising or sales promotion. At Saatchi's March annual meeting he reiterated his belief that in the future
the big global companies will want *all* their services right around the
world from the same company – not just advertising, but banking and
management help as well. 'Thirty great companies now work with us
across five or more types of service, and a fifth of all new business

projects now arises when existing clients of one member of the group begin to work with another.'

The job of proving the Saatchi 'supermarket' theory falls to Millar, who in turn argues it with what one observer describes as 'a painfully logical approach'. The *New York Times* reported that in his first speech as Saatchi's communications chief 'Mr Millar lost some of his audience with his abstract theories and dry presentation' and contrasted him unfavourably with the 'stout Britisher' Simonds-Gooding whom he replaced and who 'had the requisite flash to get along in the ad world'. The brothers, however, do not necessarily need flash and charm from Millar; they want him to make their philosophy work in practice. Millar's energies are therefore devoted both to looking for new acquisitions – when I interviewed him in Washington in January 1988 he had some twenty consulting firms on his books – and to finding 'synergy' between the existing Saatchi businesses. There are plenty of unbelievers, both inside and outside the organisation, prepared to argue that the Saatchis are wrong; that the concept of offering a client the great battery of services is no more than pie in the sky, a justification for the Saatchi desire to own more and more companies. Millar hosts regular breakfast meetings in New York between the various agency heads, urging them to find new ways of using each other's services, but not everyone is enthusiastic. 'I think they're on the right track in believing there will be world brands,' says one. 'But they haven't communicated very coherently how all the businesses that they presently own can offer something meaningful and useful to the client. I have to demonstrate to my clients that I am serving them effectively and limiting their production cost, and with some of the Saatchi clients I can do that. But I was using those companies before they ever became part of Saatchi, and nothing much has changed.'

Another agency head makes a similar point. 'If I want to do displays there are ten companies I could go to that are equally as good as Howard Marlboro [a Saatchi direct sales subsidiary]. I have to say: is there some way I can give my client the financial benefit or the performance benefit of our both being part of Saatchi? Now I don't have to apologise for Howard Marlboro or any other company in the group; but nobody yet has tied them together, and it's really very challenging to try to get together people from different organisations, different cultures and disciplines, to work on a project for a client.' The Saatchis, the executive goes on, 'are making real inroads in getting people together and exposing them to the companies that are in the system, and maybe that will show through in a benefit for the client. But everybody has their own agenda, everybody is as busy as hell and it's a natural inclination to do things you're comfortable with and not try to do things a different way.'

While achieving his 'synergy' Millar has set himself a target of $1 billion of revenues from consultancy by the year 1990 – more than five times the $198 million generated in 1987. To achieve that requires several major acquisitions which are both elusive and costly. With the stockmarket route for raising new money effectively blocked by the low share price, Millar is having to go slowly, picking up smaller and cheaper companies, filling in gaps and generally spreading the word while the brothers work out a new way of making the next big leap.

Back in London that is precisely the issue to which the brothers devote much of their working time. Jeremy Sinclair found himself sharply criticised at a City lunch one day by a fund manager who complained that they never saw the brothers. 'Why isn't Maurice here at this lunch? We're big shareholders and we've supported your big issues.' Sinclair was ready for it. 'Do you want to wreck our business?' he asked. If Maurice attended that meeting, he explained, he would have to attend twenty-five similar meetings with equally important shareholders – which would mean he was not back in the office thinking about the company's future. With many other company chairmen that would sound trite; with Maurice it is true. He does genuinely like to sit in his large airy office, read his magazines and books, and think about the future.

20

FROM MINIMAL TO MAJOR

Many of the residents in London NW8, near Regent's Park, are quite unaware of the extraordinary art gallery hidden behind a row of shops in Boundary Road. Even those who live in the street may have passed the anonymous grey steel door a thousand times without noticing it; the sole hint of what lies inside is the bell-push and the tiny notice beside it, only readable from a few feet away: 'Saatchi Collection'. Behind the door is a newly tarmacadamed yard, leading to a building which, from the outside, still resembles what it once was: a motor repair shop, later converted into a paint distribution depot. But inside the impression is stunning.

Here is one of the biggest private galleries of its kind – 30,000 square feet of exhibition space, three times as big as the Whitechapel in London's East End, ten times the size of the Serpentine. The reception area, once a loading dock, is 70 feet long, and leads on into five other large exhibition spaces – huge, roomy and starkly bare areas, purpose-designed to display the owners' taste in art.

Charles and Doris bought the site in the early 1980s and commissioned the architect Max Gordon to convert it into what one critic called 'the handsomest of London's new galleries'. It was an expensive operation. Within the old factory Gordon fitted a new skin of white plaster walls to form the background for art works which would overpower many galleries. The original sawtooth factory roof and exposed steelwork were left as they were, and the floors were clean, simple and bare. The whole space is cleverly lit by reflected light from fluorescent tubes carried by hidden metal trays in the roof structure, giving the impression of perpetual sunlight. The effect is of great, bright, uncluttered almost cavernous space, ideally suited for the works it houses.

Big as the gallery is, at any given time only a fraction of the more

than 800 pieces in the Saatchi Collection can be shown there. The
others are held in store, adorn the walls of Charles's and Doris's (now
separate) houses and the offices of the brothers or are lent out for other
shows. They are exhibited in Boundary Road on a rotational basis, with
no fixed pattern: Charles may decide it is time for a change and out
go the Schnabels and Kiefers and in come the Warhols and Serras. In
the spring of 1988, for instance, the show was called 'NY Art Now'
and featured the work of a new school of art which Charles and Doris
were buying keenly, and which had suddenly become fashionable: New
York East Village art, particularly Jeff Koons, a sculptor then famous
for his vacuum cleaners in plexiglass cases; it included outsize sinks,
one of them partially buried in earth, by Robert Gober, huge oil and
wax canvases by Ross Bleckner and moving light structures by Jonathan
Kessler. The catalogue to the show acknowledged that the art, although
of recent vintage, had already 'elicited numerous cries of "Fraud!"
and "Foul play!" from within the New York and international art
communities.' In fact, it went on, all of it had been 'dismissed as cynical,
derivative, repetitive, market-oriented, superficial, anti-humanist, cold,
obvious, over-hyped and/or a case of the emperor's new clothes.' On
the other hand it had 'held up, for the world to see, something which
the world would prefer to see concealed (or suppressed) indefinitely'.

   In other words, Charles Saatchi had, in the art world as in the
advertising world, exposed a nerve. In March 1988, when Maurice (on
his own) made the cover of *Newsweek* the magazine included a section
on the art collection which began:

> A visitor to the Saatchi Collection could be forgiven these days for thinking
> he has taken a wrong turn and walked into a somewhat quirky appliance
> store. There . . . is a display case containing two shiny new vacuum cleaners.
> Let's be clear about this. We're not talking about paintings or sculptures of
> vacuum cleaners but the real thing: honest-to-goodness Hoovers, straight
> out of the box, lovingly arranged by Jeff Koons.

Koons, at that stage a great favourite with Charles and Doris, dominated
the show. A blow-up toy rabbit, cast in stainless steel and reflecting the
other works, was even more striking than the Hoovers. So perhaps was
a series of basketballs in various different stages of suspension in glass
tanks. The experts were divided on it. One London art critic dismissed
Koons and the other East Village artists as 'designed to appeal to the
dealers, who know that the Saatchis and the followers of the Saatchis
are likely to plump for the latest, the quickest, the most fun; in their
parlance, the "sexiest" works marketable.' *Newsweek* found that such

criticism was exacerbated 'by the fact that Charles has been no more willing to talk to journalists about his burgeoning art collection than he is about his advertising business'.

In fact Charles does not talk to many people, journalists or not, about his collection. This is the private collection he and Doris have put together, essentially for their own interest; they love others to see it, but not when they're there. Some of their pleasure in it seems to go when they are asked to explain it. Charles is an intuitive art collector who does not much enjoy the intellectualising that so many in the art community feel obliged to employ. That is not to say he cannot – or does not – talk about it in private. When he wants, Charles can be a forceful, witty and eloquent conversationalist. The one recorded occasion when he did talk to a journalist about his art was in May 1985 when he agreed to discuss it (over the phone, and on the strict basis that he was not to be directly quoted) with Don Hawthorne of *ArtNews*. Hawthorne reported that as soon as the conversation turned to art Charles became 'animated, sometimes passionate. Contemporary art could find no more sincere endorsement than Saatchi's boundless enthusiasm.'

The gallery itself is an extension of the collection, the anonymous industrial building almost a modern sculpture in its own right. Here Charles and Doris can come whenever they wish (except for the two days a week when it is open to the public, a time they avoid) and see their art works displayed as they should be: the huge empty plywood boxes of Donald Judd, so large (one is 12 feet high and 80 feet long) that a wall had to be knocked down to get them in, the firebricks of Carl André that once caused a sensation in the Tate, or the immense steel plates of Richard Serra which dwarf the person standing beneath them.

Although the Saatchis share their collection with the public, that was not their intention when they began. They set off to buy works that pleased them, and soon discovered they had a collection whose importance could not be kept just for themselves. Like other collectors before them, they found that no art can be 'owned' by any individual but has a life of its own. Every week the gallery gets requests from all over the world, but particularly from the USA, to borrow works for exhibitions. Without some of the Saatchi pieces it is difficult to assemble a genuinely representative exhibition of contemporary art anywhere in the world. 'The Saatchi gallery is now a stopping-point,' says Marina Vaizey, art critic of the *Sunday Times*. 'I get a lot of telephone calls from abroad, from Americans, from Europeans, saying: "Where is the Saatchi collec-

tion? When is it open?" It's considered the showplace for art made in
the last fifteen years, because it's exclusively devoted to that, unlike
museums which have a mixed, historical collection.'

From his earliest days Charles has been a collector. His elder brother
David was surprised to discover that instead of throwing away his
Superman comics Charles was saving them – and building a collection.
Soon it seemed that all the other children were collecting Superman
comics too; they were not necessarily influenced by Charles – old
Superman comics had suddenly become a vogue. Charles just seemed
to be the first.

Later it was jukeboxes; Charles introduced one into his father's house
when he was still a teenager, and soon the whole house seemed to be
filled with them. Six months later, recalls David, it became a 'terrific
craze' to collect jukeboxes. Others who grew up with Charles also
remember his finely tuned antenna for picking up new fashions before
they were even recognised as such. Charles did not consciously spot
new trends from reading magazines or watching television, although he
did a great deal of both; he just seemed in tune with changes going on
in his generation. He did it to please himself, and more often than not
what pleased him one day would please others months later. It could
be pop music, or films, or even clothes: his family was appalled when
he first sported jeans in the late 1950s, but within a year or two jeans
were being worn by many people, even middle-aged men.

There are people like Charles in every field – market or commodity
traders who see a price trend emerging before anyone else does, more
by 'nose' or feel than by anything more tangible; fashion designers,
architects, artists, writers. All of us know someone who has this quality.

Charles combines it with an interest in collecting which goes far
beyond the young boy sticking stamps in albums which years later would
moulder forgotten in an attic. He continued to collect Superman comics
well past the time he could have been interested in reading them. In
the early 1970s, when Charles was in his late twenties, Ron Collins
recalls going into his room in Golden Square one lunchtime to show
him some art work. Charles was on the phone, so Collins waited
outside; but in that tiny office he could overhear the conversation.
Collins had never heard of anyone collecting Superman comics, so it
took him some time to work out what it was about. Charles was
bargaining with a dealer: 'No, I've got that one; how much are you
asking for the train one? Thirty bob? Too much – make it a pound . . .'

When he finished and realised Collins had overheard him he was unembarrassed, complaining about how prices of Superman comics were rising. Charles was not collecting comics to make a profit – it was the collecting that interested him.

From his teenage years on Charles was collecting cars too – an enthusiasm he shared with Maurice. At times the basement garage of Charlotte Street would be half filled with the brothers' machines. When Jaguar announced it was closing the E-type production line Charles bought one of the last three cars produced, which he still drives. Maurice bought an old 160 mph AC Cobra, and had its aluminium body restored by one of the two living panel beaters in Britain with the skill to do it. He drove it sparingly, taking it for a ritual spin on a Sunday morning. He once told me how, as he was approaching his home, he met a Post Office van in a narrow lane. Maurice arrived at his garage with a nasty dent. He was so upset by it he wept.

Maurice, however, never had the true collector's mania that Charles has – nor, as more and more of the running of the business fell to him, the time to indulge it. The art collection was something the brothers would not share. Maurice had little interest in it, saying deprecatingly, 'You can call me Phil E. Stein' when asked about it. It was never entirely true: Maurice was appreciative enough to people his own office with art – and enjoy it; and he was a keen theatre-goer from his late teens. But essentially the art collection is something Charles shared only with Doris, who is as avid a collector as he is. Doris too has always been a collector. For years before she married Charles she had specialised in what is called 'white work', white embroidered tablecloths, nightgowns and so on, a kind of specialist, almost minimal area of textiles in its own right. She showed it in a tiny gallery in Regent's Park, but essentially, like Charles's comics, it was for her own interest.

Together they have built a collection of modern art which is regarded today as perhaps the most important of its kind in the world in private hands. Charles at peak times has probably spent a third of his time (including weekends and evenings) on it; and most of his money.

He bought his first work in 1969. It was by Sol LeWitt, a New York minimalist, who came to the fore with his wall-drawing ideas: literally sets of written instructions capable of being executed by anyone who had a wall big enough. For instance there are pieces in the Saatchi collection which consist of no more than a few words, such as: 'Within 6 in. (15.2 cm) squares, draw straight lines from edge to edge, using yellow, red and blue pencils. Each square should contain at least one line. Graphite and coloured pencils.' LeWitt sculptures are often modular structures, incomplete open cubes constructed in stove enamel on aluminium for example. Many would sneer, but for devotees of minimalist art LeWitt is one of the great figures. 'LeWitt's understanding of art as activity, as an unreasonable course of action pursued reasonably, is the very soul, as opposed to the theory, of mainstream Minimalism,' says Peter Schjeldahl in the catalogue to the first Saatchi exhibition, 'Art of our Time', in 1984. LeWitt would become one of the central artists in the Saatchi collection, which now contains twenty-one examples of his work.

Charles in the late 1960s was a casual collector, with no particular knowledge of the minimalist movement then beginning to take root in New York with Andy Warhol (more correctly a 'pop' artist), Frank Stella and Carl André. Warhol was already expensive, but most minimalist art could be bought cheaply, and Charles began acquiring at a few thousand dollars a time some of the best and most characteristic works of the period. At this stage he had no interest in British or European art – all the work he acquired was American photo-realist or minimal art.

Charles's interest in art predated his marriage to Doris, in 1973, but she was influential in kindling his enthusiasm for it. A New Yorker, she had moved in the circles where Charles from the early 1970s began to become a keen buyer. In London Charles had a friend called Alain Merten who not only ran a clothes shop in the King's Road but also owned a print gallery, and he would often drop in to see what was happening. But it was his discovery of the Lisson Gallery in Marylebone which was to have the greatest influence on him. From the late 1960s the Lisson specialised in American minimal art even before it was being widely collected in New York. Charles bought many of his early paintings and sculptures there very cheaply, and developed a relationship with the Lisson which still lasts. Like everything else he did, Charles was single-minded about his art collection from the beginning; having discovered American minimal art, he bought only that. There was some photo-realist art in his early collection too, such as Malcolm Morley's detailed paintings of ships (he is an English painter who now lives in America, painting in an entirely different style), but Charles regarded photo-art as just another form of minimal art. It was at the Lisson that he bought his first Carl Andrés and his LeWitts for tiny fractions of their contemporary values.

In New York, then setting the pace for the rest of the world in contemporary art, it was a time when new vogues came and went at some speed – 'pattern' paintings, for instance, in which Charles took a passing interest. On the whole he avoided most of the short-lived trends, keeping to what he regarded as mainstream contemporary art. He had his own distinct taste and interest, which by the mid-1970s, long before he had emerged from the closed circle of the London advertising world, had already made him well known among the galleries and studios of New York's SoHo, where all the main galleries then were (the East Village galleries did not emerge until 1983 on). His interest broadened out to include examples of American figurative art (Susan Rothenburg and Eric Fischl, in particular, the two stars of figurative art). There were some mistakes and wrong turnings along the way, and Charles could lose interest in an artist as quickly as he had gained it; what he regards as his mistakes do not feature in the Saatchi Collection today (most of it has probably been sold to make way for other work). But overall his eye was remarkably sure, and works he bought then for a few thousand dollars are now seen as classic examples of the period, worth a hundred times what he paid for them.

After Saatchi & Saatchi became a public company in 1975 Charles had both more money and more time to spare for what by that stage had become a passion. He and Doris bought works by Julian Schnabel, the man who some art critics regard as among the best living artists in the world today, before he even exhibited in a proper gallery in New York. They were now regular visitors to New York, visiting the artists in their studios and often buying direct rather than through galleries. They were frequently accompanied by Michael Green and his wife Janet. Janet's collection of contemporary art is second only to Charles's in Britain – she is still a long way behind, and there are many American collections of contemporary art which would dwarf Janet Green's; there is none that compares with the Saatchi Collection. Green recalls Charles dragging them all off to an attic somewhere and glowing with excitement when he found something that caught his eye. Sometimes it would just be an old art magazine that he hadn't seen before where he might find an early article on LeWitt or Warhol; sometimes it was a new artist, or one he had passed over first time around.

The gallery owners in New York soon learned to respect this young Londoner and his American wife when they appeared at previews. Charles and Doris read as much as possible about the contemporary art scene, becoming deeply interested in every detail about the artists they followed, even if they were not in their collection. Career updates, photographs of new work, catalogues and insiders' information about art available on the market were collected assiduously by them. The New York gallery owner Leo Castelli, where the Saatchis have bought many works, says that before Charles ever appeared in his gallery 'he knew exactly what he wanted. You may think he comes in, looks around, decides to buy something. It's not that way at all. He reads the magazines, he goes to exhibitions, he comes in interested in certain pieces. Being a collector like that is a full-time business.' Others independently bear that out. Janelle Reiring of Metro Pictures says that the Saatchis 'are incredibly well informed on the artists they deal with. They're able to spot things fast, make quick decisions and go for the best pieces.' The curator of the Saatchi Collection, Julia Ernst, was working for the Sperone Westwater Gallery in New York when she first came across Charles and Doris. 'One thing I noticed from day one,' she says, 'was that they had a very specific, discriminating taste, a specific sense of connoisseurship.'

Those who know the Saatchi Collection well, and have followed its creation over the past fifteen years, divide it into separate collecting periods. The first was Charles's discovery of minimalism and his pursuit of it, which ran from roughly 1970 to 1976. 'That was what he and Doris were most effective in, and that was what they were known for,' says a friend. 'At the time no private collectors in America were buying minimal art, and there were two very big collectors in Europe – and the Saatchis. The Germans all fell in love with pop art, but for some reason it was unpopular with the Americans, and it is an extraordinary fact that the great collections of American pop art ended up in Europe.'

Then from 1976 to 1980, as he grew richer and more confident, Charles and Doris bought more adventurously, still keeping to American art but now shopping direct among the generation of young New York artists who were emerging at the time, seldom paying more than a few thousand dollars even for Schnabels (which may be worth $150,000 each today), and buying them in large numbers. That was the second phase.

Then in 1981 there was another change when they began to buy a number of works by artists they had previously ignored, particularly European ones. Nick Serota, the director of the Tate, and Norman Rosenthal, exhibitions director of the Royal Academy (both close followers of the Saatchi Collection), date this change to an exhibition they were involved in called 'The New Spirit of Painting' which they put on at the Royal Academy in London in January 1981. The Saatchis lent several works to the exhibition and took a keen interest in it. Charles was not impressed with some of the paintings Rosenthal and Serota had chosen. 'I remember his being extremely critical of an Anselm Kiefer [a major German artist],' says Serota. 'It was in part an unfamiliarity with the work.' Doris, however, loved Kiefer. She did a review of the show for the *Royal Academy Year Book*, and singled out Kiefer as one of the most exciting painters exhibited. Under her influence, Charles changed his mind six months later. Not only did he begin buying Kiefer, but visitors to his house were astonished to find that huge gloomy Kiefer landscape hanging above his bed.

'After that show he changed course, and began to go for a different type of collection in which he decided if an artist was worth representing he was worth representing in depth,' says Serota. 'And he began a very determined pursuit of major works by those emerging artists.' Serota is not strictly correct here; to a large extent, that had already happened. Charles and Doris's collection of minimal art had already been formed before that show, with ten, twelve or fifteen works by most of the big-name artists. The Saatchis had decided that they wanted to collect by concentrating on the work of particular artists. But Serota is absolutely correct when he identifies that show as a watershed for the Saatchis. 'Until that show, they were very blinkered in what they were doing,' says one of the Saatchis' art friends. 'They were only looking at New York minimal art, and then these other people emerged who they thought had found a way out of minimal art, but were still very influenced by it, and they began buying them. Then this new show arrived on the scene, and they began to look at art that was being done in Europe and Britain for the first time.'

In the mid-1970s they had bought artists such as Jennifer Bartlett (who did the tiles in the St John's Wood house), Elisabeth Murray, Joel Shapiro, Neil Jenney and then, in the late 1970s, David Salle – all of them American artists who were emerging out of the age of minimal art and beginning to paint or sculpt again. Minimal art, of course, tends to be just that: blank sculptures or blank paintings where not very much activity is visible. 'In the late 1970s there was a cry around that painting was dead and that contemporary artists had painted themselves into a corner, and no one could find anywhere else to go, because minimal art had closed all the doors,' says the art friend. 'The rather avant-garde view was that it had all been done and said, and that minimal art was the final step with all painting. I suppose that sort of sentiment happens every so often, but it was very strong at that time. Then this group of people suddenly emerged in the mid-1970s who found that there were things they could do with paint, and then there was a gigantic explosion of paint, signalled by that Royal Academy show, which had a tremendous worldwide influence. It was a show that proved that artists were painting again. And it opened a lot of people's eyes to work that was being done all over Europe.'

It certainly opened Charles Saatchi's eyes, making him suddenly aware he was following rather than anticipating trends. He had a lot of catching up to do. Says Rosenthal: 'That was the time of the real explosion of his potential, and he began to become more significant, and the art market began to boom. In the seventies the art market of the minimalists was rather esoteric, and quiet. Then suddenly grand painting seemed to begin again internationally, particularly in Germany, Italy and America, and prices started booming and the market took off. Charles Saatchi emerged as one of the leading collectors.'

In her review, Doris identified three artists as particularly impressive: two British figure painters, Frank Auerbach and Lucien Freud, and one German, Kiefer. Freud was already a big name, and was in any case a decade or two ahead of the others. But Charles did begin buying both Auerbach and Kiefer. He bought other European artists too for the first time: Georg Baselitz (known as 'Mr Upside-Down' because many of his paintings are done that way), Sigmar Polke and Francesco Clemente (two Germans and an Italian) in particular. Within a few years he had a serious group of work by the European school – twenty-four Clementes and twenty-three Kiefers, for example. He was also buying British artists at the same time, and not just the new and emerging ones: besides Auerbach, he bought Leon Kossoff and Victor Willing, both veteran painters, and Howard Hodgkin, a British painter who had been very influenced by his early visits to the Museum of Modern Art in New York. The Lisson Gallery was still important to him, and it was there that he spotted three new sculptors: Richard Deacon, Tony Cragg and Bill Woodrow.

Friends at this stage found Charles excited and passionate about his art. The discovery of the European and British artists, both old and young, had been a revelation for him. But he could barely contain himself when he came across another new movement emerging in New York at the same time, a movement which would attract a variety of labels: neo-geo, neo-futurism, neo-conceptualism, smart art or new abstraction. This group emerged in the East Village in the early 1980s in a range of new galleries which Charles and Doris now began to frequent. 'He became terribly involved in these neo-geo people in the East Village,' says the art friend. As with the minimalists a decade earlier, no one wanted the neo-geos, and the Saatchis bought in bulk, paying very little for them. It was some of these artists, including Jeff Koons, who made up the show in the Saatchi gallery in the winter of 1988.

By now the Saatchi & Saatchi share price was booming, dividends were flowing, and Charles's earnings were rising. He could afford to buy both the Europeans and the East Village artists – and what he had missed out on earlier. He began to fill in some of the gaps in the collection. He bought his first Warhols in 1982, largely because he saw Warhol as the progenitor of many other artists in the collection.

By the mid-1980s Charles and Doris Saatchi were spending at least $1 million a year on new works, much to the puzzlement of outside observers. Where did they get that sort of money from? In 1984 Charles's dividends were about £400,000 before tax – and unless he had a very clever tax scheme (which he probably had) he would have had to pay 60 per cent tax on that. His salary was £225,000, again before tax. The company provided his cars and other expenses, but even so there is a large gap between Charles's after-tax income and the money he was spending on art.

All the works shown in the Saatchi gallery are part of the Saatchi Collection; and when works are lent out they are accompanied by a discreet little card which reads: 'From the Saatchi Collection'. But not all of them are owned by Charles and Doris – Saatchi & Saatchi owns some (not many) too. Before Saatchi & Saatchi reversed into Garland-Compton and became a public company, some – possibly all – of the art collection was owned by a subsidiary of Saatchi & Saatchi called Brogan Developers, based for tax reasons in the Isle of Man. Charles bought it out. The accounts of Saatchi & Saatchi plc contain an item under 'fixed assets' called 'Furniture, equipment and works of art' (amended in the latest accounts to 'Other, including works of art') valued at £13 million. Furniture and fittings are depreciated in the accounts; works of art are not, although it is unclear if they are revalued. This confirms that some company money has been used to buy art – which is neither unusual nor indeed a bad investment. The sixth floor of the Lower Regent Street building is full of contemporary work, much of it worth many times what it was bought for. And in New York the landlord of the new Saatchi & Saatchi headquarters in Hudson Street, in Lower Manhattan, has given the mezzanine floor over as an art gallery specifically to house art owned by the company, and thereby improve the prestige of the building.

But the bulk of the collection belongs to Doris and Charles, with perhaps a fifth of it owned by the company. Shareholders have nothing to complain about – unless it is the difficulty of separating company-owned art from privately-owned works. Yet the question of how Charles pays for his art is one constantly debated in the art world.

It is actually less of a mystery than it seems. For a start, most of the works in the collection were bought at remarkably low prices; some of them have been sold later, and the money used to finance new purchases. Charles hates selling, but he will do so – and has done so – when an artist does not fit the collection any more, or if he feels the money can be better used elsewhere. His lifestyle is not exceptionally lavish, he has no other expensive hobbies, and most of his money for the past fifteen years has gone into art.

Buying and refurbishing the art gallery and the flurry of Warhols and other established artists needed other finance, however. Charles found it from a perfectly sensible source: in 1981 he and Maurice each sold several million pounds-worth of Saatchi & Saatchi shares (they bought nearly £5 million-worth again in 1987 when the share price fell), a move which went largely unnoticed because there was a share split, and the accounts published at the end of the year showed them owning more shares than at the start.

Apart from the art itself, which is controversial enough, the Saatchi reticence and unwillingness to explain has led to distrust and misunderstanding of their motives. The explanation for their collecting mania, commented one critic, 'is a powerful desire on the Saatchis' part to be important on the art scene and known as such'. Art, he added, conferred status, power, 'even intimations of mortality' on the collector. There are many who dislike the new policy of buying up large numbers of pieces by a single artist. There are more trenchant criticisms that the Saatchis lend and exhibit basically to hype the values of the works they already own, an argument which came to a head in the Tate in 1982. It was then that Charles, keen to promote the cause of contemporary art, agreed to join the Patrons of New Art, a group of rich and influential people who would, in the words of the exhibition catalogue, 'enable the Gallery to show and collect very contemporary art'. The first show organised by the patrons in 1982 included eleven Schnabel paintings, nine of them from the Saatchi Collection. The next exhibition contained six works by Jennifer Bartlett, one of them lent by the Saatchis. Charles at the same time had also become involved with the new publicly funded Whitechapel Gallery, to which he lent a number of paintings; one exhibition, Clemente's 'Stations of the Cross', included twelve Saatchi-owned works.

The visibility of these works obviously increased the interest in these particular artists – a fact which was commented on more and more in art circles in London at that time. The Saatchis were so big and so influential that merely by adding an artist to their collection the value of all the artist's work went up. 'What collectors like the Saatchis do has a tremendous influence on what other people do, and also the market,' said Leo Castelli. The disquiet over their role increased with the second Thatcher victory in 1983 – Thatcher was hated by much of the art establishment in Britain, which on the whole prefers its support to be state-directed. When it was also discovered that Saatchi & Saatchi had the advertising account for the Tate and a number of other arts institutions, the critics' anger boiled over.

It erupted in a curious way. Initially Charles got on well with Alan Bowness, the Tate director, and offered to help him when a Schnabel show was first mooted. He had, he explained, fifteen Schnabels then in the Saatchi Collection, which he was already lending to museums all over the world. 'The Tate can have access to any of this work,' he told Bowness. 'Any time you want to borrow anything, your curators can just crawl all over it and borrow whatever they want for any shows they want.' According to his friends, it never occurred to Charles that this gesture would be misinterpreted as it eventually was. 'He just thought that the artists would be very happy to be shown, and that he could help the Tate show the highlights of what was happening around the world. But he was a bit naïve not to recognise the jealousies that exist in the art world. It never occurred to him there was going to be a lot of resentment at this thirty-year-old American coming along and getting a Tate show when there are plenty of young struggling British artists who couldn't.'

The Tate made no real attempt to explain why it was showing Schnabel or, more specifically, why most of the works had come from the Saatchi Collection. Soon Bowness was being accused of giving in to the powerful Charles Saatchi, who was using the Tate for the purpose of hyping his own favourite artist, thereby increasing the value of his collection which, it was hinted, he would then begin selling at inflated prices. 'The Tate did an enormous disservice to Doris and Charles Saatchi,' says Marina Vaizey. 'They got a lot of personal abuse for lending their Schnabels and their Bartletts, and then having these little notices saying that these works had been lent by the Saatchi Collection. People attacked the Tate for validating the Saatchi Collection by showing their work, and they attacked the Saatchis for using the Tate to give the museum's blessing to their collection. That was terribly unfair, because it was a public-relations failure on the part of the Tate as much as anything else. If the Tate had made a big fanfare of it and said, "We have one of the greatest collections of contemporary art and amazingly enough it happens to live in London, and we are going to show some of this work to a wider public," then there would never have been that negative publicity which caused Charles Saatchi to withdraw from active participation in the Patrons of New Art and as a potential major supporter and sponsor of the Tate.'

Others agree with that. 'The Tate just bunged up the Schnabels and let all the little bitternesses that were being muttered build up into a real political storm,' says the art friend. 'And Charles thought that he wasn't going to put the artists through that sort of mess again, that it was unfair on them if, just because they were associated with him, people would stop looking at their work and start going on about Charles Saatchi's motives, and how he was trying to influence the Tate. He decided this wasn't helping anyone. And in any event he and Doris had decided it would be nice if they could find their own place to show their collection.'

There was another, more public Tate incident, which curiously irritated Charles and Doris far less than what they regarded as Bowness's 'wetness' over the Schnabels. The German artist Hans Haacke likes to expose what he calls the unethical and morally dubious involvements of art-world figures and institutions. None the less in early 1984 when the Tate offered him an exhibition he jumped at the opportunity. 'For an artist like me,' he said, 'who has a somewhat tenuous relationship with establishment institutions like the Tate Gallery, it is almost a question of survival, in terms of principle, to stay aloof, not to embrace the institution just because it gives you a show.' Haacke deliberately set out to expose what he felt was the Tate's weakest point: the influence of Charles Saatchi, and through him of Thatcher and the Conservative Party, anathema to large sections of Britain's arts elite.

Haacke's show included a work called *Taking Stock*, which was an attack on the Saatchis, on their advertising empire and on Mrs Thatcher. It was a picture of the prime minister painted in mock-Victorian style; behind her Haacke painted bookshelves whose volumes contained on their spines the names of major Saatchi clients: from Allied Lyons to Wrangler jeans, passing in alphabetical order through the Conservative Party, the National Gallery, the National Portrait Gallery and the South African Nationalist Party. The painting even showed a paper on the desk with details of Brogan Developers, the company which once owned the Saatchi collections, and figures from the Saatchi & Saatchi plc accounts relating to the valuation of the art. On the top shelf of the bookcase were two cracked plates, a reference to some of Schnabel's broken-plate paintings exhibited a few years before, containing pictures of Charles and Maurice Saatchi, and their initials 'CS' and 'MS'.

The painting epitomised, in Haacke's own words, the painter's view that in Charles the Tory Party had 'gained a powerful foothold inside the hallowed halls of the Tate'. Later the same painting was shown at the new Museum of Contemporary Art in New York in 1987, with accompanying text by Haacke which read: 'In July 1982, Julian Schnabel, who is known for his paintings incorporating broken plates, had an exhibit at the Tate Gallery. Nine of the eleven paintings in the show were owned by Doris and Charles Saatchi. It was the first exhibition the museum organised in collaboration with the Patrons of New Art of the Tate Gallery, a group that had been established the same year. Charles Saatchi was a driving force behind its establishment and an influential member of its steering committee.' He then went on to make the same point about the Jennifer Bartlett show, and related it all to a very contemporary New York theme: insider trading. Saatchi, accused Haacke, had bought Clementes and Morleys in bulk in front of an exhibition of their work at the Whitechapel Gallery in February 1984. He was, Haacke said, a member of the board at the Whitechapel at that time. 'It is suspected that he profited from insider information about the gallery's exhibition plans, which allowed him to buy works at a favourable moment.'

Haacke's Tate painting created a minor sensation, as he hoped it would. His research had been meticulous, but he had overlooked several key points: the first is that Charles had never spoken to Mrs Thatcher in his life, and had no desire to carry her influence into any 'hallowed halls' other than Downing Street. More fundamentally, it misrepresented Charles's whole approach to the art world. He had no more intention of engaging in the politics of the Tate or any other art gallery than he had of involving himself with the internal workings of the Conservative Party. That was completely against his nature.

Charles and Doris were philosophical about the Haacke attack; they had been warned in advance, and were also familiar with Haacke's regular attacks on sponsors and the business establishment. However, the row that followed over the Schnabels finished Charles's relationship with the Tate – though that may change again now that Nick Serota has arrived there. He opened his own gallery, where he could display his work as he wanted to: people who wanted to see it did so on his terms. 'All the great British collectors of this century have received similar treatment to the Saatchis,' says Norman Rosenthal of the Royal Academy. 'They all ended up not leaving their collections to the Tate. We're about to do the same for Mr Saatchi. They've alienated him, and in twenty or thirty years' time there'll be great regret.'

By the time the gallery opened, in 1985, the Saatchi Collection was attracting worldwide interest. It contained eleven Donald Judds, twenty-one LeWitts, twenty-three Kiefers, twenty-four Clementes, twenty-seven Schnabels, seventeen Warhols and many others – an extraordinary collection of contemporary art by any standards. 'The Saatchi Collection is one of the most complete and impressive records of the art activity of the past 20 years in private hands, or, for that matter, in any hands,' commented the magazine *ArtNews*. Norman Rosenthal echoes that: 'The Saatchis are probably the most important living collectors of modern art anywhere in the world.' The critic David Sylvester says it is only comparable in British collections with that of Ted Powers, who collected impressionists in the 1950s: 'The Saatchis and Powers are easily the two most distinguished collectors of modern art that have been produced in Britain this century.'

The New York dealer Leo Castelli reckons the Saatchis are unique among contemporary collectors; there are a few 'precedents', he says. Count Giuseppe Panza di Buomo, an Italian collector, worked in a similar way; and there is Dr Peter Ludwig, a German chocolate manu-facturer far richer than Charles Saatchi, who is seen as the only other rival anywhere in the world. Ludwig probably has a larger collection but it is different. The Saatchis follow individual artists in depth, while Ludwig collects eclectically. According to Castelli, Ludwig 'has a little bit of everything. He is, you know, omnivorous.'

There are plenty of people who see obvious links between Charles's ambition to run the biggest advertising agency in the world and his desire to collect art. In both cases, they say, it is his 'Napoleonic drive', the need to be bigger and better than anyone else at whatever he does. There may be something in that; but the Saatchi Collection – *any* decent collection – is a far more complex affair than simply buying up everything produced by a couple of dozen modern artists. 'Charles is mad about art – absolutely crazy about it,' says Rosenthal. 'Obviously, he doesn't discover things completely by himself by seeing thousands and thousands of studios, but he knows how to find good things, and he works hard at it. He's a very good collector of modern art. It's very easy to collect old masters and antique furniture if you've the money, but much more difficult to collect contemporary art.'

During 1987 there was another concern voiced over the Saatchi Collec-tion: the marriage of Doris and Charles had finally broken up and they had decided to live their own separate lives. They moved from the chapel into their own individual houses in the West End, Doris into a little mews behind Park Lane, and Charles just around the corner. So who owned what in the collection? There is no intention to try to split it up, however; and the collecting zeal for both of them does not seem in any way diminished. The art world abounds with stories, sometimes false, of whole exhibitions being bought up, of Charles buying truck-loads of art just from looking at photographs, of artists and agents spreading rumours that they are now on the Saatchi list and so on. But Charles at least is as much in the mainstream of contemporary art as ever.

21

'THE MOST IMPORTANT COMPANY'

When I first told Maurice Saatchi I was planning the present book, he was appalled. Apart from the desire to protect his and his brother's privacy, he had a basic objection. Books are written about people at the end of their careers, not at the beginning. The brothers were still only just entering their forties. 'Give us another few years at least. We haven't done anything yet.' From anyone else that would seem excessive modesty, but Maurice meant it. At that point the brothers had not taken over the big American agencies, and were still some way from being the world's largest advertising business. Even so, their achievements were considerable. Perhaps the Saatchis have a different set of measures from the rest of us.

As events turned out, this book has taken more than three years to write, during which time Saatchi & Saatchi have bought Bates, moved into consultancy, had their battle with Bell and given up the Tory Party account. Maurice's objections, however, have not changed. The book, he has insisted on a number of occasions, would be better written (if at all) ten or preferably twenty years hence when they have achieved what they have in view, when they are nearer to the ends of their corporate lives than they are to the beginning. When he came upon me in the Saatchi building interviewing one of his staff, he threw up his hands in mock horror. Surely, I must be bored by now. Again, after I had returned from interviewing in New York, Charles asked me how the book was going. I replied I was finding it 'very interesting'. He appeared startled. What could I find that was 'interesting'? Had I unearthed something he did not know about? He went away shaking his head.

Maurice has given me many hours of interviews, and also arranged for me to see anyone in his organisation I wanted. The only restriction he imposed was that I did not quote either him or any Saatchi staff directly – the same rule the brothers have always applied to journalists.

I have tried to observe that rule, and this explains why at various times I have felt obliged to attribute a quote to 'a senior Saatchi man' or 'one of the Saatchi team'. I recorded all my interviews, and have worked from transcripts of them.

Before I began this book I knew Maurice reasonably well, Charles not at all. As I got into the research, I found the reverse applying: the character and personality of Charles appeared more and more clearly from the interviews I did and the material I collected. Maurice on the other hand became more shadowy, a person more complex and more important to the story than I had initially imagined. Like most observers, I had half believed the myths: of the brilliantly creative but semi-reclusive Charles, whose gargantuan ambitions were interpreted to the world by his brother Maurice. It was never quite like that.

In many ways Maurice is more important than Charles. The cool and self-disciplined young man who joined Linday Masters and Michael Heseltine in 1967 has matured into one of the major figures in the corporate world today. Yet he is so reticent, so disdainful of anything that even borders on boastfulness, that even those who have grown up with the business see Charles as the key brother.

The reality, as both brothers confirm, is that from the beginning Maurice was just as ambitious as Charles, just as determined that whatever he did he was going to be the best at it. It did not have to be advertising. From his earliest days in school, right through the LSE and then as personal assistant to Masters and Heseltine, Maurice has always done exceptionally well. He has the ability to analyse the most complicated of problems, reduce it to a simple form, find a solution to it, then apply it. He learned some of his techniques from watching Professor Cohen at LSE, but he picked up much more afterwards. From Masters he learned the systems which made Haymarket, then a small concern, into one of the publishing successes of the past twenty years; from Heseltine he picked up the shotgun approach to takeoevers; from Procter & Gamble he learned proper business systems, and today he soaks up the experience and ideas of running a global company from Victor Millar. He never stops learning.

It is the reward of seeing theory worked out in their sixth-floor offices become reality which gives both brothers most pleasure; but the rigorous intellectual process of producing a workable doctrine and then making it happen falls largely to Maurice. Charles acknowledges this – and is keenly aware that his own special skills, essentially creative copywriting and an extraordinary eye for anticipating developing trends – are not so valuable up the management stepladder.

There is a danger that one underestimates Charles too. His contribution in the Golden Square days and up to the time of the takeover of Compton in New York is obvious enough. If one takes away the 'guru' element, his value to a worldwide group that is only partly an advertising business is less clear; yet all who work in the higher reaches of Saatchi today regard it as central. Maurice, for all his growing self-confidence and public persona, has never made a major move without the agreement and support of his brother – and would not dream of doing so now. The brothers may argue, but at the end of the day they always agree before they do anything; they have respect for each other's judgement, and when events turn against them, as they did after the Bates takeover, they also have the strength of each other's support. Charles has lost none of his ability to drive those around him, nor has he moderated his demands for more and better, and Maurice responds, as everyone else does.

In many ways Charles is an enigma. It would be a mistake to believe that because of his dismal academic record he is any less bright than Maurice. Bell, no fool himself, talked about the 'mind games' that Charles plays. Others tell of meetings with Charles when he needs no more than minutes to understand the most complicated of briefs. His taste in art is not universally shared, but his love of contemporary art is deep and long-lasting, not just a passing worship of something fashionable. His friends are successful, self-made men in business, the arts and entertainment; he became a friend of David Puttnam when they were both unknown youngsters at Collett Dickenson Pearce and now most days the two share their thoughts on the battles of Hollywood and Madison Avenue. His friends from the world of business are men like Michael Green of Carlton Communications, and Gerald Ratner, who says that Charles had a huge impact on him as he developed his family jewellery business into one of the biggest in the world. In the arts, Charles's relationships are with leading figures such as Nick Serota, the new director of the Tate, Norman Rosenthal of the Royal Academy and a dozen gallery owners in London and New York – as well as the artists themselves. He does not discuss art on the same intellectual plane as them, but they respect his knowledge and his 'eye'. Charles's response to art is more intuitive than academic, not dissimilar to his approach to advertising.

How does one equate all this with his miserable time at school? There are those who see in Charles the classic signs, much less often recognised in 1950s Britain than they are today, of a specific learning difficulty, a person whose formal written and examination work falls short of his obvious mental ability. The short attention span, the over-powering impatience and frustration, the quick bursts of anger, the short-term memory, the unwillingness to read long reports or sit through long meetings, combined with an outstanding visual ability, might well be interpreted today as a form of dyslexia. Thirty years ago, no one in Britain knew much about specific learning difficulties, and there are many successful people in public life today who only recognise their own symptoms when they are diagnosed in their children. Charles would probably be appalled at the suggestion that he ever had any such difficulty. How could he become the best copywriter of his generation if that were so? Any remedial teacher, however, would give him the answer to that.

Maurice has less of his brother's pent-up energy. He has a clinical, academic approach to problem-solving, best demonstrated by his achievement in getting up the share rating of Saatchi when the brothers decided they needed to use the City to finance their expansion. Problem: Saatchi needed money to expand by acquisition. Difficulty: investors despise advertising industry, and rate is so lowly that stock market is a prohibitively expensive source of new capital. Solution: change inves-tors' view of advertising industry. Action: PR blitz on City and financial press getting across message that advertising industry is historically stable, fast-growing, and contains bright and financially astute young men. Result: Saatchi shares rise 100-fold, there are multi-million-pound placings of new shares, and companies are bought all around the world. Advertising becomes a respectable sector for the City and Wall Street, and dozens of other advertising groups go public too.

In the election campaign of 1979 it was Maurice, rather than any of the whizzkids in the Tory Party, who first put down on paper precisely what Thatcherism stood for. His disciplined approach extends even into his gardening: before the first shovel was put into the ground of his present home, Maurice made himself an expert on roses, and carefully worked out where each variety and each colour would be. As with the growth of the company, he then took pleasure as much from seeing his ideas translated into reality as in the roses themselves. For Maurice gardening is not the physical therapy it is for the amateur; there is no question of him getting home, putting on his gardening clothes, and getting out the spade. Other people do that under his direction. His pleasure is in the planning and design – and seeing it work.

Maurice also relies on another strength: his charm. Charles acknowl-edges without jealousy that Maurice has a better way with people than he has. Simonds-Gooding, sitting comfortably in the role of chief executive of Whitbread, remarks wonderingly that he gave it all up when 'the most charming man in the world called Maurice Saatchi climbed in my window with a rose between his teeth'. Talented people joined Saatchi as much because of Maurice's sales job on them as they did because of Charles's creative reputation. Both brothers had a natural instinct for good people. Jeremy Sinclair wandered in off the street with a portfolio typed on a sheet of paper and one ad that Charles liked; he was given a test, then a job. The brothers chose Bell, with all his remarkable range of talents, and Sorrell who probably has the best financial brains to work in the advertising industry; they chose Hegarty, Collins, Warman and Bannister, Muirhead and many others. As Maurice would say, they have always tried to get together the best management and creative talent they could find. 'To do that you have to have the resources to get them, motivate them and incentivise them in order to get them to do their best work.' The brothers in the early days did not have the resources, at least as measured in money terms, but they still managed to motivate; money on its own would never have produced the devotion that Bell in particular gave them. Today they have all the resources they need.

Over and above these attributes, probably the most potent force in the Saatchi drive to the top was their clear single-mindedness. Their ambition has always been of a different order from that possessed by anyone else in the advertising industry. Ogilvy tried his hand at half a dozen different jobs before he strayed into advertising; the great figures of Bates or Bernbach never had the same early devotion to the business that Charles had – or the management skills of Maurice. Where did it come from? At the very least, the Saatchi brothers have in their genes generations of the bazaar, of Middle Eastern traders who almost invented the world of commerce thousands of years ago. If they ever had any of the insecurity of the immigrant, no one, not even their wives, ever glimpsed it; yet they are inheritors of a culture which may have given them an advantage over the less highly motivated society into which they settled.

There is also the fact that the two brothers, middle brothers at that, are so close they operate almost as a single person. David is seven years older than Charles, Maurice seven years older than Philip, so in effect the three years that separate them – they were both born in June, both Geminis – made them the closest. Neither can ever remember disagreeing about a major decision, at least not for more than a week, in their lives. Again their background may partly explain this: family in

Baghdad tended to mean something more than it does to most modern-day European societies. Philip, launching himself on to the world of pop music, refused to accept the help of his elder brothers, but was greatly touched by their interest. 'They have both been incredibly supportive but we live separate lives, we are separate people linked by blood and bound by unconditional love,' he says. As Tim Bell found, blood and unconditional love between Charles and Maurice left no room for him.

The original *Sunday Times* ad of 1970 made the point that there was a number of small bright agencies, and there were big firms which were a bit dull; wouldn't it be nice if somebody could combine the two? That objective has never changed. The challenge for them has been to create what inevitably would become a large company but which would also remain dynamic. They both become agitated at the suggestion that they keep a tight control on everything in the organisation, insisting the reverse is true – Maurice's 'tight/loose' principle describes best their system of control, with a tight financial system but considerable autonomy for the subsidiaries. Even in Golden Square, when Charles was writing the advertisements and Maurice telephoning potential clients and doing presentations, they were consciously planning how they would 'work ourselves out of a job'.

From the beginning, they say, they saw the company 'as an institution' from which they could stand back, rather than as a personal operation. Others will find that strange, since it is their name above the door, their absolute insistence that no other name join it. Their line of reasoning on this also strikes one as a neat way of aligning their working lives with their preferred work style. Because they get bored so easily, they insist on keeping themselves stimulated. And that is only accomplished by fresh challenges, creative, financial or intellectual. It is torture for them to stand still and do nothing.

As *Campaign* remarked in that article in September 1970, 'each is caught up in the infectious enthusiasm of the other. If they become aware that you are accusing them of over-simplification or platitudes, they are sure that you will still accept that what they are saying is true and unique to their thinking.' *Campaign* remarked wonderingly on the 'self-confidence, conviction and innocence' with which the brothers were about to launch their agency, and the seemingly impossible target that they become a public company within three years. In the event it took longer – five.

This applied to every other target too: in every instance the brothers have defined the objective, worked out a way of achieving it, and then set out to do it. Ask them how, and they reply simply that 'if you want something enough, you will get it'. There is a chilly single-mindedness about that, but they mean it. They wanted a public company, and they got one; they wanted to be number one in Britain and they got there. They wanted a major American advertising company, and they got that. Then they set out to become the world's number one, and they got there too. Now their ambitions are focused on the consultancy business where again they have carefully defined the objective, have committed the resources in terms of people, time and money and are some way down the road already. It may take five years, but given their record and their determination to get there, it would be a brave man who bet against them.

At the end of the day, one has to ask: just what *have* they achieved? How important are the Saatchi brothers? Have they really changed an industry, influenced or composed new philosophies? Are they anything more than just another couple of young entrepreneurs who have done well for their shareholders and made a bit of money along the way?

In *Confessions of an Advertising Man*, David Ogilvy quotes Frances Cairncross of *The Economist* saying, 'The common characteristic of success is the deliberate creation of a corporate culture.' Ogilvy claims that the factor which differentiates Ogilvy & Mather from any of its competitors is that it is the only agency in the world with a real corporate culture. This is simply not true. Ogilvy may not like Saatchi's corporate culture, but it is clearly defined, stated and understood through the group, even among the new arrivals. The brothers have indeed been very deliberate in creating and fostering it, even at the expense of losing some of the identity of agencies they have taken over. On that criterion, the Saatchis are without doubt a success.

In terms of their importance and impact on the industry, there is not much question about that either. In London advertising circles now it is fashionable to talk about the 'second'- and 'third'-wave agencies; Saatchi, along with Collett Dickenson Pearce and Boase Massimi Pollitt, are 'first' wave', agencies such as WCRS and Lowe Howard-Spink & Bell are 'second', on the basis that they were founded mostly by people who left the 'first' wave to go it alone. In the last five years a 'third' wave has come along, created by refugees from the 'second' – which makes Saatchi & Saatchi a grandfather agency. These successive waves have made London a considerable centre of creative and imaginative advertising. Even Ogilvy, in his updated version of *Confessions,* acknowledges it. When he originally wrote his book twenty-five years ago, he says, 'advertising people still looked to Madison Avenue as Muslims look to Mecca'. And today? Now, says Ogilvy, they look to London. 'They hire British copywriters and have their television commercials produced in England.' Ogilvy does not like what the Saatchis stand for, but in writing that he has to be referring to them, because it was the Saatchi who led the way. Before they took up the charge across the Atlantic, British advertising was generally disregarded in New York. And if New York agencies did look to London for ideas, who had the creative reputation in the 1970s and early 1980s?

The Saatchi influence is by no means universally regarded as beneficial. Bob Jacoby argues that it was the Saatchi takeovers which has made every agency in New York more profit-conscious and efficient – which may be a good thing for the shareholders but not necessarily for the client. There are also plenty of advertising men, as we have seen, who blame them for the great mega-merger phase which reshaped the American industry in a space of a few months, with a large number of redundancies and a shrinkage in competition. Time may show that these are changes for the good, but right now the argument is still: what does it do for the client? It may take longer to persuade the customer that the services 'supermarket' is good for him than it does actually to accomplish it.

In the meantime the Saatchis remain the major talking point of the industry. As I write this in May 1988 I have the latest issue of *Campaign* in front of me. On page one there is a story about Saatchi & Saatchi, another on page two, two on page three, a picture of the brothers on page four with a story saying Robert Maxwell might be about to take them over, a full-page profile of Roy Warman and Terry Bannister, just appointed to the main board of the holding company, on page 18, and another story on the back, where a table of new business winners shows the London Saatchi & Saatchi agency gaining more than twice as much new business so far in 1988 – followed by KHBB, another Saatchi agency. It is a typical week.

'In ten years time, Saatchi & Saatchi could be the most important company in Britain,' Maurice told Sir Kit McMahon during the course of their two-hour meeting to discuss the takeover of the Midland Bank. McMahon was puzzled. 'Why do you want to be the most important company? I can see it if it were the biggest, the most profitable, the smartest, the most interesting – but the most important? What does that mean?'

McMahon saw it as 'marketing man thinking', the view that the image mattered more than the substance. Maurice would see it differently. Only by becoming all those things – biggest, most profitable, smartest, most interesting – will Saatchi become 'the most important'. That is the logical extension of the targets they have so far set themselves – and achieved.

It was George Orwell who remarked that one cannot 'succeed' at life. But the Saatchi brothers are having a shot at it.

BIBLIOGRAPHY

Barnet, Richard & Muller, Ronald – *Global Reach* (Simon and Shuster, New York, 1974)

Birmingham, Stephen, *Our Crowd* (Harper & Row, 1967)

Brittan, Samuel, *The Economic Consequences of Democracy* (Maurice Temple Smith, 1977)

Butler, David & Kavanagh, Dennis, *The British General Election of 1979, The British General Election of 1983, The British General Election of 1987* (Macmillan)

Central Office of Information, *Advertising and Public Relations in Britain*

Corina, Maurice, *Trust in Tobacco* (Michael Joseph, 1975)

Clark, Eric, *The Want Makers* (Hodder & Stoughton, 1988)

Davis, William, *The Innovators* (Ebury Press, 1987)

Della Femina, Jerry, *From Those Wonderful Folks Who Gave You Pearl Harbor* (Pitman, 1971)

Drucker, Peter F., *Management* (Heinemann, 1974)

— *The Age of Discontinuity* (Heinemann, 1969)

Fallon, Ivan & Srodes, James, *Takeovers* (Hamish Hamilton, 1987)

Galbraith, John Kenneth, *The Nature of Mass Poverty* (Harvard 1979)

— *Annals of an Abiding Liberal*

Heller, Robert, *The Supermarketers* (Sidgwick & Jackson, 1987)

Henry, Brian, *British Television Advertising, The First 30 Years* (Century Benham, 1986)

Kleinman, Philip, *Advertising Inside Out* (W. H. Allen, 1977) *The Saatchi & Saatchi Story* (Weidenfeld & Nicholson, 1987)

Levitt, Theodore, *The Marketing Imagination* (The Free Press New York, 1983)

MacGregor, Ian, (with Rodney Tyler), *The Enemies Within* (Collins, 1986)

Mayer, Martin, *Madison Avenue U.S.A.* (Penguin, 1958)

McMillan, James & Harris, Bernard, *The American Takeover of Britain* (Leslie Frewin, 1968)

Naisbitt, John, *Megatrends* (Macdonald & Co., 1984)

Nevett, T. R., *Advertising in Britain* (Heinemann, 1982)

Ogilvy, David, *Confessions of an Advertising Man* (Longman, 1964)

—*Ogilvy on Advertising* (Pan Books, 1983)

—*The Unpublished David Ogilvy* (Crown Publishers New York, 1986)

Packard, Vance, *The Hidden Persuaders* (Penguin, 1981)

Pearson, John and Turner, Graham, *The Persuasion Industry* (Eyre & Spottiswoode, 1965)

Piggott, Stanley, *OBM 125 Years* (1975)

Reeves, Rosser, *Reality in Advertising* (Alfred Knopf, New York, 1961)

Rejwan, Nissim, *The Jews of Iraq* (Weidenfeld & Nicolson, 1985)

Townsend, Robert, *Up the Organisation* (Michael Joseph, 1970)

Turner, Graham, *The Leyland Papers* (Eyre & Spottiswoode, 1971)

Tyler, Rodney, *Campaign* (Grafton Books, 1987)

Schjeldahl, Peter, *Art of Our Time, The Saatchi Collection* (Lund Humphries, 1984)

Worcester, Robert & Harrop, Martin, *Political Communications* (Allen & Unwin, 1982)

Day, Barry, *100 Great Advertisements* (Times Newspapers Ltd, Mirror Group & *Campaign* Magazine, 1978)

Articles and Periodicals

Theodore Levitt, (Prof. Business Administration, Harvard Business School), 'Marketing Myopia' (Harvard Business Review, 1974); 'The Globalization of Markets' (Harvard Business Review, 1983)

Jagdish N. Sheth, (Prof. Research & Marketing U.C.L.A.), 'The future of the advertising agency.'

Douglas C. West, 'The London Office of the J. Walter Thompson Advertising Agency 1919–1970' (Business History, Vol. XXIX, April 1987)

INDEX

Index compiled by Jean Maund